Recommended

COUNTRY INNS®

NEW ENGLAND

Connecticut / Maine / Massachusetts
New Hampshire / Rhode Island / Vermont

Seventeenth Edition

by Elizabeth Squier
revised and updated by Eleanor Berman
illustrated by Olive Metcalf

The
Globe
Pequot
Press

GUILFORD, CONNECTICUT

Contents

HELP US KEEP THIS GUIDE UP TO DATE

Every effort has been made by the author and editors to make this guide as accurate and useful as possible. However, many things can change after a guide is published—establishments close, phone numbers change, facilities come under new management, and so on.

We would love to hear from you concerning your experiences with this guide and how you feel it could be improved and kept up to date. While we may not be able to respond to all comments and suggestions, we'll take them to heart, and we'll also make certain to share them with the author. Please send your comments and suggestions to the following address:

The Globe Pequot Press
Reader Response/Editorial Department
P.O. Box 480
Guilford, CT 06437
Or you may e-mail us at:
editorial@globe-pequot.com

Thanks for your input, and happy travels!

A Few Words about Visiting New England Inns

When I first started writing *Recommended Country Inns: New England* back in 1973, country inns were relatively scarce. Since that time, however, the number of country inns has been rapidly growing as more and more people have tired of the monotony of motels and thruway hotels and have begun searching for the infinitely more warming pleasure of a good country inn.

New England is full of good country inns. Its four seasons are ideal for inn-goers to discover all the joys of the region—the glorious fall foliage colors; the brisk days of winter as crowds converge on the multitude of downhill ski slopes or cross-country ski areas; spring with its dogwoods, daffodils, and tulips in bright array wherever you look; and the warm, blue-sky'd days of summer, when the myriad lakes and rivers and the miles of seashore offer plenty of opportunities for excitement or relaxation. I love the way so many old New England houses have been turned into gracious country inns, offering guests the opportunity to thrive on history, interesting architecture, and a unique ambience. When you're a guest in New England, you find a diversity of things to do—visiting a historical site, climbing a mountain, sailing on a lake, biking on a country road past farms and pastures, walking in a national forest, picking apples in an orchard, browsing in antiques shops, and much more. And finally, New England is a small region, so it doesn't take very long to travel from one area to another, offering travelers the opportunity to discover all its joys even on a short vacation.

With the constantly growing number of New England inns, it has become more and more difficult for me to wade through the volumes of mail from new country inns. I have had to be increasingly selective in choosing the best inns in each state. Do not be distressed if an inn you like is not in this guide. Please understand that my definition of a country inn is that it must have lodging as well as good food, and it must have a certain ambience that appeals to me. I prefer that the inns I select serve at least two meals a day and be open most of the year, but I have made exceptions when an inn seems just too special to leave out of this guide.

By my descriptions and comments, I have tried to indicate the type of atmosphere you can expect in an inn, including whether it would be a fun place to bring your children or whether it would be more appropriate to leave the children at home. Do not forget that the very reason you are passing up a motel or a hotel is for the bit of adventure and surprise you will find sitting in a weathered farmhouse, eating country cooking, chatting with a newly discovered friend, and finding new delight in a very old tradition.

So, enjoy! This *Recommended Country Inns—New England* was compiled for you, fellow lovers of New England country inns.

—Elizabeth

Key to Icons Used in This Book

 a top pick

 caters to business travelers

 a best buy

 especially family friendly

 romantic inn

How to Use This Inn Guide

This inn guide contains descriptions of country inns in the six New England states. You'll find them in alphabetical order by state—Connecticut, Maine, Massachusetts, New Hampshire, Rhode Island, and Vermont—and alphabetically by town within each state. Preceding each state listing are a map and a numbered legend of the towns with inns in that state. The map is marked with corresponding numbers to show where the towns are located.

I have personally visited every inn in this book. There is no charge of any kind for an inn to be included in this or any other Globe Pequot country inn guide.

Indexes: At the back of the book are various special-category indexes to help you find inns on a lake, inns that serve Sunday brunch, inns that have cross-country skiing on the property, and much more. There is also an alphabetical index of all the inns in the book.

Rates: With prices fluctuating so widely in today's economy, I quote an inn's current low and high rates only. This will give you a good, though not exact, indication of the price ranges you can expect. Please realize that rates are subject to change. I have not included the tax rate, service charge, or tipping suggestions for any of the inns. Be sure to inquire about these additional charges when you make your reservations. The following abbreviations are used throughout the book to let you know exactly what, if any, meals are included in the room price.

Abbreviations:

EP: European Plan. Room without meals.

EPB: Room with full breakfast. (The copy notes when continental rather than full breakfast is included.)

MAP: Modified American Plan. Room with breakfast and dinner.

Credit cards: MasterCard and Visa are accepted unless the description says "No credit cards." Many inns also accept additional cards.

Personal checks: Inns usually accept personal checks unless the description says "No personal checks."

Reservations and deposits: At most of the inns, be prepared to pay a deposit when you make your reservation. Be sure to inquire about refund policies.

Meals: Meals included in the cost of the room are indicated with the rates; other meals available at the inn will be in the "Facilities and activities" section of an inn's description. I list some of my favorite foods served at an inn to give you a general idea of the type of meals you can expect, but please realize that menus are likely to change.

Children: Many inns are ideal for children, but you know your child best; an inn's description will help you decide if it's a place where your child will be happy.

Pets: Pets are not permitted at the inns unless otherwise stated in the description. If you need to find a place to leave your pet, call the inn before you go. They may be able to make arrangements for you.

Wheelchair accessibility: Some inns have wheelchair accessibility to rooms or dining rooms, and some have at least one room specially equipped for the handicapped. Check the index in the back of the book for inns with rooms for the handicapped. You might also want to call to check for updated information.

Air-conditioning: The description will indicate if an inn has rooms with air-conditioning. Keep in mind that there are areas of New England where air-conditioning is usually unnecessary.

Alcoholic beverages: Some inns permit their guests to bring their own bottle (BYOB), especially if there is no bar service. If this fact is of interest to you, look in the inn's description for a mention of a bar, liquor license, or BYOB.

Smoking: If you see "No-smoking inn" in an inn's description, you will know that no smoking is permitted anywhere in the inn. There are other inns that may restrict smoking to certain designated areas indoors. All Vermont inns, for instance, prohibit smoking in their restaurants and common areas in adherence to the state's Clean Indoor Air Act. Call an inn directly to find out about its exact smoking policies.

The prices and rates listed in this guidebook were confirmed at press time. We recommend, however, that you call establishments before traveling to obtain current information.

Recommended

COUNTRY
INNS®

NEW ENGLAND

Connecticut

Connecticut

Numbers on map refer to towns numbered below.

* A Top Pick Inn

The Inn at Chester

Chester, Connecticut 06412

INNKEEPER: Leonard Lieberman

ADDRESS/TELEPHONE: 318 West Main Street; (860) 526–9541 or
(800) 949–7829

WEB SITE: www.innatchester.com

ROOMS: 40, plus 2 suites; all with private bath and air-conditioning;
some specially equipped for handicapped.

RATES: $105 to $160, double occupancy; $185 to $215, suites; continental breakfast.

OPEN: All year.

FACILITIES AND ACTIVITIES: Lunch, dinner, Sunday brunch. Bar and
tavern, elevator, sauna, exercise room, tennis court, conference room,
art gallery.

BUSINESS TRAVEL: Located 40 minutes from Hartford; 40 minutes
from New Haven. All rooms with phone; conference rooms, audiovisual
equipment, and fax available; corporate rates.

*J*ohn D. Parmelee, the original owner of this inn built from 1776 to
1778, would not know the place today, but he'd probably enjoy it.
The old house now serves as a private dining room and has a private
suite, and an L-shaped bar now graces the tavern, called Dunks Landing (after
the boat landing of the same name in the yesteryear shipbuilding heyday of
the town of Chester on the Connecticut River). The tavern serves light dinners
and daily specials, plus lunch. Try the spareribs grilled with an Oriental barbecue sauce, chicken wings Cajun-style, or crab cakes and more, while you listen to live music and enjoy your favorite cocktail. The tavern also makes stone
pies—a fancy name for pizza. When I was there, there was a chicken one with
roasted garlic, mozzarella, basil, and pomodoro sauce—so good.

There is much to do in the inn. Downstairs is the Billiard Room, where
you can play billiards, backgammon, or cards. The book-filled library is a
nice place to have nearby. There is an exercise room with weights, stationary
bikes, a treadmill, a Nordic ski machine, and a sauna. On the grounds are
tennis courts, and there are bicycles for your riding pleasure.

Each of the inn's rooms is individually appointed with Eldred Wheeler reproductions. The rooms really are lovely and include telephone, television, and air-conditioning.

The chef of the inn's Post and Beam restaurant is very talented. Try Mediterranean fish soup, warm duck salad, or entrees like fillet of beef, pork loin, lamb stew (so nice to have this on the menu), and lots of other wonderful dishes. The breast of duck sautéed in port wine with peaches, blueberries, and nutty wild rice sounds scrumptious.

This is a lovely inn in a beautiful part of Connecticut. Bentley, the inn dog, is a golden, and what a beauty. Well-behaved pets are welcome here by prior reservation.

HOW TO GET THERE: Take exit 6 off Route 9 and turn west on Route 148. Go 3²⁄₁₀ miles to the inn. By private plane, fly to the Chester Airport.

The Swinging Bridge

Driving into East Haddam on Route 154, you cross the Connecticut River on a metal bridge that pivots to a position parallel to the banks to allow large boats to pass. Some say this is the world's longest swing bridge; it certainly is the longest one in New England. One of just a handful of bridges linking the eastern part of the state to the west, the bridge also links the two sides of East Haddam, the only river town that has land on both sides of the Connecticut. The bridge dates back to 1913. During World War I a militia unit was housed in the opera house at Goodspeed Landing to protect the bridge from sabotage by German submarines.

The Gelston House 📱

East Haddam, Connecticut 06423

INNKEEPER: Bill Murphy

ADDRESS/TELEPHONE: Route 82 (mailing address: Box 456); (860) 873–1411; fax (860) 873–9300

ROOMS: 3, plus 3 suites; all with private bath, phone, and air-conditioning.

RATES: $100 to $125, double occupancy; $225, suites; continental breakfast.

OPEN: Mid-February to December 31; closed Monday and Tuesday.

FACILITIES AND ACTIVITIES: Lunch, dinner, Sunday brunch. Terrace Cafe, bar, lounge, theater, banquet facilities, gift shop.

BUSINESS TRAVEL: Located 35 minutes from Hartford. All rooms with phone; small conference room; computer hookup and fax available; corporate rates.

When you approach the iron swing bridge to cross the Connecticut River, the first thing you see is the Goodspeed Opera House. Right next to it is The Gelston House. Let me tell you, it is an impressive sight. Built in 1853, the inn has seen many changes, not only to itself but to the surrounding area. In 1853 a room at the inn plus a meal cost travelers $2.50, which was very expensive at the time.

It was so nice to be able to put this inn back in the book a few years ago after it was totally redecorated. It's beautiful. The Swan Room is a suite overlooking the river and the beer garden. The William Gillette Room has a view of this lovely village. All accommodations are lovely and have queen-size beds.

Dining here, watching the Connecticut River as it flows by, is very relaxing. The floor-to-ceiling windows are lovely. Menus change seasonally, but I will give you a few ideas of the selections.

Lunch might begin with Maine crab cakes or a baby mesclun salad, followed by Norwegian salmon with artichoke dill pesto or a grilled chicken foccacio served with savory fries.

Elegant dinner menus feature appetizers such as calamari or tempura shrimp and main courses from carmelized breast of duck to Chilean sea bass. The reasonably priced prix-fixe dinner changes daily but always offers soup and salad, plus special dishes such as roast prime rib of beef, grilled tuna, or a crabmeat and spinach stuffed fillet of sole and a pasta choice. The "demi sweet" of the day might be assorted biscotti served with coffee.

In past summers, the beer garden looking out on the river was very popular. Now it's back and named The Beer Garden Terrace. There are a lot of choices—hamburgers and you name it—and beer. There is fun for all, and it is very reasonable.

While you're in East Haddam, you really shouldn't miss seeing a play at the Goodspeed. It's where *Annie* and *Man of La Mancha* began many years ago.

HOW TO GET THERE: From I-95 take exit 69 onto Route 9 north, or from I-91 take Route 9 south. Follow Route 9 to exit 7 and follow the signs to the Goodspeed Opera House.

Griswold Inn 📱
Essex, Connecticut 06426

INNKEEPERS: The Paul Brothers; Sarah Grader, general manager

ADDRESS/TELEPHONE: 36 Main Street; (860) 767-1812; fax (860) 767-0481

E-MAIL: griswoldinn@snet.net

WEB SITE: www.griswoldinn.com

ROOMS: 30, including 12 suites; all with private bath and phone; some with fireplace.

RATES: $95 to $125, double occupancy; $145 to $200, suites; continental breakfast.

OPEN: All year except Christmas Eve and Christmas Day.

FACILITIES AND ACTIVITIES: Lunch, dinner, Sunday brunch, children's menu, bar.

BUSINESS TRAVEL: Located 15 minutes from railroad station. All rooms with phone; fax available; meeting rooms.

*E*ssex is a very special town right on the Connecticut River. Although it was settled long before the Revolution, Essex is still a living, breathing, working place, not a re-created museum of a town. The first warship of the Continental Navy, the *Oliver Cromwell*, was built and commissioned here in 1776.

"The Gris," as the inn is fondly called by everyone, is the highlight of anyone's trip to Essex. When you come in from the cold to the welcome of crackling fireplaces, you are doing what others have done before you for more than 200 years.

You can lunch or dine in the cool dimness of the Library or the Gun Room, the latter of which houses a collection of firearms going back to the fifteenth century. This note from a father to a son is in here:

7th month 7th day 1776

"My dear son Girard,

I send you this little gun

Do not handle it in fun

But with it make ye British run

Join ye ranks of ye Washington

And when our independence is won

We will drink of good old rum"

—JOHN FRANCIS PUTNAM

Another special spot is the Steamboat Room, where the mural on the far wall floats gently, making you feel that you really are on the river. The inn's collection of Currier & Ives steamboat prints is of museum size and quality.

There is music every night—old-time banjos, sea chanteys, Dixieland jazz, or just good piano, but never rock 'n' roll.

In the bar is a great, old-fashioned popcorn machine. There is popcorn for all. Do ask for some. It's one of many personal touches that make this nice inn such a special place.

The Hunt Breakfast is the renowned Sunday brunch at the inn. This bountiful fare is worth a trip from anywhere. The selection is extensive, with enough good food to satisfy anyone's palate. Dinner just gets better every time I visit. I've enjoyed osso buco and fettucine with two-mushroom sauce. The chicken stew with dumplings is a favorite. The Awful Awful New York strip sirloin steak is awful big and awful good.

The guest rooms are all different, and suites are lovely. The Fenwick Suite, across the street, has a great bath, a small living room, and a bedroom with a king bed, two wing chairs, and a porch. The Hayden House 1801 is next door and has been totally redone. It has two suites. There is also a beauty of a suite over the coffee house across the street. The Garden Suite, also located across the street, has a fireplace, a wet bar and refrigerator, and two double beds. Very nice.

HOW TO GET THERE: Take I-95 to exit 69, and follow Route 9 north to exit 3. Turn left at the bottom of the ramp to a traffic light, turn right, and follow this street right through town to the river. The inn is on your right, about 100 yards before you get to the river.

Marine Art in Essex

In addition to its fine collection of steamboat prints by Currier & Ives and other important New York lithographers, the Griswold Inn houses an outstanding collection of marine oils by Antonio Jacobsen. Sixteen canvases painted around the turn of the twentieth century are displayed in three rooms specially decorated to showcase these works. Marine art aficionados should look in the Essex Room, the Ward Room, and the Library.

Visitors should also explore Essex's Connecticut River Museum (860-767-8269), just steps from the inn. Located at the foot of Main Street in a restored 1878 dock house, it also houses a notable collection of marine art, including paintings and ships' models, as well as a replica of the 1775 *American Turtle* and many objects and photographs related to river history.

The Homestead Inn
Greenwich, Connecticut 06830

INNKEEPERS: Theresa and Thomas Henkelmann

ADDRESS/TELEPHONE: Field Point Road; (203) 869-7500

ROOMS: 17, plus 6 suites; all with private bath, color TV, clock radio, and phone.

RATES: $250 to $395 EP.

OPEN: All year.

FACILITIES AND ACTIVITIES: Full breakfast, lunch Monday through Friday, dinner seven days a week. Bar.

BUSINESS TRAVEL: Located 45 minutes from New York City. Phone and desk in room; small conference center; audiovisual equipment, fax, computer available.

There are very good reasons why this lovely 1799 inn has been chosen as one of the best country inns in the country. One of them is that the entire staff makes you feel like royalty. I think we all need this kind of treatment once in a while.

The inn's rooms are beautifully refurbished and redecorated. William Inge wrote *Picnic* while staying at the inn in the 1950s, in Room 26. I stayed in this one, too. Room 32 has delicate stencils on the walls; the stencils were found under six layers of wallpaper dating back to 1860. Room 23 has a king-size, four-poster bed and a marvelous eighteenth-century highboy.

The Inn-Between is the newest building on this lovely property. There are eight glorious rooms out here. The bathrooms are large and have tub, shower, and bidet. All the rooms have porches, and the furnishings are wonderful. The cottage has a meeting room and two bedrooms, all very nice and quiet.

The inn's superb contemporary French restaurant, Thomas Henkelmann, is named for its enormously talented chef. The food is more than fabulous—a few years ago this establishment was named one of the top restaurants in America by *Esquire* magazine. The restaurant is elegant in a rustic fashion—hand-hewn chestnut beams, brick walls, fireplaces, skylights, and well-spaced tables with comfortable chairs.

The presentation of the food is so picture perfect, you could almost eat the plate. The fine china and beautiful stemware are exquisite. The presentation plates are objets d'art themselves, commissioned from an artist in France. The restaurant is known for its spectacular flower arrangements.

Besides the extensive menus, there are many specials. One that I had was fresh Dover sole, the best I have ever eaten, sautéed with puree of artichoke. The restaurant is noted for its fresh fish and splendid, tender veal prepared in many interesting ways. One of the luncheon dishes is escallops of veal, served with fettuccine, basil, and tomatoes. Some of the hors d'oeuvres are ravioli of seasonal mushrooms with a sauce of tomatoes and fines herbes, and sautéed calamari dressed with an aioli sauce. The desserts, needless to say, are spectacular. You must try the warm chocolate soufflé with a liquid chocolate center and housemade vanilla bean ice cream—wow!

HOW TO GET THERE: From New York take I-95 north to exit 3. Turn left at the bottom of the ramp, then left again at the second light onto Horseneck Lane. Turn left at the end of the lane onto Field Point Road. The inn is ¼ mile on the right.

From Boston take I-95 south to exit 3. Turn right at the bottom of the ramp. Turn left at the first light onto Horseneck Lane and proceed as described above.

Copper Beech Inn
Ivoryton, Town of Essex, Connecticut 06442

INNKEEPERS: Eldon and Sally Senner

ADDRESS/TELEPHONE: 46 Main Street; (860) 767–0330 or (888) 809–2056

WEB SITE: www.copperbeechinn.com

ROOMS: 4 in inn, 9 in carriage house; all with private bath and telephone; carriage house rooms with whirlpool tub, deck, and TV.

RATES: $110 to $180, double occupancy; continental breakfast.

OPEN: All year.

FACILITIES AND ACTIVITIES: Restaurant closed on Monday; Tuesday in winter; Christmas Eve, Christmas Day, and the first week in January. Dinner, full license. Victorian-style conservatory.

One of the most beautiful copper beech trees in Connecticut shades the lawn of this lovely old inn and is the reason for the inn's name.

Eldon, an expert gardener, has done wonders with the property. There is an authentic English garden, many bulbs and perennials are in bloom at different times of the year, and everything is just breathtaking.

Sally is an interior designer, and her expertise really shows in this inn. There is a lovely parlor on the first floor, with bookcases and a table for playing cards or writing or whatever. Very warm and comfortable.

Accommodations at the Copper Beech are wonderful. There are four rooms in the inn itself, and they have unbelievable old-fashioned bathrooms. The towels are soft and fluffy. Nine more guest rooms are in the carriage house, and each one has a Jacuzzi tub, so delightful after a day of exploring the lovely towns of Essex, Mystic, and other area attractions. The carriage house has an elegant country atmosphere. The halls have very nice early-nineteenth-century botanical prints. In fact, there is nineteenth-century art all over the inn, as well as a wonderful collection of fine Oriental porcelain. The facilities are not well suited for children under twelve years of age.

The four dining rooms have comfortable Chippendale and Queen Anne chairs. The Garden Porch, which is a favorite place for me, features white wicker and nice Audubon prints on the walls. The spacious tables are set far apart for gracious dining. Fresh flowers are everywhere, and the waiters are friendly and courteous.

The menu features hearty French country cuisine and changes with the seasons. Elegant hors d'oeuvres might include Caviar aux Blinis or escargots with a roasted garlic, sun-dried tomato, and basil cream, served in a puff pastry coustade. The lobster bisque is always spectacular.

Good fresh fish is used for entrees. The lobster is always easy to eat; no struggling with it here. I had it on my last trip, and on another evening I had one of the veal dishes. The veal was so tender I didn't need to use a knife. A special that caught my eye was roasted breast of pheasant, boned and filled with a mousseline of pheasant, sun-dried tomato, and fine herbs, served with a port wine and pheasant glaze. The dining room has won the AAA four-diamond award—is there any wonder? The food and service are superb.

I love chocolate and raspberries, so my favorite dessert here is the Gâteau au Chocolat, a heavenly chocolate fudge cake with hazelnut and raspberry truffle filling, served with fresh raspberries and a raspberry sauce.

The Victorian conservatory is a wonderful addition to this fine inn. It's so nice for an aperitif before dinner or for coffee and cognac after.

HOW TO GET THERE: The inn is located 1 ¾ mile west of Connecticut Route 9, from exit 3. Follow the signs to Ivoryton. The inn is on Ivoryton's Main Street, on the left side.

The Inn at Lafayette
Madison, Connecticut 06443

INNKEEPER: Caterina

ADDRESS/TELEPHONE: 725 Boston Post Road (mailing address: Box 852); (203) 245-7773; fax (203) 245-6256

WEB SITE: www.allegrecafe.com

ROOMS: 5, all with private bath, TV, and phone.

RATES: $100 to $200, double occupancy EP.

OPEN: All year.

FACILITIES AND ACTIVITIES: Lunch, dinner, bar, lounge. Piano music in lounge Thursday, Friday. Nearby: Long Island Sound for swimming, fishing, and boating. Restaurant closed Monday.

BUSINESS TRAVEL: Thirty minutes from New Haven. Meeting facilities; copier, fax, audiovisual equipment available.

This inn was built in 1837 as the Madison Methodist Church, complete with local timber and all hand fitted by local craftsmen. In 1879 the infamous Rev. Hayden was tried for the murder of a young parishioner, but he was acquitted. Rumor has it that his ghost still hangs around the attic. The building was converted into an inn in the 1920s.

The inn's rooms and suites have private marble bathrooms. One has a whirlpool tub. All the accommodations have cable television, two state-of-the-art telephones complete with hands-free "do not disturb" conference and voice box capabilities, computer plug-in, and fax port. Add Egyptian cotton linens, bathrobes, Waterford crystal and Lenox vases, and down-filled comforters—well, I cannot say enough about the rooms. They are truly lovely.

The Colonial-style dining rooms of the inn's restaurant, Cafe Allegre, are decorated with hand-woven rugs and grand murals, a fitting backdrop for a fine dining experience. Selections include a dozen different appetizers, including a terrific hot shellfish sampler. One of the dinner favorites is Vitello Casa Nova, veal scaloppini with a thin layer of fresh tomato and mozzarella in a light garlic and lemon cream sauce, a house specialty. If you are a chocolate lover like me, don't miss the Black Forest cake, served with a white and milk chocolate sauce artfully done in a checkerboard pattern.

HOW TO GET THERE: Take exit 61 off I-95. Turn onto Route 79 going toward Route 1 and Madison center. Go left on Route 1. The inn is on the left.

Madison Beach Hotel 📱
Madison, Connecticut 06443

INNKEEPERS: Lorraine Casula, manager; Betty and Henry Cooney Sr., Kathleen and Roben Bagdasarian

ADDRESS/TELEPHONE: 94 West Wharf Road; (203) 245-1404; fax (203) 245-0410

ROOMS: 31, plus 4 suites; all with private bath, air-conditioning, cable TV, and phone.

RATES: In-season, $115 to $140; suites, $150 to $225; double occupancy; continental breakfast. Off-season, $80 to $90; suites, $125 to $175; double occupancy; continental breakfast.

OPEN: March through December.

FACILITIES AND ACTIVITIES: Lunch, dinner. Bar, lounge; private beach on Long Island Sound.

BUSINESS TRAVEL: Located 20 minutes from New Haven. Phone and modem in room; conference room with overhead projector; fax available; corporate rates.

*I*f you are fortunate enough to own a boat, do come to Madison, drop your anchor, and row right in to the Madison Beach Hotel. If you don't own a boat, come anyway. The hotel is very easy to reach and should not be missed.

This Victorian beauty dates back to the 1800s. It has had many uses and lots of names, but it has never been better than it is today. The whole inn has been refurbished with an abundance of tender loving care.

Each of its rooms and magnificent suites has its own entrance and balcony overlooking the Long Island Sound and beach. The rooms are large and airy and furnished with antique oak bureaus and wicker and rattan furniture. Soft puffs cover the wicker, so you just sink into comfort. The four suites are absolutely breathtaking; each has its own kitchen, and the views from all of them are just wonderful.

There is a distinct nautical flavor to The Wharf dining room and the lovely Crow's Nest dining room on the upper level. The luncheon menu is extensive. The lobster salad roll is huge, and even I could not quite finish it.

Several cold salad plates are offered; these are so nice on a hot day. For dinner there are queen- or king-size cuts of roast prime rib of beef served with horseradish sauce—such a nice way to serve beef. The Wharf Surf and Turf is excellent. From the sea there is a good choice of entrees, each one sounding more enticing than the next. Among the desserts, black-bottom pie caught my eye and the crème brûlée was excellent; of course, there are more. And on Friday and Saturday nights, there is live music on the upper level.

The staff, starting with Lorraine at the desk to the guys and gals who wait on you, are very nice.

The beach is private, 75 feet of it. The water is clear with no undertow, so the children are safe. There is good fishing off the inn's pier. Or sit on the porch in one of the many wicker rockers and just enjoy where you are.

HOW TO GET THERE: From I-95 turn right onto Route 79 if coming from New York and left if coming from Rhode Island. Go right at the third traffic light onto Route 1. Turn left at the Madison Country Club. The inn is at the end of the road, on the water.

Tidewater Inn 🏵
Madison, Connecticut 06443

INNKEEPERS: Jean Foy and Rich Evans

ADDRESS/TELEPHONE: 949 Boston Post Road; (203) 245-8457; fax (203) 318-0265

ROOMS: 9, all with private bath.

RATES: $80 to $185, double occupancy, EPB. Business rates available.

OPEN: All year.

FACILITIES AND ACTIVITIES: Nearby: Restaurants, biking, hiking, canoeing, tennis, swimming, fishing.

*T*here are very few inns in this guide that do not serve dinner, but this area and the inn itself should not be ignored. Hammonassett State Park is close by, as are the Madison town beaches. The inn provides beach passes, chairs, and towels for your use. The innkeepers also have menus for nearby restaurants and will help you with reservations.

The inn is a former stagecoach stop that was built in the middle nineteenth century. The accommodations are lovely. There are kings, queens, doubles, and twins. Some are four-posters, and two have canopies. All rooms have telephones, clocks, and televisions. Two of the rooms have fireplaces, and one offers a Jacuzzi. On the second floor is a nice touch, a small refrigerator for guests' use.

The sitting/dining room has a bow window and a nice fireplace, along with a couch and chairs. There are tables for breakfast, and Jean prepares a good one. It always starts with fruit, and then it might be waffles, breakfast breads and muffins, coconut French toast with bacon, blueberry pancakes, sausages, or eggs of some sort. An English garden with benches and tables is a nice spot in the summer for a picnic.

There are very pretty things in the inn and a lot of Oriental pieces. Two small pillows in the Bushnell Room have these quotes on them: "Money is the root of all evil and every woman needs roots," and "Life is short; eat dessert first."

HOW TO GET THERE: From the north, take exit 62 off I-95. Go left to the light at Route 1. Turn right and go 1¼ miles to the inn, on your right. From New York take exit 61 off I-95. Take a right at the exit onto Route 79. At the third light go left onto Route 1. The inn is 1 mile on your left.

Shopping the Shoreline

If sunbathing isn't your cup of tea, you might want to explore the charming shops of Madison and Clinton. Madison is well known for its independent boutiques, its Front Parlour Tea Room—yum—at the British Shoppe (203-245-4521), its coffeeshops, and its outstanding bookstore, R. J. Julia Booksellers (203-245-3959), one of the best independent bookstores in the nation. Located just east of Madison, the town of Clinton is famed for its many antiques shops. Just drive or walk down Route 1 from shop to shop—you'll find plenty of treasures. Also in Clinton is a premium outlet mall of seventy top designers and manufacturers. Called Clinton Crossing (860-664-0700), it has bargains on Ralph Lauren, Liz Claiborne, Tommy Hilfiger, Jones New York, Anne Klein, Waterford/Wedgwood, Le Creuset, Coach, Dooney and Bourke, and many others. You'll find it off I-95, exit 63.

The Inn at Mystic
Mystic, Connecticut 06335

INNKEEPER: Jody Dyer

ADDRESS/TELEPHONE: Routes 1 and 27; (860) 536-9604; restaurant, (860) 536-8140 or (800) 237-2415; fax (860) 572-1635

WEB SITE: www.innatmystic.com

ROOMS: 9 in the inn and gatehouse, all with private bath.

RATES: $165 to $295, double occupancy, EP.

OPEN: All year.

FACILITIES AND ACTIVITIES: Breakfast, lunch, Sunday brunch, dinner every night except Christmas Eve. Bar, lounge, room service, swimming pool, tennis, canoes, sailboats, walking trails. Nearby: Mystic Seaport Museum, Mystic Marinelife Aquarium, charter boats and tours, miniature golf and driving range; Foxwoods Casino is about a half-hour north in Ledyard.

*E*very time I think about this beautiful spot, I want to go back there. The views from the inn extend from Mystic Harbor all the way to Fishers Island; they are absolutely breathtaking.

The inn, comprised of an elegant 1904 mansion and gatehouse, sits amid pear, nut, and peach trees and English flower gardens, at the top of a fifteen-acre hillside complex that also includes a large, upscale motor inn with many facilities, such as a pool and tennis court, that are shared by inn guests. From the Victorian veranda—furnished, of course, with beautiful old wicker—the view of the natural rock formations and ponds (I watched birds have their baths) and beyond to the harbor is worth a trip from anywhere.

The large living room has walls covered with magnificent pin pine imported from England and contains lovely antiques and comfortable places to sit. The rooms in both the inn and the gatehouse are beautifully done. Some have a fireplace. My room had a canopy bed, and was it ever comfortable! Each room has an interesting bath with hair dryer and whirlpool soaking tub or Thermacuzzi spa. One has a view across the room to the harbor. Now that's a nice way to relax. Look south out the windows and you'll see Mason's Island; on a clear day you can see Long Island and Montauk.

The mansion is listed on the National Register of Historic Places. It adds to the romantic mystique to know that Humphrey Bogart and Lauren Bacall spent part of their honeymoon here in the 1940s.

The modern motor inn also offers well-decorated rooms and some with views of the water; the east wing closest to the inn duplicates the inn's room decor.

The Flood Tide restaurant has long been one of the finest in the Mystic area, with a French and continental menu that is consistently first-rate. The luncheon buffet is lavish, and the Sunday brunch is a bountiful affair. Afterwards you can retreat up the hill to your mansion and enjoy the view for dessert.

The lounge is pleasant for lighter fare and is right at the swimming pool. A piano player provides music on a parlor grand piano every night and during Sunday brunch. A wedding up here would be ambrosia. The inn, combining old-world charm with modern amenities, will create the wedding of your dreams.

Mystic Attractions

You might never want to leave the Inn at Mystic, but lots of attractions are in this popular tourist area. In the summer months, there's even a shuttle that will pick you up at the inn and take you from place to place to help you avoid the traffic and enjoy the sights.

Mystic Seaport Museum (888–9SEAPORT) is one of the nation's leading maritime museums. See an entire nineteenth-century village re-creation, tall ships, and much more. The Mystic Marinelife Aquarium (860–572–5955; www.mysticaquarium.org) is newly expanded and totally redone with lots of new exhibits about the ocean and its creatures. See a 750,000-gallon beluga whale pool, an amazing coral reef display, and much more.

You might also enjoy the Denison Pequotsepos Nature Center (860–536–1216), with 7 miles of hiking and cross-country skiing trails, a trail-side museum, a gift shop and bookstore, and lots of guided walks and talks for visitors of all ages. In nearby Groton, across the Thames River, you can visit the Historic Ship *Nautilus* and the Submarine Force Museum (800–343–0079).

HOW TO GET THERE: Take exit 90 from I–95. Go 2 miles south through Mystic on Route 27 to Route 1. The inn is here. Drive up past the motor inn to the inn at the top of the driveway.

Roger Sherman Inn
New Canaan, Connecticut 06840

INNKEEPERS: Thomas and Kay Weilenmann; Rudi Granser, general manager

ADDRESS/TELEPHONE: 195 Oenoke Ridge; (203) 966–4541; fax (203) 966–0503

WEB SITE: www.RogerShermanInn.com

ROOMS: 17, all with private bath, air-conditioning, TV, and phone.

RATES: $95 to $135, single, $140 to $300, double; continental breakfast.

OPEN: All year except Christmas Day.

FACILITIES AND ACTIVITIES: Lunch, dinner, Sunday brunch, piano bar. Nearby: Golf, tennis, nature center.

*S*et amid gardens and towering maple trees, this local landmark, built in 1740, has been nicely restored and remodeled without losing its historic charm. Spacious guest rooms in the main house and the recently renovated carriage house provide comfortable Colonial-style accommodations with nice features like cozy wing chairs for reading and desks with ample work space. The inn is within easy walking distance of New Canaan's town center.

The dining room, with its columns and paintings of historic events, is a properly elegant setting for chef Raymond Péron's continental menu, which features many Swiss specialties. His soufflés are legendary. After dinner, folks gather around the sociable piano bar in the library lounge.

The restaurant is a year-round favorite. In warm weather, you can dine outdoors on the porch. On alternate Sundays from mid-January to mid-March, chef Péron offers a Swiss cheese raclette, the perfect dish for a cold winter's night.

Six function rooms of varying size and decor make the inn a popular choice for private events and weddings.

HOW TO GET THERE: The inn is located on Route 124 North in New Canaan.

The Birches Inn on Lake Waramaug
New Preston, Connecticut 06777

INNKEEPERS: Karen R. Hamilton and Frederic Faveau (also the chef); Nancy Conant, general manager

ADDRESS/TELEPHONE: 233 West Shore Road; (860) 868–1735 or (888) 590–7945; fax (860) 868–1815

WEB SITE: www.thebirchesinn.com

ROOMS: 12, all with private bath, phone, air-conditioning, and cable television.

RATES: $95 to $350, double occupancy, EPB.

OPEN: Inn open all year; dining room closed January and February.

FACILITIES AND ACTIVITIES: Dinner Thursday through Monday. Service bar, private beach, canoes. Bicycles are available for guests. Nearby: Horseback riding, fishing, hiking, cross-country skiing, antiques shops, art galleries, and numerous points of historic interest.

The Birches Inn has been around for a long time, but not like this. Restored in 1995 after being closed for several years, it's a winner today. There are five glorious rooms on the second floor of the inn. All of them have queen- or king-size beds, two face the lake and have picture windows, two have doors to the deck, and two have small sitting areas. The other three rooms are in the lake house and have private decks. Very nice indeed. Four new rooms were added in 2001.

The dining room overlooks the lake. White napery, wood trim, and a touch of jade green in the carpet make the room pretty; the chairs are very comfortable. The breakfast room is next to the dining room and also overlooks the lake and the lovely porch that is used in season. A couple of the appetizers are crispy oysters with red Asian slaw and roasted garlic custard with balsamic caramel, grilled portobello mushrooms, and baby arugula. Entrees may be grilled Atlantic salmon, penne pasta, pan-seared chicken breast, or grilled marinated leg of lamb with Parmesan polenta, sautéed mustard greens, date chutney, and roasted garlic sauce. Their wines are glorious, and there is a very good selection.

In the living room there's a fireplace and a player piano with a lot of music rolls, and in the stairwell an artist has painted birch trees. I cannot imagine how she got up there to do this work.

HOW TO GET THERE: From New York take I–84 to Route 7 in Danbury. Follow it north to New Milford. Take a right onto Route 202 to New Preston. Take a left onto Route 45 and a left at the stop sign onto West Shore Road. The inn is 2²⁄₁₀ miles on the left.

Boulders Inn ♥
New Preston, Connecticut 06777

INNKEEPERS: Kees and Ulla Adema

ADDRESS/TELEPHONE: Route 45; (860) 868–0541 or (800) 55–BOULD; fax (860) 868–1925

E-MAIL: boulders@bouldersinn.com

WEB SITE: www.bouldersinn.com

ROOMS: 17, including 2 suites, 8 guest house rooms; and 3 carriage house rooms; all with private bath; many with fireplace; 4 with double whirlpool; 1 specially equipped for the handicapped.

RATES: $210 to $380, double occupancy, EPB.

OPEN: All year.

FACILITIES AND ACTIVITIES: Swimming, boating, bicycling, hiking, cross-country skiing, billiards room, library, Victorian bar.

The stone boulders from which the inn was made jut right into the inn, thus the name Boulders Inn. If you have the energy, take a hike up Pinnacle Mountain behind the inn. From the top of the mountain, you'll be rewarded with a panorama that includes New York State to the west and Massachusetts to the north. Nice to enjoy the woods without having to go very far.

If you're not a hiker, you can partake of the marvelous countryside right from the inn. There is an outside terrace where, in summer, you may enjoy cocktails, dinner, and spectacular sunsets. The spacious living room has large windows, and its comfortable chairs and couches make it a nice place for tea or cocktails. The dining room is octagonal and provides a wonderful view of the lake. Some very good food is served here. There are some different appetizers, like diver sea scallops with chestnut puree and balsamic red wine reduction. On a recent springtime visit, I had first-crop asparagus salad with truffle oil and Parmesan cheese. And the entrees—oh my! Roasted rack of lamb with black olive mashed potatoes and sun-dried tomato sauce. Salmon and duck. The list goes on and on.

An added reason to go to the inn: It has received *Wine Spectator*'s Award of Excellence and has some 300 wines on its list.

All the guest accommodations have a view either of the lake or of the woods and are tastefully furnished. There are eight cozy guest house rooms, all with fireplaces. Four of the guest houses have double whirlpool tubs, and the furnishings are lovely. Say hello to Mouse, Oscar, and Socksie, the inn cats.

Kees and Ulla have done nice things to the inn. They have interesting paintings, Quimper pottery made in France is on display, and the cut and pierced lampshades were all made by Ulla.

HOW TO GET THERE: From New York take I-84 to Route 7 in Danbury; follow it north to New Milford. Take a right onto Route 202 to New Preston. Take a left onto Route 45, and you will find the inn as you round onto the lake.

The Hopkins Inn on Lake Waramaug
New Preston, Connecticut 06777

INNKEEPERS: Franz and Beth Schober and son Toby

ADDRESS/TELEPHONE: 22 Hopkins Road; (860) 868-7295

ROOMS: 11, plus 2 apartments; 8 with private bath.

RATES: $77 to $87, double occupancy; EP.

OPEN: All year.

FACILITIES AND ACTIVITIES: Breakfast, lunch, dinner (breakfast only meal served January–late March). Bar, lounge; private beach on lake. Nearby: Golf, tennis, horseback riding, biking, and hiking.

*S*urrounded by majestic trees on particularly beautiful grounds, this inn has glorious, unmatched views of lovely Lake Waramaug. In season there is dining under the magnificent maple and horse chestnut trees. The inn has a trout pond where you can pick the fish you fancy. The trout meunière is delicious; fresher fish would be hard to find.

Franz is the chef, and a few of his specials include lamb curry, veal piccata or milanaise, and boeuf bourguignonne. Those are for lunch. For dinner how about bay scallops in a special garlic sauce, and backhendl with lingonberries? And there is always a special or two. On Sunday, instead of brunch, they have Sunday dinner all day with wonderful lamb and pork roasts. Many Austrian dishes are served here. Strawberries Romanoff, meringue glacé, coupe aux marrons, and homemade cheesecake. Need I say more?

The dining rooms are cheerful. The fireplace has ceramic square tiles across the mantel, and the decorations are wine racks full of wines from all over the world. Naturally, the wine list is quite impressive and pleasantly, fairly priced.

There is a private beach down at the lake for use by inn guests. Bicycling, hiking, horseback riding, golf, and tennis are available nearby.

The air-conditioned rooms are clean, neat, and country-inn comfortable.

Almost all of the rooms have a view of the lake.

HOW TO GET THERE: Take I–84 to Route 202 east to Route 45 in New Preston. Turn left on Route 45 and follow it 2 miles past the lake. Take your first left after the lake, then take the second right onto Hopkins Road.

Silvermine Tavern ♥
Norwalk, Connecticut 06850

INNKEEPER: Francis C. Whitman Jr.

ADDRESS/TELEPHONE: 194 Perry Avenue; (203) 847–4558; fax (203) 847-9171

WEB SITE: www.silverminetavern.com

ROOMS: 10, all with private bath.

RATES: $85, single; $120 to $150, double; continental breakfast.

OPEN: All year.

FACILITIES AND ACTIVITIES: Lunch, dinner, Sunday brunch. Restaurant closed Tuesday. Bar; TV in parlor.

*A*lthough the Colonial crossroads village known as Silvermine has been swallowed up by the surrounding Fairfield County towns of Norwalk, Wilton, and New Canaan, the Silvermine Tavern still lies at the heart of a community of great old-world beauty. It has a remarkable way of sweeping you worlds back in time.

This is one of the most popular dining places in the area, known for delicious New England traditional food. Thursday night is set aside for a fantastic buffet supper featuring steaks, fried chicken, and many salads, all of which you top off with a great array of desserts. Sunday buffet brunch features twenty different dishes. Some of the inn specialties are grilled rack lamb chops with charred tomato, scallion, and mint salsa, and old-fashioned New England chicken potpie. The food can be savored in one of the six dining rooms or on the riverside deck, which is open from June through September. On the old millpond below, the ducks and swans wait, hoping for some leftovers. Live jazz adds to the fun after 9:00 P.M. on Friday and Saturday.

Silvermine Tavern is furnished with old Oriental rugs, antiques, old portraits, and great comfortable chairs and sofas surrounding the six huge fireplaces. The main dining room is decorated with more than 1,000 antiques, primarily old farm tools and household artifacts. Also in here is an 1887 Regina music box. The drop of a coin will turn a huge disk, and the music will begin. This is a really fun antique. In the front parlor, in front of a cheery fire, you can enjoy sherry and petit fours at the end of your day. This is the life.

The guest rooms are comfortably furnished, many of them with old-fashioned tester beds. One of my favorite rooms has its own deck overlooking the lovely millpond.

If you wish, you can stroll by the waterfall and feed the ducks and swans on the

millpond. Across the road from the tavern you will find the Country Store, run by Frank's wife. Do take a leisurely drive around the back roads near the inn, too. They are a delight. Also in this area you have the well-known Silvermine Guild of Artists.

Bee and Thistle Inn 💜 📱
Old Lyme, Connecticut 06371

INNKEEPERS: Marie and Philip Abraham

ADDRESS/TELEPHONE: 100 Lyme Street; (860) 434–1667 or
(860) 622–4946; fax (860) 434–3402

ROOMS: 11, plus 1 cottage; all with private bath and phone.

RATES: $79 to $165, double occupancy; $210, cottage; EP.

OPEN: All year except Christmas Eve, Christmas Day, New Year's Day,
and three weeks in January.

FACILITIES AND ACTIVITIES: Breakfast. Lunch and dinner every day
except Tuesday. Sunday brunch. Afternoon tea, November 1 to April 30.
Bar, lounge, library.

BUSINESS TRAVEL: Located 20 minutes from New London, 45 minutes
from New Haven. All rooms with phone; fax available; meeting space for
small groups; corporate rates.

This lovely old inn, built in 1756, sits on five and a half acres bordering the Lieutenant River in historic Old Lyme, Connecticut. During summer the abundant flower gardens keep the inn filled to overflowing with color.

The guest rooms are all air-conditioned and tastefully decorated. Your bed, maybe a four-poster or canopy, is covered with a lovely old quilt. The bath towels are big and thirsty—how I love them! The cottage has a reading room, a bedroom with queen-size bed, a kitchen, a bath, and a large television room. A deck goes around the outside. There are also a fireplace and a private dock on the river.

There are six fireplaces in the inn. The one in the parlor is most inviting— a nice place for a cocktail or just good conversation. On weekends there is music by A Wrinkle in Time, a wonderful duo who make magic with their music. There is also a harpist on Saturday nights.

Breakfast in bed is an especially nice feature of the inn. Freshly squeezed orange juice is a refreshing way to start any day. Muffins made fresh each day, buttery crepes folded with strawberry or raspberry preserves, and much more. Lunch is interesting and inventive. Try the scallops risotto, Maryland-style crab cakes, or the Bee and Thistle shepherd's pie. Sunday brunch is really gourmet. Chicken mushroom crepes, potato-encrusted salmon, three different omelets—I could eat the menu. And, of course, dinners here are magnificent, with candlelit dining rooms, a good selection of appetizers and soups, and entrees such as pork medallions, shrimp, scallops, veal, and rack of lamb. The list goes on and on. Desserts are wonderful. The menu changes seasonally, each time bringing new delights.

Afternoon tea is served from November 1 through April on Monday, Wednesday, and Thursday from 3:30 to 4:30 P.M. The tea service is beautiful; coffee and aperitifs are also available.

The inn just keeps winning awards. *Connecticut* magazine voted the inn Best Overall Restaurant, Best Dessert, and Most Romantic Place to Dine in Connecticut. Wow! Let me tell you, the inn does deserve it.

This is a fine inn in a most interesting part of New England. You are in the heart of art, antiques, gourmet restaurants, and endless activities. Plan to spend a few days when you come.

HOW TO GET THERE: Traveling north on I–95, take exit 70 immediately on the east side of the Baldwin Bridge. At the bottom of the ramp, turn left. Take the first right at the traffic light, and turn left at the end of the road. The inn is the third house on your left. Traveling south on I–95, take exit 70; turn right at the bottom of the ramp. The inn is the third house on your left.

Old Lyme Inn

Old Lyme, Connecticut 06371

INNKEEPER: Keith Green

ADDRESS/TELEPHONE: 85 Lyme Street (mailing address: P.O. Box 787); (860) 434-2600 or (800) 434-5352; fax (860) 434-5352

ROOMS: 13, all with private bath, phone, clock radio, and TV.

RATES: $99 to $158, double occupancy; continental breakfast.

OPEN: All year.

FACILITIES AND ACTIVITIES: Lunch, dinner, Sunday brunch. Bar and dining room.

BUSINESS TRAVEL: Located 45 minutes from Hartford. Phone in every room. Meeting rooms; fax available; database for computers.

*S*assafras was the inn cat who has a neat lounge named after her. Winslow is the current inn cat, named after the huge Winslow Homer mural in the dining room. In the lounge you'll find television, games, books, and a lovely fireplace for your enjoyment, along with comfortable chairs and couch. The Victorian barroom has a back bar that is more than one hundred years old and was found by the innkeeper in Philadelphia. There is a beveled mirror over it that most museums would covet. A raw bar is offered in here for light suppers. A very cozy and comfortable room.

The rooms here at the inn are grand, especially the eight in the new wing. The beds are four-posters, and all rooms have telephone, clock radio, and Victorian couch and/or delightful wing chairs. You will find mints on your pillow at night.

There are four separate dining areas, and the food is superb. The menu, of course, changes with the seasons, but I'd like to give you just a few ideas. Several appetizers, soups, and salads are offered. New England crab cake was one; another was imported escargots. I had spinach Waldorf salad with roasted chicken, chopped apples, and walnuts. It was excellent. They also have—get this—Wild American Meatloaf. It's wild boar and buffalo blended into a meat loaf and served with mashed potatoes and mushroom gravy.

Dinner is spectacular. The Old Lyme Inn Pasta is so divine I won't even describe it. You must come and try it. There are nine appetizers, no one bet-

Getting an Impression of Old Lyme and Lyme

At the turn of the twentieth century, Miss Florence Griswold of Old Lyme welcomed a group of artists to summer at her pretty yellow mansion on the Lieutenant River. Soon a colony was established there, as now-famed painters like Childe Hassam, William Chadwick, and many others studied the light and shadows of the woods and shoreline. The Lyme Art Colony was responsible for a new style of painting known as American Impressionism. Now Miss Florence's house is a growing museum devoted to American art and the history of the colony and the region. Open year-round, the Florence Griswold Museum (860-434-5542) is just steps away from both the Bee and Thistle Inn and the Old Lyme Inn.

If you'd prefer to get your own impression of the area, explore the Old Lyme Historic District on foot, then explore Route 156 by bicycle or car. North on this roadway is the beautiful hamlet of Hamburg Cove on the Eight-Mile River. You might even see an artist with an easel painting at the riverside—a frequent sight here. Devil's Hopyard State Park, Selden Neck State Park, and the Nehantic State Forest are all nearby. Ask your innkeepers for tips on visiting these areas.

ter than the others. And soups—well, I had dilled carrot bisque with bay shrimp, and it was quite inventive. Sole and crab imperial is excellent; planked swordfish is different and so pretty; rack of lamb is very good. Of course, there is much more, and there are specials every night. The desserts have been written up in food magazines and have won awards—that's how good they are.

The luncheon menu, too, offers wonderful food. Try the Oriental chicken salad or the grilled pizza. Whatever your selection, do come and sample some of this grand food.

Enjoy your meal along with the music of a jazz guitarist on the weekends. Continental breakfast is served to guests every day except weekends, when a breakfast buffet is offered.

The inn can handle small conferences, weddings, parties, reunions, and such. It would be a lovely place to have a wedding and is easy to find just off

I-95. There is much to do and see in this pretty town and area.

Many of the paintings in the inn represent the Old Lyme School of artists who, at the turn of the twentieth century, resided a few doors down the street at Florence Griswold's home, now the

Florence Griswold Museum. In addition, there are paintings purchased from current artists featured at the Lyme Art Association shows.

HOW TO GET THERE: Traveling north on I-95, take exit 70 immediately on the east side of the Baldwin Bridge. At the bottom of the ramp, turn left. Take the first right at the traffic light, and turn left at the dead end. The inn is on the right. Traveling south on I-95, take exit 70. At the bottom of the ramp, turn right. The inn is on the right.

Saybrook Point Inn and Spa
Old Saybrook, Connecticut 06475

INNKEEPER: Stephen Tagliatela; Karin Nelson, restaurant manager; David Dixon, general manager

ADDRESS/TELEPHONE: 2 Bridge Street; (860) 395-2000 or (800) 243-0212 (outside Connecticut); fax (860) 388-1504

E-MAIL: info@saybrook.com

WEB SITE: www.saybrook.com

ROOMS: 81, including 16 suites and 1 lighthouse apartment; all with private bath, phone, TV, air-conditioning, and refrigerator; 55 with working fireplace. Some smoke-free rooms and suites.

RATES: $159 to $299, double occupancy; $259 to $549, suites; EP. Package plans available.

OPEN: All year.

FACILITIES AND ACTIVITIES: Breakfast, lunch, dinner, Sunday brunch. Banquet and meeting facilities; health club with whirlpool, sauna, and steam; spa; indoor and outdoor pools; marina with 120 slips and floating docks. Nearby: Charter boats, theater.

BUSINESS TRAVEL: Located 10 minutes from railroad station. All rooms with phones; suites with data ports for computers and fax machines; meeting rooms; secretarial services available.

"Experience the magic at Saybrook Point Inn." These are the inn's words, and they're so true. The panoramic views of the Connecticut River and Long Island Sound are magnificent. From the moment you walk into the lobby, the Italian marble floors, beautiful furniture, and glorious fabrics let you know this is a special inn. Even the carpet is hand-loomed.

Most of the guest rooms and suites have a water view and a balcony. They are lavishly decorated with eighteenth-century–style furniture, and Italian marble is used in the bathroom with whirlpool bath. Also in the rooms are a miniature wet bar and refrigerator; double-, queen-, or king-size bed; and hair dryer. The suites feature VCR and data ports for personal computers and fax machines. Secretarial services are also available, as is an exercise room with life bikes.

There is a full spa, with indoor and outdoor pools, steam room, sauna, and whirlpool. The licensed staff will pamper you with a therapeutic massage, European facial, manicure, pedicure, or even a quality makeup application.

Planning a wedding or business conference? No problem. The inn has banquet facilities for all occasions. The ballroom seats 240 people. Smaller meetings would be ideal in the library, which holds up to sixteen people, or in the executive suites.

Breakfast, lunch, and dinner are served in an exquisite room that overlooks the inn's marina, the river, and Long Island Sound. There was a full moon the evening I dined here. What a beautiful sight to enhance the memorable food! Appetizers like smoked Norwegian salmon, escargots, smoked pheasant, and beluga caviar are an elegant way to begin your dinner. Pastas are cannelloni, linguine, or wild mushroom. I had one of the best racks of lamb I have ever had. There is always a fresh seafood special. My friend had shrimp Provençale—shrimp sautéed with garlic, shallots, and scallions. A flower may be a garnish on your plate; you can eat it.

Do try to save room for dessert. I had chocolate–chocolate chip cake, which was dark and beautiful and delicious. The service is also superb.

Sunday brunch is a winner. Too much to list, but believe me, you will not go away hungry. I was here for Easter, and the food was glorious.

HOW TO GET THERE: From I–95 northbound take exit 67 (southbound, take exit 68) and follow Route 154 and signs to Saybrook Point.

Stonehenge
Ridgefield, Connecticut 06877

INNKEEPER: Douglas Seville

ADDRESS/TELEPHONE: P.O. Box 667; (203) 438–6511

ROOMS: 14, plus 2 suites; all with private bath, color TV, phone.

RATES: $75 to $120, single; $90 to $160, double; $200, suite; continental breakfast. Winter rates available.

OPEN: All year except New Year's Day.

FACILITIES AND ACTIVITIES: Breakfast, dinner, service bar, lounge. No dinner on Monday.

The setting for Stonehenge is serenely beautiful. Outside the inn is a lovely pond, which is bedecked with swans and aflutter with Canada geese and ducks stopping in on their migratory journeys. When I visited here in the spring, the red and yellow tulips were at their best.

In June 1988 the lovely old farmhouse that was the main building of the inn was destroyed in a terrible fire. But now a new Stonehenge has risen. The rooms, all different, are beautiful. No matter whether you're in the guest house or cottage or inn, the accommodations are elegant, color coordinated, and comfortable. The suite has facilities for light cooking. Most of the rooms have a queen- or king-size bed. All overlook the pond and wooded hillside.

A lovely continental breakfast is brought to you in your room, along with a copy of the morning newspaper. The breakfast consists of freshly squeezed juice, delicious muffin or Danish pastry, and coffee.

The common room has a fireplace flanked by bookcases. The large dining room has picture windows overlooking the pond and terraces. It has always been justifiably famous for its gourmet dinners. The original Stonehenge shrimp in crisp beer batter with a pungent sauce is still here—and glorious. Some of the appetizers are a crepe of wild mushrooms with Gruyère cheese, and fresh hearts of palm wrapped in prosciutto. There are good salads to choose from, followed by entrees like crisply roasted duckling with wild rice and black currant sauce, or breast of chicken filled with fresh spinach and Gruyère cheese, wrapped in puff pastry and served with a champagne sauce. You could even have roast baby suckling pig (five days' notice for this one). The desserts are stupendous. Do come and try some. Decaffeinated espresso gets my vote.

This is a beautiful place for a wedding or any other special function. The Terrace Room is available for corporate meetings.

HOW TO GET THERE: From the Merritt Parkway take exit 40. Go north on Route 7. The inn's sign is in 13 miles, on the left. From I-84 go south on Route 7. The inn's sign is 4½ miles on the right.

West Lane Inn and The Inn at Ridgefield
Ridgefield, Connecticut 06877

INNKEEPERS: M. M. Mayer and Deborah Prieger; Henry Prieger, owner of the restaurant

ADDRESS/TELEPHONE: 22 West Lane; (203) 438-7323; Ridgefield, (203) 438-8282

E-MAIL: westlaneinn@aol.com

WEB SITE: www.westlaneinn.com

ROOMS: 15, all with private bath, air-conditioning, phone, and TV; some with fireplace.

RATES: $130, single; $145 to $190, double; EPB.

OPEN: All year.

FACILITIES AND ACTIVITIES: Lunch, dinner, Sunday brunch; bar, lounge; piano nightly.

*W*e have a first here: two separate inns next door to each other. West Lane Inn has the rooms and serves breakfast and a light menu from the pantry. The Inn at Ridgefield serves delicious lunch and dinner.

Rich oak paneling and lush carpeting, along with a crackling fire, greet you as you enter West Lane. The bedrooms are luxurious, with individual climate control, color television, radio, and telephone with voice mail and modem jacks. Each room has either one king- or two queen-size beds. Some have a working fireplace. These are really nice on a cold night.

The breakfast room is bright and cheerful, serving freshly squeezed orange juice. A West Lane breakfast special is yogurt with bananas, honey, and nuts. Cold cereals in the summer, hot cereals in the winter; Danish, muffins, or toast; or a poached egg is offered. Everything is done very nicely. The pantry selections are available from noon until late in the evening. There are tuna fish salad plates, several sandwiches like grilled cheese—even peanut butter and jelly—and more. There also are desserts.

The ends of the old wooden wine and whiskey crates that line the porch of The Inn at Ridgefield let you know there are good things inside. Dinner features hors d'oeuvres like pâté of pistachio and truffles with sauce Cumberland, onion soup Calvados gratinée, and vichysoisse. Then entrees such as frogs legs (they are really good), fresh Dover sole, chateaubriand, and roast rack of spring lamb follow. There are wonderful salads and desserts. Crepes suzettes for two is an old favorite. And believe me, there are more, plus good coffees.

Both inns are just around the corner from the famous Cannon Ball House, which was struck by a British fieldpiece during the Revolution. There are quite a few stores to browse in, as well as antiques stores. The Aldrich Museum is in town, and you are close to several fine summer theaters. Ridgefield is such a pretty town to visit.

HOW TO GET THERE: Coming north from New York on Route 684, or Route 7 from the Merritt Parkway, get off on Route 35 and follow it to Ridgefield. The inns are on Route 35 at the south end of town.

Old Riverton Inn
Riverton, Connecticut 06065

INNKEEPERS: Pauline and Mark Telford

ADDRESS/TELEPHONE: P.O. Box 6; (860) 379–8678 or (800) 378–1796; fax (860) 379–1006

ROOMS: 12, all with private bath.

RATES: $90 to $195, double occupancy; EPB.

OPEN: All year except the first week of January and the first two weeks of March.

FACILITIES AND ACTIVITIES: Lunch, dinner Wednesday through Sunday. Dining room has wheelchair accessibility. Bar.

*T*he Old Riverton Inn was originally opened in 1796 by Jesse Ives. It was on the post road between Hartford and Albany and was known as Ives Tavern. It has passed through many hands since then, and the hands that have it now are very capable.

The Grindstone Terrace was enclosed to make it useful all year. The floor of this room is made of grindstones that, according to century-old records, were quarried in Nova Scotia and sent by ship first to Long Island Sound and then up the Connecticut River to Hartford. From there they were hauled by oxen to Collinsville, where they were used in the making of axes and machetes. A lot of history is here. Once Riverton was known as Hitchcocksville, because the famous Hitchcock furniture factory is here. It is open Monday through Saturday until 6:00 P.M., til 5:00 P.M. on Sunday.

The Colonial dining room has, of course, Hitchcock chairs and a lovely bow window chock-full of plants. I sat here for luncheon one day and had delicious broiled scrod. The menu offers a lot of choices. Chicken salad plate looked really enticing. Dinner appetizers, such as the homemade soups, also are good. I had the onion soup, and it was delicious. There are several seafood entrees, each one looking better than the last. Other specialties of the inn include boneless breast of chicken marengo, veal Français, and veal maison.

Chef Leo Roy really has a way with food.

A stained-glass window is in the bar. Murals in here were painted by Bobby Walsh, who created murals at the New York World's Fair in the late '30s. As the Telfords say, they "provide hospitality for the hungry, thirsty, and sleepy."

One of my favorite guest rooms has a working fireplace, a sitting area, and queen-size bed. A few rooms have canopy beds. A comfortable lounge and library are on this floor, providing you with games, tons of books—and lots of quiet.

HOW TO GET THERE: The inn is 3½ miles from Winsted. Take Route 8 or Route 44 to Winsted. Turn east on Route 20, and it is approximately 1½ miles to the inn.

A Riverton Ramble

Antiques, galleries, the delightfully old-fashioned Riverton General Store, the Hitchcock Museum, the Hitchcock Chair Factory Store, the Village Sweet Shop, and the Catnip Mouse Tea Room are all on the lovely stretch of Route 20 that is Riverton's main street. All are well within walking distance of the Old Riverton Inn, and most are open year-round or at least from April through December.

The Hitchcock Museum (860-738-4950) is in the Old Union Church. A visit here reveals the history and handiwork of Lambert Hitchcock, who began producing his notable style of hand-painted American chairs in 1818. You can also visit the factory store (860-379-4826), located in Lambert's original factory building along with Buckingham Galleries.

Down the street are such shops as Antiques and Herbs (860-379-4729), perfect for browsing for treasures. Stop for a treat at the sweet shop or the tearoom—boy, are they good.

Under Mountain Inn
Salisbury, Connecticut 06068

INNKEEPERS: Marged and Peter Higginson

ADDRESS/TELEPHONE: Route 41; (860) 435-0242; fax (860) 435-2379

ROOMS: 7, all with private bath.

RATES: $180 to $215, double occupancy; MAP.

OPEN: All year.

FACILITIES AND ACTIVITIES: For inn guests, dinner is available every night. Nearby: Swimming, canoeing, skiing, fishing, golf.

*U*nder Mountain Inn was built in the early 1700s. Wood found in the attic was known as "king's wood" because of its special width. It now is the paneling on the front of the bar.

The house is Colonial in style and has been lovingly restored. Each of the seven guest rooms has Posturepedic mattresses. There are doubles, queens, and kings, so take your choice. Marged has a wonderful collection of stuffed animals, and you will find one or two on your bed. What a homey feeling this added touch provides. You will also find sherry in your room for your enjoyment. Beautiful canopies are on most of the beds.

There are three acres of grounds, so in the summer you can wander out under the trees and enjoy their beauty. Shading the inn and terrace is a tree that is rumored to be the oldest thorned locust in Connecticut. Sneakers is the inn cat.

The dining rooms are charming; there are three. Peter, who hails from England, is the chef. You can start with Scottish salmon or one of Peter's good soups. Go on to traditional British entrees such as roast goose with chestnut stuffing, shepherd's pie, bangers and mash, beef steak and kidney pie . . . I could go on and on. Desserts are homemade and scrumptious. The menu, of course, changes seasonally. In the morning you are served a full English breakfast.

Arabelle's Lounge is small and so comfortable, with a VCR and a wonderful collection of British movies.

There is much to do in this area of Connecticut. The inn has brochures to help you plan your day. You will find canoeing, fishing, swimming, horseback riding, tennis, skiing, and more. There are also many good private schools in this area.

HOW TO GET THERE: Take Route 41 north for 4 miles from Salisbury. The inn is on the left. From New York State take I-684 to Route 22, then Route 44 to Route 41.

The White Hart
Salisbury, Connecticut 06068

INNKEEPER: Scott Bok

ADDRESS/TELEPHONE: Box 545; (800) 832-0041 or (860) 435-0030; fax (860) 435-0040

ROOMS: 23, plus 3 suites; all with private bath, cable TV, phone, and air-conditioning; 1 specially equipped for handicapped.

RATES: $99 to $205, double; $169 to $195, suites; EP.

OPEN: All year.

FACILITIES AND ACTIVITIES: Breakfast, lunch, dinner. Tavern room, garden room, Riga Room restaurant, private function and meeting rooms. Nearby: Swimming, boating, skiing, horseback riding; Tanglewood and Jacob's Pillow.

How nice to have this old beauty back in the book! Looking sharp and refurbished in a grand style, the inn now boasts an extra wing, and a sprinkler system has been added. The lobby and common rooms are beautifully furnished. A small upholstered child-size wing chair is a lovely touch in a corner of the lobby. Along with it are a pair of adult-capacity wing chairs and nice couches, too.

To the left of the lobby is the Hunt Room, used primarily for receptions, but with a chess table guests can enjoy when the room is not in use.

Accommodations are fine—either two double beds or a queen-size bed in each room—and very comfortable. My room on my last visit was the Ford Room, named for Edsel Ford, the owner of the inn many years ago when his son went to the Hotchkiss School. He wanted to be assured of a pleasant and convenient place to stay when he visited his son.

The restaurants include the Garden Room and the Old Tavern. Breakfast, lunch, and light dinners are served here.

I had my breakfast in the Garden Room. Sunshine and pretty plants added to the good food. Fresh-squeezed orange juice, eggs, French toast, oatmeal, and more. Sunday breakfast, of course, is grand, with thick-sliced brioche French toast with walnut streusel, grilled New York strip steak, and eggs and much more.

Lunch has lots of goodies. French Brie baked in puff pastry, blackened chicken Caesar salad, or a portobello mushroom sandwich on olive bread are just a few of the great choices.

The Riga Room is a wonderful restaurant for fine dining and Sunday brunch. Italian fabric was used for the bar stools, chairs, and banquettes, then color-coordinated with the walls and drapes. It is lovely. Prince Edward Island mussels with white wine saffron and cream isn't a bad way to start dinner. Entrees include pan-roasted venison tender- loin, roasted breast of duck, or rack of lamb. Desserts—I do not know where I found the room, but I was glad I did. Go and enjoy.

On a summer day there is no nicer pastime than watching the world go by from the wicker chairs on the front porch of this classic New England Inn.

HOW TO GET THERE: Go north from the Merritt Parkway (Route 15) to Route 7. The inn is on the Green in Salisbury, at the intersection of Routes 44 and 41.

Simsbury 1820 House

Simsbury, Connecticut 06070

INNKEEPER: Diane M. Ropiak, general manager

ADDRESS/TELEPHONE: 731 Hopmeadow Street; (860) 658-7658 or (800) 879-1820; fax (860) 651-0724

WEB SITE: www.simsbury1820house.com

ROOMS: 33, plus 3 suites, in 2 buildings; all with private bath, phone, and TV with VCR, complimentary movie rental; 2 with wheelchair accessibility.

RATES: $145 to $205, double occupancy; continental breakfast.

OPEN: All year.

FACILITIES AND ACTIVITIES: Dinner Monday through Thursday; lounge. Nearby: Shopping, antiquing.

BUSINESS TRAVEL: Located 25 minutes from Hartford. All rooms with phone; conference rooms; fax, computer, and overhead projector available; corporate rates.

Built in 1820, Simsbury House recently stood vacant for twenty-four years; vandals, time, and weather took their toll. But today, after a lot of hard work, frustration, and expense, it has been beautifully transformed into a fine inn and restaurant.

Relatives of the former owners provided old photographs of the house that were a good reference as it was restored. Two local craftswomen made leaded-glass windows to match the originals. The furniture consists of antiques and fine handmade reproductions from England. For example, the four-poster mahogany beds were carved by English cabinetmakers, and they are beauties. Some of them are king-size and oh, so comfortable.

Twelve hundred rolls of wallpaper and 5,000 yards of fabric were used in restoring the inn and carriage house. The color schemes—blue, beige, and gold—recur among the rooms. The suites in the carriage house are sumptuous. One has a whirlpool tub. This is the life! All the rooms are different, and some have an outside terrace.

The modernized inn has a sprinkler system throughout, as well as smoke detectors. There are two rooms for the handicapped.

The inn's cafe is open Monday through Thursday from 5:00 P.M. to 8:00 P.M., with a pleasant dinner menu; the dining room is reserved for private parties on Friday and Saturday evenings.

One of the most popular dishes, the chef's seasonal crepe, which changes daily, can be ordered as an appetizer or an entree. Seafood and meats done on the grill are another specialty, served with a variety of interesting sauces, and there are some interesting dishes such as shrimp and sea scallops served on a julienne vegetable crispy noodle cake with a Thai-inspired broth. Save room for dessert; you won't want to miss it.

HOW TO GET THERE: From I-84 take exit 39 onto Route 10 and go to Simsbury. The inn is on the left.

Skating with the Stars in Simsbury

Not far from the Simsbury 1820 House, on Simsbury's main Route 10, also known as Hopmeadow Street, the International Ice Skating Center of Connecticut (860-651-4500) draws crowds of skaters and spectators who would like to share the ice with or simply watch in awe such champion figure skaters as Ekaterina Gordeeva, Viktor Petrenko, Oksana Baiul, and Scott Davis. This world-class twin-rink facility is their home base. Visitors can skate, take lessons, and see both figure skating and hockey events and practices. A cafe, a restaurant, and coffee shop are all here. It's open year-round from 6:00 A.M. to midnight; call for public skating sessions. Rent some skates and have fun.

The Mayflower Inn

Washington, Connecticut 06793

INNKEEPERS: John Trevenen; Adriana and Robert Mnuchin, owners

ADDRESS/TELEPHONE: 118 Woodbury Road (mailing address:
P.O. Box 1288); (860) 868-9466; fax (860) 868-1497

ROOMS: 18, plus 7 suites; all with private bath; some with balcony;
some with fireplace.

RATES: $400 to $650, double occupancy; $700 to $1,300, suites; EP.

OPEN: All year.

FACILITIES AND ACTIVITIES: Breakfast, lunch, dinner. Bar and lounge,
gift shop, spa, heated pool, tennis.

BUSINESS TRAVEL: Phones in rooms; conference area. The teahouse is
fully equipped for meetings or conferences.

The Mayflower Inn is glorious. The entrance hall is huge and well
appointed with antiques, Persian rugs, and many works of art.
Much of it has been collected by the Mnuchins over the years during their travels. There is a cherry-paneled library off this, and the other side
has a large game room full of beautiful things.

The Shop at Mayflower has unusual vintage jewelry, cashmere gloves,
sweaters, and silks; it is just grand.

There are rooms in three buildings: the Mayflower, the Standish, and the
Speedwell. Facilities are sumptuous, with feather beds and down comforters
and pillows. Frette linens grace the beds, which are either queens, kings, or a
pair of twins. Some rooms
have a balcony, and others
have a fireplace. There is
also nightly turndown service.

You can dine in one of
three dining rooms or, if
the weather is nice, outside
on the dining terrace that
overlooks the grounds and

woods. The English pub-style lounge, which has a piano, leads out to the porch, where in summer there is wicker furniture. It is called the "drinking porch."

The teahouse is an executive retreat and a wonderful place for conferences. The spa, with a very strong emphasis on massage, is a plus—I had a massage, and it was wonderful. There are special classes, and personal trainers are also available.

Dining here is grand. I had a nice thick veal chop and salad. The inn has special Mayflower mashed potatoes, and boy, are they good! The menu changes not only seasonally but frequently. Foods from the local farms are used. There is not enough room to elaborate on breakfast, or the luncheon specials, or even dinner. But wow, save room for the desserts!

Everyone who works here has a smile, and all are more than willing to make your stay a pleasant one.

Orchids are everywhere, the *New York Times* is brought to your door, and a minibar is in your room. One night was not enough, so I stayed for two.

HOW TO GET THERE: From Hartford take I-84 west to exit 15, Southbury. Follow Route 6 north through Southbury to Woodbury. It is exactly 5 miles from I-84 to "Canfield Corners" (an 1890s building on your right). Go left here on Route 47 to Washington. It is 8²⁄₁₀ miles to the inn.

Water's Edge Inn

Westbrook, Connecticut 06498

INNKEEPER: Andy Abels, general manager

ADDRESS/TELEPHONE: 1525 Boston Post Road; (860) 399-5901 or (800) 222-5901 (outside Connecticut)

ROOMS: 100 rooms, 65 villas; all with private bath, cable TV, and phone.

RATES: $135 to $275, double occupancy; EP.

OPEN: All year.

FACILITIES AND ACTIVITIES: Breakfast, lunch, dinner, Sunday brunch. Bar, lounge; room service; entertainment on holidays and special occasions; spa; indoor and outdoor pools; banquet rooms; tennis; private beach on Long Island Sound.

BUSINESS TRAVEL: Located 30 minutes from New Haven. All rooms with phone; six conference rooms.

There is a song that says, "This one's for me." Well, here it is, and what a gem! Sitting up high, overlooking Long Island Sound, the inn is like a turn-of-the-twentieth-century resort. With its own sparkling private beach, it offers swimming, plus boating on the inn's fleet of catamarans, sailfish, and paddleboats.

The dining room is decorated in soft shades of peach, rose, and gray. The food is magnificent. The seafood and lobster bisque with crab is excellent. There is a choice of several salads. I had the scrod entree one night and duckling another. Both were very good. I love the way the food is arranged so prettily on the plates.

Sunday brunch is a delight. It is so popular that reservations are a must. Chefs make Belgian waffles to order, as well as omelets with a choice of ingredients inside. Roast beef, roast turkey, fish, fruit, and vegetables are also offered. The pastries are really good!

There's an outdoor patio for cocktails and dining in summer, called Le Grille. It is just fabulous, with its view of the Sound. The lounge is warm in feeling and has a nice fireplace, besides. The bar sports comfortable chairs and has the style of a pub.

The rooms and suites are sumptuous. Most of them have a king- or a queen-size bed. All have comfortable chairs and views of something pretty. Some have a balcony, and there is a wet bar in the suites.

The health club has the latest equipment, day and night tennis courts, indoor and outdoor swimming, and sauna. There are banquet and conference rooms for ten to 350 persons. The inn's grounds are very nice for a walk. And there is much to do in this lovely area—marinas, state parks, the lovely town of Essex nearby, and much more.

HOW TO GET THERE: From I-95 take exit 65 at Westbrook. Go south to Route 1, then go east approximately ¼ mile and look for the inn's sign.

Select List of
Other Connecticut Inns

Bishopsgate Inn

7 Norwich Road
P.O. Box 290
East Haddam, CT 06423
(860) 873–1677

5 rooms, 1 suite with sauna; all rooms with private bath; 4 with fireplace; 1818 Colonial within walking distance of Goodspeed Opera House and Connecticut River.

Wake Robin Inn

104–106 Sharon Road (Route 41)
Lakeville, CT 06039
(860) 435–2515
Fax (860) 435–2000
Web site: www.wakerobininn.com

40 rooms in 1896 main inn, all with private bath; 15 rooms in motel.

Whaler's Inn

20 East Main Street
Mystic, CT 06355
(860) 536–1506 or (800) 243–2588

41 rooms, all with private bath; historic inn near Mystic River.

Randall's Ordinary

Route 2
P.O. Box 243
North Stonington, CT 06359
(860) 599–4540 or (877) 599–4540 (toll free)

18 rooms in 300-year-old Colonial house and renovated 1819 barn; suite in silo has fireplace and a winding staircase up to a Jacuzzi. Authentic seventeenth-century open-hearth cooking in restaurant.

Three Chimneys Inn

1201 Chapel Street
New Haven, CT 06511
(203) 789-1201 or (800) 443-1554
Fax (203) 776-7363

10 rooms, all with private bath; 3 with nonfunctional fireplaces; all with air-conditioning, TV, phone, data port for computer; on-site parking; within walking distance of Yale University.

The Elms Inn

500 Main Street
Ridgefield, CT 06877
(203) 438-2541 (phone and fax)

20 rooms, including 5 suites; all with private bath, TV, phone; 1760 Colonial on a site of the Battle of Ridgefield in the Revolutionary War.

The Inn at Longshore

260 Compo Road South
Westport, CT 06880
(203) 226-3316

12 rooms, including 3 suites; all with private bath; 1890s seaside inn with extensive outdoor sports facilities and views of Long Island Sound.

The Inn at National Hall

2 Post Road West
Westport, CT 06880
(203) 221-1351 or (800) 628-4255
Fax (203) 221-0276

15 rooms, including 7 suites; all with private bath; luxurious 1873 National Register of Historic Places Italianate building overlooking Saugatuck River.

Maine

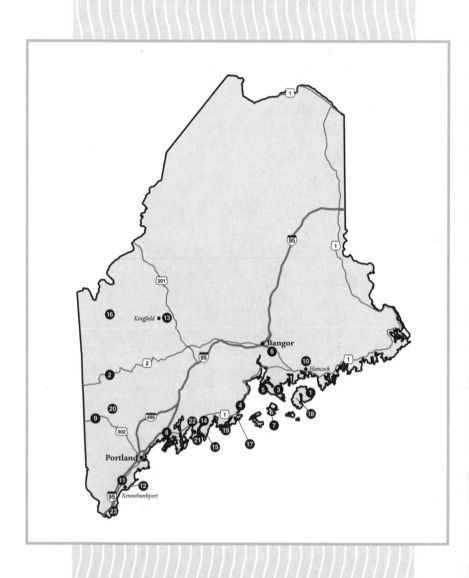

Maine

Numbers on map refer to towns numbered below.

* A Top Pick Inn

Bar Harbor Hotel–Bluenose Inn
Bar Harbor, Maine 04609

INNKEEPER: David J. Witham

ADDRESS/TELEPHONE: 90 Eden Street; (207) 288-3348 or
(800) 445-4077

WEB SITE: www.bluenoseinn.com

ROOMS: 97 rooms and suites, all with private bath; 41 with gas fireplace, phone, cable TV, air-conditioning, minifridge

RATES: $129 to $399, double occupancy; EP. Lower off-season rates,
great packages.

OPEN: Late April to late October.

FACILITIES AND ACTIVITIES: Breakfast and dinner, bar, lounge. Indoor
and outdoor heated pools. Fitness center, spa. Nearby: Boating, parks,
and beauty.

*W*hy it's taken me so long to get back to Bar Harbor I may never
know, but I'm here now, and the place is breathtaking. This inn is
large but made very comfortable by the owner and his staff.

The Mizzentop, built in 1995, has the registration office, a great room
and bar, a function room, fifty-two of the guest rooms, and Raspbeary's gift
shop. A lot of bears and bunnies, all handmade, live here.

Stenna Nordica, another
building, has forty-five rooms, a
glass front elevator, and much
comfort. All the rooms have
views of Frenchman Bay.

The third building has the
heated indoor pool, and it's a
beauty, with classic columns and
arched windows; the spa and fitness center are also here. The
Rose Garden restaurant is also out here, and it's lovely—AAA-rated and good
food. For starters there are Maine lobster bisque with sweet brandy cream,
crab cakes with tomato coulis and herb oil, pan-seared Hudson Valley foie
gras—these should give you an idea or two. The salads are grand, and entrees

may be fresh Maine lobster (of course), grilled salmon fillet, or sautéed halibut with saffron risotto, asparagus bundles, and roasted red pepper sauce. There's also rack of lamb, fillet of beef, and more. Desserts? Well, come on up and see.

The bar's a beauty of handcrafted cherry wood; the great room has a huge wood fireplace. There are fresh flowers everywhere and good couches and comfortable chairs. There are glorious chandeliers everywhere you look.

The property, all of it, has Mobil's four stars. No wonder—it's grand. There are thirty-nine suites, and I was in one on the fourth floor that had a fireplace, two televisions (one for the sitting area, one for the bed area), and a porch overlooking the bay. The standard rooms are beauties, and the suites are fabulous.

Acadia National Park is a short drive away, and the dock for the *Cat* ferry to and from Nova Scotia is 600 yards away. The *Cat* is a high-speed ferry that gets to Nova Scotia in 2½ hours.

There's also the *Bay Lady,* an 85-foot schooner. Listen to the wind in the rigging while you sail Frenchman Bay. Watch for whales and puffins.

This inn is perfect for conferences, weddings, bridal showers, and much more. Dinner meetings in the Rose Garden can seat as many as fifty guests.

HOW TO GET THERE: Northbound travelers follow I-95 over the bridge into Maine and continue on I-95 to exit 45A. Take this exit and follow Route 395 East to Route 1A to Ellsworth. Go straight on Route 3 to Bar Harbor. Pass the *Cat* Ferry Terminal. The Bar Harbor Hotel–Bluenose Inn is 600 yards beyond the ferry terminal on the right, across from the College of the Atlantic.

Southbound travelers take I-95 to exit 45A and follow northbound directions. The hotel sits high on an elevated site overlooking Frenchman Bay.

The Bethel Inn and Country Club
Bethel, Maine 04217

INNKEEPERS: Dick Rasor; Allen Connors, manager
ADDRESS/TELEPHONE: P.O. Box 49; (207) 824–2175 or (800) 654–0125
E-MAIL: info@bethelinn.com

WEB SITE: www.bethelinn.com

ROOMS: 137, all with private bath, phone, and cable TV; 56 with fireplace; 2 specially equipped for handicapped.

RATES: $70 to $189, per person, double occupancy; MAP. Package rates available.

OPEN: All year.

FACILITIES AND ACTIVITIES: Lunch, bar, lounge. Golf, tennis, swimming pool, lake house with kayaks and canoes, cross-country skiing, saunas, exercise room, indoor games, supervised activities and summer day camp for children. Own walking-tour guide. Wheelchair access to lobby, conference center, dining room. Nearby: Downhill skiing at Sunday River and Mt. Hebron.

*T*he Bethel Inn faces the village common of Bethel, Maine, which is a National Historic District complete with beautifully restored churches, public buildings, and private homes. The rear of the inn overlooks its own 200 acres and eighteen-hole championship golf course.

Guest rooms have private baths and direct-dial telephones. They are well done and very comfortable. A number of rooms have been redecorated with country-print wallpaper, thick carpeting, and fresh paint. The Bingham Suite, where I stayed the last time I was at the inn, has a fireplace and a Jacuzzi—glorious!

The huge lobby, the Gibson room, and library are beautifully furnished for the utter comfort of the guests. The piano, by the way, is a Steinway.

Dining is a pleasure, either in the charming main dining room or on the year-round dining veranda overlooking the golf course. You'll find such entrees as prime rib, roast duck, and lobster and crabmeat casserole on the

Oliver Metcalf

extensive menu. Just before sunset, look out over the golf course. You'll see literally hundreds of swallows diving into the chimney of the utility building next to the course.

Downstairs is the MillBrook Tavern. Mill Brook cuts through the golf course and was the site of Twitchell's mill, erected in the early 1700s in Sudbury, Canada, which is now Bethel, Maine.

Down here in the bar and lounge is a light supper menu that is nice for the late hiker or skier. In the winter you can have hot cider, hot buttered rum, and glögg. Lunch is nice in the screened-in terrace lounge, but the drinks are even better. They're called the Kool Krazy Bouncy and Hot drinks. I managed to taste three of them—oh boy!

The lake house, 3 miles away on Lake Songo, features clambakes and barbecues and all water sports.

Skiing is super up here, with Sunday River (I love that name) and Mt. Abram right at hand. The inn has special ski packages. Do check them. And as a special special, the inn has more than 25 miles of groomed cross-country trails for your pleasure.

The recreation center has a heated, ninety-two-degree outdoor swimming pool for use all year, plus saunas, exercise room, lounge, and game room. You'll never be at a loss for something to do at The Bethel Inn.

Afternoon teas, punch parties, and lobster bakes are nice to find at an inn.

HOW TO GET THERE: Bethel is located at the intersection of U.S. Route 2 and Maine Routes 5 and 26. From the south take exit 11 off the Maine Turnpike at Gray and follow Route 26 to Bethel. The inn is on the town common.

The Sudbury Inn
Bethel, Maine 04217

INNKEEPERS: Bill and Nancy White

ADDRESS/TELEPHONE: Main Street (mailing address: P.O. Box 369); (207) 824-2174 or (800) 395-7837; fax (207) 824-2329

E-MAIL: sudbury2@thesudburyinn.com

WEB SITE: www.thesudburyinn.com

ROOMS: 16, plus 5 suites in 2 buildings; all with private bath, air-conditioning, and cable TV.

RATES: $70 to $110, double occupancy; EPB.

OPEN: All year.

FACILITIES AND ACTIVITIES: Dinner, bar, lounge. Nearby: Skiing, ice skating, canoeing, tennis, golf, hiking.

This inn is located in the very pretty village of Bethel in the mountains of western Maine. The town is home to Gould Academy, one of Maine's foremost prep schools, which was founded in 1836. Near the inn are miles of maintained cross-country ski trails, downhill skiing, ice skating, canoeing (flat and white-water), tennis, golfing, and hiking the Appalachian Trail. The inn provides easy access to the White Mountain National Forest. The fall foliage around this area is breathtakingly beautiful.

The front of the inn was built in 1873, and the rear was added in the early 1900s. The inn recently has been completely refurbished, and the Whites, who purchased the property in June 2000, have installed modern amenities like air-conditioning and cable TV in every guest room. The furnishings remain simple, homey, and comfortable, and the comfy rockers remain on the front porch.

Another big change is a fine new chef, Randall Smith, who was named chef of the year for the state of Maine a few years ago. The warmth and comfort of the main dining room and its enormous fireplace remains, but the menu is all new. Appetizers include treats such as potato and wild mushroom lasagna, and a fabulous lobster and artichoke dip served with grilled focaccia bread points.

Smith's specialty is cioppino, a fish stew featuring Maine lobster, rock crab claws, jumbo shrimp, and fresh mussels served in a spicy seafood bouillon with fresh vegetables and tomato. Divine! Other entrees include beef tournedos, rack of lamb, and roast duckling topped with Maine maple syrup and wild blueberry glaze. Some favorite homemade desserts are classic crème brûlée or Chocolate Perfection, a flourless chocolate torte with a touch of rum, served in an oatmeal crust. A cup of espresso completes a great meal.

How can I think of breakfast? Well, how can you resist Belgian waffles? Or eggs any way you like them, fresh yogurt with fruit, and French toast seasoned with nutmeg? And I wonder how I gain weight on these trips!

Subs Pub, on the lower level, was created when the

old granite-walled basement was dug out and expanded. A lighter menu is served down here, along with thirty draft beers, featuring Maine microbrews. The pub, a longtime favorite with the après-ski crowd, offers live entertainment Friday and Saturday nights during ski season. Thursday night year-round is "Hoot Nite," when locals show of their musical talent in an open-mike format. It's unpredictable, but always fun.

HOW TO GET THERE: Take exit 11 off the Maine Turnpike and follow Route 26 to Bethel. The inn is on lower Main Street.

Blue Hill Inn
Blue Hill, Maine 04614

INNKEEPERS: Don and Mary Hartley

ADDRESS/TELEPHONE: Route 177; (207) 374–2844 or (800) 826–7415

E-MAIL: bluhilin@hotmail.com

WEB SITE: www.bluehillinn.com

ROOMS: 11, all with private bath; 3 with fireplace; 1 luxury suite with raised-hearth fireplace; 1 specially equipped for handicapped. No-smoking inn.

RATES: In-season, $148 to $255, double occupancy; EPB. Special package available. Lower rates in off-season.

OPEN: Mid-May through October 31; weekends and Thanksgiving in November.

FACILITIES AND ACTIVITIES: Breakfast and hors d'oeuvres daily. Four wine dinners offered in May, June, September, and October. Wheelchair access to dining room, parlor. Full license. Nearby: Cross-country skiing, swimming, boating, concerts.

*B*lue Hill Inn is another no-smoking inn. This is really nice. The inn was built in 1830 as the home of Varnum Stevens and has been an inn since 1840. It is located just up the hill from the head of the bay. There are tall beautiful elms all around the property. The garden area is lovely, and during the summer cocktails are so pleasant out here.

There are two common rooms to relax in. You can feel free to curl up in a chair and read—the fireplaces are so nice up here on a cold night. A variety of accommodations is available. All the rooms are comfortable, and all have their own private bath. You'll find some queen- and king-size beds and some fireplaces in the rooms. The furnishings are nineteenth-century antiques. The inn's facilities are not well suited to children under thirteen.

The inn offers a variety of packages each season, featuring sailing or cruising, concerts, hiking, or antiquing. Packages including wine dinners are a special treat. The dinners are eight-course affairs served by candlelight, with each course accompanied by a wine carefully chosen to complement the foods.

There is an 1850 pump melodeon in the inn for you to play. The horse-drawn sleigh rides in this beautiful area are just grand.

Every evening before guests depart for dinner, they are invited to the innkeepers' reception, where hors d'oeuvres are served and cocktails are available. The inn guests enjoy meeting one another and making new friends.

Breakfasts are hearty and filling, with freshly squeezed orange juice, omelets, Maine blueberry pancakes, and more.

There's a new suite, the Cape House, with a kitchen, king-size bedroom and bath, living room with a raised hearth fireplace, cable TV, phone, air-conditioning and heat, and a private deck. Make sure you see the tree out here.

HOW TO GET THERE: From Belfast follow Route 3 East through Searsport to Bucksport. Bear right after crossing the Bucksport Bridge. After a few miles, turn right onto Route 15 South to Blue Hill. Turn right on Main Street, then bear right again onto Route 177 West. The inn is the first building on your left at the top of the hill.

Blue Harbor House
Camden, Maine 04843

INNKEEPERS: Jody Schmoll and Dennis Hayden
ADDRESS/TELEPHONE: 67 Elm Street; (207) 236–3196 or (800) 248–3196; fax (207) 236–6523
E-MAIL: balidog@midcoast.com

ROOMS: 10, including suites; all with private bath and phone; some with TV; some with air-conditioning; suites with kitchen. No-smoking inn.

RATES: $95 to $165, double occupancy; EPB. Special packages available.

OPEN: Mid-May through December.

FACILITIES AND ACTIVITIES: Afternoon refreshments, dinner ($38.50) by reservation. Nearby: Tennis, golf, boating.

Camden, Maine, is called the jewel of the Maine coast with very good reason: It's just beautiful. Blue Harbor House is a restored 1810 New England cape. At one end of the large glass-walled sunporch are a television, bookcases, and comfortable couches and chairs.

The guest rooms have kings, queens, doubles, or twins, some of which are canopied. You're sure to like the quilts on the beds. All the rooms have telephones, and some have their own television. In the front rooms, where there is noise from Route 1, the innkeepers have installed a white-noise generator and added air-conditioning and soundproofed windows. The carriage house suites have a sitting room, kitchen, king-size bed, television, gas fireplace, and whirlpool tub.

Breakfast is a joy and just a bit different. Jody and Dennis have Apple Bakers, and a baked apple never tasted so good. It's filled with vanilla ice cream, of course. You could also start your day with fat-free stuffed French toast. Or blueberry pancakes with blueberry butter—the way to go!

Dinner offerings include a Downeast Lobster Feast, stuffed rack of lamb, and other regional specialties.

It's just a short walk to the picture-perfect waterfront, with its shops and great boats. Take your car, and Dennis will direct you to Route 52; it's a really beautiful drive. Or go to the top of Mt. Battie and take a look at Camden Harbor from 900 feet up.

HOW TO GET THERE: Coming from the south, take exit 6A from the Maine Turnpike to I-295, which joins I-95 just north of Portland. A few miles north of Freeport, take exit 22 (Coastal Route 1, Brunswick). Continue north on Route 1 through Waldoboro. Six miles past Waldoboro turn left onto Route 90 and follow it for 10 miles until it rejoins Route 1. Turn left onto Route 1 and continue for 2 miles toward Camden. Blue Harbor House is on your left as you come into town.

Camden Harbour Inn
Camden, Maine 04843

INNKEEPERS: Sal Vella and Patti Babij

ADDRESS/TELEPHONE: 83 Bay View Street; (207) 236-4200 or (800) 236-4266; fax (207) 236-7063

E-MAIL: info@camdenharbourinn.com

WEB SITE: www.camdenharbourinn.com

ROOMS: 22, all with private bath; 8 with fireplace; 8 with balcony or deck.

RATES: $195 to $255, peak season (mid-June to mid-October); $105 to $195, off-season; double occupancy; EPB.

OPEN: All year.

FACILITIES AND ACTIVITIES: Dinner served daily May to October, rest of year extended weekends. Wheelchair access to dining room. Bar; TV in lounge. Meetings, conferences, and special events. Nearby: Golf, skiing, sailing, hiking.

Camden Harbour is one of the best-known ports in Maine, and it's one of the prettiest, too. In the late nineteenth century, when Camden was bustling with cargo and fishing schooners, the inn was built to accommodate passengers who traveled from Boston to Bangor by steamship. Today, boats of yesteryear, both sail and power, as well as modern-day beautiful yachts, moor here by the rolling mountains that come right down to the rocky shores. The inn sits up high above all this and provides a panoramic view all around. The porch is terrific, and guests enjoy it from early morning coffee to evening nightcaps.

All the guest rooms are different in character. They are furnished with period antiques, Victorian pieces, and wicker. Many overlook the harbor and bay and have outside decks. There is a suite with a foyer, a wet bar, a sitting room adjacent to a large deck, and a comfortably furnished bedroom with a working fireplace. Another room has a large sitting area and a brick patio that overlooks the outer harbor. Other rooms have a fireplace, and some have a private outside entrance with reserved parking. The inn is equipped with sprinklers and heat and smoke detectors.

If dinner with a view is to your liking, the full-service restaurant probably has a table for you. The inn's logo is the tail of a whale, and the restaurant's name is Cetacea, which in Latin means "a family of whales." The menu is simple, yet done with a nice flair. Appetizers range from chowder to fresh Maine crab cakes and good salads. Entrees include grilled native salmon, sauté of Maine lobster meat, veal marsala, the fresh catch of the day and a pasta and vegetarian dish of the day, and, of course, steamed lobster. And don't forget to save room for the pastry chef's sinful creations.

This is a wonderful town to muddle about in for days. I was here for two wonderful days, and I had such a nice time—wonderful innkeepers and help.

There are walking tours, bicycle trips, and nature walks in and around Camden. There is hardly a spot in this whole lovely Maine town that is not worth a visit.

HOW TO GET THERE: From Route 1, which runs through the center of town, turn up Bay View Street to number 83.

Mt. Battie and Camden Hills State Park

A 25-mile hiking trail system and a 1⁶⁄₁₀-mile auto road in Camden Hills State Park (207–236–3109) have helped to open this beautiful area to the thousands of visitors who come here yearly to see the glorious views of Penobscot Bay. A stone mountain tower at the peak marks the location of the former Summit House, built as a hotel in 1887 by Camden resident Columbus Bushwell. Such notables as Theodore Roosevelt and poet Edna St. Vincent Millay climbed to the top of the mountain on an old carriage road that is now a part of the trail system. Visitors today can hike that same footpath year-round or drive up on the auto road from May 1 through November 1. Hikers agree that the view is worth every step. In winter the park offers snowshoeing, cross-country skiing, and downhill skiing at the Camden Snow Bowl.

In addition to Mt. Battie, the 6,500-acre park includes Mt. Megunticook. The highest point on the Camden Hills as well as one of the highest elevations on the whole Eastern Seaboard, Megunticook is also a popular destination for hikers and picnickers. A small admission fee is charged at the park entrance on Route 1.

The Castine Inn
Castine, Maine 04421

INNKEEPERS: Tom and Amy Gutow

ADDRESS/TELEPHONE: P.O. Box 41; (207) 326–4365; fax (207) 326–4570

E-MAIL: relax@castineinn.com

WEB SITE: www.castineinn.com

ROOMS: 19, all with private bath.

RATES: $75 to $210, double occupancy; EPB.

OPEN: May 1 through October.

FACILITIES AND ACTIVITIES: Full breakfast daily, dinner daily in season. Pub, sauna, perennial gardens. Nearby: Harbor.

Castine is a beautiful town, and the inn is a lovely focal point on a hill overlooking the harbor. The porches have chairs for watching and resting. The inn was built in 1898, and guests are as warmly received now as in the past, when they came by boat. Some still do.

There are a lot of gardens, and they are a pleasure to see. You enter a large front hall and a parlor with a wood-burning fireplace that is routinely lit in the evening to ward off the chill of coastal Maine. Books and games await if you want diversions.

The dining room, from which you can glimpse the water, has a hand-painted mural of Castine, covering all four walls, done by a former innkeeper. The food served here is very good. Some appetizers may be Penobscot Bay crabmeat cake with a mustard sauce, celery root soup, or a good salad. Entrees may be haddock, salmon, loins of lamb, and chicken. Desserts include crème brûlée, ice cream, and more. There are good wines. Breakfast ideas? How about pancakes with blueberries, eggs, and cereals. The pub is cozy.

Guest rooms are cheerful; many have harbor views. The nice wide halls have a full sprinkler system.

Castine itself is picturesque. The Maine Maritime Academy is the town's only "industry." The International Guild of Miniatures Artisans holds a

conference here each June. The harbor is dotted with sailing ships, yachts, and windjammers. Penobscot Bay is lovely.

HOW TO GET THERE: Take I-95 to Augusta and Route 3 east to the coast. Connect with Route 1 at Belfast, and follow Route 1 north to Bucksport. In 2 miles turn right onto Route 175. Follow it to Route 166, which takes you into Castine.

The Pentagöet Inn
Castine, Maine 04421

INNKEEPERS: Jack Burke and Julie Van de Graff

ADDRESS/TELEPHONE: P.O. Box 4; (207) 326–8616 or (800) 845–1701;
fax (207) 326–9382

WEB SITE: Pentagoet@Hypernet.com

ROOMS: 15, plus 1 suite; all with private bath; suite with fireplace.
No-smoking inn.

RATES: $75 to $150, double occupancy; EPB.

OPEN: May 1 to November 1.

FACILITIES AND ACTIVITIES: Breakfast only meal served. Full-service
bar, afternoon tea, and high tea. Nearby: Fishing, sailing, golf.

*T*he Pentagöet is an 1894 Victorian charmer on the shore of beautiful Penobscot Bay, complete with turret, gables, and a wraparound porch with wicker chairs and a swing. The window boxes
overflow with flowers. Fresh flowers are also for sale, but typical of the
warmth here, you buy on the honor system, depositing your money in a box
on the porch.

As you come in the door of the main inn, there is a sitting room to the left
with a wood-burning stove and a window in the turret looking down on the
harbor. To the right is a pub with a small, cozy oak bar; restful armchairs; and
Empire-style sofas. One wall is lined with books and collectibles; the others
are filled with paintings and old photos from travels to exotic places.

The guest rooms are lovely. Some have little alcoves with views of the
town and harbor. Some are small and have odd shapes, but this goes well
with a country inn. Seven rooms have king-size beds.

The building next door, Ten Perkins Street, is also part of the inn, and is

more than 200 years old. I stayed in
the suite here, and it's a gem with a
working fireplace. Wood is supplied
so that you can light yourself a fire
if there's a chill in the air.

The breakfast is hearty, usually
with Maine blueberries picked fresh
at a local farm that morning. All the
baking is done by the owner, Jack,

who had an acclaimed pastry shop in Philadelphia for twenty years.

Good food is served in an intimate dining room, in the pub, or on the porch. The inn offers nightly suppers featuring local seafood and New England specialties. The lobster pie and saffron-scented Spanish seafood stew are two favorites.

Castine is the Maine of your imagination. It was founded as a French trading colony in 1613, nine years before the Pilgrims landed at Plymouth. The town square is lined with stately elms and classic New England buildings straight from a Norman Rockwell drawing. Five times a day you can hear the whistle from the steamboat *Laurie Ellen* that serves the town, and the sound of bell buoys lulls you to sleep.

HOW TO GET THERE: Take I–95 to Augusta; take Route 3 East to coast. Connect with Route 1 at Belfast and follow Route 1 north to Bucksport. Two miles beyond, turn right onto Route 175. Take Route 175 to Route 166, which takes you into Castine.

The Lucerne Inn
Dedham, Maine 04429

INNKEEPERS: Jeff Carey; Bion Foster, owner

ADDRESS/TELEPHONE: Route 1A; (207) 843–5123 or (800) 325–5123; fax (207) 843–6138

ROOMS: 22, plus 8 suites; all with private bath, phone, TV, fireplace, and whirlpool tub.

RATES: $99 to $199, high season; $59 to $159, off-season; double occupancy, continental breakfast. Call for midseason rates and packages including brunch.

OPEN: All year.

FACILITIES AND ACTIVITIES: Sunday brunch, dinner, full license, bar. Meeting room for up to 150 people; pool; golf.

The regal mountains around The Lucerne Inn make such a beautiful picture that you feel as if you could be in Switzerland, especially if you catch a special sunset. Situated on ten scenic acres overlooking Phillips Lake, the buildings were originally a farmhouse and stable but have been serving guests as an inn since 1814.

The location is convenient for touring. It's just forty-five minutes from Acadia National Park and Bar Harbor, ninety minutes from Camden, and twenty minutes from Ellsworth and Bangor, where you'll find theaters and shopping.

But why leave? Besides the lake, the inn also has an outdoor swimming pool, and a golf course is right here.

This is quite an inn. There are still reminders of its long history in the guest and common rooms, in the form of "distinguished" antiques. The rooms have everything you could want—fireplaces, telephones, televisions, private baths, heated towel bars, whirlpool tubs, wonderful views, comfortable beds, and nice furniture.

The dining room has a pleasant view of the lake to accompany the delightful food. A few of the appetizers are crab-stuffed mushrooms with lobster sauce, smoked seafood sampler, baked onion soup, and a soup du jour. One of the entrees that's a real beauty is vegetable primavera—assorted vegetables simmered in cream and tossed with pasta. Lobster is prepared in a few different ways, salmon comes broiled, and the rack of lamb is stunning.

Dessert anyone? Come on up to see what they have.

HOW TO GET THERE: The inn is on Route 1A between Bangor and Ellsworth. Take I-95 to exit 45A, just south of Bangor. Take I-395 to Route 1A East. In about 10 minutes you will see the inn on your right.

The Pilgrim's Inn
Deer Isle, Maine 04627

INNKEEPERS: Jean and Dud Hendrick

ADDRESS/TELEPHONE: Main Street; (207) 348-6615;
fax (207) 348-7769

ROOMS: 13, plus 2 cottages; 10 with private bath.

RATES: $175, private bath; $150 to $215, shared bath; double occupancy; MAP. Ginny's House $205 MAP, $135 EPB; double occupancy.

OPEN: Mid-May through mid-October.

FACILITIES AND ACTIVITIES: Bar, lounge. Wheelchair access to dining room. Nearby: Bicycles, sailboats for charter, swimming. Golf or tennis at the island country club as the inn's guest.

*I*n 1793 Ignatius Haskell built this lovely house, following the specifications of his wife, who demanded the luxuries of city living on their country estate. He had his own sawmill nearby and built the house out of northern pine. Today you are welcomed to this rambling inn by the glowing hearths of its many fireplaces.

All the rooms are different and have a view of the pond or Northwest Harbor. The third floor has the best views and one really great room. Actually, there are five rooms on the third floor, but one in particular is huge.

The inn has all the right touches, such as tons of books, a huge fireplace, and soft, well-worn wood floors and walls in the common rooms and taproom. There is a small service bar; here the honor system is in effect. If it's before the 6:00 P.M. cocktail hour, you know to leave your tab on the bar.

Crisp linen and flowers are on the tables of the dining room, which once was a barn. In the soft light of the oil lamps, it just glows. Dinner may be poached salmon or tenderloin of beef, done many ways. There is a different special every night of the week. Soups are interesting—billi-bi, cream of celery, and more—accompanied by a different bread each night. All the baking is done right here.

A full breakfast is served. It is a sumptuous buffet, with baskets of muffins, homemade granola, meats and cheeses, melons, and fruit. You are also offered eggs.

Isle au Haut is accessible by mail ferry from the inn—a visit there makes an excellent day trip.

Ginny's house has two very private separate units. Each one has a living room with cable TV, gas stove, kitchenette and dining area, queen-size bedroom and bath, and a deck with a view.

HOW TO GET THERE: From Route 1 turn right after Bucksport onto Route 15, which goes directly to Deer Isle. In the village turn right on Main Street. The inn is on your left.

Harraseeket Inn
Freeport, Maine 04032

INNKEEPERS: Nancy and Paul Gray

ADDRESS/TELEPHONE: 162 Main Street; (207) 865–9377 or (800) 342–6423

WEB SITE: www.stayfreeport.com

ROOMS: 84, all with private bath, TV, phone, and wheelchair accessibility; some with Jacuzzi, fireplace, woodstove, or wet bar; 4 specially equipped for handicapped; 9 extended-stay town houses.

RATES: $95 to $235, double occupancy; EPB. Special packages available.

OPEN: All year.

FACILITIES AND ACTIVITIES: Lunch, high tea, dinner. Elevator; wheelchair access to dining room. Tavern, full liquor license, function rooms. No smoking in the dining room. Nearby: Shopping, nature walks, fishing, boating, skiing.

BUSINESS TRAVEL: Conference rooms. All rooms with phone and modem for personal computers.

The inn is named for the Harraseeket River, which runs through the town and into Casco Bay. It was built in 1850 and is Greek Revival in style. Everything about it is elegant, which is not a surprise, as its sister inn is the very elegant Inn at Mystic in Mystic, Connecticut.

Freeport has long been known for L. L. Bean and a ton of other famous outlet stores, all of which are just a short walk from the inn. If shopping is not your thing, however, nearby are Casco Bay and South Freeport Harbor, where you can rent a boat and go sailing or fishing. Nature lovers will be in heaven at the Audubon Sanctuary and Wolf Neck Woods State Park.

The rooms and suites are grand. There are canopied beds, antiques, telephones, cable television, and even modems for personal computers. Twenty-four rooms have a Jacuzzi, sixteen have a fireplace, and one has a woodstove. Whatever you're looking for, it's all here. You can even arrange a meeting or business conference at the inn, as there are function rooms accommodating up to 250 people that overlook the terrace.

Your day begins with a superlative breakfast buffet. Early birds can have coffee at 6:00 A.M. It's nice to find inns that serve lunch. I had crepes, and my friend had the chicken stir-fry. The lunch menu is extensive, and you can even ask for a lunch basket to take along if you're headed out for the afternoon. The dinner menu is even larger. There are appetizers, soups, salads, and lots of entrees, including "Tableside Classics" that are prepared and carved at your table. You can have a whole chicken, roast rack of baby lamb, chateaubriand, and various fruits of the sea. There's even two-tailed lobster, honest. The maple-syrup-braised loin of pork is just one of the feasts from the land. Desserts—well, by now you can imagine. Each one is better than the last. The chocolate fondue is an orgy. The Broad Arrow Tavern has its own lighter menu of burgers, pastas, lobster salad, sandwiches, and even a bucket of steamed clams. I could go on and on. The inn also has a grand room-service menu.

This whole inn is just splendid. The innkeepers are native to Maine, and though this is a large inn, it has not lost its charm.

In the living room, where tea is served, is a player piano, seated at which is the largest stuffed polar bear I've ever seen. There's a lovely fireplace in here, too.

Or, if you want another kind of warmth, there's an indoor pool kept at a toasty eighty-five degrees.

HOW TO GET THERE: Take I-95 north to exit 20 to Freeport. The inn is on Main Street.

Mast Landing Sanctuary

The Maine Audubon Society maintains this 150-acre preserve with field, forest, and tidal marsh habitats. This area was once logged for its tall pines that were used to make masts for the ships of the British Navy, thus the name. The sanctuary is open year-round from dawn to dusk. Self-guided trails take visitors past old apple orchards and millstreams, through woods and meadows. A 1-mile loop trail is a nice walk for brief visits. Enjoy the picnic area if you can stay a while. No fee is charged for parking. The sanctuary is on Upper Mast Landing Road, off Bow Street.

The Oxford House Inn
Fryeburg, Maine 04037

INNKEEPERS: John and Phyllis Morris

ADDRESS/TELEPHONE: Route 302; (207) 935-3442 or (800) 261-7206; fax (207) 935-7046

WEB SITE: www.oxfordhouseinn.com

ROOMS: 4, all with private bath and cable TV.

RATES: $110 to $125, double occupancy; EPB.

OPEN: All year.

FACILITIES AND ACTIVITIES: Dinner. Lounge with a full license. Nearby: Canoeing, swimming, fishing, antiquing, hiking, biking, scenic drives, outlet shopping.

*J*ohn and Phyllis have a lot of innkeeping experience and know just how to make an inn inviting and comfortable. There's one thing for sure: They have put together a marvelous brochure. It says that this is the way The Oxford House might have appeared back in 1923, looking through the windows of a spanking new Jordan motorcar.

The rooms are charming and very restful. All of them are named after the names of rooms on the original blueprints. Perhaps you'll sleep in the Sewing Room or the old-fashioned heated Porch Room. All have antiques and king- or queen-size bed, and three rooms offer mountain views.

At dinnertime you'll delight as I did in the outstanding and creative dishes offered on the menu. For example, turkey Waldorf is an entree you'll not find many places. It is medallions of turkey breast sautéed with apples and walnuts, then splashed with applejack and cream. Pork, pears, and port is another entree, done in a rich port and ginger sauce. How about veal Oxford? Very nice indeed. Three innovative steaks are also offered as well as fresh Maine seafood. House pâté of the day might be how you'd like to begin your meal. I think it's nice to find variations in pâtés. Or maybe Maine crab chowder will catch your eye. It's good and different. Needless to say, the desserts are all homemade.

On those cold Maine nights, the tavern is very inviting. It has a television, books, and a woodstove.

In warm weather the front porch is used for dining. I really like porches, and this one is a beauty. There is also a glassed-in heated porch at the back of the house with gorgeous views. You can sit here and look out at the beautiful surrounding mountains or the lovely gardens. Peace and quiet are at hand.

HOW TO GET THERE: The inn is on Route 302 in Fryeburg, 8 miles east of North Conway.

Le Domaine
Hancock, Maine 04640

INNKEEPER: Nicole L. Purslow

ADDRESS/TELEPHONE: Box 496, Route 1; (207) 422–3395, or (207) 422–3916, or (800) 554–8498; fax (207) 422–2316

E-MAIL: nicole@ledomaine.com

WEB SITE: www.ledomaine.com

RATES: $200, double occupancy; MAP.

OPEN: June to end of October.

FACILITIES AND ACTIVITIES: Bar, lounge. Badminton, walking trails. Nearby: Boating, swimming, fishing, hiking, Acadia National Park.

Hidden behind the hedges on busy Route 1 is a lovely surprise, an authentic bit of France in Downeast Maine. The inn is best known for its restaurant, but upstairs are charming rooms named after towns in Provence—Sault, Arles, Les Baux, Mausanne, and St. Remy—and decorated in the style of each village, with Provençale furnishings, antiques, and art. Eqyptian cotton bedding and goose-down pillows make for a luxurious feel, and guests are pampered with breakfast in bed, on their private balcony overlooking the gardens, or seated in the garden. Freshly baked croissants, French butter, and Nicole's own honey, jam, and jellies are a special treat in any setting.

A graduate of the Cordon Bleu school of cooking in Paris, Nicole is carrying on the tradition begun by her late mother, who founded the inn more than fifty years ago. The country French cuisine has been lauded in many publications. The inn also has a notable 500-bottle wine cellar.

The menu changes with the seasons. Paté de foie maison and *saumon fumé d'Ecosse* may be among the appetizers. Move on to dishes such as coquilles St. Jacques Provençale or steak bordelaise. I can't say enough about this food; it is divine.

There are many things to do in the area, including exploring Acadia National Park. But you may be content roaming the inn's many acres, where a wooded trail leads from the lawn to a secluded pond, or maybe just settling into a wicker chair in the lovely garden. It's hard to imagine a nicer oasis.

HOW TO GET THERE: The inn is about 9 miles above Ellsworth on Route 1.

The Kennebunk Inn
Kennebunk, Maine 04043

INNKEEPERS: John and Kristen Martin

ADDRESS/TELEPHONE: 45 Main Street; (207) 985–3351

ROOMS: 26, plus 4 suites; all with private bath and air-conditioning; some with TV and/or phone.

RATES: Off-season, $60 to $120; in-season, $100 to $160; double occupancy; EP. MAP is available.

OPEN: All year except Christmas Day.

FACILITIES AND ACTIVITIES: Dinner every day. Wheelchair access to dining room. Bar, lounge. Nearby: Fishing, swimming, boating.

The inn is located in the heart of town, convenient to everything. Even the beaches are very close at hand. The accommodations are very nice. The beds are comfortable, and all the rooms are air-conditioned. There are telephones in some rooms, a plus for busy people. Some rooms even have a television.

The upstairs foyer is a nice place to gather. There are couches and chairs, puzzles, games, books, and a television.

You have your choice of the four-star dining room or the informal pub. The interesting formal menu begins with choices like wild mushroom strudel with Madeira wine and boursin cheese or bruschetta of grilled game sausage. Many of the entrees feature fresh local seafoods. Not to be missed is the pan-seared jumbo sea scallops set with a shiitake spring roll over a curry, ginger, and lime pan sauce.

In the pub, you can enjoy a cold microbrewed draft beer and a bowl of lobster bisque or burgers, burritos, or barbecued ribs. When the weather is mild, you can top it off with coffee and homemade dessert on the garden patio.

HOW TO GET THERE: Take exit 3 from I–95 (the Maine Turnpike) to Kennebunk. Follow Main Street to the inn at number 45.

The Captain Fairfield Inn
Kennebunkport, Maine 04046

INNKEEPERS: Janet and Rick Wolf

ADDRESS/TELEPHONE: Corner of Pleasant and Green Streets (mailing address: P.O. Box 2690); (207) 967-4454 or (800) 322-1928

E-MAIL: jrw@captainfairfield.com

WEB SITE: www.captainfairfield.com

ROOMS: 9, all with private bath and air-conditioning; some with fireplace.

RATES: $110 to $275, double occupancy; EPB and afternoon refreshments, beach passes, and towels. Data port and fax available.

OPEN: All year.

FACILITIES AND ACTIVITIES: Guest refrigerator, off-street parking. Nearby: Ocean, shopping, restaurants, fishing, art galleries.

*T*his inn—an 1813 Federal mansion—was given as a wedding present to James Fairfield and his bride from his father-in-law. They knew how to do things right in those days! Today the inn is listed on the National Register of Historic Places. The gardens are striking, and so are the towering trees. There are numerous other lovely captains' houses in the neighborhood, and you are within walking distance of town, the water, shops, and restaurants.

There's an inviting living room with a wood-burning fireplace and tons of comfort. The captain's portrait hangs over the mantle. The music room features an ebony grand piano and comfortable leather seating, an invitation to enjoy music, reading, and camaraderie. The guest rooms are furnished with antiques and period furniture, including four-poster and canopy queen-size beds. All rooms have private bathrooms, and some have fireplaces. All the amenities are there—firm mattresses, down comforters, generous towels, special soaps, bottled spring water, hair dryers, and garden flowers.

Breakfast, which is the only meal served here, is generous. Janet and Rick bake all their own breads and pastries. Maine blueberry crepes, skillet frittatas with harvest vegetables, or eggs Benedict with their own special hollandaise sauce are among the scrumptious choices.

This area offers many things to do—whale watching, coastline excursions, fishing, golf, shopping, art galleries, and beautiful sandy beaches. Go and enjoy.

HOW TO GET THERE: Take exit 3 off I–95. Turn left onto Route 35 South, and follow it through Kennebunk to the intersection with Route 9. Go left onto Route 9, over the river and into Dock Square. Turn right onto Ocean Avenue. In 5 blocks go left just past the village green onto the one-way street. The inn is 1 block ahead on your right.

Christmas Prelude

Kennebunkport and its neighbors are delightful places to be at Christmastime. A ten-day holiday festival called Christmas Prelude (207–967–0857) is launched in the Kennebunks on the first weekend in December. If you are not in the spirit when you arrive, you will soon be caught up in the magic. A Christmas tree in Kennebunkport's historic Dock Square is decorated with the buoys of local lobstermen, and a community caroling event is held on the first Friday evening. Shopkeepers offer holiday refreshments, Santa arrives by lobsterboat, and the restaurants prepare special Prelude menus. Sleigh rides or hayrides carry revelers through the streets, pageants and concerts are offered at a variety of locations, and twinkling lights are draped on doorways, trees, and shop windows. Before the last two weeks of the Christmas rush begin, Kennebunk reminds visitors of the true meaning of the holiday. Its Walk through Bethlehem is a candlelight procession of 500 carolers led by the Three Wise Men. Do come—it's grand.

The Captain Jefferds Inn
Kennebunkport, Maine 04046

INNKEEPERS: Pat, Dick, and Jane Bartholomew

ADDRESS/TELEPHONE: (207) 967–2311 or (800) 839–6844;
fax (207) 967–0721

WEB SITE: www.captainjefferdsinn.com

ROOMS: 14 rooms, including 6 suites; all with private bath.

RATES: $135 to $285, double occupancy; EPB.

OPEN: All year except mid-December until a few days after Christmas.

FACILITIES AND ACTIVITIES: Full breakfast. BYOB. Nearby: Boating, whale watching, and much more.

The inn was built in 1804. There is a widows' walk on top, built so that the wife of Captain Jefferds could watch for her husband's ship to return from sea. There's a ton of history here.

This beauty has a lot going for it. The rooms are named for favorite places of the owners. The Italian suite has a king-size bed and an indoor water garden—not many of these around. The Monticello room is in the oldest part of the inn and features Indian shutters and a working fireplace. All the rooms are very lovely.

Breakfast is full and in fall and winter is served by candlelight in front of a warm fire, or in summer on the many terraces overlooking the gardens. Some of the breakfast goodies are pumpkin hazelnut soup, raspberry coffee cake, blueberry yogurt pancakes with lemon sauce, apple crisp with vanilla ice cream, pumpkin walnut muffins, and eggs Florentine with cheddar cheese sauce.

Hot mulled cider and home-baked sweets are served in the garden room every afternoon; and upon your return from whatever, the inn's golden retriever, Kate, will greet you. There are a few inn cats, my loves.

Much to do here: fishing and sailing, whale watching, hiking, antiquing, canoeing and rafting, biking, horseback riding, beaches, museums, and cross-country skiing. Just ask, and these innkeepers have the answers.

HOW TO GET THERE: Take exit 3 from I-95 to Highway 35 South. Follow the signs through Kennebunk to Kennebunkport. Take a left at Route 9 and cross the bridge. Turn right at the monument in dock square to Ocean Avenue. Go 5 short blocks, then turn left on the one-way street just past the green. Take another left at the first corner; look for the inn's white fence on the left.

Captain Lord Mansion
Kennebunkport, Maine 04046

INNKEEPERS: Beverly Davis and Rick Lichfield

ADDRESS/TELEPHONE: Ocean Avenue (mailing address: P.O. Box 800); (207) 967-3141; fax (207) 967-3172

WEB SITE: www.captainlord.com

E-MAIL: captain@biddeford.com

ROOMS: 19, plus 1 suite; all with private bath, phone, working fireplace, and whisper-quiet air-conditioning.

RATES: $199 to $399, double occupancy; EPB.

OPEN: All year.

FACILITIES AND ACTIVITIES: Breakfast only full meal served. Afternoon tea. BYOB. Gift shop. Nearby: Perkins Cove and Rachel Carson Wildlife Refuge.

BUSINESS TRAVEL: Conference room. All rooms with phone.

This is a truly grand inn, a mansion built in 1812. Some of the original Lord furniture is in the house. For example, the handsome dining-room table with carved feet and chairs belonged to Nathaniel Lord's grandson, Charles Clark, and is dated 1880. Throughout the inn are portraits of past owners in the Lord family.

A three-story suspended elliptical staircase, a gold vault, and double

Indian shutters are but a few of the wonderful things to be found in the inn. There are fireplaces, Oriental rugs, old pine wide-board floors, and claw-footed tables. It's almost a comfortable museum and thus is not well suited to children under twelve. Rick knows the history of the house and loves to tell it.

All of the guest rooms in the inn have working fireplaces. Most of the rooms have padded, deep window seats, a great place to relax and daydream. One of the beds is a four-poster 12 feet high. Rugs and wallpaper, thanks to Beverly's eye for decoration, are well coordinated, thirsty towels are abundant, and extra blankets and pillows help make your stay better than pleasant.

There's a grand suite with a huge bathroom, a double Jacuzzi, and a canopy king-size bed. There are heated tile floors in some bathrooms. This truly is a grand inn.

Breakfast is the only meal served in the inn, but what a meal! It is served family style. Two long tables in the kitchen are set with Wedgwood blue. There are two stoves in here side by side, a new one and a coal one about a hundred years old. The breakfast bell is a hundred-year-old music box. You'll start your day with good baked food like rhubarb nut bread, French breakfast puffs, pineapple nut upside-down muffins, oat and jam muffins, or strawberry bread. The recipes are available in the lovely gift shop, so now I can bake some of these yummies at home. In addition you'll have eggs, cereal, and

fruit—all this, plus an exquisite mansion, good staff, and great innkeepers.

Want more? Gourmet coffees, Swiss water decaf, chocolate cappuccino—or how about Snickerdoodle? Have fun.

This is a bring-your-own-bottle inn, and from the scenic cupola on its top to the parlors on the first floor, you will find many great places to enjoy a drink.

The inn has received *Mobil Travel Guide*'s four star rating.

HOW TO GET THERE: From I-95 take exit 3 off the Maine Turnpike to Kennebunk. Turn left on Route 35 and drive through Kennebunk to Kennebunkport. Turn left at the traffic light at the Sunoco station. Go over the drawbridge and take the first right onto Ocean Avenue. Go ³/₁₀ mile and turn left at the mansion. Park behind the building and take the brick walkway to the guest entrance.

The Inn at Harbor Head
Kennebunkport, Maine 04046

INNKEEPERS: Eve and Dick Roesler

ADDRESS/TELEPHONE: 41 Pier Road; (207) 967–5564;
fax (207) 967–1294

ROOMS: 2, plus 2 suites; all with private bath and air-conditioning.

RATES: $155 to $330, double occupancy; EPB.

OPEN: All year except December 10 to Valentine's Day. Weekends only
in February and March.

FACILITIES AND ACTIVITIES: Breakfast only meal served, afternoon
refreshments. BYOB.

This inn is a beauty. It sits in a lush area on Cape Porpoise Harbor.
There's a dock on the property. The gardens alone are worth the
trip. The views of this quaint fishing village are terrific.

The breakfasts are a grand affair. Here's a sample of the menu, just to
tease your palate: fresh-squeezed orange juice, herbed scrambled eggs, sage
sausage, fresh fruit, pecan French toast, bacon, wild mushroom tart, asparagus with hollandaise, honey waffles with whipped cream and raspberries,
ham, mushroom strata, quiches, and crepes. There's always fruit, and it's
served very differently.

Accommodations are neat. The Summer Suite has a king-size wicker bed,
gas fireplace, and a deck with a view. The bathroom has a Jacuzzi. There are
robes in the rooms. The Harbor Suite offers a king-size canopy bed, a fireplace, couches, hand-painted walls and ceiling, and a small deck overlooking
the harbor. The Garden Room has an Oriental feel and French doors overlooking the ocean, while the Greenery is in a Victorian mood, with a king-
size bed and a lovely bath with hand-painted tile and a whirlpool tub.

The sitting room features couches and a wing-back chair. The dining
room has a table for eight. There are inn birds—love birds, of course. A library
has a copper Japanese fountain and a picture window with a view; very nice
indeed.

A wonderful restaurant, called Seascapes, is run by former innkeepers of
the Kennebunk Inn and can be found down the street a bit from this inn.

The menu is great, and so is the spot. What a grand water view, grand people, and delicious food.

HOW TO GET THERE: Get off the Maine Turnpike at exit 3 (Kennebunk) and follow Route 35/9A to Kennebunkport. Take a left at the intersection of Routes 9 and 35. Cross the bridge and follow Route 9 east through Dock Square to the stop sign. Take a right on Maine Street and a left on School Street. Continue on Route 9 about 1½ miles past a school and through some woods to the village of Cape Porpoise. Just after Bradbury's Market, leave Route 9 (don't make the sharp left) and go straight ahead, entering Pier Road. Pass the Wayfarer Restaurant, and go around the head of the cove. From there, the Inn at Harbor Head is ²⁄₁₀ mile on the right—watch for the sign. If you miss it, don't worry—the road ends in ¼ mile, and you'll find it on the way back.

The Kennebunkport Inn
Kennebunkport, Maine 04046

INNKEEPER: Debbie Lennon

ADDRESS/TELEPHONE: One Dock Square (mailing address: P.O. Box 111); (207) 967–2621 or (800) 248–2621

ROOMS: 34, all with private bath, TV, air-conditioning, and phone.

RATES: $84.50 to $325, double occupancy; EP.

OPEN: All year.

FACILITIES AND ACTIVITIES: Breakfast and dinner served daily May through October. Bar, lounge, pool. Nearby: Beaches, boating, fishing, tennis, golf, shopping.

The Kennebunkport Inn was built in the late 1890s by Burleigh S. Thompson, a wealthy coffee and tea merchant. It was magnificent then, and it still is. It was turned into an inn in 1926, various changes were made, and today it is noted for its charm, warmth, and grace.

Born to shop? Well, you are right in the heart of all the fine shops of Kennebunkport—antiques, arts and crafts, clothing, and lots more. One year I ordered some cut lampshades from one of the shops, and they arrived at my home in fine shape. The town also offers fine beaches, tennis, fishing, boating, golf, theaters, and much more. The inn has a nice swimming pool.

The inn is elegant, a true nineteenth-century mansion. The River House, built in the 1930s as an annex to the inn, is a lovely place to be, but then so are all of the rooms in the inn. Every room has a color television and lots of comfort, and the inn rooms are air-conditioned. Coming back to your room after shopping or sight-seeing in busy Kennebunkport is a joy.

The piano bar–lounge is open daily in the summer and fall and Friday and Saturday in the spring. It has a neat fireplace, a friendly bartender, and a pub menu. The piano is played every night from June till the end of October.

There's a lovely terrace alongside of the inn, and dinner is served out here in the summertime. Dinner is also elegantly served by candlelight in two dining rooms, on tables covered with white napery. It is a meal you will truly enjoy. Ask Rick to recommend some wine to complement your dinner. He is a connoisseur of fine wines and has developed an excellent wine list. The breakfast buffet has lots of goodies—melon, cereal, muffins, and more.

Martha and Rick are very good innkeepers. They work at it, and it shows. On my last visit I met the Griffin girls, Alexis and Lydia, a pair of charmers.

HOW TO GET THERE: Take exit 3 from the Maine Turnpike. Turn left on Route 35 and go south to Kennebunkport. At the traffic light at the junction of Route 9, turn left, go over the bridge, and the inn is ahead on the left.

Old Fort Inn
Kennebunkport, Maine 04046

INNKEEPERS: David and Sheila Aldrich

ADDRESS/TELEPHONE: P.O. Box M; (207) 967–5353 or (800) 828–3678; fax (207) 967–4547

ROOMS: 16, all with private bath, air-conditioning, TV, phone, and wet bar; 4 with Jacuzzi, 4 with gas fireplaces.

RATES: $135 to $285, double occupancy; EPB.

OPEN: Mid-April to mid-December.

FACILITIES AND ACTIVITIES: Breakfast only meal served. BYOB. Swimming pool, tennis, antiques shop, 1 block from the ocean.

*W*hen you enter the Old Fort Inn, you are in an excellent antiques shop. Next you are in a huge living room with a covered porch that overlooks the swimming pool. (The pool has a solar cover that enables the inn to stretch its swimming season a bit.) This is a lovely, comfortable living room with a fireplace, a super spot to curl up and read a book.

The rooms are charming. The beds are lovely canopy or four-poster ones with good, comfortable mattresses. The towels are plush, which I always love. There is a nice library in the foyer. One of the suites has a sitting room, two bedrooms, and two bathrooms. There is a television in each room, and four rooms have Jacuzzis. All have telephones and wet bars.

The breakfast buffet is superb. You can pick and choose from all types of teas and juices, fresh fruit, baked breads, croissants, sticky buns, and hot entrees. The hot dishes change daily.

The inn provides a laundry. Until you have been on the road a week or so, you do not know how convenient such a facility is. The inn also provides a place to shower and change if you are checking out and still want to swim in the pool or the ocean.

The Carriage House has very interesting shadow boxes displaying nineteenth-century clothing. The living room over here is so comfortable and quiet. On the other hand, in the main house's living room you must meet Walter, who "plays" the piano. The inn was awarded four diamonds from AAA.

HOW TO GET THERE: Take I-95 to exit 3. Turn left on Route 35 for 5½ miles. Go left at the Route 9 intersection, into Dock Square; take the first right along Ocean Avenue for ⁹⁄₁₀ mile. Take a left in front of the Colony Hotel, then go right at the T junction; follow signs for ³⁄₁₀ mile to the inn.

The Tides Inn by the Sea
Kennebunkport, Maine 04046

INNKEEPERS: Marie Henrikson and Kristin Blomberg

ADDRESS/TELEPHONE: 252 Goose Rocks Beach; (207) 967-3757

WEB SITE: www.tidesinnbythesea.com

ROOMS: 22, plus 3 suites; 21 with private bath.

RATES: $125 to $285, double occupancy; EP. Family rooms, $285; EP.

OPEN: Mid-May to Columbus Day weekend.

FACILITIES AND ACTIVITIES: Breakfast, dinner, and drinks at the inn's Belvidere Club overlooking the ocean. Nearby: Ocean, fishing, boating, harbor cruises.

*L*ocation, location, location. This inn certainly is in a beautiful one. A Victorian inn on the white sands of Goose Rocks Beach, it looks over the sea. Since its beginning at the turn of the twentieth century, it has hosted Teddy Roosevelt and Sir Arthur Conan Doyle, the creator of Sherlock Holmes.

The inn's brochure says it well: "Wake to the plaintive cries of seagulls; stroll miles of sandy beaches, and search for shells; doze to the sounds of the surf. You won't find televisions or telephones in the rooms (there is one in the front parlor) and you won't find rooms that look like any other."

The rooms for the most part are small; so what? In this area, who wants to stay inside? Almost all have a view of the Atlantic Ocean. The inn also has very spacious oceanfront suites with kitchens that rent by the week.

The inn is a short ride from Kennebunkport, where there are sailboat charters, harbor cruises, fishing, tennis, and more. Timber Island, just off shore, is for exploring. You can see harbor seals basking on the rocks at Goose Rocks. Do bring your camera.

When you enter the inn, the reception desk is on the left, and on the right is a really lived-in living room with a television, magazines, and comfort. The food is very good at the inn's Belvidere Club. Regional specialties include pan-sautéed crab cakes, oysters on the half shell, seafood chowder, and steamed clams and lobster. Sip a cocktail on the veranda and enjoy the intoxicating views of Goose Rocks Beach

Kristin and Marie, a mother-daughter team, have been innkeeping for more than thirty years, and they've gotten it down to perfection.

HOW TO GET THERE: From the Maine Turnpike take exit 3. Follow Route 35 to Route 9 through Dock Square. Follow Route 9 east for 3 miles, to Cape Porpoise. Turn left on Route 9, continue 2½ miles, and turn right at "Clockfarm" onto Dyke Road to its end. Turn left to the inn.

White Barn Inn 📱
Kennebunkport, Maine 04046

INNKEEPERS: Maureen Violette; Laurie J. Bongiorno, owner

ADDRESS/TELEPHONE: Beach Avenue (mailing address: P.O. Box 560-C); (207) 967–2321; fax (207) 967–1100

E-MAIL: innkeeper@whitebarninn.com

WEB SITE: www.whitebarninn.com

Seashore Trolley Museum

Take a trip back in time at the Seashore Trolley Museum (207-967-2800), which houses a collection of more than forty fully restored trolleys, streetcars, buses, and subway cars. Board an open-air car for a ride on the old Atlantic Shore interurban trolley line that linked Kennebunkport to Kittery and Biddeford. Visit the restoration shop and watch artisans and mechanics work on the vehicles stored in the car barns. Enjoy a treat at the snack bar or buy a souvenir at the gift shop. Children will especially enjoy the chance to sound the motorman's whistle or even operate the car itself. Special events are held on weekends and holidays throughout the season, from early May through early October. Admission is charged, but you can ride all day if you want to. The museum is on Log Cabin Road, about 3 miles from Dock Square.

ROOMS: 16, plus 9 suites; all with private bath; some with phone, TV, and Jacuzzi; 13 with fireplace.

RATES: $230 to $575, double occupancy; continental breakfast and tea. Packages available.

OPEN: All year.

FACILITIES AND ACTIVITIES: Dinner, full license. Meeting room, bicycles. Nearby: Beach, shops, galleries, golf, tennis.

BUSINESS TRAVEL: Located 25 minutes from Portland. Writing desk and phone in room; conference room; fax and audiovisual equipment available.

A pre–Civil War farmhouse and its signature white barn have been transformed into this lovely inn. It is just a short walk from the beach and the charming village of Kenne-bunkport, with its colorful shops, galleries, and boutiques. When you consider the inn's exquisite food and its warmth and graciousness, it comes as no surprise that it is the only Maine member inn of *Relais et Châteaux,* the exclusive worldwide association of luxury inns.

Hospitality is evident throughout the inn. When you enter your room, you find a basket of fruit, flowers, luxurious toiletries, and a robe for you to wear. At night your bed is turned down and a treat is left on the pillow.

The rooms in the inn itself are attractively decorated with antiques, armoires, and brass and iron beds in a variety of sizes. The Gate House's rooms are large, with cathedral ceilings, ceiling fans, dressing areas, queen-size beds, and wing chairs. May's Annex has six suites with king-size four-poster beds and large sitting areas with fireplaces. There are oversized marble baths with whirlpool baths and separate showers. The towels are large and lush.

The breakfast room is large and cheerfully decorated with flower arrangements. The main dining room is the barn; a lovely lounge and piano bar are here, too. Candlelight, linen, and soft music are nice touches. The menu changes weekly.

When I think about the food, I want to go back for more. The restaurant has received five diamonds from AAA and four stars from the Mobil guide; these are prestigious awards and well deserved. The menu changes weekly in order to offer the freshest and finest of ingredients. I know the greens are fresh—I watched them being picked. Soups are amazing: A light cream soup of potato, leek, and watercress is scented with thyme; lobster minestrone comes with black beans, roasted tomatoes, olive oil croutons, and a bacon pistou.

The appetizer of homemade ravioli is glorious. Dinner choices the week I was here included pan-seared striped bass with sautéed eggplant, Niçoise olives, and basil oil in a roasted tomato broth. The veal rib chop came grilled with glazed baby turnips, Swiss chard, garlic-roasted Parisienne potatoes, and an herb sauce. You can guess there are more seafood offerings from this Maine inn—lobster, halibut, and salmon were also on the menu.

No matter what size your party—two or eight— when your dinner is ready, that number of waiters arrives to stand behind each diner's chair and on cue serves everyone simultaneously. What a sight.

The little bar is copper, with eight upholstered chairs. The piano bar has a huge flower arrangement in its center.

After dinner, go relax in the living room with a glass of port or brandy, a book from the inn's well-filled bookshelves, or one of the many current magazines. Or you could be ambitious and go for a ride along the beach on one of the inn's bicycles. I took one and sure did enjoy it.

There's a wine room, and it's a beauty for large parties or small, I'm sure. Please invite me, I'd love to come.

There's a pool, and the area around it is grand. Sodas and lunch are served to guests out here. There is also a fly-fishing school, offered in conjunction with Orvis—wonderful packages for anglers.

HOW TO GET THERE: From the Maine Turnpike, take exit 3 to Kennebunk. Follow Route 35 south 7 miles to Kennebunkport, then continue through the traffic light onto Beach Avenue. The inn is in ¼ mile, on the right.

The Inn on Winter's Hill
Kingfield, Maine 04947

INNKEEPERS: Richard and Diane Winnick and Carolyn Rainaud

ADDRESS/TELEPHONE: RR 1, Box 1272; (207) 265-5421 or (800) 233-9687; fax (207) 265-5424

WEB SITE: www.winterhill.com

ROOMS: 20, in 2 buildings; all with private bath, phone, coffee machines, and cable TV; 1 specially equipped for handicapped.

RATES: $75 to $150, double occupancy; EP. Golf, skiing, and fly-fishing packages available.

OPEN: All year.

FACILITIES AND ACTIVITIES: Dinner for public daily, by reservation. Wheelchair access to dining room. Bar, lounge, meeting and banquet facilities. Hot tub, indoor and outdoor swimming pools, tennis, cross-country skiing, ice skating. Nearby: Downhill skiing, hunting, fishing, hiking, golf, canoeing, Stanley Steamer Museum, dogsled rides.

The Inn on Winter's Hill, located in the midst of western Maine's Bigelow, Sugarloaf, and Saddleback Mountains, sits on top of a six-acre hill on the edge of town. This Neo-Georgian manor house was designed by the Stanley (steam car) brothers and built at the turn of the twentieth century for Amos Greene Winter as a present for his wife, Julia. It is listed on the National Register of Historic Places. Today it is owned by a brother and sister who are doing a great job as innkeepers, following a long-time tradition of casual elegance and warm hospitality.

Accommodations are varied and range from the turn-of-the-twentiethcentury luxury rooms in the inn to the modern rooms in the restored barn. Every one is very comfortable, with nice bathrooms, wonderful views, cable television, and telephone.

Julia's Restaurant is elegant, and the food served here is excellent. The night I was here, for appetizers I had crackers and garlic cheese spread and pineapple wrapped in bacon. My garden salad with house dressing was followed by a light sorbet and then Sole Baskets, which were superb. Salmon in phyllo, Atlantic salmon fillet baked in phyllo with a Parmesan-cheese cream sauce, is a special dish. Desserts are grand. Oh, it's all so good, it's hard to choose!

In the lounge area is an old piano; it came by oxcart from Boston for Julia Winter. It took two and a half months to arrive.

Spring, summer, fall, or winter, there is so much to do up here. Winter brings cross-country skiing from the door, and downhill skiing at Sugarloaf is minutes away. Hunting, fishing, canoeing, and hiking along the Appalachian Trail welcome outdoors people in the other seasons. If those do not appeal to you, try the pool table in the bar area. Television is here, too. All is watched over by Ming Lee and Kismet, the Shih Tzu inn dogs.

HOW TO GET THERE: Kingfield is halfway between Boston and Quebec City, and the Great Lakes area and the Maritimes. Take the Maine Turnpike to the Belgrade Lakes exit in Augusta. Follow Highway 27 through Farmington to Kingfield. The inn is on a small hill near the center of town.

The Newcastle Inn
Newcastle, Maine 04553

INNKEEPERS: Howard and Rebecca Levitan

ADDRESS/TELEPHONE: River Road; (207) 563–5685 or (800) 832–8669; fax (207) 563–6877

WEB SITE: www.newcastleinn.com

ROOMS: 14, including 4 suites; all with private bath; some with fireplace; suites with Jacuzzi or soaking tub. Inn suitable for older children. No-smoking inn.

RATES: $125 to $250, double occupancy; EPB. Packages available.

OPEN: All year.

FACILITIES AND ACTIVITIES: Dinner served on Friday and Saturday from November through the end of May and daily (except Monday) from June through October. Pub. Nearby: Walking trails, beaches, bicycling, bird-watching, boating, cross-country skiing.

The Newcastle Inn is in the lovely Boothbay region, only 14 miles from Boothbay Harbor and 16 miles to Pemaquid, with its famous lighthouse, fort, and sandy beach. This is a very interesting and distinctive part of Maine.

The beautiful flower known as the lupine is the signature of the inn. A native to this part of Maine, it grows just two weeks in June. Make sure you see the watercolor painting of lupines on the wall in the stencil room.

A 40-by-16-foot cedar deck at the rear of the inn overlooks the gardens and the Damariscotta River. It is used in season for the inn's multicourse breakfasts and very special Downeast lobster bakes. Every summer night on the deck and in the pub, the innkeepers host a reception for their guests, with hors d'oeuvres and beverages of every kind.

Dinner is served most evenings in the summer. Here's a sample of the menu's offerings: appetizers like Newcastle Inn crab cakes and mussels in saffron cream and entrees like baked salmon with horseradish crust, baked stuffed lobster, and breast of chicken. For dessert try the apricot almond tart or the chocolate mousse. The chef's cooking is glorious.

The pub is open every night, and the wine list features selections from around the world. This room has a gas fireplace, a deck, and lovely water views.

Each of the inn's rooms is special. All are named after the lighthouses on the coast of Maine. Many have a canopied four-poster bed. Some have a fireplace. The newest suite offers a king-size bed, a soaking tub for two, and a fireplace in the sitting room. Every night guests are left a gift of Godiva chocolates as part of the inn's turndown service.

Howard and Rebecca have a goal for each visitor: "Come as our guests and leave as our friends." Very nice indeed. Do say hello to Jasper, the inn's Maine coon cat. There is much to see and do up here. All you have to do is ask.

HOW TO GET THERE: Going north on Route 1, take the Newcastle exit to the right. About 7 miles north of Wiscasset, take Newcastle River Road; the inn is ½ mile down, on the right.

The Bradley Inn at Pemaquid Point
New Harbor, Maine 04554

INNKEEPERS: Beth and Warren Busteed

ADDRESS/TELEPHONE: 361 Pemaquid Point (mailing address: 3063 Bristol Road); (207) 677-2105 or (800) 942-5560; fax (207) 677-3367

E-MAIL: bradley@lincoln.midcoast.com

WEB SITE: www.bradleyinn.com

ROOMS: 12, plus 1 cottage, 3 rooms in carriage house; all with private bath. Rooms with phone and TV; 5 with gas fireplace.

RATES: $135 to $195 in season, double occupancy; EPB. Off-season $105 to $160, double occupancy; EPB. Special packages available.

OPEN: All year except Christmas Eve and Christmas Day.

FACILITIES AND ACTIVITIES: Dinner. Bicycles and helmets. Wedding facilities. Nearby: Ocean, tennis, golf.

BUSINESS TRAVEL: Phone with private line in room; conference facilities.

*P*emaquid, a Native American word meaning "long finger," is an appropriate name for the point of land that extends farther into the Atlantic Ocean than any other on the rugged Maine coast. What a wonderful ride it is out here! And once you arrive, the terrain is breathtaking. You're just a short walk from the Pemaquid Lighthouse or the beach with its lovely white sand. In the nearby seaside village of New Harbor, you can watch the working boats. Fort William Henry is close by. I drove around the point, parked my car, and watched the surf beating on the rocks below. It was quite a sight.

On this visit I scrambled down to the water's edge and back up. It was a bit scary but well worth it.

The inn is more than eighty years old. There's an attractive living room with a fireplace and a baby grand piano. On Friday and Saturday there is live piano music. A folk singer also performs on Friday nights. The taproom has a long, custom-made bar of Portland granite with a mahogany rail.

The Bradley Inn Restaurant is decorated with some beautiful ship models and a huge ship's wheel. Some of the appetizers are chilled Spiney Creek oysters and smoked salmon terrine. Entrees may be filet mignon, Maine lobster, and sea scallops. The menu changes monthly. The wine list is impressive, and the dessert that won my vote was Chocolate Decadence cake.

The rooms are charming and very comfortable. The view from some of the second- and third-floor rooms is of Johns Bay or the gardens. The cottage has heat and a wood fireplace, a limited kitchen, a bedroom and bath, living room, screened-in porch, and a TV. Chloe, a love of a yellow lab, is the inn dog.

The carriage house has three lodging options. On the second floor is a large apartment with a kitchen, bedroom, bath, and a loft—a great place for children. On the first level is a bedroom with a private bath and another bedroom with a private bath and sitting room. The carriage house is available in summer only.

There's also a nice yard with lounge chairs. There's much to do and see out here, so come on up.

HOW TO GET THERE: Take the Maine Turnpike to exit 9, the Falmouth–Route 1 interchange. Take I-95 for 21 miles to Brunswick. Continue on Route 1 for 27 miles to Damariscotta, and from there follow Route 130 for 14 miles to the inn.

The Rangeley Inn
Rangeley, Maine 04970

INNKEEPERS: David and Rebecca Schinas

ADDRESS/TELEPHONE: P.O. Box 160; (207) 864–3341 or
(800) MOMENTS (666–3687); fax (207) 864–3634

E-MAIL: rangeinn@rangeley.org

WEB SITE: www.rangeleyinn.com

ROOMS: 52, all with private bath; 5 have double whirlpool tubs;
2 specially equipped for handicapped.

RATES: $64 to $140, single; $69 to $119, double occupancy; EP. MAP
available.

OPEN: All year.

FACILITIES AND ACTIVITIES: Breakfast, dinner, bar, lounge, banquet
facilities. Dining room closed Easter to Memorial Day and Thanksgiving to Christmas. Pub open seven days with a pub menu. Wheelchair
access to dining room, lounge, and public rest room. Nearby: Fishing,
boating, swimming, hiking, tennis, golf, hunting, skiing, snowmobiling.

*W*hat a wonderful trip it is just to get up here in this beautiful country. The first thing you see when you arrive at the inn is its welcoming long veranda that gives a nice old-fashioned feel of a
long-ago summer hotel. Well, it's been here since 1907 and is on the shore of
Haley Pond.

The bar and lounge area is quite large. A pool table is in here, as is a huge
rock fireplace and several comfortable bar stools. A pub menu is offered
seven nights a week. The television room has a big-screen and a VCR—all very
comfortable, good chairs and couches.

Almost all of the rooms are carpeted, and all are very clean. The baths
have wonderful claw-footed tubs. A bath in an old tub is heavenly. You can
be up to your neck in water. Try this in a modern one—no can do! Some
rooms have showers. Five rooms have double whirlpool tubs.

The dining room is large and very comfortable. Breakfast is huge—eggs
any way, corned beef hash, all kinds of pancakes and waffles and French
toast. Cold cereal, hot cereal, and tons of side things to order. A wondrous
espresso machine, and what coffees and latte! Dinner starters—how about

ostrich? It's marinated, grilled, and served on a bed of braised greens. Wow. There are more goodies and entrees like pasta primavera, steak, chicken, salmon, and rack of lamb. Save room for dessert.

There are nature hikes. A sunrise canoe trip starts at 5:00 A.M. I'm told it's so beautiful it takes your breath away, but I don't think I'll try it.

Spring brings superb fishing for brook trout and landlocked salmon. Some brooks are open only to fly-fishing. Wildflowers and migrating birds are plentiful, so bring a camera. Summer is ideal for boating, swimming, hiking, tennis, and golf. Fall brings spectacular foliage and hunting. Winter, of course, brings snow activities. Saddleback Mountain is nearby for downhill skiing, and cross-country skiing and snowmobiling are everywhere.

In any season of the year, Angel Falls, 20 miles away, is impressive and worth a visit. It is a 50- to 60-foot fall. Beautiful!

HOW TO GET THERE: From the Maine Turnpike take exit 12 at Auburn. Pick up Route 4 and follow it to Rangeley.

Capt. Lindsey House Inn
Rockland, Maine 04841

INNKEEPER: Terry Wagner; Capts. Ken and Ellen Barnes, owners

ADDRESS/TELEPHONE: 5 Lindsey Street; (207) 596–7950 or (800) 523–2145; fax (207) 596–2758

E-MAIL: lindsey@midcoast.com

WEB SITE: www.lindseyhouse.com

ROOMS: 7 rooms and 2 suites, all with private bath, cable television, telephone, air-conditioning, and hair dryer; 1 room specially equipped for the handicapped. No-smoking inn.

RATES: In season, $120 to $175; off season, $65 to $110. Packages available.

Gourmet continental breakfast and afternoon tea included.

OPEN: All year.

FACILITIES AND ACTIVITIES: Available for small conferences and retreats. Nearby: Shopping districts of Rockland and Camden; the Farnsworth Museum; cross-country skiing; golfing at the Samoset golf course; six-day Windjammer cruises aboard the historic schooner *Stephen Taber.* (Twenty-two passengers; no children under 14. For reservations call 800-999-7352.)

BUSINESS TRAVEL: Access to fax machine and copying services; computer port in library.

he Capt. Lindsey House Inn is located in Rockland's harbor district. Built in 1837, it was Rockland's first inn. It is certainly one of its best.

There is a story behind the inn's simple brick facade. You see, the bricks were hand-burned on site by the original owner. Imagine that! The inside is simply grand. The decor here is all in deep greens, wines, and creams, with polished oak floors and rich Oriental rugs throughout. It is all tastefully decorated with fine antiques and family heirlooms.

The living room is quite inviting. It has a cozy fireplace and comfortable couches. There is also a library with a good selection of books. You're invited to take one home if you're still reading it when you're ready to leave.

Accommodations are bright and homey. Each bedroom is done right. There are wide beds, warm down comforters, tapestry bedspreads, and good pillows. My room had two comfortable reading chairs and original hardwood floors. The large sea trunk at the foot of my bed has been in the Lindsey family since anyone can remember.

In the morning there is a gourmet continental breakfast, with homemade granola, muffins and croissants, fresh fruit, juices, and more. What a nice way to start the day. It is served in the cheerful oak-paneled breakfast room.

Afternoon tea is an especially nice feature of the inn. You may choose tea, sherry, or port. In the summer there is a lovely selection of scones, fresh fruit, tea cookies, sweet breads, and cucumber sandwiches. In the winter you'll find hot chocolate and an assortment of cookies.

I had a wonderful dinner with Ken and Ellen Barnes next door at their

WaterWorks Pub and Restaurant. Dining is always a pleasure here, and it is quite a family affair. You see, their daughter, Susan, is the chef here. The *Boston Globe* called WaterWorks a "place not to be missed in Midcoast Maine." I can understand why.

You'll enter the restaurant through large oak doors with leaded-glass windows. Notice the wide floorboards and beamed ceilings. The two funny wooden monkeys you see are genuine movie stars! They were once props on a Hollywood soundstage. Well, here you must make a choice. To your right is a casually elegant restaurant with intimate tables. To your left is an English-style pub with long oak trestle tables and a grand stone fireplace.

The menu? Where should I begin? I had pan-fried salmon with an oak crust and a leek and cider sauce. Simply divine. One popular entree is called "Whale Bones." These are very large prime rib bones slow-cooked in a rum barbecue sauce. And you must leave room for dessert. Susan's apple crisp with cinnamon ice cream is a special favorite. Oh boy, is it yummy!

Rockland is some area. Take a stroll around the lovely harbor, and you'll see the schooner *Stephen Taber*. It was built in 1871 and is the oldest merchant sailing vessel in continuous service. Ken and Ellen serve as captain and cook on six-day sails from Windjammer Wharf. Ken tells wonderful sea stories. Ellen cooks all of the schooner's gourmet meals on a vintage woodstove in the galley. Maine blueberry pancakes with warm maple syrup is a popular breakfast choice. If you sign up for a sail, you'll even feast on steamed lobsters with all the fixings on a midweek stop on a deserted island. You can find Ellen's recipes in her book, *A Taste of the Taber*. The trips are very popular. You must reserve early.

HOW TO GET THERE: From the south take the Maine Turnpike (I–95) to exit 22, coastal Route 1, into Rockland. From the north take coastal Route 1 through Camden to Rockland. Call the inn for directions once you reach Rockland.

The Claremont
Southwest Harbor, Maine 04679

INNKEEPER: John W. Madeira Jr.

ADDRESS/TELEPHONE: P.O. Box 137; (207) 244–5036 or (800) 244–5036; fax (207) 244–3512

E-MAIL: clarhotel@acadia.net

WEB SITE: www.theclaremonthotel.com

ROOMS: 24 in the inn, 6 in Phillips House, 14 cottages; all with private bath.

RATES: In-season: $200 to $225, double occupancy, MAP; $150 to $155, double occupancy, EPB. Off-season: $130 to $190, double occupancy, MAP; $89 to $115, EPB. No meals with cottages. No credit cards.

OPEN: Early June to mid-October. Cottages from mid-May to mid-October.

FACILITIES AND ACTIVITIES: Lunch in-season, dinner, full license. Tennis court, dock and moorings, croquet courts, badminton, bicycles, rowboats, library. Nearby: 3 golf courses, sailing, freshwater swimming, summer theater, Acadia National Park.

The Claremont has been a landmark on the shores of Somes Sound, the famous fjord of beautiful Mount Desert Island, for more than a century. It was entered on the National Register of Historic Places in 1978. I saw an ad that describes the inn well: "For over 100 summers, upholding the traditions of hospitality and leisure on the Maine coast."

There is so much to do and see up here. The Claremont Croquet Classic—the home of nine-wicket croquet—is held every summer.

You can sit in a cozy chair at a bay window upstairs and watch this event in sheer comfort. Bring your binoculars and you can see all the way to Northeast Harbor. Watch for all the lobster boats, sailboats, and yachts that sail by.

I was here in mid-June and boy, did the fireplace in the lovely living room feel good! The library–game room also has a nice fireplace. There are a lot of places to sit down and just relax at The Claremont. If you look hard, you can find a television, but why bother, with all of this beauty around you?

Most activities center on the boathouse and waterfront, where a dock, float, and deep-water moorings are available for guests. The boathouse is

open June 25 through August and is nice for lunch and predinner cocktails. What a view you get from here!

The guest rooms in the inn are comfortable and decorated simply. There are also two guest houses. The Phillips House has six large rooms, including a suite, a large living room with a fireplace, and a veranda with views. The Clark House has an additional suite. There are also fourteen housekeeping cottages, each of which has a Franklin stove or a stone fireplace. Most of these have views of the Sound.

The dining room is lovely, with candlelight, linens, fresh flowers, and attentive service. Gentlemen are asked to wear jackets. The food is excellent. You can order char-grilled salmon, Maine crab cakes, sautéed duck breast, and beef, but, of course, the king of all is lobster. An extensive breakfast buffet is served daily.

HOW TO GET THERE: Take the Maine Turnpike to Augusta, exit 15. Follow Route 3 east through Ellsworth to the Trenton Bridge and Mount Desert Island. Once over the bridge, take Route 102 to Southwest Harbor and follow signs to The Claremont.

The East Wind Inn
Tenants Harbor, Maine 04860

INNKEEPER: Tim Watts

ADDRESS/TELEPHONE: 149 Mechanic Street (mailing address: P.O. Box 149); (207) 372-6366 or (800) 241-VIEW

E-MAIL: info@eastwindinn.com

WEB SITE: www.eastwindinn.com

ROOMS: 26, including 3 suites and 4 apartments, in 3 buildings; 16 with private bath, all with phone.

RATES: $82 to $110, double occupancy; includes continental breakfast.

OPEN: All year. From December 1 to April 1, the inn is available only to groups.

FACILITIES AND ACTIVITIES: Breakfast, Sunday brunch, dinner. Wheelchair access to dining room and meeting room. Lounge with full liquor license, meeting room, deep-water anchorage for boats, sailboat charter. Nearby: Golf, tennis, swimming, cross-country skiing.

The inn was built in 1890 and stood vacant for twenty years. Tim, a native of the town, watched the old house deteriorate and dreamed of restoring it so others could share the charm of "the country of the pointed firs." He's been able to do just that.

Today you can sit on the wraparound porch of the inn and enjoy the view. Tenants Harbor should be on a postcard, it's so beautiful. The inn is within walking distance of the village, where you will find a library, shops, post office, and churches.

The Meeting House is so nice for a relaxed conference or seminar. The guest rooms are very clean. Some have oak bureaus and Victorian side chairs, while others have brass beds. All the rooms have water views. The Ginny Wheeler cottage has three apartment accommodations, and there is another apartment in the meeting house, all ideal for families.

The view and the food compete for your attention here. Dinner has marvelous specialties from the sea—fresh daily, as you'd expect. Desserts—of course, they are excellent.

You'll no doubt be tempted to get out on that beautiful water, and that's easy to do. The friendship sloop *Surprise* sails three times a day from the pier at The East Wind. These are three-hour cruises on a 33-foot ketch, with comfortable accommodations for up to six persons. The captain really knows these waters and can tell you all you want to know. Go and enjoy.

HOW TO GET THERE: From Route 1, just east of Thomaston, take Route 131 south for 9½ miles to Tenants Harbor. Turn left at the post office and continue straight to the inn.

The Waterford Inne
Waterford, Maine 04088

INNKEEPERS: Barbara and Rosalie Vanderzanden

ADDRESS/TELEPHONE: P.O. Box 149; (207) 583-4037

E-MAIL: inne@gwi.net

WEB SITE: www.waterfordinne.com

ROOMS: 10; 7 with private bath.

RATES: $85 to $125, double occupancy; EPB.

OPEN: All year.

FACILITIES AND ACTIVITIES: Breakfast, dinner. BYOB. Nearby: Hiking, hunting, fishing, swimming, bird-watching, golf, skiing.

*T*his is a beautiful part of the world. It is secluded, quiet, and restful. The inn offers a fireplace in the parlor and a library full of books and good music for your relaxation. And when the weather is warm, you can while away your days in the rockers on the porch.

But if you're looking for activity, The Waterford Inne can offer that, too. The area provides hiking, hunting, fishing in the summer and winter, downhill and cross-country skiing, swimming, and bird-watching.

The mother and daughter who are the innkeepers bought the inn in 1978 and have done a masterful job of restoring and renovating it. There are antiques in all the rooms, nice wallpapers, and some stenciling. For your comfort there are electric blankets in the winter, and for your visual pleasure there are fresh flowers in the summer. The Country Fair room, all pine and posters, is the latest addition and very refreshing.

Rosalie, the mother, does the cooking. The dinner is a fixed price with one entree served each evening. She is a very good and creative chef. All baking is done right here, and all the vegetables are grown in the inn's garden. Barbara does the serving, and you may be seated at a table for four in the attractive dining room with a fireplace or in a secluded corner just for two.

Snuffy and Simba are the two inn cats lucky enough to live in this glorious part of the world.

HOW TO GET THERE: From Norway, Maine, take Route 118 west for 8 miles to Route 37. Turn left and go ½ mile to Springer's General Store. Take an immediate right up the hill. The inn is in about ½ mile.

The Lawnmeer Inn
West Boothbay Harbor, Maine 04575

INNKEEPERS: Jim and Lee Metzger

ADDRESS/TELEPHONE: P.O. Box 505; (207) 633–2544 or
(800) 633–7645

WEB SITE: www.lawnmeerinn.com

ROOMS: 32, all with private bath, cable TV, and phone; some with
sundeck or air-conditioning.

RATES: $95 to $195, double occupancy; EP.

OPEN: Mid-May to mid-October.

FACILITIES AND ACTIVITIES: Full breakfast, dinner, Sunday brunch.
Bar, lounge, boat dock. Nearby: Boothbay Harbor activities, boat tours,
aquarium, theater.

The inn is nicely located on the island of Southport in the Boothbay Harbor region. As you sit on its porch or relax in the Adirondack chairs on the lawn, you are looking at Townsend Gut and
watching the masts of the moored sailboats sway with the winds and tides.

The accommodations range from modern rooms in a new wing to comfortable inn suites and rooms. Lee's handiwork is evident in many rooms; her
grapevine wreaths, potpourri, and stenciling are a pretty touch. Some rooms
have a television and a sundeck overlooking the water. The views are really
lovely and tranquil—nearly every room has a view to savor.

There are delightful sitting areas. One has a fireplace to ward off early
spring or fall chills. The common room has a television and is full of wicker
furniture and baskets of books. Rescued bears collected from far and wide
and nearby also reside in baskets around the inn. Spike, the inn's coon cat,
keeps them company. The bar and lounge add to the inn's charm. The two
dining rooms are attractive, with their nice napery and tall ladder-back
chairs. One has a fireplace.

A breakfast of hot oatmeal is nice, and the inn offers a full breakfast, too.
I had orange French toast made with a hint of Triple Sec. It was very good.
The brunch menu has quiches, crepes, eggs prepared many ways, fresh-
squeezed orange juice, fresh blueberry muffins, and more.

For dinner there are lobster and baked or broiled seafood selections and
plenty of them. The native sea scallops are grand. Of course, there are meat
and chicken dishes for the landlubbers. Lawnmeer's seafood pasta with four
or five kinds of deep-sea catches over linguine with an Alfredo sauce is a win-

ner. So is the sautéed veal in wine and mushroom sauce. If you're worried about your health or weight, the chef will cook to order according to your dietary needs.

The inn has been operating since 1898. It is the oldest continually operated inn in the Boothbay area. Come see the puffins, craggy cliffs, coon cats, and lighthouses. It's all yours to enjoy.

The windjammers arrive in late June every year, and I was lucky enough to be here then. What a treat!

HOW TO GET THERE: Take exit 22 from I-95 onto Route 1. Just north of Wiscasset turn on Route 27 south. Go through Boothbay Harbor onto the island of Southport. The inn is on Route 27, 3/10 mile from the Southport Bridge.

The Squire Tarbox Inn
Wiscasset, Maine 04578

INNKEEPERS: Karen and Bill Mitman

ADDRESS/TELEPHONE: 1181 Main Road, Westport Island; (207) 882-7693

ROOMS: 11, all with private bath.

RATES: $164 to $251, double occupancy, MAP; $98 to $185, double occupancy, EPB.

OPEN: Mid-May through late October.

FACILITIES AND ACTIVITIES: Full license. Bicycles. Nearby: Beaches, harbors, museums, antiques shops.

Everyone knows how I feel about inns and animals. Well, here they are really different. Among their farm animals Karen and Bill have Nubian goats, which are very pretty animals. Much of the inn's baking is done with the milk, and the goat cheese is shipped all over the country. The barns are scrupulously clean, as these goats are fastidious.

The inn is old, circa 1763, and is listed on the National Register of Historic Places. Many of the original boards and timbers remain today. There are eight fireplaces in the inn. Four are in the bedrooms, which are nicely furnished and comfortable. If you'd like to bring your children to the inn, the innkeepers suggest you telephone first.

A five-course dinner is served at 7:00 P.M. There are two entrees, and the menu changes daily. One dinner featured pear or cucumber soup, whey buns, roast pork tenderloin, Parmesan potatoes, broccoli, acorn squash, and chocolate cake with brandied strawberries. Another night: potage Portugaise, orange and grapefruit nut salad, whey buns, scallops Rebecca (scallops in a wine-Parmesan sauce), cranberried red cabbage, and Sin Pie. As they say, it's the ultimate chocolate dessert. Other menus include fresh seafood, chicken, beef, and more. The inn caters to those on special diets, and alternative choices are offered each evening.

You wake up to a full breakfast, featuring really fresh eggs from free-range chickens. Count on some divine quiches and pancakes.

The sitting areas are neat, with a woodstove, books, and puzzles. The music room has a player piano with lots of rolls. You'll find much to do here.

There are sand dunes, museums, and flea markets. I'd just sit and enjoy. I just love the deck, with its bird feeders—it's such fun to watch the many varieties of birds that come here. And there is a path to the water where a rowboat awaits you.

HOW TO GET THERE: From Route 1 between Bath and Wiscasset, turn onto Route 144 and follow it 8½ miles to the inn, which is on Westport Island.

York Harbor Inn
York Harbor, Maine 03911

INNKEEPERS: Nancy and Gary Dominquez

ADDRESS/TELEPHONE: P.O. Box 573; (207) 363–5119 or (800) 343–3869; fax (207) 363–7151

E-MAIL: info@yorkharborinn.com

WEB SITE: www.yorkharborinn.com

ROOMS: 40, plus 2 suites in 2 buildings; all with private bath, air-conditioning, and phone; some with TV and fireplace; 4 with Jacuzzi.

RATES: High season April to November, $119 to $249, double occupancy, EPB; low season $99 to $249. Harbor Cliffs, $159 to $229, double occupancy, EPB. Very special packages available.

OPEN: All year.

FACILITIES AND ACTIVITIES: Lunch in-season, dinner, Sunday brunch, bar, full license. Nearby: Public beach, fishing, boating, golf, tennis.

BUSINESS TRAVEL: The inn offers more than 5,000 square feet of meeting space and has an inventory of state-of-the-art audiovisual equipment including a computer video data projector.

*W*ow! Three dining rooms with a view of the Atlantic. This is a cozy and comfortable inn, with good food and good grog. Sitting there looking over the Atlantic should be enough, but when you add the excellent food, it is heaven.

Everything is made to order and baked right here. Chef Gerry Bonsey, named chef of the year by the local chapter of the American Culinary Federation one year, by his own admission creates incomparable soups.

The appetizers, such as Portobello Pizza and Maine crab cakes (I had these on my last trip, and they're delicious), are glorious. Entrees include baked stuffed haddock, Yorkshire lobster supreme, lobster-stuffed breast of chicken, roast rack of lamb, beef tenderloin, and, of course, boiled lobster and scallops. Do save room for the desserts.

The wine cellar, which once was a livery stable, is the lounge. The bar is a beauty, made of unstained cherry wood joined with holly and ebony woods. The carpenter even put an inlaid tulip in a corner—out of tulip wood, of course. Happy hour is very happy, featuring good food and conversation with a lot of local people. There is entertainment here on Wednesday, Friday, and Saturday.

Parts of the inn are very old; 1637 is the date of the cabin room. Originally a fisherman's house, it has sturdy beams in the ceiling—not for holding up the roof but instead for holding up wet sails to dry before the large fireplace. It was moved here.

The rooms are comfortable, and from some you can see the sea. On a quiet night you can hear the surf breaking on the generous beach below the inn. The carriage house next door is handsomely decorated. All rooms have private baths and two have working fireplaces. All are air-conditioned and have a complete sprinkler system.

The Harbor Cliffs next door is a real beauty, offering seven rooms, all with private bath, four with wood fireplaces, two with Jacuzzis, one with a large deck. You can see the ocean very well from here. The ocean is so beautiful, and so are these rooms.

The inn dogs, Annie and Sam, are handsome springer spaniels. Bring your camera—it's beautiful up here. Come up for York's Christmas Prelude—the first two weekends in December.

HOW TO GET THERE: Going south on I-95, take the Yorks/Berwicks exit; going north on I-95, take the Yorks/Ogunquit exit. Turn right at the blinking light, left at the first traffic light (Route 1A), and go through the village about 3 miles. The inn is on the left.

Nubble Light

The town of York's most visited—and most photographed—site is the Nubble Light at Cape Neddick, the rocky promontory that stretches nearly a mile into the Atlantic Ocean. On its own little island at the tip—or "nubble"—of the peninsula, the 1879 lighthouse is at the end of Nubble Road off Route 1A at York Beach. English navigator Capt. Bartholomew Gosnold landed at this site in 1602; Capt. John Smith came to chart the area in 1614. It is he who coined the term "knubble." Now automated and maintained by the U.S. Coast Guard, the white iron-sheathed brick tower had a keeper until 1987. Its black-capped light is 88 feet above the high-water mark, still protecting seafarers off Maine's rugged coast.

Select List of
Other Maine Inns

Mira Monte Inn & Suites
69 Mount Desert Street
Bar Harbor, ME 04609
(207) 288-4263 or (800) 553-5109; fax (207) 288-3115

13 rooms in 1864 main building, 11 with fireplace, all with private bath; 3 suites in other buildings, all with private bath, fireplace, balcony.

Spruce Point Inn
Atlantic Avenue
Boothbay Harbor, ME 04538
(207) 633-4152 or (800) 553-0289; fax (207) 633-7138
E-mail: thepoint@sprucepointinn.com
Web site: www.sprucepointinn.com

75 rooms, all with private bath; main inn has restaurant and lounge.

Maine Stay
22 High Street
Camden, ME 04843
(207) 236-9636; fax (207) 236-0621
E-mail: innkeeper@mainestay.com
Web site: www.mainestay.com

8 rooms, all with private bath; 200-year-old farm complex.

English Meadows Inn B&B

Port Road
Kennebunk, ME 04043
(207) 967-5766 or (800) 272-0698

12 rooms, 10 with private bath; Victorian farmhouse.

Old Granite Inn

546 Main Street
Rockland, ME 04841
(207) 594-9036 or (800) 386-9036
E-mail: ogi@midcoast.com
Web site: www.midcoast.com/~ogi

11 rooms, 8 with private bath; federal Colonial B&B.

The Surry Inn

Route 172
Surry, ME 04684
(207) 667-5091
Web site: www.surryinn.com

13 rooms, 11 with private bath. A lovely 1834 inn on Contention Cove, chef-owned with dinner served seven days. Wonderful sunsets.

Edwards Harborside Inn

Box 866, Stage Neck Road
York Harbor, ME 03911
(207) 363-3037 or (800) 273-2686; fax (207) 363-1544

10 rooms, 8 with private bath; Victorian waterfront estate.

Stage Neck Inn

22 Stage Neck Road
York Harbor, ME 03911
(207) 363-3850 or (800) 222-3238; fax (207) 363-2221

58 rooms, all with private bath; 2 dining rooms; indoor pool; Jacuzzi; fitness room.

Massachusetts

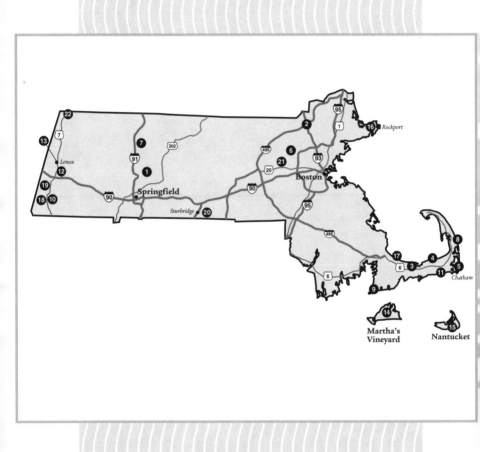

Massachusetts

Numbers on map refer to towns numbered below.

*A Top Pick Inn

The Lord Jeffery Inn
Amherst, Massachusetts 01002

INNKEEPER: Michael Maderia

ADDRESS/TELEPHONE: 30 Boltwood Avenue; (413) 253–2576 or (800) 742–0358; fax (413) 256–6152

E-MAIL: info@lordjefferyinn.com

WEB SITE: www.lordjefferyinn.com

ROOMS: 40 rooms, 8 suites; all with private bath, TV, and phone.

RATES: $79 to $139, double occupancy; $129 to $189, suites; EP.

OPEN: All year.

FACILITIES AND ACTIVITIES: Breakfast, lunch, dinner, Sunday brunch, tavern, room service for all meals. Elevator. Nearby: Skiing, golf, tennis, antiquing, Emily Dickinson house.

*T*he Lord Jeffery Inn, located on the historic common in Amherst, is named for Lord Jeffery Amherst, a hero of the French and Indian War. When you arrive here, you'll think the inn is so impressive with its whitewashed brick exterior.

The common rooms on the first floor are huge and comfortable. Cozy couches and chairs, beautiful flowers, and wonderful fireplaces are all around. The former living room has become the Windowed Hearth restaurant. I also like the tavern, with its small bar, tables, and windows looking out over the gardens. A patio is in front of the building off the tavern.

A comforting thing to know about this old building is that its halls have sprinkler systems and that smoke alarms are everywhere. The rooms here come in all sizes—small, medium, and large. Some are small suites. All have Colonial decor, comfortable mattresses, television, and telephones with data ports. Some of the rooms overlook the lovely Colonial gardens, and others have a view of the Amherst common. Eight of the garden rooms have porches.

The inn, especially the Grand Ballroom, is a popular place for weddings and other special events. Six function rooms in all can accommodate up to 225 guests.

Breakfast here is a great way to start the day—excellent baked goods, omelets, eggs, sausage, bacon, and lots more. Lunch is hearty. When I last visited I had a delicious thick tomato and spinach soup and a salad so generous I could not finish it. The dinner menu in the Windowed Hearth varies with the season but often features duck, lobster, rack of lamb, and chateaubriand, a yummy favorite of mine.

If you are in the mood for something lighter, pub fare is available in the Elijah Boltwood Tavern.

There is much to do in this area. Besides Amherst College, many other colleges are in the area. Skiing, golf, tennis, and more are all nearby.

HOW TO GET THERE: Take I–91 to the Amherst exit (exit 19), then go east 8 miles on Route 9 to Amherst.

Andover Inn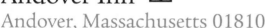
Andover, Massachusetts 01810

INNKEEPER: Henry Broekhoff

ADDRESS/TELEPHONE: Phillips Academy campus; (978) 475–5903; fax (978) 475–1053

E-MAIL: andover1@tiac.net

WEB SITE: www.andoverinn.com

ROOMS: 11, plus 4 junior and 2 executive suites; all with private bath, air-conditioning, TV, phone, wheelchair accessibility.

RATES: $105, single; $120, double; $160 to $195, suite; EP.

OPEN: All year.

FACILITIES AND ACTIVITIES: Breakfast, lunch, dinner, Sunday brunch. Dining room closed on Christmas Day. Bar, elevator, barbershop.

BUSINESS TRAVEL: Located 30 minutes from Boston. Phone in all rooms, desk in some; conference room; fax available.

The Andover Inn is part of the campus of Phillips Academy. It is privately owned and offers twenty-four-hour desk service, an elevator, dry-cleaning services, photocopying, and box lunches. Room service is available, as are taxis and wake-up service.

You expect ivy-covered buildings here, and you get them in abundance. Upon entering the inn you are in the reception area, with a fireplace and comfortable couches. The bar is in the right corner of this room, and it is one of the nicest I've visited. The stools with armrests are overstuffed, and honest, you hate to leave them.

The rooms have modern conveniences, such as color television, air-conditioning, direct-dial telephone, and full bath. All of them have nice views of the campus.

The dining rooms are lovely, and the china used is Villeroy and Boch. Siena is the pattern. It is porcelain and looks just like pink marble. The breakfast menu is extensive. Freshly squeezed orange or grapefruit juice is a nice way to start the day. Dinner selections include hot and cold appetizers, salads, and entrees from the sea or land. Try the specialty of the inn, scampi flambé.

From early May to the end of June, there is a white asparagus festival. The asparagus comes fresh from the Netherlands twice a week to the inn. Grown underground and harvested by hand, it's a rare treat.

Sunday brings rijsttafel, an original Indonesian dish served late in the day. It consists of dry steamed rice and an indefinite number of side dishes and sauces. The menu tells you how to eat it. I was overwhelmed and delighted by it. Do go and give it a try. It's worth a trip from anywhere, and reservations are a must.

Monday through Thursday and Saturday evenings, guests enjoy light classical music on the grand piano. Friday evening are dinner and dancing to the sounds of the big-band era. Sunday brunch features classical guitar music.

HOW TO GET THERE: The inn is 25 miles north of Boston on Route 28, near the intersection of I–93 and I–495.

Cobb's Cove 🖤
Barnstable Village, Massachusetts 02630

INNKEEPERS: Evelyn Chester and Henri-Jean

ADDRESS/TELEPHONE: Powder Hill Road (mailing address: P.O. Box 208); (508) 362–9356 or (877) 378–5172 (same number for fax).

E-MAIL: evelyn@cobbscove.com

WEB SITE: www.cobbscove.com

ROOMS: 6 suites, all with private bath.

RATES: $149 to $189, double occupancy; EPB.

OPEN: All year.

FACILITIES AND ACTIVITIES: Dinner by reservation only to houseguests. BYOB.

The moment you walk in the door and are greeted by Evelyn and Henri-Jean, you know you have happened on a distinctive and delightful inn. You are taken to your suite, and what a marvelous view you have! The third-floor suites have an immense dormer with glass on three sides and a million-dollar view. There is a couch in front of this dormer where you can sit and see all of Cape Cod Bay, Sandy Neck, and all the way to Provincetown Light. The other suites also have grand views, deliciously comfortable beds, and all the extras you expect at an extraordinary inn. The baths all have whirlpools—so relaxing after a day of travel. The soaps and bubble bath are pear scented, a nice touch. There are plenty of big towels and good, soft pillows.

The inn is on a very secluded and scenic piece of property. The bay is right at hand. The inn was built of 12-by-12-inch rough-cut timbers, and many of the walls are done in rough burlap. The keeping room has a large Count Rumford shallow fireplace, comfortable chairs, and wonderful smells that come from Henri's kitchen. There is a terrace full of bird feeders made by Harry Holl of the Scargo Pottery. Harry also made many of the kitchen things Henri uses, including a huge

Cape Cod by Land and by Sea

Traffic on Cape Cod can be a real misery at the height of the tourist season. Let someone else do the driving whenever you can. Landlubbers can tour a part of the Cape by excursion train. The Cape Cod Central Railroad hooks up three vintage railway cars to make a 42-mile round-trip from Hyannis (just south of Barnstable) to the Cape Cod Canal. The two-hour ride includes grand scenery and an interesting narrative on the various sights. A special three-hour Dinner Train is a romantic option; it includes a five-course dinner and a sunset stop at the world's widest sea-level canal. For a schedule and reservations, call (508) 771-3800 or (888) 797-RAIL, or check the Web site www. cape-train.com.

Lovers of the sea may want to leave the driving to a licensed captain. Walk down to Barnstable Harbor off Mill Way and book passage on a Hyannis Whale Watcher cruise (508-362-6088 or 800-287-0374). The four-hour trip to and from Stellwagen Bank may include a look at humpbacks, minkes, finbacks, and more. An on-board naturalist points out the sights. The 100-foot boat has both open and enclosed decks and a galley for snacks and drinks. Cruises are April through October.

salad bowl that is a rare beauty. In summer breakfast is served on the terrace, and it's quite a sight with all the birds on the feeders.

The dining room–library has a long hutch table that seats fourteen quite comfortably. Dinner is served in three or five courses. One night I was there it started with delicious mussels, then a special cauliflower dish done Henri's way. This was followed by a fish (cod, I believe, and you can only believe because Henri reveals no kitchen information at all) so white and so tasty you wondered why you had ever eaten meat. Next came a salad, and finally a crème caramel for dessert, topped off by a great cup of espresso coffee, an Henri specialty.

This is fine dining, and believe me, the innkeeper who joins you for every course is the reason this inn is such a success. It also has the best view in Cape Cod. I must add, however, that Henri cooks dinner only when he feels like it.

HOW TO GET THERE: Take exit 6 off Route 6. Turn left on Route 132 north to Route 6A. Turn right, go about 3 miles, and pass through the light in the middle of Barnstable Village. After you pass the church on your left, turn left onto Powder Hill Road. Take the first driveway on the left, marked EVELYN CHESTER.

High Brewster
Brewster, Massachusetts 02631

INNKEEPERS: Tim and Catherine Mundy

ADDRESS/TELEPHONE: 964 Satucket Road; (508) 896-3636

ROOMS: 8, in 4 buildings; all with private bath.

RATES: $115 to $250 (for cottages), double occupancy; expanded continental breakfast. Weekly rates available.

OPEN: April through November.

FACILITIES AND ACTIVITIES: Dinner, wine, beer. Fishing. Nearby: Biking, ocean, antiques stores, state parks with nature walks.

The grounds of High Brewster are beautiful. There are lush lawns, glorious flowers, and tables on the terrace overlooking Lower Millpond. There are three and a half acres in all. In spring the herring come up Herring Run Creek to spawn. There are walkways along the creek.

The original property had three houses, one of which stands today. Referred to as the Main House, it was built in 1738. That's old, folks; and the way the floors tip and tilt upstairs, you know it's old. There are two rooms upstairs—the Red Room and the Green Room.

There are guest rooms in three other buildings. Pond Cottage overlooks the pond and has one bedroom, a service kitchen, and a wonderful screened-in deck with a view of the pond. The living room in Brook House has a lovely fireplace, a dining table, and a picture window overlooking the pond. It also has two bedrooms and one bath, plus a deck where you can sit and listen to the creek on its way down to the pond. Then there is the barn, which has a bedroom, a sleeping loft, one and a half bathrooms, a kitchen, and a fireplace.

You have a choice of three dining rooms. Fresh flowers are on the tables. The kitchen is spotless and the food is grand. The menu changes at least every six weeks and sometimes more often.

There were four of us on my last trip here, and we started our dinner with an array of appetizers. One I really liked was Portobello Pot Stickers, filled with chicken, goat cheese, and leeks, with a light Oriental glaze.

We all had lamb chops grilled with garlic mashed potatoes and vegetables and a good salad. Other menu choices include grilled leg of lamb with different sauces each day, medallions of veal, shrimp, scallops, and black Angus tenderloin of beef.

For dessert I had the best rhubarb and strawberry crisp with ice cream that I've had in many a country mile.

HOW TO GET THERE: Take Route 6 to exit 11. Go left on Route 6A to a blinking amber light. Turn on Stony Brook Road and go about 1 mile. Just past the gristmill and creek, take the first left and turn into the inn's driveway.

The Queen Anne Inn
Chatham, Massachusetts 02633

INNKEEPERS: Guenther and Dana Weinkopf

ADDRESS/TELEPHONE: Queen Anne Road; (508) 945–0394 or (800) 545–4667; fax (508) 945–4884

ROOMS: 31, all with private bath, phone, and TV.

RATES: $198 to $345 per room, double occupancy; continental breakfast.

OPEN: All year except January to February 14.

FACILITIES AND ACTIVITIES: Dinner. Tennis courts, swimming pool. Nearby: Boating, fishing tours can be arranged.

*I*magine receiving this lovely place as a wedding gift. True. It happened in 1840. Now Guenther has a fine inn. The rooms are so very comfortable. On the garden side the rooms have private balconies, which are a nice addition to the inn. Rooms looking south have a good view of Oyster Pond Bay.

There is a very pleasant lounge to relax in. The artist James Parker has done a grand mural of Native Americans here in the lounge; there are others in various rooms and in the spa. And then there is the Earl of Chatham, the dining room, serving the most unbelievable food you can imagine. The wait-staff are beautifully trained. The chef has a briefing with them each night, so they can explain each course to their diners.

The appetizers are great—fried native oysters with roasted corn salsa and horseradish butter, or crispy shiitake mushroom and soft polenta sandwiches with basil-tomato fondue. The salads with field greens or arugula are so pretty and good. Entrees include roasted halibut with garlic mashed potatoes, spinach, fried onion rings, and red-wine butter sauce. There are also oven-roasted salmon, grilled tenderloin of beef, breast of chicken, and more. Do remember, though, that the menus change, so you may find different choices.

I needed a walk, and there are pleasant places to go. The water is close at hand, and every Friday night band concerts are held in nearby Kate Gould Park. What a nice way to meet the other guests!

The spa downstairs has a stunning mural that surrounds the hot tub; a mermaid, fish, and plants are depicted in soft and very restful colors. There are lounge chairs and comfort in here. The next room has a large television and good books.

The inn also has three all-weather Har-Tru tennis courts in a beautiful parklike setting, a resident tennis pro, pro shop, and private lessons. There's a lovely swimming pool, and a service bar in the lower lounge. Add to all this the inn dog, Tip, who's a pip.

This is a beautiful area of the Cape. See the lighthouse and windmills, listen to the bells chiming from the church steeples, and watch the surf thundering on Nauset Beach and Monomoy Island.

HOW TO GET THERE: From Route 6 (Mid-Cape Highway) take exit 11, go south on Route 137 to its end, and take a left on Route 28 to Chatham Center. At your first traffic light, in about 3 miles, go right on Queen Anne Road. The inn is on your right.

The Town House Inn
Chatham, Massachusetts 02633

INNKEEPERS: Russell and Svea Peterson

ADDRESS/TELEPHONE: 11 Library Lane; (508) 945-2180 or (800) 242-2180

E-MAIL: chathamthi@capecod.net

WEB SITE: www.chathamtownhouse.com

ROOMS: 26, plus 2 air-conditioned cottages; all with private bath, TV, VCR, refrigerator, and phone. No-smoking inn.

RATES: $135 to $365, double occupancy; EPB.

OPEN: All year except January.

FACILITIES AND ACTIVITIES: Dinner May to the end of October. Full liquor license, lunch in-season. Heated pool, spa, cabana bar. Nearby: Friday-night band concerts, golf, tennis, beaches.

The front porch that overlooks Main Street beckons me. The Fourth of July parade, one of the summer's biggest events, goes right by the front door. Best seat in town is the porch of this inn. The original structure dates back to the 1820s. Remains of the foundation can still be seen in the cellar, and some of the original woodwork is here. The carved moldings and wood trim depict harpoon and oar motifs. The floors are made of hemlock, and the original walls, recently exposed, have hand-painted scrolling. Check out the stencils in the rooms. Some of the shell stencils are really beautiful.

The rooms are immaculate; matter of fact, the whole inn is. The beds are queens and doubles. There are four-poster canopy beds in several rooms. All of the linens and towels are laundered right here by Svea. There are irons and ironing boards in each room. Each room also has a television with a clock radio, VCR, and a refrigerator. Hair dryers, too, are in every room; this is a really nice touch. The cottages have a fireplace and air-conditioning. Children are welcome in the cottages, and baby-sitters are available.

Breakfast is not a ho-hum thing here. Russ bakes the muffins and Svea does wonders with Scandinavian goodies. Favorites are Svea's Finnish pancakes with a fresh fruit mélange on top and her French toast with apricots.

The restaurant is called Two Turtles. Using her mother's recipes, Svea prepares Swedish pickled herring and Swedish meatballs as well as desserts.

Her son, David Peterson, is a certified chef and serves glorious food. There are nine choices of appetizers, followed by good soups and salads. He prepares entrees like baked scrod with lemon butter, Nantucket scallops, scampi, grilled lamb chops, salmon, and much more. The desserts are sinful. Two Turtles flourless chocolate cake with lightly sweetened whipped cream is just one.

David is also the restaurant manager and beverage coordinator. Son Russell oversees the cabana, with glorious frozen margaritas and lots more. He's also a captain and offers sportfishing excursions on the *Liveliner*.

HOW TO GET THERE: Take Route 6 (Mid-Cape Highway) to exit 11, Route 137 South, to Route 28 and east to the center of downtown Chatham. Watch for the Eldredge Library on your left. The inn is next door, at 11 Library Lane.

Wequasset Inn
Chatham, Massachusetts 02633

INNKEEPER: Mark Novata

ADDRESS/TELEPHONE: Route 28, Pleasant Bay, Cape Cod;
(508) 432–5400 or (800) 225–7125; fax (508) 432–5032

E-MAIL: reservations@wequasset.com

WEB SITE: www.wequasset.com

ROOMS: 104, including 7 suites; all with private bath; most with private
patio or deck.

RATES: $195 to $895, single or double occupancy; EP.

OPEN: April to late November.

FACILITIES AND ACTIVITIES: Breakfast, lunch, dinner. Croquet court,
5 all-weather PlexiPave tennis courts plus pro shop and lessons, fitness
center, conference center, heated swimming pool, fishing, 18-hole
golf course.

aking its name from the Native American word meaning "Cres-
cent on the Water," Wequasset is a country inn resort that
includes twenty separate buildings and is worth a trip from anywhere. Tucked between a secluded ocean cove and a twenty-two-acre pine
forest, the lands around Wequasset were once used by native peoples as a
summer campground.

A nineteenth-century sea captain's home now houses the inn's main din-
ing room, the Square Top, named for the building's unusual roof line. There is a spectacular view of Pleas-ant Bay from here, a nice complement to the inn's glorious food, which has been awarded Mobil Travel Guide's four-star rating. The breakfast menu offers so many choices that you

could eat all day. At lunch there are many different salads, great burgers, and a deli board. One sandwich I liked was the Yorkshire—thinly sliced roast beef, creamy horseradish, and lettuce and tomato piled high on a kaiser roll. Way to go, Elizabeth—right to the fat farm. Of course, they do have a fitness platter. Well, maybe next time. There's also a lovely selection of really different drinks on the lunch menu.

The dinners? Well, you can imagine. Tons of appetizers, hot and cold. I can taste the lobster salad now. The seafood is wonderful, as are the meat and poultry. Desserts—are you ready? Wequasset Inn's chocolate truffle cake. I do not know where I put it, but it was all gone. There are many specialty coffees along with the regular ones.

In summer, lunch and dinner are also served at the Outer Bar and Grille, and informal restaurant on the waterfront where you can order anything from clam chowder to a sirloin steak.

The accommodations are unique. Each room has its own bath and entrance, simply styled pine furniture, traditional fabrics, and lots of charm. There are heating and cooling units, color television, and patios and decks. Suites feature fresh flowers, minibar, and VCR.

It would be hard to beat the serenity of sitting on the porch overlooking the bay at any time of the day, but oh, the early-morning calm!

HOW TO GET THERE: Wequasset Inn is on Pleasant Bay, midway between Chatham and Orleans on Route 28. If you are driving from the north, take Route 6 east to exit 11. Turn left at end of exit ramp; go 25 yards to Pleasant Bay Road (your first left). Go straight through the first stop sign, and when you reach the second stop sign, you have arrived at Wequasset Inn.

Concord's Colonial Inn
Concord, Massachusetts 01742

INNKEEPERS: Jurgen and Rebecca Demisch

ADDRESS/TELEPHONE: 48 Monument Square; (978) 369–9200 or (800) 370–9200; fax (978) 371–1533

WEB SITE: www.concordscolonialinn.com

ROOMS: 45, plus 9 suites; all with private bath, air-conditioning, phone, and TV.

RATES: $135 to $425 per room; EP.

OPEN: All year.

FACILITIES AND ACTIVITIES: Breakfast, lunch, dinner, Sunday brunch, afternoon tea. Tavern, lounge; gift shop; jazz or folk music daily.

BUSINESS TRAVEL: Located 18 miles from Boston, 20 miles from Logan Airport. Phone in room; conference room; corporate rates.

The history of Concord's Colonial Inn (1716) is tied to the history of young America in famous Concord, Massachusetts. Here was fired the "shot heard 'round the world." Here lived some of the nation's literary greats—Henry David Thoreau, Ralph Waldo Emerson, Louisa May Alcott, Nathaniel Hawthorne. They are all laid to rest on Author's Ridge in Sleepy Hollow Cemetery, a short walk from the inn. There is so much history in Concord, it would take days to see it all.

High tea means sandwiches of cucumber and radish, cream cheese and chives, smoked salmon and watercress, plus crumpets and scones, cream and fresh berries, miniature cakes and fresh fruit tarts—afternoons here are done right.

The whole inn was refurbished a few years ago, and it's lovely. The main dining room is beautiful, with its white napery, windows full of plants, and beamed ceiling. The lunch menu is extensive with four different salads, good soups, and choices of hot or cold sandwiches. You'll also find shrimp scampi, steak au poivre, and poached salmon. Dinner, of course, is grand, as are the desserts. The staff is very nice.

The taproom and Liberty and Village Forge lounges are three rustic lounges that, until 1967, served men only. Women are welcome today but at their own risk. Ho, ho. I wasn't scared. Many years ago, however, I stayed in Room 24. Now they tell me it's haunted. Well, the lights came on in the wee hours and woke me. I knew I hadn't turned them on, but I certainly did turn them off—after a while. I wonder who it was?

HOW TO GET THERE: Take Route 2 east to Route 62 east to Concord Center to Monument Square. The inn is at 48 Monument Square.

Deerfield Inn 📱
Deerfield, Massachusetts 01342

INNKEEPERS: Karl and Jane Sabo

ADDRESS/TELEPHONE: Main Street; (413) 774–5587 or (800) 926–3865; fax (413) 775–7221

E-MAIL: frontdesk@deerfieldinn.com

WEB SITE: www.deerfieldinn.com

ROOMS: 23, all with private bath, air-conditioning, phone, and color TV. No-smoking inn.

RATES: $122.00 to $156.50, double occupancy; EPB.

OPEN: All year except December 24 to 26.

FACILITIES AND ACTIVITIES: Lunch, dinner. Tavern, two living rooms, elevator, color TV in lounge. Nearby: Museums, Deerfield Academy, historic house tours.

BUSINESS TRAVEL: Phone in room; conference rooms; audiovisual equipment and fax available.

*T*his is an inn that has been welcoming travelers since 1884, one of the few structures in New England continuously offering food and lodging for such a long time. Is stands in the center of the beautiful avenue known simply as "The Street," lined with more than sixty fine Colonial and Federal homes, many of them open to the public as house museums. Deerfield is such a rare town that the entire village has been declared a National Historic Landmark.

The rocking chairs on the front porch of the inn somehow let you know how lovely things will be inside. The parlors are beautifully furnished, with mostly twentieth-century copies or adaptations. The Beehive Parlor, done in shades of blue, is a restful place for a cocktail or two. The main dining room is spacious, serving the kind of food befitting the setting. The chef prepares a daily special, taking advantage of seasonal and local market offerings. He also does magical things with veal, chicken, and fish. Fresh fish is brought in three times a week.

The luncheon menu has some interesting and quite different offerings, such as a beautiful summer salad (the raspberry vinaigrette is glorious) and a very good casserole of fresh fish baked in wine and garden herbs. At dinnertime try the tasty gravlax with a sauce of honey mustard and dill. There's also broiled venison on the menu.

The bedrooms are true joys—Beautyrest mattresses, matching bedspreads and drapes, comfortable chairs, and good lights for restful reading or needlework. The baths have been color-coordinated with the rooms they serve. The towels are large and fluffy. Little to nothing has been left to chance in this restoration. Even European hair dryers have been added; they have magnifying mirrors on them.

A coffee shop on the lower level leads out to an outdoor garden: a perfect spot for informal meals and a place the children will love.

Take a carriage ride down the street and around Historic Deerfield. Browse through Memorial Hall Museum, one of the nation's oldest, and through the museum shop. Take time to tour the homes around here—they hold some of the finest collections of Early American furnishings in the country.

Historic Deerfield

The Deerfield Inn is smack-dab in the middle of one of the nation's best-preserved historic sites. The village of Deerfield was founded in the 1660s at the edge of the frontier claimed by the British. Attacked several times and nearly destroyed twice by Native American and French raids, the settlement was rebuilt throughout the eighteenth century. Now it stands as a monument to two centuries of colonial and early American life and architecture.

Along the mile-long main street of Old Deerfield are many beautiful private homes and more than a dozen museum homes. Visit the Hall Tavern Information Center at Historic Deerfield: A Museum of New England History and Art (413-774-5581) to see a lovely short film on the history of the village and its restoration, then buy tickets to tour the homes that are open to the public. There are also museums displaying colonial artifacts, textiles, silver and metalware, costumes, and much more. A charming museum store right next to the inn offers beautiful reproductions, needlework, fabrics, books, and other gifts that you can buy as a memento of your visit here.

HOW TO GET THERE: From I–91 take exit 24 northbound. Go 6 miles north on Route 5. At the sign for Old Deerfield Village, take a left. The inn is on your left, just past Deerfield Academy.

Nauset House
East Orleans, Massachusetts 02643

INNKEEPERS: Diane and Al Johnson, Cindy and John Vessella

ADDRESS/TELEPHONE: 143 Beach Road (mailing address: Box 774); (508) 255–2195

ROOMS: 14; 8 with private bath.

RATES: $75 to $140, double occupancy; EPB; afternoon refreshments.

OPEN: April 1 to October 31.

FACILITIES AND ACTIVITIES: Full breakfast. Dinner by special arrangement. BYOB. Nearby: Ocean.

Nauset Beach at East Orleans is the first of the great beaches that rim Cape Cod. Rolling dunes, dashing surf, and wide swaths of sand run southward for more than 10 miles. Quiet, out-of-the-way coves offer the beachgoer an ideal place to sun and picnic or just relax and enjoy. If you prefer freshwater, dozens of inland ponds are at hand.

At Nauset House the conservatory, circa 1910, is from an estate in Greenwich, Connecticut, and was reassembled here in the late 1970s. Very charming with its dolphin fountain, plants and flowers, and nice wicker furniture, it is a pleasant place to while away a summer's evening.

The inn, which includes nine guest rooms, dates back to the 1800s and was a farm in those years. The carriage house, with four more guest rooms, is the farm's original barn. There is also a one-room cottage called Outermost House. All of the rooms are very comfortable, and many are enhanced by lovely hand-painted furniture. You might find irises on a wall and on a bookrack.

Breakfasts are good, and the innkeepers have printed a recipe book with loads of great ideas to take home. Every afternoon wine and cranberry juice are served with hors d'oeuvres. Diane has done spontaneous dinners such as lobster feasts and pasta by candlelight. In addition, there are good restaurants nearby.

The inn has a good map of the Cape, and the innkeepers are very helpful with arrangements. Red the cat and Wiley the inn dog will be there to greet you.

HOW TO GET THERE: Take exit 12 (Orleans-Brewster) off Route 6. Turn right at bottom of ramp, then right at first traffic light. Proceed straight, past the next light and across route 28, Tonset Road. At the next light, turn right onto Main Street. Proceed to the fork and bear left onto Beach Road. The inn is $^8/_{10}$ mile on the right.

Coonamessett Inn
Falmouth, Massachusetts 02541

INNKEEPERS: Linda and Bill Zammer Jr.; Jim Underdah, general manager

ADDRESS/TELEPHONE: 311 Gifford Street; (508) 548-2300; fax (508) 540-9831

E-MAIL: cmi.cathi@aol.com

WEB SITE: www.capecod.com/coonamessett

ROOMS: 25 suites, plus 1 cottage; all with private bath.

RATES: $89 to $260, double occupancy; EP.

OPEN: All year.

FACILITIES AND ACTIVITIES: Lunch, dinner, bar. Parking.

In 1796, in a rolling field that sloped gently down to a lovely pond, Thomas Jones constructed a house and barn that was to become Coonamessett Inn (a Native American word for "the place of the large fish"). The original residence, barn, caretaker's quarters, and carriage house still stand, on six acres of scenic grounds. The framework of the main house is finished with wooden-peg joints, and much of the interior paneling is original. Many of the bricks in the old fireplaces are thought to be made of ballast brought from Europe in the holds of sailing ships.

The inn is best known for its restaurant, and the food is excellent, offered from a large, varied menu and served by friendly waitresses. Luncheons attract a lot of people, as the inn's food reputation travels far and wide. The famous Coonamessett Onion Rings are glorious. Dinner appetizers are many, including Maine crab cakes and Prince Edward Island mussels. A real winner, and judged to be the best in the East, is the lobster bisque, and I'll second it. It's really almost better than I make! And dinner entrees are great, especially the fresh lobster, served steamed or baked and stuffed. There are other seafood dishes, and meat eaters are not forgotten either. There are beef, lamb, and veal entrees, plus the chef's special homemade fresh pasta of the day. (Note: The innkeepers also own Bally's Restaurant in North Falmouth and the Flying Bridge Restaurant overlooking Falmouth Harbor.)

The most famous of the three dining areas is the Cahoon Room, named for a renowned local folk artist and featuring eighteen of his paintings, many of them of the inn itself. This attractive room has high vaulted and beamed ceilings and lighting fixtures in the form of hot-air balloons made of brass and copper. The balloons reflect one of the themes in Cahoon's paintings.

The Cape Cod Room is the newest addition at the inn. Used for private functions, it is large and grand, with windows along one wall overlooking the pond. Outside the Cape Cod Room and the main dining room is a deck large enough for alfresco dining and glorious enough for a wedding ceremony.

The guest suites have a sitting room, bedroom, modern bath, color television, and telephone. They are furnished with country pine and pleasant print and paisley fabrics. These are cottage suites, as there are no guest rooms in the inn itself.

I love the Cape in the off-season, and it's good to know that no matter what day I decide to come, I will receive a cordial welcome here. The inn grounds are beautiful and are kept in mint condition year-round. All around you will see the loveliest array of grass, trees, flowers, shrubs . . . and peace. Don't forget the peace. I wish I lived closer.

HOW TO GET THERE: Take Route 28 at the bridge over the canal, and go into Falmouth. Turn left on Jones Road, and at the intersection of Gifford Street, you will see the inn.

Thornewood Inn
Great Barrington, Massachusetts 01230

INNKEEPERS: Terry and David Thorne

ADDRESS/TELEPHONE: 453 Stockbridge Road; (413) 528–3828 or (800) 854–1008

WEB SITE: www.thornewood.com

ROOMS: 12; all with private bath, telephone, and TV; 3 with fireplace.

RATES: $95 to $250, double occupancy; EPB.

FACILITIES AND ACTIVITIES: Dinner, Sunday brunch at Spencer's Restaurant. Jazz entertainment on special weekends, taproom, swimming pool, massage therapist. Nearby: Skiing, Tanglewood, summer theater, museums.

The inn, a Dutch Colonial built in 1920, has been restored with care. The rooms have twin, double, queen , or king beds, some of which are four-posters and canopies. All the rooms are comfortable and furnished with antiques and fine reproductions. Three prize rooms offer fireplaces and French doors leading to balconies overlooking the beautiful Berkshire hills.

Spencer's Restaurant, named for the Thornes' grandson, is quite elegant, with seasonal "country continental" cuisine, beautifully presented. Many of the fresh fruits and vegetables are from the inn gardens. The dining room has wonderful views of the Berkshires and the Housatonic River in the distance. The restaurant was closed for redecorating when we last visited; can't wait to see the results.

The inn is minutes away from Tanglewood, summer playhouses, museums, and antiques shops. Winter brings skiing, and summer is ideal for relaxing in the inn's own pool.

HOW TO GET THERE: The inn is at the junction of Routes 7 and 183 in Great Barrington.

Windflower Inn

Great Barrington, Massachusetts 01230

INNKEEPERS: Barbara and Gerald Liebert, Claudia and John Ryan

ADDRESS/TELEPHONE: 684 South Egremont Road; (413) 528–2720 or (800) 992–1993

E-MAIL: wndflowr@windflowerinn.com

WEB SITE: www.windflowerinn.com

ROOMS: 13, all with private bath, air-conditioning, and phone; many with a working fireplace.

RATES: $100 to $200, double occupancy; EPB.

OPEN: All year.

FACILITIES AND ACTIVITIES: Swimming pool. Nearby: Golf, tennis, downhill and cross-country skiing, music, theater. BYOB.

Great Barrington was settled in the eighteenth century, and today it is a lovely resort town. The inn was built in the 1850s and is Federal style.

I like the large living room. It has a white brick fireplace, couches, and a huge coffee table covered with magazines. Very conducive to loafing. There is also a reading or game room with a piano for anyone who knows how to play. There are tons of books to read.

The guest rooms are spacious. Most of the beds are queens, and some have canopies. Two rooms have twin beds that can be made into kings. Fireplaces are in some of the rooms. The room on the first floor has its own entrance from the terrace and a large stone fireplace. It's a lovely room.

The dining room features Currier & Ives snow scenes on the walls and works done by local artists. One of them, by Gerald, is of his granddaughter holding a balloon. It's very dear.

The vegetable garden is a 70-by-90-foot spread of delights. John was ready to go out and pick raspberries when I saw him. He is the only one who picks them, because he's so careful that they don't get bruised.

The country club across the street is available for golf. The inn's own swimming pool is very relaxing, and in summer you have Tanglewood, Jacob's Pillow, and the Berkshire Theater nearby.

HOW TO GET THERE: The inn is on Route 23, 3 miles west of Great Barrington.

Augustus Snow House
Harwichport, Massachusetts 02646

INNKEEPERS: Joyce and Steve Roth

ADDRESS/TELEPHONE: 528 Main Street; (508) 430–0528 or (800) 320–0528

ROOMS: 5; all with private bath, fireplace, phone, TV, and ceiling fan.

RATES: $105 to $190, double occupancy; EPB.

OPEN: All year.

FACILITIES AND ACTIVITIES: BYOB. Lawn games, croquet, badminton. One block from private beach.

Built in 1901, the Augustus Snow House is a romantic Queen Anne Victorian mansion that's a real beauty. It has gabled dormers and a wraparound porch with a screened gazebo.

The parlor has the original fireplace, nice couches, and an interesting old organ. A small dining room for inn guests is off this room. Guests are provided with a full gourmet breakfast.

Up the stairs is a cabinet full of old Cabbage Patch dolls and five exquisite rooms. The wallpapers all through the inn are glorious. Three rooms have whirlpools. All have televisions and ceiling fans. One room has the most unusual commode I have ever seen, and I surely have seen a lot of them. This is Sara's Room.

Melissa's Room has beautifully curved bay windows, a fireplace, and a grand bath. Amy's Room is Country French, with yellow-striped wallpaper, and has the house's original bathroom with a claw-footed tub. Belle's Room has a private entrance, a king-size bed, and tons of charm. Rose's Room is soft pink and has a water view, a four-poster queen-size bed, and abundant charm.

There's a patio with white iron furniture. In-season, dining is out here for those who wish. The grounds are beautiful, and a private beach is just 1 block away.

HOW TO GET THERE: Take exit 10 off the Mid-Cape Highway (Route 6). Proceed south on Route 124/39 to Main Street in Harwich Center. Turn left onto Main Street and then take your first right onto Bank Street. Follow Bank Street to Route 28 and turn right. The inn is about ½ mile on your right.

The Morgan House
Lee, Massachusetts 01238

INNKEEPERS: Kimberly and Wesley Bookstaver

ADDRESS/TELEPHONE: Main Street; (413) 243–3661; fax (413) 243–3103

E-MAIL: morgan@vgernet.net

WEB SITE: www.morganhouseinn.com

ROOMS: 11; 6 with private bath.

RATES: $75 to $175, per room; EPB.

OPEN: All year.

FACILITIES AND ACTIVITIES: Lunch, dinner, tavern. Nearby: Tanglewood, Jacob's Pillow, golf, tennis, swimming, hiking.

The Morgan House is a great in-town inn. It has a long and interesting history dating back to 1817, when it was built as a private home. In 1855 it was converted into a stagecoach inn by Edwin Morgan, and an inn it has remained.

Many illustrious guests enjoyed a stay here during the inn's early years, including Ulysses S. Grant, George Bernard Shaw, and Grover Cleveland.

Though nicely renovated, the guest rooms still speak of the past with period furnishings. No two rooms are alike.

You'll also step back to the stagecoach era in the Colonial dining room, which has both tables and old-fashioned high-back booths. Lunch offers soups, salads, and grand sandwiches. The dinner menu has something for everyone—pasta, chicken, salmon, duck, filet mignon, and more. Save room for the dessert, because the chocolate cake is irresistible, as are the tarts, pies, and cobblers.

The tavern serves lighter fare for lunch and dinner, and locally brewed beers. Piano music livens things on Friday and Saturday nights.

My favorite spot here is the enclosed porch featuring Stickley furniture, where you can settle in with a book or watch the world go by on Main Street.

HOW TO GET THERE: From the Massachusetts Turnpike take exit 2. Follow Route 20 west 1 mile, to the center of Lee. The inn will be on your left.

The Gateways Inn
Lenox, Massachusetts 01240

INNKEEPERS: Rosemary and Fabrizio Chiariello

ADDRESS/TELEPHONE: 51 Walker Street; (413) 637–2532; fax (413) 637–1432

E-MAIL: gateways@berkshire.net

WEB SITE: gatewaysinn.com

ROOMS: 10, plus 1 suite with fireplace; all with private bath, phone with data port, TV, and air-conditioning; 8 with gas fireplace; some with VCR.

RATES: In-season, $185 to $260, room; $400, suite; off-season, $100 to $180, room; $325, suite; EPB.

OPEN: All year.

FACILITIES AND ACTIVITIES: Restaurant closed Monday to Wednesday in winter. In summer dinner by reservation preferred. Open for lunch weekends in summer. Nearby: Berkshires attractions.

The Gateways was built as a summer mansion for Harley Proctor. That's Proctor of Proctor and Gamble, so you can imagine that he had the wherewithal to do something grand. The square building shape with a flat top almost resembles Mr. Proctor's favorite product, Ivory Soap. The oval windows beside the front door and the magnificent stairway alone are worth a visit.

The Chiariellos have done extensive work on the inn, turning it into a luxury property that Mr. Proctor no doubt would have approved. Each guest room has its own theme. The Blue Danube is done in blue with prints and paintings of European waterways, rivers, and canals. The Proctor Garden Room has floral motifs, and the Berkshire Room is properly Colonial, with a four-poster bed, hand-knotted canopy, and Georgian-style dressers and chairs. The Fiedler Suite has its own Jacuzzi. All the bathrooms are stocked with terry robes and plush Egyptian cotton towels.

The dining room is the pride of the inn. The innkeepers and staff work with local farmers and dairies to use their fresh products whenever possible. The menu changes often, but to give you an idea of the possibilities, you might start with seared foie gras with a fig compote or asparagus and scallop ravioli with fresh herb and butter sauce.

Main courses may be boneless Long Island duck breast served with wild rice, sesame crusted fillet of Atlantic salmon, or rack of lamb. Save room for the apple pie—it's an award winner—unless you'd rather have tiramisu, or a chocolate-chocolate torte in a hazelnut crème sauce. The nightly cheese selection is always tempting, and if you want something lighter, you can choose Italian gelati and sorbets or a cookie and biscotti plate.

A nice recent addition to the inn is the Terrace Room, with tall French windows all around. The bar has also been enlarged to offer comfortable armchair groupings.

One thing that needed no improvement is the inn's location in the heart of Lenox, one of the loveliest villages in New England and the home of Tanglewood, where the Boston Symphony spends the summer.

HOW TO GET THERE: Take Route 7 to Route 7A. The inn is on Route 7A, 1 block from the intersection of Routes 183 and 7A.

Jacob's Pillow Dance Festival

This ten-week summer festival celebrates the work of some of the nation's most talented and innovative dance companies. Performing in the rustic country setting of the world-class dance school named Jacob's Pillow, Paul Taylor, Alvin Ailey, Merce Cunningham, Meredith Monk, Twyla Tharp, Margot Fonteyn, and many other dance greats have wowed audiences at both indoor and outdoor theaters. On a hilltop former farm in the town of Becket, just east of Lee, are studios where you can watch rehearsals, a cafe where you can enjoy a light meal, and picnic areas where you can relax while you watch developing dancers practice their art. Performance tickets are $15 to $40. Call (413) 243-0745 for the schedule or tickets.

The Village Inn
Lenox, Massachusetts 01240

INNKEEPERS: Clifford Rudisill and Ray Wilson

ADDRESS/TELEPHONE: 16 Church Street; (413) 637-0020 or (800) 253-0917; fax (413) 637-9756

E-MAIL: villinn@vgernet.net

WEB SITE: www.villageinn-lenox.com

ROOMS: 32, all with private bath, air-conditioning, TV/VCR, hair dryer, and phone; 6 with fireplace; some with whirlpool tubs; 1 room for the handicapped.

RATES: $55 to $255, double occupancy; EPB and MAP rates available.

OPEN: All year.

FACILITIES AND ACTIVITIES: Breakfast, afternoon tea, dinner Tuesday through Sunday in summer and fall and Thursday through Sunday rest of the year. Village Tavern. Nearby: Skiing, tennis, golf, swimming, horseback riding, fishing, hiking, Tanglewood, Jacob's Pillow, many museums, historic homes.

There is a saying here at the inn: "If you can't be a houseguest in the Berkshires, be ours." This surely would be a fine choice. The inn was built in 1771 and is the oldest surviving house in Lenox. While it has been extensively renovated, the historic character remains. The living room is a delightful place to sit and listen to the grand piano being played. There are Oriental rugs on the maple floors, stenciled walls, and lots of antiques, here and throughout the house.

Rooms range from lavish, with 25-inch televisions, canopy beds, handsome armoires, and whirlpool baths to simple accommodations, something for every budget. Each has antiques, period wallpaper, and a VCR, with a free lending library of videos, a really nice touch.

Another treat is an authentic English afternoon tea, complete with homemade scones and Devonshire-style clotted cream, served daily in summer and fall and on Saturday in winter and spring.

The inn restaurant serves a tasty and generous breakfast buffet daily in summer and fall and every weekend, with goodies like Belgian waffles or farmer's omelets. A continental breakfast is offered midweek in winter and spring.

The dinner menu is grand, and classical music in the background adds to the charm. First courses might be poached "Beggar's Purse" with shrimp, scallops, and lobster or home-made spinach ravioli. Don't miss the house specialty, pecan-breaded breast of chicken. Some other favorites include crab cakes, roasted duckling, and a pistachio-encrusted rack of lamb. The desserts? Just divine.

The downstairs Village Tavern is another cosy setting, a nice place for an English draught beer or ale and a light snack.

The Berkshires are chock-full of activities year-round, and the inn offers special winter and spring packages. Come when the crowds leave and have this beautiful part of the world all to yourself.

HOW TO GET THERE: Take Route 7A off Route 7 and turn on Church Street in Lenox. The inn is on the right.

Wheatleigh 🎔
Lenox, Massachusetts 01240

INNKEEPERS: Susan and Linfield Simon; François Thomas, general manager

ADDRESS/TELEPHONE: Hawthorne Road; (413) 637–0610; fax (413) 637–4507

E-MAIL: wheatleigh@taconic.net

WEB SITE: www.wheatleigh.com

ROOMS: 19, all with private bath, air-conditioning, TV, VCR, and phone; 9 with working fireplace.

RATES: $365 to $1,150, double occupancy; EP.

OPEN: All year.

FACILITIES AND ACTIVITIES: Lunch, dinner, Sunday brunch. Lounge. Swimming, tennis, cross-country skiing, massage and fitness center.

Wheatleigh is a unique and fabulous property, a summer mansion built in 1893 for a countess and modeled after a sixteenth-century Italian palazzo. The house stands overlooking a lake, amid lawns and gardens, on twenty-two self-contained acres in the heart of the picturesque Berkshires. Patios, pergolas, porticos, and terraces surround the mansion to make the most of the view.

But those who knew Wheatleigh in the past will find dramatic changes. The mansion has just undergone a multimillion dollar renovation updating its image. The creative architects working with owners Susan and Lin Simon were Calvin Tsao and Zack McKown, whose eclectic previous work has included the VIP lounge of Virgin Atlantic Airways, the fifth floor of Bergdorf Goodman in New York, and the sleek Mercer Hotel in Manhattan's SoHo.

The furnishings now have a fresh, understated look, and abstract paintings by local artists adorn the walls. The new, more modern palette is a calming mix of mustard, wheat, sage, and cypress, planned to blend with the natural beauty just outside the great arched windows. The grand but formal Great Hall has been softened with intimate seating arrangements and warm lighting. Everywhere are lovely small details garnered from around the world—an antique Japanese vase, lacquered boxes from China, light fixtures from Paris.

The architects have also worked their magic on the main dining room, where the outdoor courtyard has been enclosed with glass walls between Palladian columns, extending the room and making the most of the wonderful setting outside. In the main dining room, longtime executive chef Peter Platt offers a choice of prix-fixe menus, a three-course dinner, a four-course vegetarian Tasting Menu, and the Grand Menu Degustation, a multicourse extravaganza. On a recent dinner menu, you could choose among appetizers like seared medallion of Hudson Valley foie gras with apple, celery root, and raspberry vinegar sauce or Roquefort cheese soufflé with a red beet salad and hazelnut vinaigrette. Entree offerings such as roast rack of lamb, crispy skin black bass, or seared loin of veal preceded a dessert line-up with temptations such as *tarte fine aux pommes,* a thin apple tart with cinnamon and vanilla ice creams; lemon crème brûlée tart and a fallen almond soufflé.

Another major change is the modern look of The Library, which now serves as an intimate, less formal dining room, furnished with velvet sofas and high-back leather chairs. Mahogany cabinets show off Susan's handsome collection of blue-and-white china. A tasty choice of sandwiches, salads, and pastas is available for lunch, and a newly trendy dinner menu offers choices from Yankee pot roast to Scottish salmon teriyaki. The fresh fish of the day is served with mussels, shrimp, and littleneck clams in a mild lobster green curry broth.

Guest rooms at Wheatleigh are tranquil, with contemporary decor and more intriguing details, such as the bathtubs purchased in a London antiques shop, and handblown sconces to provide the softest of lighting. Many rooms are large, with high ceilings. Some have fireplaces, balconies, and wonderful vistas.

Susan's description of the inn is "elegance without arrogance," and Lin's is "the ultimate urban amenity." Mine is "a perfect country inn." Wish I lived closer!

HOW TO GET THERE: From Stockbridge at the Red Lion Inn where Route 7 turns right, go straight on Prospect Hill Road, bearing left. Travel about 4½ miles, past the Stockbridge Bowl and up a hill to Wheatleigh.

From the Massachusetts Turnpike take exit 2 and follow the signs to Lenox. In the center of Lenox, take Route 183, pass the main gate of Tanglewood, and then take the first left on Hawthorne Road. Go 1 mile to Wheatleigh.

The Charlotte Inn
Martha's Vineyard (Edgartown), Massachusetts 02539

INNKEEPERS: Gery and Paula Conover

ADDRESS/TELEPHONE: 27 South Summer Street; (508) 627-4751

ROOMS: 23, plus 2 suites; all with private bath, air-conditioning, and phone, some with fireplace; TV in most rooms.

RATES: In-season, $250 to $650; interim-season, $165 to $550; off-season, $145 to $395; suites, $495 to $650. Double occupancy, continental breakfast.

OPEN: All year.

FACILITIES AND ACTIVITIES: In-season, dinner. Off-season, dinner on weekends. Reservations a must. Gift shop and gallery. Nearby: Sailing, swimming, fishing, golf, tennis.

*T*his is an island haven of total luxury, an exquisite complex of four buildings amid lush gardens with a restaurant that has long been considered the best in town.

The main house dates to 1864 and gives the feeling of a more elegant era. The foyer is hung with fine nineteenth-century paintings, and guests are greeted at a grand mahogany desk, where they sign an old-fashioned ledger.

Choosing where to stay is a pleasant dilemma. The Carriage House offers private terraces, fireplaces, French doors, and old brick courtyards. The second-floor suite has a fireplace I could live in.

A pathway through the rose garden leads to the Coach House, where a special suite offers glimpses of the harbor through a Palladian window. The veranda of the Summer House is a favorite spot to catch the breeze, and some of the bathrooms are as large as a normal bedroom. The Garden House has an enchanted feel, surrounded by plantings inspired by the traditional English perennial garden, a sign of Paula's talents as a gardener.

Wherever you stay, the rooms are sumptuous. Four-poster brass and sleigh beds are piled with goose-down pillows and comforters. Most of the furnishings are late-nineteenth-century English, with accents like marble-topped dressers, silk and linen formal draperies, antique trunks, sterling-silver dresser sets, and brass and crystal lamps.

The famous French restaurant here is L'Etoile. On one of my visits here, four of us had dinner here, and the food was exquisite.

Capon breast stuffed with duxelles, spinach, and sun-dried tomatoes with coriander mayonnaise was the best I have had. I tasted everyone's food— nice occupation I have. Rack of lamb, served rare, with red wine–rosemary sauce and accompanied by potato and yam gratin was excellent. During my last visit I had grilled Angus filet mignon—it was glorious. My friend Audrey had a halibut fillet. They also have a special or two, but then everything is so special, the word does not fit. The menu changes monthly. Desserts the week I was there included blackberry and lemon curd napoleon and rhubarb and raspberry tart—oh my! For breakfast I had a strawberry crepe that I can still remember vividly. Freshly squeezed juices and fruit muffins . . . heaven!

Not the least of the pleasures of a vacation here is the forty-five minute ferry ride to Martha's Vineyard. It's wise to make early reservations for your automobile on the ferry. Or, if you prefer not to take your car, you'll find taxis waiting when the ferry docks.

Gery and Paula are special innkeepers, but they do need the help of Ozzie and Jezebel, a pair of goldens.

HOW TO GET THERE: Reservations are a must if you take your car on the ferry from Woods Hole, Massachusetts. Forty-five minutes later you are in Vineyard Haven. After a fifteen-minute ride, you are in Edgartown, and on South Summer Street is the inn.

The Daggett House
Martha's Vineyard (Edgartown), Massachusetts 02539

INNKEEPER: Stephen Warriner; John Chirgwin and Jim Chirgwin, owners

ADDRESS/TELEPHONE: 59 North Water Street; (508) 627–4600 or (800) 946–3400; fax (508) 627–4611

WEB SITE: www.mvweb.com/daggett

ROOMS: 31, plus 4 suites; all with private bath, TV, and phone. No-smoking inn.

RATES: Rooms $175 to $275, double occupancy, mid-May to mid-October; $115 to $275 mid-October to mid-May. Suites $240 to $575 year-round; EP.

OPEN: All year.

FACILITIES AND ACTIVITIES: Breakfast and lunch April through October; full license. Boating and swimming.

The Daggett House, built in 1660, has an interesting history. It was the first tavern on Martha's Vineyard licensed to sell beer and ale. It has been a store, a lodging for sailors, an accounting house in whaling days, and a privately owned mansion. In 1948 it was purchased by the Chirgwin family and became an inn.

The location on the water is splendid, and the ferry to Chappaquiddick Island is right here. Yachts and sailboats sail by the inn's private dock.

The inn consists of three buildings. The Garden Cottage is down by the water. It once was a schoolhouse and later became an artist's studio. It is open from April to November. One room has a large picture window and a comfortable chaise lounge. Another has white wicker furniture and a lovely white canopy bed. All of the beds are comfortable.

The Captain Warren House, which is also open April to November, is across the street. Built around 1850, it has lovely

Ferrying to Martha's Vineyard

Sailing from "America," as the islanders call the mainland, to Martha's Vineyard is easily accomplished on one of the ferries that ply the waters between the island and Falmouth, Hyannis, Woods Hole, and New Bedford. All of the ferry services offer parking lots for both day-tripping and overnight travelers.

The **Steamship Authority** (508-477-8600 or 508-693-9130) out of Woods Hole offers the only car-and-passenger service to the island, sailing year-round to Vineyard Haven and from May to September to Oak Bluffs. The crossing takes forty-five minutes, and car reservations are required.

The *Island Queen* (508-548-4800) is a passenger ferry that makes daily trips from Falmouth Harbor on Cape Cod to Oak Bluffs on the Vineyard from late May to mid-October. This crossing takes only thirty-five minutes. This open-air vessel offers a spacious sun deck and a complete snack bar on board as well as secure parking in a private lot not far from the Falmouth dock. Day-trippers and other seasonal visitors can bring bicycles aboard and cycle along the island's shore path and into Oak Bluffs, Vineyard Haven, and Edgartown. Island tours can also be arranged through this ferry service.

Also in season only, from May through October, the **Cape Island Express Lines** (508-997-1688) runs the 600-passenger *Schamonchi* from Billy Woods Wharf in New Bedford to Vineyard Haven. The Hy-Line Ferry (508-778-2600) sails from Hyannis to Oak Bluffs.

rooms, nice wallpapers, and interesting tiles in the tubs.

Some of the rooms have ceiling fans, and all have televisions and telephones. The third floor has a large suite, with two bedrooms and baths, living room, dining room, and kitchen. Up on the roof the widow's walk has a view that won't quit and a hot tub and chairs. Why go anywhere else? This is as close to heaven as you will get.

The dining room is in the main inn. It has a beehive fireplace that dates back to 1660 and a bookcase that swings open to reveal a hidden stairway leading to a guest room. Of course, it's named the Secret Staircase Room. The Chappaquiddick Suite has a view of the island and a hot tub. There's another room called the Red Canopy Room, which, of course, has a red canopy as well as a view of the harbor.

The breakfast menu is ample. There are omelets, waffles, eggs Benedict, and Grapenut French toast. The recipe for the Grapenut Bread is yours for the asking and came from the owner's mother. The lunch menu offers tasty soups, salads, and sandwiches. On sunny days, you can have lunch on the patio.

HOW TO GET THERE: Take the ferry to Martha's Vineyard. In Edgartown go down Main Street to North Water Street. Turn left, and the inn is on the right.

Lambert's Cove Country Inn
Martha's Vineyard (West Tisbury), Massachusetts 02568

INNKEEPERS: Katherine and Louis Costabel

ADDRESS/TELEPHONE: Lambert's Cove Road (mailing address: Box 422, RFD, Vineyard Haven, MA 02568); (508) 693-2298; fax (508) 693-7890

ROOMS: 15, all with private bath.

RATES: In-season, $185 to $250; off-season, $90 to $210; double occupancy, EPB.

OPEN: All year.

FACILITIES AND ACTIVITIES: Dinner daily in-season, Thursday through Sunday interim season. BYOB. Tennis court. Nearby: Swimming, cross-country skiing, ice skating.

*A*t the end of a tree-shaded country road, you will find this gem of an inn. The original house was built in 1790. Over the years it was enlarged and a carriage house and barn added. Today the carriage house and barn have been beautifully renovated for guest use, and half of the rooms are here.

One of the rooms in the carriage house has a greenhouse sitting room at one end. Nice to have your cocktails in here and look up at the stars. All of the rooms in the inn are done with imagination. There are plenty of comforts, too, like soft pillows and lush towels.

When you enter the inn, you are in an elegant center hall. Up a magnificent staircase and you are in a restful sitting area, with an overstuffed couch and chair and bookcases full of books. There is also a delightful library, a huge room with walls lined with volumes of books and furnished with tables for games and really comfortable furniture. On a cold day a fire in the fireplace here feels great.

A big deck opens from the library and dining room and looks out on an apple orchard. There are five decks in all at this inn. The English garden is lovely, and flowers are everywhere you look.

Getting to Nantucket

Flying and ferrying are the two preferred methods of traveling to Nantucket, unless you happen to have your own sturdy boat or the means to charter one. Flights are available to Nantucket from Hyannis, Providence, Boston, New York, and Newark. For current airlines flying these routes, contact Nantucket Memorial Airport (508–325–5300; www.nantucketairport.com) or the Nantucket Chamber of Commerce (508–228–1700; www. nantucketchamber.org).

Ferries run year-round from Hyannis only. The Steamship Authority (508–477–8600) offers car-and-passenger, two-and-a-quarter-hour-trips and a "fast ferry" high-speed boat that makes the trip in one hour. Hy-Line (508–778–2600) sends its high-speed cat *Grey Lady* on one-hour crossings year-round and its slower MV *Great Point* ferry on two-hour crossings from mid-May to late October. Reservations for cars are a must.

Maybe you'd like to come for dinner. The menu tempts with dishes such as pan-fried crab cakes with Key lime mango sauce or walnut-crusted rack of lamb with blackberry mint lamb demi-glace. All the desserts are made right here. The one I had on my last visit was white chocolate mousse with fresh raspberries. The choices change daily, but no matter what you order, it will be good.

This is real country. Walk twenty minutes to the Lambert's Cove beach, or just walk anywhere. It's just a beautiful part of the world, and it would be a wonderful spot for a wedding.

HOW TO GET THERE: Take the ferry to Martha's Vineyard from Cape Cod. After driving off the ferry, take a left, then a right at the next stop-sign intersection. Stay on this road for 1½ miles to Lambert's Cove Road, on your right. Three miles from this point, look for the inn's sign, on the left.

Jared Coffin House
Nantucket, Massachusetts 02554

INNKEEPERS: Philip and Peg Read; John S. Cowden Jr., V.P. and general manager

ADDRESS/TELEPHONE: 29 Broad Street; (508) 228–2400 or (800) 248–2405; fax (508) 228–2400

E-MAIL: jchouse@nantucket.net

WEB SITE: www.jaredcoffinhouse.com

ROOMS: 60; 11 in main house, 16 simpler rooms in Eben Allen Wing, 3 rooms in Swain House connected to the Eben Allen Wing, 12 rooms in Daniel Webster House across the patio, 18 rooms in 2 houses across the street.

RATES: $85 and up, single; in-season, $150 to $375, double occupancy; off-season, $100 to $150, double occupancy; EP.

OPEN: All year.

FACILITIES AND ACTIVITIES: Breakfast, lunch, dinner, taproom. Eben Allen Room for private parties. Nearby: Swimming, tennis.

BUSINESS TRAVEL: Meeting rooms; fax, e-mail, overhead projector available.

*I*t is well worth the 30-mile trip by ferry, or the plane trip from Boston or New York, to end up at the Jared Coffin House. Built as a private home in 1845, the three-story brick house with slate roof became an inn only twelve years later. The inn passed through many hands before it came to the extremely capable ones of Philip and Peg Read.

The public rooms at the inn reflect charm and warmth. The furnishings are Chippendale and Sheraton; showing the results of the worldwide voyaging by the Nantucket whalemen are Chinese and Japanese objets d'art and furniture.

To add to the charm are many fabrics and some furniture that have been made right here on the island. In addition to the main house, there are several other close-by houses that go with the inn. All are done beautifully for your every comfort. The size and the quantity of the luxurious bath towels in the guest rooms please me greatly. The housekeeping staff does a wonderful job, and the exquisite antiques reflect their loving care.

The taproom, located on the lowest level, is a warm, happy, fun place. Here you meet the local people and spin yarns with all. Old pine walls and hand-hewn beams reflect a cozy atmosphere. Luncheon is served down here, with good burgers and great, hearty soups. During the winter this is a nice spot for informal dinners.

The main dining room, papered with authentic wallpapers, is quiet and elegant. Wedgwood china and pistol-handled silverware make dining a special pleasure and reflect the good life demanded by the nineteenth-century owners of the great Nantucket whaling ships.

The inn is located in the heart of Nantucket's Historic District, about ⅛ mile from one public beach and 1 mile from the island's largest public beach and tennis courts. It's a very pleasant 3-mile bicycle ride through the district to superb surf swimming on the South Shore.

HOW TO GET THERE: To get to Nantucket, take a ferry from Hyannis (April through January) or Woods Hole (January through March and summer months). First call (508) 540–2022 for reservations. Or take a plane from Boston, Hyannis, or New York. The inn is located 2 blocks north of Main Street and 2 blocks west of Steamboat Wharf.

The Woodbox Inn
Nantucket, Massachusetts 02554

INNKEEPER: Dexter Tutein

ADDRESS/TELEPHONE: 29 Fair Street; (508) 228–0587; fax (508) 228-7527

E-MAIL: woodbox@nantucket.net

WEB SITE: www.woodboxinn.com

ROOMS: 3 queens, plus 6 suites in 2 buildings; all with private bath.

RATES: $175 to $305, double occupancy; EP. No credit cards.

OPEN: Memorial Day to Columbus Day. Weekends only from Columbus Day to January 1.

FACILITIES AND ACTIVITIES: Full breakfast, dinner, beer and wine license. Wheelchair access to sunrooms, dining rooms. Nearby: Swimming, boating, biking, tennis.

For more than forty-five years there has been a Tutein running this inn. Built in 1709, it is the oldest inn on Nantucket Island. What a treat to be here!

The suites are unique. In an old building like this, you cannot change the structure to modernize it, so the bathrooms have been very inventively fit in. Very pretty and comfortable. The suite I was in had a fireplace in the living room; two bedrooms, one with a huge canopy bed; and a lovely little private patio. It was hard to leave.

There are three dining rooms in the inn. I'm sure I had dinner in what must be the oldest public dining room in New England. The room has two "king's boards" on the wall of the immense, almost walk-in fireplace. Today the fireplace holds an old cradle with dried flowers. The china is old, and there are nice touches on the tables, like your own pepper mill. Tall candlesticks add to the charm of this inn.

The inn is famous for its popovers, and I can understand why, having devoured quite a few. The food is truly gourmet. Naturally, the entrees include the catch of the day; I had fresh sea bass that was delicious. My dinner companion had the veal chop, saffron rice, and glazed pear chutney. The house salad dressing is ex-cellent. And for dessert, well, the best crème brûlée I have ever had.

The inn's breakfast is a great way to start the day—choose Belgian waffles or pancakes or the eggs Benedict—an inn tradition. The pancakes and waffles come with pure maple syrup, blueberries, strawberries, peaches, or apples. Those wonderful popovers come with any egg dish. The chef has cooked several times at the James Beard Foundation in New York City. The inn is also a five-time winner of the *Wine Spectator*'s Award of Excellence. One night during our stay, Dexter took us to a real Nantucket hot spot for a very unusual dinner at Black Eye Susan's (508–325–0308) at 10 India Street—do go try this one.

The powder room must be seen. There are no words to describe it.

HOW TO GET THERE: Take the ferry to Nantucket or fly from Hyannis. The inn is at 29 Fair Street. You can walk to it from the ferry.

Yankee Clipper Inn
Rockport, Massachusetts 01966

INNKEEPERS: Bob and Barbara Wemyss Ellis; Carl Kosko, general manager

ADDRESS/TELEPHONE: 96 Granite Street; (978) 546–3407 or (800) 545–3699; fax (978) 549–9730

E-MAIL: info@yankeeclipperinn.com

WEB SITE: yankeeclipperinn.com

ROOMS: 26, including 6 suites, in 3 buildings; all with private bath, air-conditioning, cable TV, and phone. Some baths have Jacuzzis.

RATES: $109 to $319, double occupancy; EPB. MAP is available.

OPEN: March 1 to November 15.

FACILITIES AND ACTIVITIES: Dinner. Small function room, heated saltwater pool. Nearby: Fishing, boating, shopping, whale watching.

When you are lucky enough to be here and see a sunset, you will be overwhelmed. It's a golden sea and sky, with the town of Rockport in the distance. No camera could truly capture this scene. Wait a while longer, and the moonlight on the sea is an awesome sight.

Three buildings make up the Yankee Clipper. The inn is an oceanfront mansion. Here the rooms have antique furniture, Oriental rugs, and some canopy beds. Some rooms have porches. You're sure to enjoy the television lounge, with cable television and a really big screen. All meals are served in this building.

The Quarterdeck has large picture windows, providing a panoramic view of the ocean. Upholstered chairs are placed in front of the windows. Sit back and relax; it's almost like being on a ship that does not move. All of the rooms in this building are beautifully furnished. Some of the rooms in the Bullfinch House have water views.

The special occasion room is a lovely spot. For any sort of function from small weddings to executive meetings, it has a wonderful water view, a big-screen TV and VCR, and everything you'd need for your meeting.

The Veranda dining room has marvelous views that are matched by the marvelous food, a contemporary take on regional American dishes, with lots of excellent seafood. Remember to bring your own wine; Rockport is a dry town.

The Captain's Quarters is a private, fully furnished house. Rented by the week, it sleeps six. It costs $2,500 without housekeeping, $2,800 with.

To work off some of the calories, you might want to swim in the heated saltwater pool at the inn. In the area there are whale-watching trips, fishing, and, in the town of Rockport, fantastic shopping. It really is fun to walk around here.

HOW TO GET THERE: Take Route 128 north and east to Cape Ann. Route 128 ends at traffic lights. Turn left onto Route 127. Drive 3 miles to where Route 127 turns left into Pigeon Cove. Continue on Route 127 for $1\frac{2}{10}$ miles to Yankee Clipper in Pigeon Cove.

The Dan'l Webster Inn
Sandwich, Massachusetts 02563

INNKEEPER: Steve Catania

ADDRESS/TELEPHONE: Main Street; (508) 888–3622 or (800) 444–3566

WEB SITE: www.danlwebsterinn.com

ROOMS: 54, in 3 buildings; all with private bath, phone, TV, and air-conditioning; many with whirlpool tub and fireplace.

RATES: $149 to $329, double occupancy; EP.

OPEN: All year except Christmas Day.

FACILITIES AND ACTIVITIES: Breakfast, lunch, dinner, Sunday brunch. Bar, lounge, swimming pool, gift shop. Nearby: Doll museum, glass museum, Heritage Plantation, beaches, golf.

A more than 250-year-old linden tree, complete with bird feeders, stands outside the Conservatory, one of the inn's three lovely dining rooms, and an aquarium filled with beautiful fish is in the wall on the way to the Conservatory dining room. This is a glassed-in room, overlooking a beautifully landscaped courtyard and swimming pool. The dining menu is a bit different. There are half dinners, and, believe me, you will not go away hungry.

The Webster Room has a portrait of Daniel Webster's second wife and china cabinets to display old Sandwich glass on loan from the museum. The Heritage Room has a huge open fireplace and a grand piano for your entertainment.

These dining rooms provide the perfect atmosphere for the excellent food. Breakfasts are hearty, with eggs, six different omelets, sausage, croissants,

fruit, and much more. The lunch menu lists salads, sandwiches, and quite a few hot choices. Dinner is an adventure. The hors d'oeuvres list is extensive. Appetizers include tasty oysters Webster and lobster chowder, a house specialty. Then you can choose fresh local seafood, chicken, or veal dishes. The daily chef's specials are always a good bet. I had chateaubriand—very nice because it was served for one. It was very good. Desserts are sinful, and there are special coffees.

The Tavern at the inn is a cozy spot, with stained-glass windows and very nice wooden bar stools. There are tables and chairs here for those who are not barflies.

All the guest rooms are a little different. Most have Hitchcock furniture. All have a four-poster or canopy beds. The Webster Suite on the third floor of the inn has two bedrooms and two bathrooms. One bath has a Jacuzzi, and the other has a steam tub.

In the lovely Fessenden House next door are four suites. I was in the Captain Ezra Nye Suite. A whirlpool tub is in each of these suites, as is a marble fireplace. They are beautifully furnished with classic antiques. I had to go up two steps to get into bed. Oh my, I do like it here. Eight recently added suites are even more luxurious, with elegant antique beds, balconies, heated tile floors, and oversized whirlpool tubs.

A split of sparkling water is provided in each guest room. The beds are turned down in the evening, and a chocolate is left on the pillow. What nice touches!

The John Carver Inn, in Plymouth, Massachusetts, is sister inn to this one. It's larger, and there's only a short walk to the "rock" (25 Summer Street; 508-746-7100 or 800-274-1620).

HOW TO GET THERE: Go over the Bourne Bridge to a rotary; go three-fourths of the way around it, taking the Route 6A exit that parallels the canal. Stay on this road until you come to the third set of lights. This is Jarves Street. Go right, then right again onto Main Street. The inn is on the right, close to the corner.

The Egremont Inn
South Egremont, Massachusetts 01258

INNKEEPERS: Karen and Steve Waller

ADDRESS/TELEPHONE: 10 Old Sheffield Road (mailing address: Box 418); (413) 528-2111 or (800) 859-1780; fax (413) 528-3284

WEB SITE: www.egremontinn.com

ROOMS: 19, plus 1 suite; all with private bath, phone, air-conditioning; some with whirlpool. Smoking in common rooms only.

RATES: $90 to $215; EPB on weekends.

OPEN: All year.

FACILITIES AND ACTIVITIES: Dinner Wednesday through Sunday in the dining room and tavern. Live entertainment on Thursday and Saturday. Discounted ski tickets.

Built in 1780, this inn is true New England. It is in the quiet corner of the southern Berkshires. When you walk in, you are in a huge living room, called the Pine Room, with a large fireplace, good couches and chairs, and the start of a stuffed animal collection that you'll find all over the inn. Albert the Duck and Winston A. Bear are there waiting. Yes, Karen has named them all. I relate to this as I've got tons of bears.

To the right of this room is another lovely room with a fireplace, plus a sitting room with another fireplace, with a couch right in front of it, and a television. This is where you'll find a lot of board games and a toy chest for children.

The main dining room is warm and attractive. The napery is white, and there are lots of plants and another fireplace.

The food is grand. Among the five appetizers, wild mushroom soup is excellent. The menus change often and seasonally and feature a variety of fish and meats, and nightly specials.

The comfortable tavern has its own less formal menu.

This is a wonderful old building with tilty floors and delightful accommodations.

Do take the walking tour through town, because there is a lot to see. The lovely village is on the National Register of Historic Places. The inn is, too.

HOW TO GET THERE: From New York go north on Route 22 or the Taconic Parkway to Route 23 east. After the town of South Egremont, turn right at the small island. The inn is 200 yards ahead. From Boston take the Massachusetts Turnpike to exit 2. Follow Route 102 west to Route 7 south. After going through Great Barrington, take Route 23 west to South Egremont. In $3^{3}/_{10}$ miles, bear left at the small island. The inn is straight ahead.

The Weathervane Inn
South Egremont, Massachusetts 01258

INNKEEPERS: Jeffrey and Maxine Lome

ADDRESS/TELEPHONE: Main Street (Route 23); (413) 528–9580 or (800) 528–9580; fax (413) 528–1713

E-MAIL: innkeeper@weathervaneinn.com

WEB SITE: www.weathervane.com

ROOMS: 10, including 1 suite with fireplace; all with private bath, air-conditioning; 2 rooms with wheelchair accessibility. No-smoking inn.

RATES: $135 to $165 ($245 suite), double occupancy; EBP. On weekends, $115 to $150, double occupancy; EBP. Minimum of two nights' stay on weekends, three nights on holiday weekends and in the summer. Special seasonal or group packages available, some with dinner.

OPEN: All year except Christmas Day.

FACILITIES AND ACTIVITIES: Breakfast and afternoon tea; optional catered dinner for small groups. Swimming pool, outside games. Nearby: Antiques stores, fishing, hiking, bicycling, golf, tennis, skiing.

BUSINESS TRAVEL: Fully appointed meeting room; audiovisual equipment; copying, faxing, Internet access available.

The Weathervane began its existence as a farmhouse in 1785 and is listed on the National Register of Historic Places. The original fireplace, which served as a heating and cooking unit, boasts a beehive bake oven. These are rarely seen today but were a real necessity in early times.

What better way to celebrate the old farmhouse's history than with a hearty country breakfast? Innkeepers Jeff and Maxine Lome offer a homemade French toast with maple syrup from local farmers. It's to die for! Or you can savor fresh-baked muffins, like their applesauce strudel muffins, in addition to other hot-off-the-griddle breakfast fare. Don't miss the homemade preserves prepared from fruit grown on the premises. Talk about flavorful! You'll enjoy this feast while looking out over ten beautifully landscaped acres of gardens and trees.

After a day of sight-seeing, sports, shopping, or even snoozing (!), don't

miss the afternoon tea put out each day. Have a cup of your favorite tea, or try spiced cider or hot chocolate in season. There are always homemade goodies to tempt you, maybe Toll House cookies or fresh banana bread. Dinner is available only by special arrangement, usually for groups of ten or more, although the inn sometimes offers family packages that include a family-style dinner. Ask ahead of time if you're interested.

Guest rooms feature cheerful flowered wallpapers, colorful patchwork quilts, comfortable reading chairs, and queen- or king-size beds, some of them four-poster. A new suite has a king-size bed, in-room fireplace, and television with VCR. Luxurious!

Norman Rockwell Museum

Overlooking the Housatonic River in Stockbridge is a museum honoring one of America's most beloved illustrators. Norman Rockwell was a resident of the town for fifty years while he painted magazine covers for *Saturday Evening Post, Look, McCalls,* and *Colliers.* In this beautiful museum, see permanent displays of Rockwell's original artwork, his own studio, and changing exhibitions of other noted illustrators. Stroll the thiry-six-acre grounds to see sculptures by son Peter Rockwell. The museum is open year-round. Call (413) 298–4100 for hours and admission.

All the public rooms are comfortable, and there is so much to do in this area all year that you could stay and stay. Be sure to visit the antiques dealer in the barn. In winter downhill or cross-country skiers will not have far to go. Bicycling or hiking in the area is awesome. Riding horses or fishing the lakes is also a nice thing to do in this beautiful countryside.

HOW TO GET THERE: Follow Route 7 to Route 23 west. You are now 3 miles from South Egremont. The inn will be on your left.

The Red Lion Inn
Stockbridge, Massachusetts 01262

INNKEEPER: The Fitzpatrick family, owners; Brooks Bradbury, innkeeper

ADDRESS/TELEPHONE: Main Street; (413) 298–5545; fax (413) 298–5130

E-MAIL: innkeeper@redlioninn.com

WEB SITE: www.redlioninn.com

ROOMS: 111, plus 20 suites; 90 with private bath; most with wheelchair accessibility.

RATES: $65 to $300, winter; $75 to $350, summer; double occupancy; EP.

OPEN: All year.

FACILITIES AND ACTIVITIES: Breakfast, lunch, dinner, bar. Heated outdoor swimming pool. Elevator. Pink Kitty Gift Shop, country curtains shop. Nearby: All the museums and performing arts of the Berkshires.

The Red Lion Inn is a four-season inn. In summer you have the Berkshire Music Festival at Tanglewood and the Jacob's Pillow Dance Festival, both world-renowned. The inn's own heated outdoor swimming pool is a nice warm-weather attraction. Fall's foliage is perhaps the most spectacular in New England; in winter there is snow on the hills; in spring come the lovely green and flowers. All go together to make this a great spot any time of year. And right down the street is the Corner House, once the home of Norman Rockwell.

The inn is full of lovely old antiques. The halls are lined with antique couches, each one prettier than the last. From a four-poster canopy bed to beds with great brass headboards, all the rooms are marvelously furnished and comfortable as sin. Whether in the inn itself or in one of the inn's many adjacent houses, you will love the accommodations. All rooms have extra pillows, which I love.

During one visit, I stayed in a century-old village firehouse. This also was the subject of a Norman Rockwell painting, which hangs here in the Old Stockbridge firehouse (1899) that has been converted into a spacious suite. The firemen used to gather around their antique pool table; now the place is furnished with a beautiful king-size bed, part of a lovely wicker set from an old estate. The bathroom has a double whirlpool bath and a huge shower. Downstairs the doors for the fire engines are still here.

A newer old house (circa the 1940s), 2 Maple Street, is where I was lodged on my most recent visit. It has a living room, fully equipped kitchen, bedroom, bath, a porch, and private parking. Very nice.

The Lion's Den is downstairs in the main inn, with entertainment nightly and its own small menu. In warm weather the flower-laden courtyard, with

its Back of the Bank Bar, is a delightful place for food and grog. There's a wonderful collection of old birdcages out here. And the chef really knows what to do with scrod.

Another place to eat is the Widow Bingham's Tavern.

There is an almost hidden booth designed for lovers in here.

More excellent food is served in the lovely dining room. The poached salmon is divine. The vegetable plate is a very nice touch. The inn also serves New England favorites like old-fashioned chicken potpie and roast native turkey. The menu changes with the seasons. Do you still want to know more? Well, in the morning you'll find many breakfast choices, starting with freshly squeezed orange juice.

Be sure to find an opportunity to visit The Red Lion Inn and listen to the authentic country-inn cricket in the lobby. Honest, he lives here.

HOW TO GET THERE: Take exit 2 from the Massachusetts Turnpike and follow Route 102 west to the inn.

Colonel Ebenezer Crafts Inn
Sturbridge, Massachusetts 01566

INNKEEPER: Albert Cournoyer

ADDRESS/TELEPHONE: Fiske Hill Road (mailing address: P.O. Box 187); (508) 347–3313 or (800) PUBLICK

ROOMS: 7, plus 1 suite; all with private bath.

RATES: $79 to $99, double occupancy; $109 to $145, suites; continental breakfast.

OPEN: All year.

FACILITIES AND ACTIVITIES: Afternoon tea. Publick House nearby for other meals. Small swimming pool. Nearby: Old Sturbridge Village.

*I*n Colonial times the finest homes were usually found on the highest points of land. Such a location afforded the owners commanding views of their farmland and cattle. It also set them above their contemporaries. So in 1786 David Fiske, Esquire, a builder, built this house high above Sturbridge. The house was magnificently restored by the management of the Publick House and named after the inn's founder, Col. Ebenezer Crafts.

Accommodations are wonderful. There are two queen-size canopy beds that are real beauties. Some beds are four-posters. Terry cloth robes are placed in your room for your comfort. The wallpapers are subtle and elegant. The suite joins the main inn by a short breezeway. It has a living room, bedroom, bath, and color television.

Provided for your relaxation is a nice living room with a baby grand piano, a color television with a VCR and movies, and a good library of books and *National Geographic* magazines that are always a pleasure to read or look through.

Your breakfast of freshly baked muffins, fresh fruit, juice, and coffee comes with a copy of the morning paper. In the afternoon, tea, sherry, and sweets are served. Or you can go 2 miles down the road to the famous Publick House in Sturbridge for a full breakfast. Here, too, you can have lunch and dinner and enjoy the lovely bar and cocktail lounge. You will find a gift shop and an incredible bake shop. Do not miss taking some treats home.

If you want to plan a business conference or family gathering, the entire house is available for up to twenty-two people.

Ask someone to show you the Underground Railroad of Civil War days. The slave hole is still here.

HOW TO GET THERE: Take exit 3 from I–86, and bear right along the service road into Sturbridge. Continue to Route 131, where you turn right. Turn left at Hall Road and then right on Whittemore Road, which becomes Fiske Hill Road.

Publick House 📱
Sturbridge, Massachusetts 01566

INNKEEPER: Albert Cournoyer

ADDRESS/TELEPHONE: P.O. Box 187; (508) 347–3313 or
(800) PUBLICK; fax (508) 347–1246

E-MAIL: info@publickhouse.com

WEB SITE: www.publickhouse.com

ROOMS: 15, plus 2 suites; all with private bath, air-conditioning, phone.

RATES: $90 to $135, double occupancy; $130 to $155, suites; EP.
Package rates available.

OPEN: All year.

FACILITIES AND ACTIVITIES: Breakfast, lunch, dinner, bar. Wheelchair
access to restaurant. Gift shop, swimming pool, tennis courts, jogging
trail, shuffleboard, children's play area. Nearby: Old Sturbridge Village,
golf, fishing, cross-country skiing.

BUSINESS TRAVEL: Meeting rooms; phone in all rooms; fax available;
corporate rates.

*I*t's a real pleasure to me to keep coming back to the Publick House
and finding it always the same, always excellent. As a matter of fact,
very little has changed here in the past 230 years. The green still
stretches along in front of it, and the trees still cast their welcome shade. The
Publick House is still taking care of the wayfarer, feeding him well, providing
a comfortable bed, and supplying robust drink.

The Publick House calendar is fun to read. Throughout the year there are
special celebrations for holidays. They do keep the spirit of Christmas alive
here. All twelve days of it. The Boar's Head Procession is truly unique, complete with a roast young suckling pig, a roast goose, and plum pudding.
Wow!

Winter weekends are times for special treats, with chestnuts roasting by
an open fire, and sleigh rides through nearby Old Sturbridge Village, a happy
step backward in time.

The guest rooms are decorated with period furniture, while the pent-
house suite has the modern conveniences of a television and king-size bed.

The wide floorboards and beamed ceilings have been here since Col. Ebenezer Crafts founded the inn in 1771.

The barn, connected to the main house with a ramp, has been transformed into a restaurant. Double doors, topped by a glorious sunburst window, lead into a restaurant that serves hearty Yankee cooking, such as delicious lobster pie. There is a little musician's gallery, still divided into stalls, that overlooks the main dining room. Beneath this is an attractive taproom where a pianist plays.

A blueberry patch and a garden that covers more than an acre of land provide the inn with fresh fruit and vegetables and beautiful roses during the summer.

I found my way by following my nose to the Bake Shoppe, where every day fresh sticky buns, deep-dish apple pies, corn bread, and muffins come out of the ovens to tempt me from my diet! Take some along for hunger pangs along the road.

And from home you can order the inn's good jams, mustards, relishes, chowders, and more. They are beautifully packaged and mailed to you wherever you wish. A country village picnic can also be arranged.

HOW TO GET THERE: Take the Massachusetts Turnpike to exit 9. The Publick House is located on the Common in Sturbridge, on Route 131. From Hartford take I–84 to I–86, exit 3, which brings you right into Sturbridge.

Longfellow's Wayside Inn
Sudbury, Massachusetts 01776

INNKEEPER: Robert Purrington

ADDRESS/TELEPHONE: Wayside Inn Road; (978) 443–1776 or (800) 339–1776

E-MAIL: innkeeper@wayside.org

WEB SITE: www.wayside.org/wayside

ROOMS: 10, all with private bath, air-conditioning, and phone.

RATES: $96 to $120, single; $112 to $155, double; EP.

OPEN: All year except Christmas Day and July 4.

FACILITIES AND ACTIVITIES: Breakfast for houseguests only, lunch, dinner, bar. Horses boarded. Gift shop, museum.

BUSINESS TRAVEL: Located 22 miles from Boston. Phone, table, and chairs in room; conference room; fax available.

*G*enerations of travelers have found food and lodging for "man and beast" at the Wayside Inn. Route 20 is the old stagecoach road to Boston, now well off the beaten track. The inn looks much as it did more than 280 years ago and still supplies the traveler with hearty food and drink and a comfortable bed.

As with many old buildings, "improvements" were made to the inn in the nineteenth century, but a complete restoration in the 1950s afforded the opportunity to put many things back the way they were in the beginning. Now part of the inn serves as a museum with priceless antiques displayed in their original settings.

There are a large dining room and several smaller ones, a bar, a gift shop, and a lovely walled garden. At the end of the garden path is a bust of Henry Wadsworth Longfellow, who was inspired by the inn to link a group of poems known to all schoolchildren as *Tales of a Wayside Inn*.

Henry Ford bought 2,995 acres surrounding the inn in 1923, and since then this historic area has been preserved. A little way up the road stand a lovely chapel, the little red schoolhouse that gained fame in "Mary Had a Little Lamb," and a stone gristmill that still grinds grain for the rolls and muffins baked at the inn. I bought some of their cornmeal because the muffins I ate at the inn were exquisite. This is a most interesting building to visit, as all of the equipment in the mill is water powered.

As a final touch, the inn boasts the oldest mixed drink in America. It is called Coow Woow. You must taste it to discover how well our forefathers lived.

HOW TO GET THERE: From Boston take the Massachusetts Turnpike west to Route 128 North. Take exit 26 west onto Route 20. Wayside Inn Road is 11 miles west, just off Route 20. From New York take the Massachusetts Turnpike to Route 495, and go north to Route 20 East. It is approximately 8 miles to Wayside Inn Road.

Le Jardin
Williamstown, Massachusetts 01267

INNKEEPER: Walter Hayn

ADDRESS/TELEPHONE: 777 Cold Spring Road; (413) 458–8032

ROOMS: 6, all with private bath.

RATES: $75 to $95, double occupancy; EP.

OPEN: All year.

FACILITIES AND ACTIVITIES: Breakfast, dinner, Sunday brunch, bar, trout pond.

*T*he grounds are so pretty at this inn. The backyard has picnic tables, and in front are Hemlock Brook and a nice pond. A lot of sugar maples shade the property, and Walter taps them and then makes his own maple syrup.

The rooms are lovely. There are four working fireplaces with glass doors for safety. One of the rooms, the one where I always want to stay, has a whirlpool tub. What heaven it is to relax in! Another room has a deck extending into the woods.

There is also a nice bar and lounge. It's a most attractive room, with comfortable bar stools and tables.

Terry is the manager of the dining rooms—real beauties—and she does a superb job. Fresh, crisp napery; a fresh flower on each table; and plants hanging in the windows provide the perfect cozy, but still elegant, atmosphere for the magnificent food. The cuisine is French. Some of the hors d'oeuvres are snails in garlic butter, oysters baked with spinach and Pernod, and beluga malossol caviar. I had the onion soup baked in a tureen. Very hot and good. The frogs legs were done to perfection. There are also jumbo shrimp baked with a hint of garlic and crisp Long Island duckling with apples. An excellent choice is sirloin flamed in cognac and laced with coarse black pepper. Rack of lamb is beautifully served with tender vegetables and fresh mint sauce. There's a wonderful and extensive wine list. It's so nice when both the food and the wine are exceptional.

And the desserts . . . well, just imagine a French restaurant. I'm not about to spill the beans and tell you what to expect. Come on up and see for yourself.

A nice feature on the property is the trout pond. You may try to catch your own. Can't get them much fresher than that.

HOW TO GET THERE: The inn is right on Route 7, just 2 miles south of Williamstown, on the right.

Sterling and Francine Clark Art Institute

Here in the hollows of the Berkshires, far from big-city museums, is one of the finest art collections in the nation. The French Impressionists are among the most notable works—see Monet, Pissarro, Degas, and Renoir. American paintings and sculpture by Sargent, Homer, and Remington are here along with European pieces dating back to medieval times. The museum itself is grand, and admission is free. Lectures, concerts, poetry readings, and outdoor musical performances in the summer are on the yearlong calendar of special events. A gift shop and seasonal cafe are also here. Call (413) 458-2303.

Select List of
Other Massachusetts Inns

The Captain's House Inn
369-371 Old Harbor Road
Chatham, MA 02633
(508) 945-0127 or (800) 315-0728; fax (508) 945-0866
E-mail: capthous@capecod.net
Web site: captainshouseinn.com

19 rooms, all with private bath; 13 with fireplace, TV/VCR; 4 with whirlpool tub; 1839 Greek Revival B&B decorated in Williamsburg style.

Walker House
64 Walker Street
Lenox, MA 01240
(413) 637-1271 or (800) 235-3098; fax (413) 637-2387
E-mail: phoudek@vgernet.net
Web site: www.walkerhouse.com

8 rooms, all with private bath; B&B in 1804 Federal Colonial decorated with antiques; each room named for a composer.

Spray Cliff on the Ocean, a B&B Inn
25 Spray Avenue
Marblehead, MA 01945
(781) 631-6789 or (800) 626-1530; fax: (617) 639-4563
E-mail: spraycliff@aol.com
Web site: www.spraycliff.com

7 rooms, all with private bath; 3 with fireplace; B&B in early 1900s oceanfront house 1 mile from town.

Seven Sea Street Inn

7 Sea Street
Nantucket, MA 02554
(508) 228-3577 or (800) 651-9262; fax (508) 228-3578
E-mail: seast7@nantucket.net
Web site: www.sevenseastreetinn.com

11 rooms, 2 suites, all with private bath; serves breakfast; newly constructed inn with authentic Nantucket ambience, red oak post and beam construction.

Fernside B&B

162 Mountain Road
P.O. Box 303
Princeton, MA 01541
(978) 464-2741 or (800) 545-2741; fax (978) 464-2065
E-mail: innkeeper@fernsideinn.com
Web site: www.fernsideinn.com

4 rooms, 2 suites, all with private bath; 1835 Federal mansion.

New Hampshire

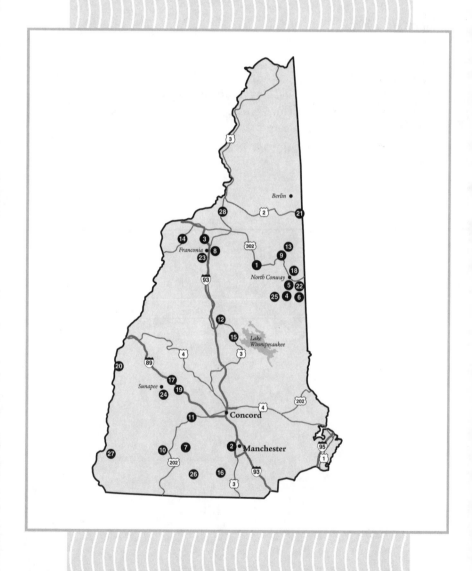

New Hampshire

Numbers on map refer to towns numbered below.

*A Top Pick Inn

A Top Pick Inn

The Notchland Inn
Bartlett, New Hampshire 03812

INNKEEPERS: Les Schoof and Ed Butler

ADDRESS/TELEPHONE: Route 302; (603) 374–6131 or (800) 866–6131; fax (603) 374–6168

E-MAIL: notchland@aol.com

WEB SITE: www.notchland.com

ROOMS: 7, plus 6 suites; all with private bath and fireplace; 1 specially equipped for handicapped.

RATES: $235 to $345, double occupancy; MAP. B&B is available.

OPEN: All year.

FACILITIES AND ACTIVITIES: Full liquor license. Hot tub. Hiking, canoeing, swimming, fishing, bicycling, cross-country skiing, sleigh rides, snowshoeing, and ice skating. Nearby: Downhill skiing. Dinner is not served on Monday.

*T*he inn was built in 1862 by a wealthy Boston dentist, Samuel Bemis. He used native granite and timber, and you can bet that the construction of this building was some job. Seventeen fireplaces are in the inn, and all of the rooms have a working fireplace. Some of the suites have a two-person spa bath. One suite has an exquisite Japanese wedding kimono posted on a wall, and a few suites are in the schoolhouse. The Carter Suite is grand; it has a deck, a wood-burning fireplace, a Jacuzzi tub in a large bathroom, a queen-size bed, and a nice living room.

There are high ceilings and beautiful mountain views. The front parlor was designed by Gustav Stickley, a founder of the Arts and Crafts movement. The music room is inviting with its piano and stereo, and the sunroom is full of beautiful plants and a fountain. The dining room dates back to 1795, has a raised hearth fireplace, and looks out onto the pond and gazebo.

Every evening dinner is served at 7:00, and patrons are offered a choice of two soups, two appetizers, three entrees, and three desserts. To give you an idea of the varied menu, soup might be lightly curried sweet potato and butternut squash, orange-scented tomato with a fresh herbed yogurt, or Szechuan carrot. Appetizers might be crab cakes or three-tier vegetable pâté with a red pepper coulis. Entrees might be filet mignon with béarnaise sauce, chicken champagne, poached catfish, or poached salmon stuffed with scallops and herbs. And dessert might be very lemon pie, apricot cheesecake, or chocolate walnut tart. If you can even think about breakfast after such a dinner, you'll delight in the full country breakfast that will start your day right.

There's so much to do in this area that you may have a hard time deciding where to start. The hiking is by far the nicest you'll find almost anywhere. There are beautiful waterfalls and granite cliffs to scale. The Saco River is the place for swimming, fishing, or canoeing, and two swimming holes are on the inn's property. White-water class III and IV are here in the spring, so come on up with your kayak. Or bring your bicycle, as biking is fun here. Skiing of all kinds is very close by (there are 45 miles of ski trails)—or do you want to try snowshoeing? This is the place for it, or you can go ice skating on the inn's pond. If more sedentary activities suit your fancy, gliders on the porch are ideal for reading and needlework.

The innkeepers love animals as much as I do. Dolly is a Belgian draft horse. DC and Sid are the llamas. Coco and Abby, their Bernese mountain dogs, are loves and even have "Coco Loco" cookies to give to guests—boy, are those good! Coco's Corner is in the inn's newsletter, and what a wag she is! She reports on all of the animals that visit—ducks, bears, and birds. Keeps her busy.

While you are here, do read the history of the inn; it's a fascinating story. When you come in the door of the inn and turn left, there is a living room with a puzzle going at all times; it's always fun to work on it.

HOW TO GET THERE: Follow Route 302 from North Conway to the inn. It is 20 miles north of North Conway.

Attitash Bear Peak

Outdoor recreation lovers will enjoy the multiseason activities at Bartlett's Attitash Bear Peak (603–374–2368) on Route 302. This year-round recreation area and ski mountain has forty-five downhill ski trails, including a vertical drop of 1,750 feet for thrillseekers and a novice trail for beginners. There are complete snow-making capabilities, pay-by-the-run lift tickets, a ski school with classes for ages four to adult, and instruction for snowboarding at the site's snowboarding park and halfpipe.

In the warm months visitors can enjoy the mountain's ¾-mile alpine slide with rider-controlled sleds. Water slides and kiddie pools are also part of the fun here. For a breathtaking view of the countryside, you can take the chairlift to the 2,350-foot summit of the mountain, then climb to the top of the White Mountain Observation Tower. In addition, the downhill ski trails are opened to mountain bikers. A 3-mile downhill trail challenges experienced bikers. A less difficult trail traces the banks of the beautiful Saco River and includes interpretive information stops and picnic areas. Bike rentals are available. A base lodge has a cafeteria and rest room facilities. Fees are charged for all the mentioned activities.

The Bedford Village Inn
Bedford, New Hampshire 03102

INNKEEPER: Jack Carnevale

ADDRESS/TELEPHONE: 2 Village Lane; (603) 472–2001 or (800) 852–1166; restaurant, (603) 472–2001; fax (603) 472–2379

ROOMS: 12 suites, plus 2 apartments; all with private bath, TV and phone.

RATES: $200 to $375, double occupancy, EP.

OPEN: All year.

FACILITIES AND ACTIVITIES: Breakfast, lunch, dinner, Sunday brunch, taproom. Elevator.

"Country elegant" is the way to describe this inn. It was a farmhouse built before the American Revolution, and it still retains the original wide fireplaces and wide pine boards.

In what was once the hayloft, there are sumptuous suites, each with a bathroom of Italian marble and a Jacuzzi. The fixtures are gold finish—very pretty. The suites are well furnished. There are nice lamps with three-way switches, a too-often-forgotten detail. Each suite has three telephones, one at the desk, one by the bed, and one in the bathroom. A deck off the luxury suite in the barn's peak overlooks the meadow. One of the apartments has two bedrooms.

The original milking room has become a common area for inn guests, furnished with couches, lounge chairs, and a nice table for games or whatever. It is a very comfortable room.

Breakfast at the inn includes all of the usual items plus treats such as frittatas with crab, lobster, fresh herbs, and Havarti cheese, and vanilla-bean crepes topped with seasonal fruit sauces. The pastries are beautiful and come straight from the inn's own bakery. The taproom has its own menu.

There are several dining rooms, each one lovely. The oldest dates back to around 1700 and has a huge fireplace. Lots of windows make it light and airy. The luncheon and Sunday brunch are ambrosia, and dinner is a delight. Traditional New England foods are served here, and the menu changes regularly. The inn boasts an 800-bottle wine cellar. Special dinners at the inn include a Christmas feast and wine dinners.

Oriental carpets, antique four-poster beds, comfortable chairs, and old fireplaces all add up to a wonderful country inn.

HOW TO GET THERE: The inn is on Route 101, just west of Manchester.

Adair
Bethlehem, New Hampshire 03574

INNKEEPERS: Bill and Judy Whitman

ADDRESS/TELEPHONE: 80 Guider Lane; (603) 444-2600 or
(888) 444-2600; fax (603) 444-4823

E-MAIL: adair@connriver.net

WEB SITE: www.adairinn.com

ROOMS: 10, plus 1 suite and 1 two-bedroom cottage; all with private
bath. No-smoking inn.

RATES: $165 to $345, double occupancy; EPB.

OPEN: All year. Restaurant closed in April and November and on Monday and Tuesday.

FACILITIES AND ACTIVITIES: Dinner (Tim-Bir Alley restaurant). Beer
and wine, or BYOB. Tennis. Nearby: Hiking, skiing, golf, mountain biking.

*A*dair was built in 1927 as a gift to Dorothy Guider from her
father. She lived in this hilltop mansion until her death in 1991.
The house was converted into a glorious inn the next year. It is
surrounded by 200 acres of sheer beauty in a picture-postcard setting.

The landscaping, de-
signed by the Olmsted
brothers (Sons of Fredrick)
of Boston Common and
Central Park fame, is magnificent. The walking paths
offer grand views of the Presidential and Dalton moun-
tain ranges. A very nice patio
overlooks the tennis court.

You enter a formal entry
hall. On one side is a large
living room recently redecorated by the Whitmans. They have added
antiques and original art throughout the inn. To the left is a lovely dining
room.

At 8:45 in the morning, piping-hot popovers are served, followed by good
things such as pumpkin pancakes with bacon, ham and cheese frittatas, a
variety of juices, and low-fat yogurt for the diet-conscious.

The Tim-Bir Alley restaurant's menu changes every week. Beer and wine are served, but you can bring other beverages. The restaurant is separate from the inn. Two of the appetizers are sautéed shrimp on corn pancakes and lamb and smoked cheddar ravioli. Entrees may be catfish with avocado-lime salsa, or tournedos of beef with mozzarella and sun-dried tomato. Chocolate-glazed banana cake with white chocolate sauce is one of the desserts that caught my eye.

The Granite Taproom is a good spot for relaxing or playing a game of pool. Television and a VCR with a variety of movies are here, too, as is a private telephone.

On the way upstairs to the luxurious guest rooms is a library. The rooms are named for the mountain ranges, and all of them have a view of either mountains or the beautiful grounds. Bathrooms have been recently upgraded, and some now have two-person soaking tubs. A collection of great hats decorates the second-floor landing.

HOW TO GET THERE: From I–93 take exit 40, which takes you directly to Adair's driveway. From Route 302 Adair is 3 miles west of the center of Bethlehem village.

Stafford's in the Fields
Chocorua, New Hampshire 03817

INNKEEPERS: Ramona and Fred Stafford

ADDRESS/TELEPHONE: P.O. Box 270; (603) 323–7766 or (800) 833-9507

E-MAIL: staffordsinthefield@acornworld.net

ROOMS: 11 in main building, 6 with private bath; 3 to 4 cottages, all with bath.

RATES: $120 to $240 per person, double occupancy; MAP.

OPEN: All year.

FACILITIES AND ACTIVITIES: Liquor license; trail lunches available. Function barn for weddings, parties, concerts. Sleigh rides, cross-country skiing. Wheelchair access to dining room and cottage.

*A*t the end of a quiet country lane sits a really lovely country inn. It comes with a babbling brook, has forests at hand, and overlooks rolling fields. You will also find a barn with truly unusual acoustics. It can hold up to 250 people; what a great spot for a wedding! The inn's Oliver Twist Tap Room is an intimate place to relax in an Old English atmosphere.

Ramona Stafford likes to cook in a sort of French country style with wine and herbs and spices and, best of all, great imagination: pork tenderloin with prunes, and stuffed chicken breast with almonds and raisins.

Breakfast is the way to start your day. Omelets are different—sour cream with green chives, mild country cheddar, or cheddar and salsa. You will not go wrong trying the huevos rancheros or fresh sweet rolls. Ramona serves well-balanced meals. Smoking is not permitted in the dining room.

The inn is immensely comfortable, with cross-country skiing right on the fields, and just utter peace. As Fred Stafford says, there is an inexhaustible supply of "nature things to do." Just sitting, watching the swallows swoop or a leaf spin slowly to the ground, restores what you may have lost in the hustle and bustle of today's world.

Turn in the lane some snowy evening and see Stafford's glowing in the field, waiting to welcome you from a world well left behind. Pita, the inn dog, and Celeste, the goose, will be waiting to greet you. So will Buddy the Bear—he's stuffed, of course—who wears Fred's father's World War I helmet.

HOW TO GET THERE: Take Route 16 north to Chocorua Village, then turn left onto Route 113 and travel 1 mile west to the inn. Or, from I-93, take exit 23 and travel east on Route 104 to Route 25, and then to Route 16. Proceed north to Route 16 to Chocorua Village.

Darby Field Inn 🍷 ♥
Conway, New Hampshire 03818

INNKEEPERS: Marc and Maria Donaldson

ADDRESS/TELEPHONE: Off Route 16 on Bald Hill (mailing address: 185 Chase Hill Road, Albany, NH 03818); (603) 447–2181 or (800) 426–4147 (outside New Hampshire); fax (603) 447–5726

E-MAIL: marc@darbyfield.com

WEB SITE: www.darbyfield.com

ROOMS: 14, with private bath.

RATES: $70 to $118, per person, double occupancy, MAP; $55 to $115, per person, double occupancy, EPB. Package plans available.

OPEN: All year except April.

FACILITIES AND ACTIVITIES: Bar, TV, library, swimming pool, outdoor hot tub, 12 miles of cross-country ski trails, hiking.

*S*et high atop Bald Hill in New Hampshire's White Mountains with spectacular views of this wonderful country is Darby Field Inn. Located 1,000 feet above Mount Washington Valley and only 3 miles from Conway Village, the inn delights wanderers adventurous enough to leave the beaten path.

The inn borders the White Mountain National Forest, where guests are welcome to cross-country ski, snowshoe, hike, or walk to nearby rivers, waterfalls, and lakes. The inn dog, Gorby, and the bunny, Fluffy, love this beautiful country.

Rooms are charming, some with four-poster beds and wall-to-wall rugs. All rooms have private baths, and they are tucked away wherever space was available. How do you feel about an L-shaped shower stall? Deluxe accommodations have Jacuzzis, fireplaces, and a wonderful view.

The inn's huge cobblestone fireplace is the center for warm conversation. The pub has a wood-burning stove.

Candlelit dinners begin with fine wine and a smashing sunset view up the valley. The food reflects the careful preparation of the chef. You'll always find a chef's special and fresh fish du jour. Whatever you order up here will be excellent. Desserts are interesting. You must try Darby cream pie, quite different. The Irish Revolution will really end your day nicely.

Darby Field, a notorious Irishman, was the first white man to ascend Mount Washington. Had the inn been here in 1642, it is doubtful whether Mr. Field would ever have passed the pub.

HOW TO GET THERE: Turn on Bald Hill Road, a ½ mile south of the Kancamagus Highway, off Route 16, then go 1 mile up the hill and turn right onto a dirt road. The inn is 1 mile beyond.

Conway Scenic Railroad

You can't beat the scenery and the sense of adventure when you board the excursion trains at North Conway's grand Victorian railroad depot for a ride on the Conway Scenic Railroad (603–356–5251 or 800–232–5251). Choose from a 55-minute ride or a 105-minute ride on the Valley Train, which stays in the Mount Washington Valley for trips to Conway and Bartlett and back to the depot. You can also take the Notch Train; buy a ticket for this five-hour round-trip, then hop on for the most beautiful ride of your life. This route passes through Crawford Notch on the Frankenstein Trestle, a remarkable structure that carries the train through one of the most awesome landscapes in New England.

Live narration is given on all trips; snack bars are on both trains. At least one train each day offers dining service. Coach and first-class seats are available on both trains; fares vary with the age of the passenger, the length of the trip, and the season. The Valley trip runs from May through October and on holiday runs in late November and December; the Notch Train runs from mid-June to mid-October, weather permitting. Reservations are highly recommended during September and early October when the foliage is at its peak.

Rockhouse Mountain Farm Inn
Eaton Center, New Hampshire 03832

INNKEEPERS: John R. Edge Jr. and Alana

ADDRESS/TELEPHONE: Rockhouse Mountain Road; (603) 447–2880

ROOMS: 18; 8 with private bath.

RATES: $68 per person, double occupancy; MAP. Children's rates.

OPEN: Mid-June to November 1.

FACILITIES AND ACTIVITIES: BYOB. Private beach on Crystal Lake, 450 acres to roam, animals. Nearby: Golf, tennis, weekly hayrides for kids, canoe trips down the Saco River.

Memorable summer and fall vacations and family reunions have been had at Rockhouse since 1946. There are 450 acres of pastures, woodlands, mountains, and ponds, so bring your camera. The private beach on Crystal Lake has rowboats, canoes, and sailboats. A nice added attraction is the once-a-week luncheon barbecue at Frog Rock on Swift River. Take a swim under the waterfall.

And there are animals—llamas, piglets, dogs, cats, peacocks, geese, and prize steer.

The inn provides ice, glasses, and refrigeration and hopes you will join the adults at happy hour.

Rooms here are plain but clean. There are reduced rates for children, and even a children's dining room for dinner. And speaking of dinner, one entree is served each evening. It may be roast beef or lamb, baked ham, fish, or turkey if it's Sunday, chicken at the Sugar House on Wednesday, and a steak cookout on Saturday. All breads and pastries are homemade.

The view from the living room of the mountains and trout pond is spectacular. The recreation room has Ping-Pong and shuffleboard, and the barn, with a swing, is a major attraction.

The Carriage House has three rooms, and another building, called the 20's House, has three bedrooms and a living room with fireplace. These are great accommodations for a family.

HOW TO GET THERE: From I-95 take Route 16 to Conway. Turn right on Route 153 to Eaton Center. At the Inn at Crystal Lake, take a sharp right up the road to the inn.

The Inn at Crotched Mountain
Francestown, New Hampshire 03043

INNKEEPERS: John and Rose Perry

ADDRESS/TELEPHONE: Mountain Road; (603) 588–6840

ROOMS: 13; 8 with private bath; 4 with fireplace.

RATES: $40 to $60, per person, double occupancy; EPB.

OPEN: All year except April to mid-May.

FACILITIES AND ACTIVITIES: Wheelchair access to inn and dining rooms. Bar, tennis, swimming pool, cross-country skiing. Nearby: Golf, fishing, summer theater.

*T*his Colonial house, more than 150 years old, is located on the northern side of Crotched Mountain. There is a 40-mile view of the Piscataquog Valley, complete with spacious skies. Both innkeepers have gone to school to learn their trade, and what a charming house to practice it in. They are both pretty special themselves. Rose is from Singapore, and John is a Yankee.

Come and stay: There are many things to do. There are three golf courses in the nearby valley; the fishing in the numerous streams, ponds, and lakes is great; and there is a wading pool for the young, as well as a 30-by-60-foot pool for real swimmers. Two areas provide skiing—one at the front door and another down the road. Two clay tennis courts eliminate that tiresome waiting for a playing area. And come evening there are two summer theaters, one at Peterborough and another in Milford.

Any house that has nine fireplaces needs a wood lot and a man with a chainsaw. Four of the bedrooms here have a fireplace, so remember to request one when you reserve.

Three English cockers live here, Winslow, Frances, and Lucy. Come and enjoy this wonderful countryside with the dogs. They would love to have you.

HOW TO GET THERE: Take 101A from Nashua to Milford, Route 13 to New Boston, and Route 136 to Francestown. Take Route 47 for 2½ miles, then turn left onto Mountain Road. The inn is 1 mile up the road.

Franconia Inn 👥
Franconia, New Hampshire 03580

INNKEEPERS: Richard and Alec Morris

ADDRESS/TELEPHONE: Route 116 (mailing address: 1300 Easton Road); (603) 823–5542 or (800) 473–5299

E-MAIL: info@franconiainn.com

WEB SITE: www.franconiainn.com

ROOMS: 29, plus 2 family suites and 1 "inn" suite; all with private bath; 2 with Jacuzzis.

RATES: $155 to $235, double occupancy; MAP. EP and EPB rates available.

OPEN: All year except April 1 to Mother's Day.

FACILITIES AND ACTIVITIES: Bar, lounge, game room, airfield, hot tub, swimming pool, four tennis courts, cross-country ski center, ice skating, sleigh rides, soaring center, horseback riding, bicycles, croquet, nightly movies. Nearby: Downhill skiing, golf.

This is an inn in the fine tradition of old New England hostelries. The inn is the fourth for the Morris family. It is run by third-generation innkeepers. The inn welcomes children. Never a dull moment any season of the year. While the children play or watch a movie on the big-screen TV in the movie room, you can relax in the lounge and listen to selected classical and popular music by the glow of the fireplace.

A game room and a library are here for your enjoyment, as are two verandas, one catching the sunrise over Cannon Mountain, the other for watching the sunset over Sugar Hill.

Another entertainment for you is horseback riding. There are trail rides through Ham Branch stream and around the hay fields.

The living room is paneled with old oak and, with the fireplace, is very warm and cozy. A lovely candlelit dining room, with pink and white napery, serves glorious food. The chef has treated shrimp in an innovative way. They come warmed in pancetta and served over an almond couscous timbale with basil butter. What a superb appetizer! Beer-battered softshell crabs is a winner, and so is seared duck breast with a pear, ginger, and spinach marmalade, served with wild rice.

There are 30 miles of cross-country trails right at hand on the inn's 107 acres, and they also have facilities so that you can ski from inn to inn on connecting trails. Downhill skiing is but 10 miles away. Horse-drawn sleigh rides in this beautiful winter wonderland are my idea of heaven. Do come and enjoy.

HOW TO GET THERE: Take I–91 north to the Wells River–Woodsville exit. Go right on Route 302 to Lisbon, New Hampshire. A few miles past Lisbon, go right on Route 117 to Franconia. Crossing the bridge into town, go right at the Exxon station onto Route 116, and you're 2 miles from the inn, which is on the right. Or, if you have a single-engine plane, the inn has its own FAA-listed airfield with a 3,000-foot-long runway.

The Horse and Hound
Franconia, New Hampshire 03580

INNKEEPERS: Bill Steele and Jim Cantlon

ADDRESS/TELEPHONE: 205 Wells Road; (603) 823–5501 or (800) 450–5501

ROOMS: 6, plus 2 two-bedroom units; all with private bath and phone.

RATES: $86, double occupancy; $135 for two bedrooms; EPB. MAP rates also available.

OPEN: All year except April 1 to Mother's Day, and sometimes November.

FACILITIES AND ACTIVITIES: Dinner. Bar, lounge. Skiing, soaring, biking, hiking. Nearby: Swimming, boating, fishing, golf, tennis. Wheelchair access to bar, lounge, and dining room. Well-behaved pets welcome ($8.50 charge).

*T*he Horse and Hound is located at the base of Cannon Mountain just north of Franconia Notch. Tucker Brook rushes down from the top of the mountain just past the edge of the inn's property. In winter you can set off from the door of the inn on your cross-country skis. In other seasons bicycling is a big thing here, with a 7-mile circuit for you to try. Should be fun up here in these beautiful mountains.

You can also go soaring in a plane or just take an airplane ride. What a way to enjoy the fall foliage. I did it once in a helicopter, and it was sublime.

There are three fireplaces to warm you, whether you are in the living room or the dining rooms. The library lounge has lots of books, which are well organized in categories such as bike books, children's books, and classics. There is music in here also. A miniature pool table is tons of fun, or you can enjoy checkers and other games. You might enjoy playing with Gus and Max, the inn's cocker spaniels, or Pipper and Tigger, the inn's cats.

Comfortable rooms are bright and airy and have lovely views.

The terrace in summer is so lovely for cocktails. The food is excellent. Under appetizers, escargots en croûte are good. I liked the baked French onion soup, but there is also a soup du jour. Entrees include filet mignon, lamb chops, veal, fish, the chef's Vegetarian Fancy, and daily specials. The desserts and pastries all are made here and are so good.

HOW TO GET THERE: From Boston take I–93 north, exit at Route 18, and turn left. Go 2½ miles to Wells Road, and take a left onto Wells. The inn is on the left. Coming south on I–93, take exit 38 from Franconia, go left on Route 18, travel 2½ miles to Wells Road, and take a right onto Wells.

Lovett's by Lafayette Brook
Franconia, New Hampshire 03580

INNKEEPERS: Jim and Janet Freitas

ADDRESS/TELEPHONE: Route 18; (603) 823–7761 or (800) 356–3802; fax (802) 823-8802

E-MAIL: lovetts@NCIA.net

WEB SITE: www.lovettsinn.com

ROOMS: 21; 3 in main house, 18 in cottages; all with private bath; 14 with fireplaces; 4 with Jacuzzis.

RATES: $110 to $195, double occupancy; EPB.

OPEN: All year except some weeks in April.

FACILITIES AND ACTIVITIES: Dinner, bar, outdoor pool, ten acres with 66 kilometers of trails for snowshoeing, cross-country skiing. Nearby: Skiing, tennis, golf, horseback riding, bicycling, fishing, Franconia Notch State Park.

The main building is a classic, dating from 1784 and on the National Register of Historic Places. But it is the dining room that made this inn famous. The legend began more than seventy years ago when Charles Lovett turned the old home into an inn with hospitality and cuisine that brought loyal fans back year after year.

Charlie left more than a decade ago, and things had gone downhill under a series of owners. But since the newest innkeepers, Jim and Janet Freitas, arrived more than three years ago, they have been working hard to regain that top reputation, renovating, refurbishing, stripping old paint off the handsome fireplaces, polishing up the hardwood and heart pine floors, and generally making the inn a welcoming home base. The popular bar area, featuring a spectacular marble bar, has been almost doubled in size. The sun porch is a comfortable place for watching TV.

With a background as restaurant owners and caterers in Massachusetts, the Freitas were well qualified to take over the kitchen, where Janet is winning new acclaim. Dinners served by candlelight might begin with White Mountain Brie cheese rolled in mixed nuts and baked in phyllo dough, or spinach crepes in a basil cream sauce, one of the guests' favorites. Janet's crab cakes are also popular, along with the main courses such as chicken Florentine, stuffed with spinach and goat cheese and served in a herbed cream sauce; pan-fried boneless trout with lemon caper butter; roast pork tenderloin with a currant glaze; and veal Genovese, pan seared in olive oil with herbs, garlic, and wine. Beef lovers will find planty of choices, and dishes such as pasta primavera will please vegetarians. Some of the seasonings come from the herb garden just outside the kitchen. The day begins with a hearty breakfast, always featuring fresh fruit, a choice of a vegetarian or meat omelet, plus special dishes like pancakes, crepes, or French toast. Janet will pack a bag lunch for those who want to spend the day exploring this beautiful part of New Hampshire.

The upgrading of rooms is almost complete, with many new furnishings including country antiques. Some of the choicest rooms offer queen beds, Jacuzzis, and mountain views. Most of the rooms in the cottages beside the pool and around the lawn have fireplaces, and the patios are great for gazing at Cannon Mountain. Two-room cottages are ideal for families, and one three-bedroom cottage can be rented as a unit.

In winter, the inn's expansive system of cross-country trails connects with other area inns, so you can ski from inn to inn.

HOW TO GET THERE: Take I–93 north to exit 3, Route 18, and turn left. The inn is on the left, 2 miles down the mountain.

Sugar Hill Inn
Franconia, New Hampshire 03580

INNKEEPERS: Jim and Barbara Quinn

ADDRESS/TELEPHONE: Route 117; (603) 823–5621 or (800) 548–4748 for reservations

WEB SITE: www.sugarhillinn.com

ROOMS: 10, plus 6 cottage rooms; all with private bath; suites have fireplaces, decks, and whirlpool baths. No-smoking inn. Gas fireplaces in all of the cottage guest rooms.

RATES: $145 to $255, double occupancy; MAP.

OPEN: All year except April.

FACILITIES AND ACTIVITIES: Dinner, full license. Nearby: Skiing, horseback riding, fishing, canoeing, tennis, golf, hiking, museums, antiques shops, summer theater, hot-air ballooning.

The White Mountains are so beautiful and majestic, it is a joy to find the Sugar Hill Inn tucked into this loveliness. This charming inn was built in 1789 as a farmhouse by one of Sugar Hill's original settlers, and it was converted to an inn in 1929.

The inn has been carefully restored. The innkeepers have made the most of the beautiful old beams and floors and the handsome fireplaces. They have two charming common rooms, each with original fireplaces. Each has comfortable furniture, reading materials, board games, and puzzles. A television is in one of these rooms.

In the living room is a player piano with a lot of discs. Really fun for a sing-along. A recent addition to the inn is a lovely pub dubbed "Squier's Pub."

Guest accommodations in the inn and in the country cottages are lovely. Handmade quilts, good mattresses, lovely antiques, stenciled walls, and all superclean. The closets are scented with potpourri. The rooms in the inn are not well suited to children under twelve.

Jim prepares all the meals. The breakfasts are full country ones and may include super walnut pancakes or Swiss eggs with croissant. Be sure to try the fresh muffins. I had the pumpkin raisin muffins.

Dinner starters might include a choice of mushroom dill soup or New England clam chowder. Try the chicken Washington (chicken breast stuffed with crabmeat and covered with hollandaise), French-cut rack of lamb, or roast duck with orange-cranberry sauce. Four entrees are always offered each evening. Oven-baked salmon is a winner; tenderloin of beef is grilled to order and served with bordelaise sauce. Desserts are delicious; raspberry pie, pecan bourbon pie, and chocolate mousse might be available when you're here.

A tea cart, laden with scones and sweet breads or cool drinks in summer, is in the parlor at 4:00 P.M. every day. And the hot cider on the wood-burning stove for skiers is so nice.

Bernerhof Inn
Glen, New Hampshire 03838

INNKEEPER: Sharon Wroblewski

ADDRESS/TELEPHONE: Route 302; (603) 383–9131 or (800) 548–8007 (out of state); fax (603) 383–0809

E-MAIL: stay@bernerhofinn.com

WEB SITE: www.bernerhofinn.com

ROOMS: 9, all with private bath, TV, phone, and air-conditioning; 6 with Jacuzzi; 1 with fireplace.

RATES: $75 to $175, double occupancy; EPB.

OPEN: All year.

FACILITIES AND ACTIVITIES: Breakfast, dinner in Prince Place Restaurant, bar, cooking classes. Wheelchair access to dining room. Hiking trail. Nearby: Golf, tennis, canoeing, fishing, cross-country and downhill skiing; discount shopping.

*A*s the brochure says so well, this is "an elegant small hotel in the foothills of the White Mountains." Rooms are light and airy and individually decorated. There are three king-size brass beds and six Jacuzzis. One is in a sensational window alcove. Games and puzzles await in the sitting room.

A free champagne breakfast in bed is yours on the third morning of your stay. It comes with eggs Benedict and fresh flowers. My, my!

Food in the Prince Place restaurant is something else, as you might expect since chef/owner Mark Prince runs a cooking school. The *delices de Gruyère*—a smooth blend of Swiss cheeses, delicately breaded and sautéed and accompanied by a savory tomato blend—is superb. Swiss entrees include *emince de veau Zurichoise*, Wiener schnitzel, and, of course, fondues. You might also try the sautéed rainbow trout with almonds, brandy, amaretto, and tarragon butter, or the basil cannelloni with roasted red pepper and tomato sauce. The portions are very generous.

You'll want to leave room for dessert, it's so good. Pot de crème, chocolate fondue, linzertorte, or *profiteroles au chocolat*—tiny pastries filled with ice cream and topped with chocolate. The Grand Marnier mousse is outrageously good. I could go on, but I'm getting hungry.

The Black Bear Pub at the inn welcomes guests with a cozy atmosphere. It's a lovely oak room done in the style of a European pub. A true haven for beer lovers, it also serves good food from its own menu at affordable prices. You can sip some real Gluh Wein or espresso made from freshly ground beans.

A Taste of the Mountains, a cooking school hosted by Mark Prince and other area chefs, is designed for lovers of fine food. If you want to know more, do call or write for a brochure.

HOW TO GET THERE: From North Conway take Route 16 north. At Glen, turn left onto Route 302. The inn is on your right.

The Hancock Inn
Hancock, New Hampshire 03449

INNKEEPERS: Joe and Linda Johnston
ADDRESS/TELEPHONE: Main Street; (603) 525-3318 or (800) 525-1789
(outside New Hampshire); fax (603) 525-9301
E-MAIL: innkeeper@hancockinn.com

WEB SITE: www.hancockinn.com

ROOMS: 15, all with private bath, air-conditioning, cable TV, and phone; 1 suite for handicapped. No-smoking inn.

RATES: $120 to $135, double occupancy; EPB. Special package rates.

OPEN: All year.

FACILITIES AND ACTIVITIES: Dinner, lounge. Wheelchair ramp into the inn. Parking. Nearby: Swimming, hiking, antiquing, summer theater, skiing, tennis.

*R*eceiving guests since 1789, this is the oldest inn in New Hampshire. The governor of New Hampshire has given it a commendation for its long years of hospitality. It is now in the competent hands of old friends and good innkeepers, Joe and Linda Johnston.

The name of the inn stems from the fact that John Hancock, the founding father, once owned most of the land that composes the present town of Hancock. Set among twisting hills and featuring a weathered clapboard facade, graceful white pillars, and a warm red door, the inn represents all that is good about old inns.

The new common room with its stone fireplace is a great gathering place for guests. The carefully preserved Mural Room was painted by Rufus Porter in 1825. At the end of the day, you will retire to the comfort of a four-poster bed, where the sound of the Paul Revere bell from a nearby steeple will gently lull you to sleep. This is a town that hasn't changed much in the past two centuries.

The dining rooms are lovely, and the food is superb. The inn has been awarded the best of the best award: four diamonds, designating this to be one of the top one hundred restaurants in the country in the category of American food. Appetizers like Maine crab cakes and baked Brie are followed by good soups and an excellent house salad. The famous Shaker cranberry pot roast is alone worth the trip, but perhaps you'd like to try the roasted maple duck, rainbow lake trout, or summer garden linguine. The Squire Patten Pub serves libations and comfort food to patrons.

There is much to do in the area. Climb mountains, or just sit and listen to the church chimes during foliage time. Alpine and cross-country skiing are nearby in winter. Or browse in the antiques shops on a cool spring morn.

The inn dogs are Duffy, a springer spaniel, and Maggie, his niece.

HOW TO GET THERE: From Boston take I–93 north to I–293, then Route 101 to Peterborough. Take a right onto Route 202, then a left onto Route 123. Turn left at the stop sign.

Colby Hill Inn
Henniker, New Hampshire 03242

INNKEEPERS: Cyndi and Mason Cobb

ADDRESS/TELEPHONE: P.O. Box 779; (603) 428-3281 or (800) 531-0330; fax (603) 428-9218

E-MAIL: stay@colbyhillinn.com

WEB SITE: www.colbyhillinn.com

ROOMS: 16, all with private bath and phone; 2 with working fireplace. Entire inn is air-conditioned. No-smoking inn.

RATES: $105 to $195, double occupancy; EPB.

OPEN: All year.

FACILITIES AND ACTIVITIES: Breakfast, dinner. Swimming pool, ice skating, tennis, badminton. Nearby: Canoeing, kayaking, fishing.

BUSINESS TRAVEL: Phone in rooms; fax available; meeting space.

I just love this inn. Built more than 200 years ago as a farmhouse, it leans and dips here and there, but that only adds to its charm. The wide floorboards are authentic. Over the years it has been a tavern, a meetinghouse, and a church. What a history!

In one living room is an Edison Standard phonograph that's almost a century old. It's a rare gem. Ask Mason to run it for you. The records are round, the size of a can of soup, and play for four minutes. I never saw one of these before.

The sixteen guest rooms are filled with antiques and have their own telephones and numbers. A very nice touch. The parlor has a fireplace, good magazines, a television, and a VCR. If you come in the summer, be sure to go see the pool. You go through the barn, turn right through a tunnel, and there it is. The barn is also fun to explore.

Colby Hill also offers cross-country skiing and tennis, and nearby are canoeing, kayaking, and fishing. It's a perfect spot for vacations, weddings, and conferences.

Now to the good stuff—dinner. Among the appetizers during a recent visit were seafood crepe, marinated tenderloin tips, and lobster ravioli. The lobster bisque was divine. Entrees range from loin of venison and roast

The Fiber Studio

One of the most charming aspects of journeying through New England is finding artists' studios and crafters' workshops tucked in the small towns we visit. A restored barn overlooking Henniker's Pat's Peak mountain is the home of the Fiber Studio (603-428-7830), a glorious riot of color and texture hidden in the hills. Workshops are offered year-round in weaving, dyeing, spinning, basketry, and knitting. Hand-dyed woolens, mohairs, alpacas, cottons, linens, and silks for weaving and knitting are for sale here, as are beads from around the world, buttons galore of every description, hand-crafted jewelry and jewelry-making supplies, and much more. Looms, spinning wheels, and books—you name it.

The shop is open year-round Tuesday through Saturday from 10:00 A.M. to 4:00 P.M. and on Sunday by chance. It's located at 9 Foster Hill Road in Henniker off Route 202/9.

lamb loin to baked scrod and vegetarian medley. Then there are those like me who can't wait for dessert. Apple crumb pie, brownie sundae, dessert specials—oh boy!—and then warm up with spirited coffees. This is just a sample of what to expect.

Breakfast is great, with pancakes, crepes, eggs many ways, and all so good.

HOW TO GET THERE: Take I–91 to Brattleboro, then Route 9 east to Henniker.

The Meeting House
Henniker, New Hampshire 03242

INNKEEPERS: June and Bill Davis; Cheryl and Peter Bakke

ADDRESS/TELEPHONE: Flanders Road; (603) 428–3228; fax (603) 428–6334

E-MAIL: meetinghouse@conknet.com

WEB SITE: www.meetinghouse.com

ROOMS: 6, all with private bath and air-conditioning.

RATES: $65 to $115, double occupancy; EPB.

OPEN: All year.

FACILITIES AND ACTIVITIES: Dinner. Hot tub, sauna (available at extra charge). Nearby: White-water canoeing, sailboarding, tennis, golf, hiking, indoor ice skating, cross-country skiing, downhill skiing, antiquing, summer theater.

You can sit in the restaurant of this inn and watch the skiers coming down the hill. Now that's fun. This old barn that houses the restaurant and bar is more than 230 years old.

Hanging on the walls are plastic bags in which people from all over the world have collected shells, stones, sand, and volcano dust and sent them here for display. A nice thing to do. Little white Christmas lights are all over this area. They are so pretty and unique. Only in a country inn.

When you want breakfast, it is delivered to your room in a basket, and what a surprise awaits you! (No, I'm not going to tell; you'll have to see for yourself.)

And dinner . . . well, there is fillet de Cassis, beef Wellington, duck, and lamb. Add to those choices seafood offerings you don't find very often and veal and chicken dishes, all of which looked great. The salad dressings are super. I had an excellent hot bacon dressing. The fried cinnamon apples with ice cream, flavored with apple brandy, were the perfect ending to my dinner.

The rooms are filled with treasures from June's and Bill's former homes. I was delighted to find plenty of books and magazines and plump pillows for reading in bed, a favorite pastime of mine. Grensel is the inn cat.

After a day of skiing, try the sauna and hot tub in the greenhouse. Sheer luxury! In summer, stroll around to view the flower gardens.

White-water activities are on the Contoocook River. Antiques shops are nearby, and a summer theater is in a neighboring town. This really is a nice area.

HOW TO GET THERE: In Henniker take Route 114 south for about 2 miles to Pat's Peak sign. Turn right onto Flanders Road. The inn is in about ½ mile on the right.

The Manor on Golden Pond
Holderness, New Hampshire 03245

INNKEEPERS: Brian and Mary Ellen Shields

ADDRESS/TELEPHONE: Route 3, Box T; (603) 968-3348 or (800) 545-2141; fax (603) 968-2116

E-MAIL: manorinn@lr.net

WEB SITE: www.manorongoldenpond.com

ROOMS: 25, plus 2 cottages; all with private bath; no-smoking inn.

RATES: $210 to $375, double occupancy; EPB.

OPEN: All year.

FACILITIES AND ACTIVITIES: Afternoon tea. Bar, lounge, swimming pool, tennis, ice skating, canoeing, sandy beach. Nearby: Downhill and cross-country skiing.

*I*ssac Van Horne, an Englishman, built this grand manor at the turn of the twentieth century overlooking Squam Lake and the White Mountains. It still retains the warmth of a country home, albeit a grand one.

The richly paneled living room has elegant carved wood trim and its original lead windows. Many of the bedrooms have wood-burning fireplaces and a view to take your breath away. Some have the added modern luxury of a Jacuzzi.

Breakfast is exceptional, with treats such as Belgian waffles with fresh fruit and whipped cream. What a way to start the day! And dinner is a regal experience, with choices such as quail with soy and ginger sauce, potato-encrusted salmon fillet with hazlenut butter, or maple-glazed venison chops. Afterward, you can linger over a drink in the cozy Three Cocks Pub.

The estate includes thirteen acres and 300 feet of sandy beach frontage on the lake. Among the activities on the property are a swimming pool, tennis, croquet, and canoeing. If it rains, all is not lost; tea is served every afternoon, and any time of day, it's a pleasure to be inside this beautiful mansion.

HOW TO GET THERE: Take Route 3 into Holderness. Cross the bridge, and on the right you will see the signs for The Manor on Golden Pond.

Christmas Farm Inn
Jackson, New Hampshire 03846

INNKEEPER: Bruce Campbell

ADDRESS/TELEPHONE: P.O. Box CC; (603) 383–4313 or
(800) HI–ELVES; fax (603) 383–6495

E-MAIL: info@christmasfarminn.com

WEB SITE: www.christmasfarminn.com

ROOMS: 41, including Carriage House, suites and cottages; all with private bath and air-conditioning. Phones, TV in cottages and Carriage House.

RATES: $88 to $189, per person, double occupancy; MAP. Special weekly and package rates.

OPEN: All year.

FACILITIES AND ACTIVITIES: Wheelchair access to inn and dining room. Pub, complimentary movies, game room, putting green. 80 kilometers of cross-country trails, golf, tennis, sauna. Nearby: Downhill skiing, alpine slide, canoeing on Saco River.

Yes, Virginia, there is a Christmas Farm Inn, and it has the Mistletoe Pub and the Sugar Plum Dining Room to prove it. The food is fit for any Santa and his helpers, from the hearty, full country breakfast, which includes homemade breads, muffins, and sticky buns, to gracious dinners featuring a full menu of entrees, homemade soups, and desserts made by an on-site baker. Children age twelve and under have their own special menu.

The medallions of pork MacIntosh are glorious and have a hint of brandy. The veal and chicken are so tender. Entrees from the seas are real treats. The desserts do indeed make visions of sugarplums dance in your head. How about apple pie, crème brûlée, or the Christmas Farm special sundae? From here take a quick trip to the Mistletoe Pub for a nightcap.

Separate from the main building is the Christmas Farm function center, a perfect spot not only for medium to small business meetings but also weddings, anniversaries, and the like. At one side of the room is a 12-foot-wide fieldstone fireplace. There are games of all sorts, a wide-screen television, a sauna, a bar, and four nice suites that are ideal for families.

Also separate are the cottages, each with living room, fireplace, two bedrooms, and two baths. The rooms in the main building have Christmas names: Holly, Dasher, Prancer, Vixen, Donner, Cupid, Comet, and Blitzen. There are two deluxe rooms with Jacuzzi tubs.

Sugar House, the honeymoon suite, has air-conditioning, a wood fireplace in its living room, a bedroom, and a huge bath with a two-person Jacuzzi and a shower. Five cottages have two bedrooms and baths, coffeemakers, TV, and refrigerators, plus air-conditioning. They are grand.

Jackson is in the heart of the White Mountains, so bring your skis, or come in the summer to splash in the outdoor pool, lunch at the cabana, work out in the state-of-the-art fitness center, or get a massage.

HOW TO GET THERE: Go north on Route 16 from North Conway. A few miles after Route 302 branches off to your left, you will see a covered bridge on your right. Take the bridge through the village and up the hill ¼ mile, and there is the inn.

Jackson Ski Touring Foundation

One of the best such operations in the entire Northeast, the Jackson Ski Touring Foundation maintains nearly 160 kilometers of cross-country ski trails over 60 square miles of this region. Skiers can use the trail system to ski from inn to inn; some trails are easy, and others are suited to experienced skiers. Races and workshops are held on these trails every winter weekend. Trail fees help to maintain the trails, and they were recently used to build a covered bridge to provide access to the Ellis River Trail, a 10-kilometer route from the village of Jackson to one of the inns in the area. Call (603) 383-9355 for more information.

Ellis River House
Jackson, New Hampshire 03846

INNKEEPERS: Monica and Jim Lee

ADDRESS/TELEPHONE: Route 16 (mailing address: P.O. Box 656); (603) 383-9339 or (800) 233-8309; fax (603) 383-4142

E-MAIL: innkeeper@erhinn.com

WEB SITE: www.erhinn.com

ROOMS: 14, plus 4 suites and 1 cottage; all with private bath, air-conditioning, phone, and TV; 12 with fireplace; 6 with two-person Jacuzzi.

RATES: $89 to $229, double occupancy; EPB.

OPEN: All year.

FACILITIES AND ACTIVITIES: Dinner, full license. Wedding and anniversary functions. Cross-country skiing, fishing, vineyard, swimming pool. Nearby: Shopping, downhill skiing, and much more.

Calling all snow people: Have I found an inn for you! The inn's River and Mountain View Atrium is a glass-enclosed 24-by-24-foot room with an eight-person spa in the center. Imagine relaxing in the warm spa and watching the snow coming down and cross-country skiers going by. That's the way for this inn creeper to go.

In warm weather the heated outdoor pool or trout pond will beckon you. Or perhaps you'll enjoy the gazebo off the dining room, overlooking the Ellis River and the inn's well-landscaped grounds.

The rooms here are wonderful. Twelve of them have a fireplace. Six have two-person Jacuzzis. All are air-conditioned and have cable television, classic antiques, good beds, and a ton of comfort.

A wedding here is handled beautifully. From the church, florist, photographer, horse-drawn carriages, entertainment, and dinner, it's complete.

The menu changes daily, so you can keep coming and enjoy new and excellent food every day. Some of the kitchen's first-course offerings are butternut squash soup, escargots in puff pastry, and tomato and wild mushroom soup. There are also roast tenderloin of pork, prime rib, good pasta, and fish. Roast goose is really different. Garlic mashed potatoes make my mouth water. Desserts? Why ask? They're glorious.

Breakfasts are a treat. In addition to the usual, there are homemade breads—cinnamon, oatmeal, molasses, beer, or French.

The inn has a wonderful history. It's been here since 1893, starting as a farmhouse. There's much to do in this area—factory outlet shopping, skiing, fishing, you name it.

HOW TO GET THERE: Take I–95 north to Route 16 north to Jackson. The inn is on the left, ¼ mile past the historic covered bridge.

The Inn at Thorn Hill
Jackson, New Hampshire 03846

INNKEEPERS: Jim and Ibby Cooper

ADDRESS/TELEPHONE: Thorn Hill Road; (603) 383–4242 or (800) 289–8990; fax (603) 383–8062

E-MAIL: thornhill@ncia.net

WEB SITE: www.innatthornhill.com

ROOMS: 19, in 2 buildings, plus 3 cottage suites; all with private bath and phones; 16 Jacuzzis. No-smoking inn.

RATES: $150 to $300, double occupancy; EPB. Higher in peak season.

OPEN: All year.

FACILITIES AND ACTIVITIES: Bar, swimming pool, hot tub, cross-country skiing. Nearby: Downhill skiing, golf club, tennis, horseback riding, canoeing, ice skating, sleigh rides.

Over the Honeymoon Bridge to The Inn at Thorn Hill you go, and when you get there you will find a Victorian beauty. Mountains are everywhere you look from this inn. Relax on the porch in a New England rocking chair and enjoy the view.

I loved the Victorian parlor, with a baby grand piano, and the spacious drawing room, with a woodstove and an unbelievable view. There are board games, cards, and books for you to enjoy. A cozy full-service pub with a fireplace and five bar stools has lots of cheer.

Elegant country dining by candlelight is what you get, with a changing menu offering the freshest and most innovative ingredients the season has to offer. Casually elegant service and an extensive wine list are to be found here.

Curried crepes with a roasted eggplant aponata and artichoke ricotta filling and red pepper garlic yogurt sauce is just an example of the elaborate appetizers.

The soups and salads are interesting. And the entrees are grand. Pan-seared shrimp with applewood-smoked bacon cream and wilted spinach served over buckwheat soba noodles; roasted rack of lamb served with asparagus risotto, pan jus, and sorrel mint oil . . . the list goes on. The desserts that follow are excellent.

There is a Victorian flair to all the inn rooms. A variety of beds are available—canopies, twins, doubles, kings, and queens—and all rooms have wonderful views of the mountains. The Katharine suite has a two-way fireplace. The carriage house next door has a 20-by-40-foot great room with a fireplace and seven guest rooms, so bring a gang and have some fun. The three cottages are very nice and just great for those who want more privacy. They have been beautifully refurbished, each with a Jacuzzi, front porch, wet bar, television, gas fireplace, and air-conditioning. Some have a deck and view. I stayed in one of the cottages, and, believe me, you could move right in and be very comfortable.

The inn's facilities are not well suited to small children.

There is much to do here. The inn has its own swimming pool; hiking and downhill skiing are close at hand. Cross-country skiing begins at the doorstep and joins the 146-kilometer Jackson touring network. Say hello to Snuggles, the inn dog.

No wonder the inn was one of ten winners of Uncle Ben's Best Country Inn awards! I was one of the judges.

HOW TO GET THERE: Go north from Portsmouth, New Hampshire, on the Spaulding Turnpike (Route 16) all the way to Jackson, which is just above North Conway. At Jackson is a covered bridge on your right. Take the bridge, and two roads up from the bridge on the right is Thorn Hill Road, which you take up the hill. The inn is on your right.

Whitneys' Inn 👪
Jackson, New Hampshire 03846

INNKEEPER: Bob Bowman

ADDRESS/TELEPHONE: Route 16B (mailing address: P.O. Box 822); (603) 383–8916 or (800) 677-5737

E-MAIL: whitneys@ncia.net

WEB SITE: www.whitneysinn.com

ROOMS: 28, plus 2 cottages; all with private bath and air-conditioning; cottages with living room, fireplace, and TV. Nonsmoking rooms available.

RATES: $38 to $75, per person, double occupancy, EPB. $61 to $100, per person, double occupancy, MAP.

OPEN: All year.

FACILITIES AND ACTIVITIES: Bar, lounge, TV and VCR with movies, children's play yard, outdoor heated pool, outdoor Jacuzzi, skiing, ice skating, tennis, swimming pond, badminton, shuffleboard, paddleboat.

This is an authentic mountain hideaway nestled at the base of Black Mountain ski area. You can't get much closer than this. It's pretty nice to be able to crawl out of bed, have a sumptuous breakfast, and walk across to the lifts, trails, ski shop, or ski school, all just a snowball's throw away.

Another very nice feature of the inn is the children's dinner table, available at 5:30 P.M. during busy times. It's nice to know you can spend some time alone while your children are well supervised. There is a good video library, along with board and card games and crossword puzzles. The recreation room has a Ping-Pong table. All this and fourteen acres, tennis courts, heated outdoor pool, shuffleboard, badminton, and a brook-fed pond with a sandy beach and paddleboat.

The Greenery Lounge is neat. There are six original tractor seats at the bar, and on winter weekends the Shovel Handle Pub, a 250-seat après-ski bar, is open with live entertainment.

The dining room is a casually elegant one, and the food is grand. Asparagus with tomato vinaigrette and smoked scallops are but two appetizers. Entrees include sole, scampi, roast duck, and the chef's veal (this was really good), chicken, turkey, and marinated pork. All come with a house salad.

In the morning breakfast consists of fresh eggs (egg substitutes are available), French toast, pancakes, homemade corned beef hash, omelets. . . .

There is much to do up here, and when you arrive you will receive a map listing what is going on.

HOW TO GET THERE: Go north from Conway 22 miles on Route 16. Take a right on Route 16A through a covered bridge into Jackson Village. Take Route 16B to the top of the hill to the inn.

The Wildcat Inn
Jackson, New Hampshire 03846

INNKEEPERS: Pam and Marty Sweeney

ADDRESS/TELEPHONE: Route 16A; (603) 383-4245 or (800) 228-4245

E-MAIL: wildcat@ncia.net

WEB SITE: www.wildcatinnandtavern.com

ROOMS: 14; 12 with private bath and air-conditioning, TV, and phones. Suites sleep 4. 1 cottage.

RATES: $129 to $149, double occupancy; EPB. Cottage, $350.

OPEN: All year.

FACILITIES AND ACTIVITIES: Lunch daily in-season, weekends off-season; no lunch served in April or May. Dinner, bar. Wheelchair access to dining room and tavern. Music in lounge. Nearby: Downhill and cross-country skiing, golf, hiking, tennis, horseback riding.

The brochure here at Wildcat says it so well that I'm just going to repeat it: "Everything you need for a perfect vacation is within walking distance of the inn, so leave your car out back and save gas, money, and time. Begin in the Tavern Gardens, where you will be well fed and properly wined from breakfast through last call. Tennis, your choice of one hard and three clay courts. Golf at the beautiful Wentworth Hall course. Riding lessons, shows, and trail rides through mountain forests. There are package deals for all of the above. Fishing, hiking, or just meandering through town; good shopping is up here. And both downhill and cross-country skiing are nearby."

The tavern has two big fireplaces and nice couches, and on weekends and holidays there is music. This is one of the Valley's favorite après-ski spots, whether for cappuccino or the ten microbrews on tap.

Accommodations are comfortable. All the rooms are different, and each one has a view.

The Wildcat is a very popular dining spot. In fact, some years ago the big old front porch had to be converted into a dining room to make more dining space for all the people who wanted to eat here. The food will titillate your taste buds. All meals are made to order and, as the chef says, patience is a virtue.

Breakfasts are fine, with all pastries baked right here. There are tavern specials at lunch. Lobster Benedict is different. I had it for lunch one day. Salads, burgers, spinach pie, and Reuben sandwiches are other possibilities. Be sure to read the sign with the rules of the tavern. It's very funny. There are a lot of inns in Jackson, but only this one serves lunch, though only on weekends in winter.

At dinnertime there are good appetizers and soups. One entree is called "the extravaganza," shrimp, lobster, and scallops sautéed with garlic, peppers, onions, and fresh tomatoes, served with rice pilaf or linguine—extravagant indeed! Wildcat chicken is chicken wrapped in puff pastry, a house specialty. Desserts are divine. So what are you waiting for?

HOW TO GET THERE: Take Route 16 north from North Conway. Take Route 16A to your right, through a covered bridge, and into Jackson. The inn is in the center of town.

The Ammonoosuc Inn
Lisbon, New Hampshire 03585

INNKEEPERS: Jeni and Jim Lewis

ADDRESS/TELEPHONE: 641 Bishop Road; (603) 838–6118 or (888) 546-6118

ROOMS: 9, all with private bath.

RATES: $70 to $120, double occupancy, EP; continental breakfast. MAP rates available.

OPEN: All year.

FACILITIES AND ACTIVITIES: Dinner, full license; call for reservations. Nearby: Fishing, canoeing, downhill skiing, hiking; inn adjoins a golf course.

The inn was constructed as a farmhouse in 1888. It has been restored and remodeled into an inn with fine common areas and a restaurant.

The inn sits up high and overlooks the Ammonoosuc River, which flows peacefully along. Fishing is great. Tubing down the river would be fun. The Lisbon Village Country Club is right next door and offers many activities. Its golf course was designed by Ralph M. Bartin, a renowned golf course designer. The club has its own clubhouse and lounge.

Relaxing at the inn after a day of fun is easy. The lounge has a woodstove, and the parlors are comfortable. Everything is aimed at your comfort. There is cable television for you to enjoy, or you might have drinks on the porch. The guest rooms are lovely and very tastefully decorated.

The dining room has its original wood paneling and beams. A continental-plus breakfast includes fresh-cut melon and fresh-baked goodies. Dinner is warm and quiet, with a traditional New England menu.

There is so much to do here that you should be sure to come for more than one day. If you like skiing, the inn is fifteen minutes from Cannon Mountain. I, for one, would love to go sledding on the golf course. In warmer weather the porch with rockers is my idea of peace. Just sit back and rock and watch the river.

HOW TO GET THERE: From I–91 take exit 17 (Woodsville–Wells River). Go east on Route 302 to Lisbon. Two miles past Lisbon take a left on Lyman Road for about ½ mile, then left onto Bishop Road for about ¾ mile. The inn is on the right.

Chase House at Mill Falls
Meredith, New Hampshire 03253

INNKEEPERS: Rusty McLear and Gail Batstone

ADDRESS/TELEPHONE: Route 3, (603) 279–7006 or (800) 622–6455

ROOMS: 20, plus 3 suites; all with private bath, phone, TV, fireplaces, and balconies.

RATES: $69 to $249, double occupancy; EP. Packages with meals available.

OPEN: All year.

FACILITIES AND ACTIVITIES: 150-seat conference and function center, Camp restaurant.

The newest addition to the collection of inns here is the luxurious Chase House. The rooms and suites all offer lake views, fireplaces, and romantic sitting areas, and most offer private balconies and whirlpool spas. They are beautifully decorated.

The restaurant, called "Camp" and also known as The Common Man, has a huge fieldstone fireplace and views of the lake. The innkeepers say, and I quote, "We're not very big, our kitchen is tiny, so we go to market every day, we may add an item or not have something—keeps things interesting!" The menu is fun and has lighter fare. Swasey's Back Porch over at the sister inn (see the Inn at Mill Falls) is the one for room service. Breakfast is served till 2:00 P.M.—the way to go when on vacation. Come on up here and try the inns.

HOW TO GET THERE: From I-93 take exit 23 and go east on 104 to its end. Turn left on Route 3, and in less than a mile on the left is the inn.

Inn at Baypoint
Meredith, New Hampshire 03253

INNKEEPERS: Rusty McLear and Gail Batstone

ADDRESS/TELEPHONE: Route 3; (603) 279-6455 or (800) 622-6455

ROOMS: 24, all with private bath, phone, and TV.

RATES: $69 to $249, double occupancy; EP. Packages with meals available.

OPEN: All year.

FACILITIES AND ACTIVITIES: Breakfast, lunch, dinner, Sunday brunch. Bar and lounge. Boating, swimming, and fishing in the lake at the sister inn. Indoor pool, sauna, spa, shops, and a choice of restaurants.

The inns at Mill Falls are a wonderful collection of three inns: The Inn at Mill Falls, the Chase House at Mill Falls, and this beauty on the shores of Lake Winnipesaukee. Sure wish I lived closer. The Inn at Baypoint is surrounded by more than 2,000 feet of manicured lakefront park. The views of the lake and mountains are awesome. Many of the guest rooms offer private lakeside balconies, fireplaces, and personal whirlpools.

The lake, "Granddaddy Lake" (the smile of the Great Spirit), is 72 miles square, with 200 islands and a 300-mile shoreline. As they say up here where the mountains and blue water meet sky, bring your water wings!

The MS *Mount Washington* is 230 feet long; there are a lot of choices for cruises. Special theme and dinner dances, special functions, and smaller boats that go where the big one can't.

This inn is spectacular, as are the others. You can sit on the dock and watch the boats. Try the Boathouse Grill; lunch was lovely. There are several appetizers and entrees. I had a delicious lobster salad. Other choices may be rock crab cakes, pizza of the day, soup and half a sandwich—maybe the Baypoint Club sandwich. Then, after a day of delightful wandering all over the marketplace at the sister Inn at Mill Falls—just across the street—I was back in the Boathouse for dinner. I had the chef's suggested soup, and I was so glad I did. It had beef and chicken stock, shallots and garlic, lemon, pepper, heavy cream, and veggies. There are about ten different appetizers, and dinner entrees are a grand variety—something for everyone. Desserts? Well, just save room.

HOW TO GET THERE: From I–93 take exit 23; go east on Route 104 to its end. Go left on Route 3 North. The inn is 1 mile down the hill on the right.

The Inn at Mill Falls
Meredith, New Hampshire 03253

INNKEEPERS: Rusty McLear and Gail Batstone, innkeepers; Amy Kirk, front desk manager

ADDRESS/TELEPHONE: Route 3; (603) 279–7006 or (800) 622–MILL (6455)

ROOMS: 54, all with private bath, cable TV, phone; some with a fireplace; 1 inn room equipped for handicapped.

RATES: $69 to $249; EP. Packages with meals available.

OPEN: All year.

FACILITIES AND ACTIVITIES: Full breakfast, lunch, dinner, Sunday brunch; bar and lounge. Indoor pool, sauna, whirlpool spa, shops, art gallery. Boating, swimming, and fishing in lake. Nearby: Tennis, racquetball, golf, skiing.

The inn is in what was once an old mill. It straddles an underground canal that runs from Lake Waukewan in the hills above to Lake Winnipesaukee below. Through a window near the lobby, you will see a sluice that is solid ice in winter.

The inn can accommodate banquets, seminars, conferences, and special events. Everything is here: mooring for your boat, newspapers, indoor pool, whirlpool spa and sauna, video rentals, safety deposit boxes, and boating on beautiful Winnipesaukee, the sixth-largest natural lake entirely within the United States. It is 28 miles long and 9 miles wide. The MS *Mount Washington* is an excursion ship that will take you on a 50-mile cruise. Or sail the *Queen of Winnipesaukee,* a 46-foot sloop. There are others to choose from. You prefer sports on solid ground? Golf, jogging, skiing, hiking, tennis, and racquetball are all in the area, too. And some twenty shops and an art gallery are right here if you'd rather do something less active.

The enclosed walkway leading from the lobby spans the tumbling falls and connects the inn with the Mill Falls Marketplace. This 180-year-old restored mill building is the setting for the inn's full-service tavern and restaurant. Millworks has great breakfasts, both large and small ones. At luncheon there is a good selection of sandwiches. The French onion soup offered at dinner is glorious. The salads are very choice, and the entrees are excellent. You must try it here. Mame's is a small restaurant with many interesting dishes on the menu. At Sunday brunch, the eggs Benedict are perfect.

The accommodations are comfortable, with wall-to-wall carpeting, telephones, and cable television. Well-lighted areas are provided for reading or for work (if you must). This whole inn is a wonderful vacation spot.

HOW TO GET THERE: From I–93 take exit 23. Go east on Route 104 to its end. Go left on Route 3 north. The inn is in 1 mile, down the hill on the left.

The Ram in the Thicket
Milford, New Hampshire 03055

INNKEEPERS: Andrew and Priscilla Tempelman

ADDRESS/TELEPHONE: Maple Street; (603) 654-6440;
fax (603) 654-6440

ROOMS: 9; 3 with private bath.

RATES: $60 to $75, double occupancy; continental breakfast.

OPEN: All year.

FACILITIES AND ACTIVITIES: Dinner, bar. Hot tub, indoor swimming
pool, horseback riding, hiking. Nearby: Summer theater.

*T*he unusual name of the inn is taken from the old bible story of
Abraham and Isaac. As a substitute for his dear son Isaac, Abraham finds "a ram caught in the thicket," sent by the Lord. Andrew
and Priscilla founded the inn as a substitute for a life in the Midwest from
which they wanted a change.

Luckily for all inn lovers, the Tempelmans' move has resulted in another
better-than-nice inn. This old Victorian mansion has been carefully restored
and now has lovely dining rooms with crystal chandeliers, a hand-carved fireplace, and many other Victorian touches. One dining room has lovely blue
delft tiles. (The innkeepers are Dutch.) The New Hampshire lounge has
plants hanging from the ceilings.

You will surely love the inventive and interesting dinners. Pasta e fagioli
is corkscrew pasta tossed with tomatoes, onions, favas, garbanzos, and kidney beans, seasoned with fresh oregano, thyme, and rosemary. Umeboshi
pork is Japanese. Veal Tierra del Fuego—go and see what it is. There are good
soups, salads, and desserts. The menu changes quite often.

This fine inn is set on eight acres of wonderful country for roaming.

Mandy is the inn dog, and Mog-
ley is the inn cat.

HOW TO GET THERE: Take Route
3, and just about at Nashua take
exit 7 west on 101A to 101 for
about 15 miles to Wilton. Watch
for the inn's signs. The inn is 200
yards from the Wilton line.

The Inn at Pleasant Lake
New London, New Hampshire 03257

INNKEEPERS: Linda and Brian Mackenzie

ADDRESS/TELEPHONE: 125 Pleasant Street (mailing address: P.O. Box 1030); (603) 526–6271 or (800) 626–4907

E-MAIL: bmackenz@kear.tds.net

WEB SITE: www.innatpleasantlake.com

ROOMS: 8, plus 2 suites; all with private bath. No-smoking inn.

RATES: $110 to $165, double occupancy; EPB.

OPEN: All year, except early April and early November.

FACILITIES AND ACTIVITIES: Dinner 5 nights a week by reservation. Bar. Swimming, hiking, 2 canoes, 1 rowboat, and all winter sports.

The Inn at Pleasan Lake, the oldest operating inn in the area, has taken on new life since owner/chef Brian Mackenzie arrived in 1997. A graduate of the Culinary Institute of America, Brian has turned the inn into a gourmet's destination. His five-course dinners offer a choice of a fish or meat entree, but the rest is up to the chef, varying with the seasons, and his choices are sublime.

Guests are welcomed at a predinner reception where they get to meet the chef and hear about the night's menu, before being escorted into the candlelit dining room. It's worth the tab for this exceptional cuisine, classical French with an Asian influence. Brian was recently asked to show off his prowess at the James Beard House in New York, where only the best regional chefs are invited.

The inn began its life as a farm in 1790, and still has the feel of the country, with antique furnishings and warming fireplaces. Guest rooms are country comfortable. The location couldn't be better, looking out on Pleasant Lake and Mount Kearsarge beyond, a view that is simply spectacular in the fall.

In winter you can ice skate or cross-country ski right on the property. Skiers will find Mount Sunapee, Ragged Mountain, and Whaleback each about fifteen minutes away. Guests also have privileges at the Slope and Shore Club on the lake, which offers swimming, boating, and fishing in warm weather.

One of the nicest activities here is simply gazing out of the window at those wonderful lake vistas.

HOW TO GET THERE: From I–89 take either New London exit. Halfway through New London, turn at the Lake Sunapee Bank. This is Pleasant Street. Go about 2 miles, and the inn is on your left.

New London Inn
New London, New Hampshire 03257

INNKEEPERS: Donna and Keith Pomkoski

ADDRESS/TELEPHONE: P.O. Box 8; (603) 526–2791 or (800) 526–2791; fax (603) 526–2749

ROOMS: 25, plus 2 suites; all with private bath; 1 with wheelchair access.

RATES: $95 to $150, double occupancy; EPB.

OPEN: All year.

FACILITIES AND ACTIVITIES: Dinner, bar. Wheelchair access to dining room and bar. Nearby: Skiing, theater, golf, two public beaches, water sports, shopping.

This college-town inn has been restored to the grandeur it had in 1792 when it began serving the traveler. The changes have been faithful to detail, even right down to the Federal-period sign that hangs in front of the inn. This restoration has been a tremendous job, and I applaud the effort. The gardens are lovely, as well.

As you approach the inn, you immediately appreciate the long veranda. There's also another one upstairs with the rooms. Do come up and try the rockers. Rooms in the inn are large, airy, and comfortable. Each one is decorated differently, and one is specially equipped, bathroom and all, for handicapped guests.

Cool cream and green are the colors of the dining room. It has large windows, and the original fireplace is still working. For a 200-year-old fireplace, that's a lot of fires! The dining room's gracious ambience is well suited to the wonderful food.

The dinner menu changes seasonally and features such enticing appetizers as mushrooms with seafood stuffing and scallops wrapped in bacon with maple glaze. Soups include New England clam chowder and a changing soup du jour. Innovative entrees might include veal Gregoire—sautéed veal topped with lobster, asparagus, mushrooms, and hollandaise—or pork tenderloin wrapped in bacon, finished with brown sugar–glazed apples. Fresh seafood is always on the menu. Boy, it's hard to choose just one dish! Desserts are very good and prepared daily. Breakfasts feature freshly squeezed orange or grapefruit juice.

The town of New London, home of Colby-Sawyer College, still conveys the feeling of a nineteenth-century village. From its wide main streets, fields, fences, and gracious houses to the beautiful mountains, it's just a lovely place to be. Its location in the Mount Sunapee Lake Region means that there are three lakes close by that offer all the water sports. The golf is nice because there is no waiting, and there is good skiing.

This is a beautiful part of the world at any time of the year, so come on up.

New London Barn Playhouse

In the summer months the stage of the New London Barn Playhouse is lit for a full season of dramatic and musical entertainment suitable for the whole family. Well known on the summer-stock circuit, the theater is one of the oldest in New England. Special events and children's shows are also staged here from June through August. Regular performances are at 8:00 P.M during the week, at 5:00 P.M. on Sunday, and at 2:00 P.M. on Wednesday. Call for information on the full schedule. Tickets are reasonably priced; call the box office at (603) 526–4631 or (800) 633–2276.

The 1785 Inn
North Conway, New Hampshire 03860

INNKEEPERS: Charles and Rebecca Mallar

ADDRESS/TELEPHONE: Route 16 (mailing address: P.O. Box 1785); (603) 356–9025 or (800) 421–1785; fax (603) 356–6081

E-MAIL: the1785inn@aol.com

WEB SITE: www.the1785inn.com

ROOMS: 16, plus 1 suite; 12 with private bath.

RATES: $69 to $199, double occupancy; EPB.

OPEN: All year.

FACILITIES AND ACTIVITIES: Dinner, bar, lounge. Wheelchair access to dining room. Swimming pool, cross-country skiing. Nearby: Golf, tennis, canoeing, fishing, skiing.

*T*he 1785 Inn is one of the oldest houses in all of Mount Washington Valley. It was built in 1785 by Capt. Elijah Dinsmore. Records indicate that Captain Dinsmore received a license to "keep a Publik House" in 1795. In addition to being a public house, the lovely old inn served as a stagecoach stop. The chimney and dining room fireplace with brick oven are original to the house. They form a beehive structure the size of an entire room in the center of the inn.

Guest accommodations are ample. The Mallars have completely refurbished the inn and done such a fine job. I find the in-room sinks a very nice feature in rooms with shared baths.

There are two living areas; both have fireplaces, and one has a television set. They are furnished with attractive chairs and couches for your comfort. The handsome old oak icebox is a conversation piece and a beautiful piece of furniture. The tavern has a large bar, a wood-burning stove, and good sitting areas. There is light classical music here at times.

The views from the porch–dining room are just lovely. The food is inventive and very good. One dinner dish is raspberry duck: duck roasted with a brandy-laced raspberry sauce and served on wild rice. There are several veal selections, and, of course, seafood and chicken. The desserts are wild. Chocolate velvet. Coffee butter-crunch pie, as featured in *Bon Appétit*. Becky's wondrous raspberry desserts.

Candlelight casts a romantic glow throughout the evening, so take your time and enjoy your meal and fine wines. The wine list has been called "one of the finest in the world" by *Wine Spectator* magazine.

This is a nice inn, surrounded by many activities and serving good food—what more can you want?

HOW TO GET THERE: Take Route 16 north. The inn is on the left just before you come to Route 16A.

Stonehurst Manor
North Conway, New Hampshire 03860

INNKEEPER: Peter Rattay

ADDRESS/TELEPHONE: Route 16; (603) 356–3113 or (800) 525–9100; fax (603) 356–3217

WEB SITE: www.stonehurstmanor.com

ROOMS: 15 in the manor, 10 in the annex adjoining the manor; 23 with private bath, air-conditioning, cable TV, radio.

RATES: $53 to $83 per person; MAP. Package rates available.

OPEN: All year.

FACILITIES AND ACTIVITIES: Breakfast, dinner. Wheelchair access to dining room. Bar. Pool, tennis, hot tub, cross-country skiing and showshoeing on 65 kilometers of groomed trails. Nearby: Swimming, hiking, fishing, skiing.

*T*his century-old mansion is a fine country inn. Set back from the highway among stately pine trees, it makes you think you are going back in time, and in a way you are.

The front door is huge. Once inside, you see beautiful oak woodwork and a wonderful wall-to-wall carpet. The room to the left is all wicker and all comfort. Ahead of you is the warm living room, with walls full of books and a huge fireplace. The unusual screen and andirons were made in England. To the right of the fireplace is a 12-foot curved window seat of another era. The lounge area has a two-seat bar, just the right size.

Relax in a high-back wicker chair in one of the inn's four dining rooms, which have been recommended by many publications and also won the Silver Spoon Award. Enjoy the fine gourmet dining, prepared by a chef who has twice been named New Hampshire chef of the year. There are many appetizers; the escargots are divine, as is the smoked salmon. Choose from the good soups and salads—the Caesar, prepared tableside, is glorious. The eighteen entrees are all so good. Chicken with wood-baked maple yams, roast duck with blackberry sauce, and rack of lamb for two. Oh my! There is a special wood-fired stone oven for pizzas. They are sensational, and there are a dozen different ones.

The manor staircase is a beauty, and the large rooms are meticulously appointed. Fantastic wallpapers and beautiful carpets all add to this great inn. The third-floor rooms have windows at odd angles, dictated by the roofline of the house. Some rooms have porches, and one has a stained-glass door going out to its porch. There is a lot of lovely stained glass throughout the inn. On the second floor, in one of the hall bathrooms, is a wood-enclosed steel bathtub. Be sure to take a look at it; it is quite a sight. Seven guest rooms have fireplaces. The inn was the country estate of the Bigelow carpet family, so of course the inn cat's name is Mrs. Bigelow.

Cocktails are served around the pool in the summer. Swimming or playing tennis will keep you busy, or, like me, you might want to just sit and relax.

There are a variety of walking and hiking experiences from the inn. Sixty-five kilometers of groomed trails await you.

HOW TO GET THERE: The inn is on Route 16, 1⁷⁄₁₀ miles north of North Conway Village.

Follansbee Inn
North Sutton, New Hampshire 03260 、

INNKEEPERS: Dave and Cathy Beard

ADDRESS/TELEPHONE: P.O. Box 92; (603) 927–4221 or (800) 626–4221

ROOMS: 23; 11 with private bath. No-smoking inn.

RATES: $90 to $130, double occupancy; EPB.

OPEN: All year.

FACILITIES AND ACTIVITIES: Beer and wine license, for inn guests only. Cross-country skiing from the inn, swimming, boating, bicycles. Nearby: Downhill skiing, golf, antiquing.

The Follansbee Inn is an 1840 New England farmhouse located on Kezar Lake. It has its own pier and private beach. A sailboard, paddleboat, rowboat, kayak, and canoe are provided for your pleasure. Or perhaps you'd like to take a swim in this lovely lake? The innkeepers are always willing to pack a lunch for a secluded picnic on the lake's island or for hiking up Mount Kearsarge.

A wood-burning stove makes the living room cozy and homey. One sitting room has a well-stocked service bar for houseguests. Guests are encouraged to play the piano or guitar. The rooms are recently refurbished and are nice. The innkeepers have thoughtfully purchased very good mattresses. The upstairs halls are wide enough to have space for some interesting furniture. There are plants all over the inn, no televisions, and lots of good books. The inn's facilities are not well suited to children under ten.

The dining room has comfortable captain's chairs and touches of chintz and linen. These are very pleasant surroundings in which to relax and savor the food. Breakfast, served around large tables with other guests, includes homemade granola, fresh fruit, muffins, and a hot dish such as an egg casserole or pancakes. A chalkboard menu for the night's dinner is shown at breakfast each day. One entree is served each evening. It might be rack of lamb, a chicken dish, roast pork, their special crab-and-shrimp casserole, a pasta dish, or something else equally delicious. The desserts are homemade. How about some chocolate cheesecake, chocolate eclair tart, or baked Alaska pie?

There is much to do in the area. You can go play a game of tennis or golf, take a hike or bicycle ride, or go picnicking. Maps are provided for interesting day trips, or you can just sit and relax on the front-porch rockers. In winter alpine skiing is nearby, and cross-country skiing is from the door of the inn.

North Sutton's old church is right next door. You might want to set your watch by its chiming clock.

HOW TO GET THERE: Take I-91 north to Route 9 in Brattleboro, Vermont. Continue to Henniker, New Hampshire, and go north on Route 114 for 18 miles to North Sutton. The inn is behind the church. From Boston take I-93 North to I-89 at Concord. Follow I-89 to exit 10 and turn left off the exit; continue 2 miles to North Sutton.

Muster Field Farm Museum

Farming in the New Hampshire mountains wasn't easy in the 1800s—still isn't easy now. By the late nineteenth century many farmers in the area realized they'd make a bit more money if they opened their farmhouses to paying guests, and the villages of North Sutton, Sutton, Sutton Mills, and all the other Suttons became popular destinations for travelers. The circa 1780 Matthew Harvey Homestead was one of the homes opened as a tavern of sorts, and today it and the 265-acre Muster Field Farm are open to the public as a museum.

Dedicated to educating visitors about agriculture and farm life, the museum includes farm implements and domestic utensils, an 1881 springhouse, a blacksmith shop, an 1810 schoolhouse, and demonstration flower and vegetable gardens. Activities are common throughout the summer season—you might be able to take a hay ride, for instance. Fresh eggs, milk, and locally grown berries and other produce are often here for sale. Admission is $3 for adults, $1 for children 6 to 12, and free for younger children. A craft show with more than 100 exhibitors is held here on the weekend before Labor Day. Traditional crafts and farming methods and tasks are demonstrated at this special Farm Day. Call (603) 927–4276 for hours and other information.

Home Hill Inn 💟
Plainfield, New Hampshire 03781

INNKEEPERS: Victoria and Stephane du Roure, owners

ADDRESS/TELEPHONE: River Road; (603) 675–6165; fax (603) 675–5220

WEB SITE: www.homehillinn.com

ROOMS: 7, plus 2 suites; all with private bath; 4 with working fireplaces.

RATES: $150 to $245, double occupancy; continental breakfast.

OPEN: All year except Monday and Tuesday.

FACILITIES AND ACTIVITIES: Dinner, bar, lounge. Swimming pool, tennis court, cross-country skiing, fishing in Connecticut River, walking trails. Nine-hole golf course for guests only.

The brochure said Home Hill Inn and French Restaurant, and I could hardly wait to get here. At the inn's authentic French restaurant, the food presentation is picture-perfect and the taste is elegant. No gravies, only sauces, and no flour, cornstarch, or fillers are allowed.

The contemporary menu changes every day. The continental breakfast of juice, croissants, butter, jams, and coffee is a fine way to start the day.

The rooms are charming. There are French and American antiques, reproductions, and comfort. The lounge-library is lovely; in fact, you will find it hard to find any fault with this inn.

The carriage house, also on the property, has six bedrooms, each with a bath and a fireplace. This is a nice addition to the inn. I stayed in one of these rooms during my last trip.

The inn is on twenty-five acres, only 500 yards from the Connecticut River. There are a swimming pool (a bar is out here), tennis courts, and cross-country skiing. Any season, any reason, head for Home Hill.

HOW TO GET THERE: Take I–89 to exit 20. Follow Route 12A south 3 miles to River Road and turn right. In 3½ miles you'll find the inn on the left.

Philbrook Farm Inn
Shelburne, New Hampshire 03581

INNKEEPERS: Connie Leger and Nancy Philbrook

ADDRESS/TELEPHONE: 881 North Road; (603) 466–3831

ROOMS: 19, plus 9 cottages with fireplaces; 10 rooms and all cottages with private bath. 6 cottages have housekeeping arrangements. Pets welcome in cottages. Cottages open mid-May to Columbus Day.

RATES: $125 to $155, double occupancy, MAP (private bath); $115, double occupancy, MAP (shared bath); $700 per week, housekeeping cottages; $145 per night, MAP, one-room cottages. No credit cards.

OPEN: All year except April and October 31 to December 26.

FACILITIES AND ACTIVITIES: BYOB. Wheelchair access to dining room and first floor but not to rest rooms. Library, pool table, Ping-Pong, swimming pool, cross-country skiing, snowshoeing, hiking. Nearby: Downhill skiing.

Philbrook Farm started as an inn in 1861. Now listed on the National Register of Historic Places, it is still an inn and still owned by the Philbrooks, who run it in fine New England tradition.

Everything you eat here is prepared from scratch in their kitchens. The baked goods are made daily. One entree is served each night. Roasts of everything you can want—pork, beef, turkey—and on and on. The New England boiled dinner is a favorite, as is baked bean supper on Saturday night and roast chicken dinner on Sunday.

The downstairs playroom has Ping-Pong, a pool table, a piano, and fun. A lot of reading material can be found all over the inn. Fireplaces are also all over the inn. The inn has a wonderful selection of Philbrook Farm puzzles made by Connie's grandfather. They have large, ¼-inch-thick pieces and are just beautiful. A player piano, an old pump organ—where else can you find such unique things except in an inn?

Rooms are furnished with a lot of old family treasures. There are some nice four-posters and a wonderful collection of old bowl and pitcher sets. All the cottages are different. They sure are nice if you want to linger here a while. Some have dining rooms, most have fireplaces, and all have porches. If you are staying in a cottage, you can bring along your pet.

With more than 1,000 acres, the inn has plenty of room for you to roam any season of the year. Walking trails begin in the meadow in front of the inn, taking you to the river, through a white birch grove, and on three meandering trails back home. Look across their fields to the Carter-Moriah and Presidential mountain ranges. Behind the inn rises the Mahoosuc Range. This is the Androscoggin Valley. The inn cats are Felix and Spice, and the inn dog, Valkerie, is a German shorthair pointer.

HOW TO GET THERE: The inn is 1½ miles off Route 2. From Route 2 take Meadow Road. Cross the railroad tracks and then a bridge. Turn right at the crossroads and go ½ mile to the inn, which is on North Road.

Snowvillage Inn
Snowville, New Hampshire 03849

INNKEEPERS: Kevin, Caitlin, and Maggie Flynn

ADDRESS/TELEPHONE: P.O. Box 68; (603) 447–2818 or (800) 447–4345

E-MAIL: snowvill@nxi.com

WEB SITE: www.snowvillageinn.com

ROOMS: 18, all with private bath; 4 with fireplace.

RATES: $99 to $249, per person, double occupancy; MAP available.

OPEN: All year.

FACILITIES AND ACTIVITIES: Bar, lounge, sauna, cross-country skiing, showshoeing, tennis, nature trails. Nearby: Swimming, fishing, canoeing, hiking, downhill skiing.

*I*n the winter Snowville lives up to its name. It snows, and it is pristine and beautiful all around. The view from the inn is breathtaking. Mount Washington and the whole Presidential Range greet your eyes wherever you look. In summer at the top of Foss Mountain, right at the inn, you can eat your fill of wild blueberries.

The guest rooms are comfortable and spacious, with tons of towels in luscious colors. The rooms are named after writers (funny, I did not find an Elizabeth Squier room), some have fireplaces, and all have private baths.

The living room, with its huge fireplace and nice couches, makes this an inn for rest and relaxation. There are a service bar, a lounge area, and books everywhere. A huge porch surrounds part of the inn. I could sit here all day and enjoy the incredible views.

Dinner is a delight in the very nice dining room. I could hardly decide between the home-baked sour cream rolls and rolls with sun-dried tomato and basil. Soups like fresh tomato and corn chowder or wild mushroom, apple, and pistachio bisque are delicious and lead the way to wonderful entrees like roasted duck with a blueberry green-peppercorn sauce, or medallions of veal sautéed with apples and calvados brandy cream sauce. The menu changes often, but rack of lamb, pork tenderloin, and roasted duck are almost always available, with different sauces and accompaniments.

Can you still find room for dessert? Who can resist when you have wonderful things like chocolate carrot cake or frozen lemon mousse with raspberry sauce.

You can work it off with a game of tennis on the inn court or, in winter, on 13 kilometers of cross-country trails; ski rentals are available. Sledding is also fun.

Crystal Lake is nearby for swimming, fishing, and canoeing. Remember, though, shopping is nearby.

HOW TO GET THERE: Outside of Conway on Route 153, go 5 miles to Crystal Lake. Turn left, follow the sign to Snowville, and go about 1½ miles. Turn right at the inn's sign, and go up the hill ¾ mile to the inn.

Foxglove
Sugar Hill, New Hampshire 03585

INNKEEPERS: Janet and Walter Boyd

ADDRESS/TELEPHONE: Route 117 at Lovers Lane, Sugar Hill;
(603) 823-8840; fax (603) 823-5755

E-MAIL: foxgloveinn@compuserve.com

WEB SITE: www.foxgloveinn.com

ROOMS: 6, all with private bath.

RATES: $85 to $165, double occupancy; EPB. MAP available in
foliage season.

OPEN: All year.

FACILITIES AND ACTIVITIES: Breakfast, dinner, BYOB. Conference
room for small executive retreats. Nearby: Tennis, swimming, hiking,
cross-country and downhill skiing, snowshoeing, and much, much more.

*S*ugar Hill is a wonder. When the lupine is in bloom, it's one of the
most beautiful sights I've seen—the fields are a blaze of color. This is
the village you must see to believe it's real. The meetinghouse was
built in 1831, and the post office has one room.

Foxglove, at Lovers Lane, is made for all ages of lovers. When I last spoke
to Walter, he reported a lot of snow had fallen. To be up here with it all white
has to be just beautiful. There are local cross-country trails nearby. Also not
too far away are four major ski areas. Anyone for ice skating? Local ponds
await. There's a glass porch that's really a picture window looking out at
wildlife and sheer beauty—apple trees and maybe a deer. The fireplaces are
warm and so inviting. So is dinner; some unusual choices for seating are
offered in a sitting room for two, in the innkeepers' library with a stone fireplace, on the porch, or, how about the dining room? Try the good soups—
black bean, cream of cauliflower, Belgian carrot, and more. There are good
salads; entrees may be grilled corn-cob smoked ham steak with apple cream
sauce and fresh chives served with whipped sweet potatoes and corn bread.
Maybe tenderloin of beef, shrimp, or poached salmon. The desserts are awesome; home-baked fruit pie or tart, strawberry rhubarb or maybe bittersweet
chocolate torte. Way to go, Elizabeth! Eating my way through New England.
What a life.

Accommodations are grand. Rooms are named so you won't get lost,
laughs Walter. The Garden Room has a deck, indoor and outdoor shower,
hot tub, king-size bed, and sitting area, all looking at the forest. Oh my. The

Paisley Room is lovely; the artwork in the inn is glorious. The Gingham Room is on a corner; Mrs. Harmes is a turret with magnificent views; the Blue Room is a favorite for honeymooners; and Serengheti speaks for itself. A small sitting room with a TV is between Gingham and Blue.

Breakfasts are well served. Extra-thick orange French toast is a winner, but there are also steamed eggs, pancakes, and more.

Do ask to see their beautiful cat.

HOW TO GET THERE: Take I–93 to exit 38. Go right on Route 18 for ½ mile. Go left on Route 117 to the inn, $2^3/_{10}$ miles on the right. From I–91 take exit 17. Follow Route 302 east 16 miles. Turn right onto Route 117 to the inn, $5^6/_{10}$ miles on the left.

Sunset Hill House
Sugar Hill, New Hampshire 03585

INNKEEPERS: The Henderson family: Lon, Nancy, Mary Pearl, and Adeline

ADDRESS/TELEPHONE: Sunset Hill Road; (603) 823–5522 or (800) 786–4455; fax (603) 823–5738

E-MAIL: innkeeper@sunsethillhouse.com

WEB SITE: www.sunsethillhouse.com

ROOMS: 27, plus 3 suites; all with private bath; 2 with Jacuzzi; some with fireplace.

RATES: $100 to $295, double occupancy; EPB. MAP rates available.

OPEN: All year.

FACILITIES AND ACTIVITIES: Dinner daily from mid-May to November 1 and Thursday through Sunday the rest of the year. Full license. Meeting room, art gallery, swimming pool, cross-country skiing, hiking, golf. Nearby: Almost anything you might want to do.

The Sunset Hill House is perched on a 1,700-foot ridge with unparalleled views of New Hampshire's Presidential Mountain Range to the east and Vermont's Green Mountains to the west.

The inn was built in 1832, in an era of grand hotels and resorts, and is Victorian in style. The living rooms have a view as well as fireplaces and an old piano.

There are many rooms and suites. Two have Jacuzzis, and all have private baths and views no matter which way you look. They're very nicely furnished and comfortable. Some have a fireplace, and some have a bow window.

The tavern offers lighter pub fare, including a pizza of the day and stir-fry of the day. My favorite dish was rotini and hot linguine salad tossed in a puree of olive oil, green onions, peas, garlic, sun-dried tomatoes, and cheese, and topped with marinara sauce, mixed greens, and a creamy parsley dressing. Oh my!

But there's more. A salad with apple and maple walnut vinaigrette dressing sounds wonderful. I'll have to order it the next time I come here.

The dinner menu opens with crispy duck with an Asian plum sauce, grilled crab cakes, and good soups and salads. The entrees include roast pork loin, sautéed chicken breast, broiled trout, and tenderloin of beef, or the chef will accommodate any dietary preference. All you have to do is ask.

I like what Lon and Nancy call the 3 Ms—the Majesty of the Mountains, the Magic Nature of a Country Inn, and the Management of Every Detail.

This is an inn with many special spots. I especially liked the art gallery in a wide hall. All the works are by local artists and are for sale. On the terrace level is a huge room for business meetings, weddings, and receptions. On the grounds is a lovely heated swimming pool. And just down the road a few miles is all the majesty of Franconia Notch State Park, one of the most scenic oases in New England.

HOW TO GET THERE: From I–93 take exit 38 to Route 117 to the top of Sugar Hill. Turn left on Sunset Hill Road. From I–91 take exit 17 to Route 302 East. Proceed approximately 18 miles to Route 117. Drive to the top of Sugar Hill and turn right on Sunset Hill Road.

Dexter's

Sunapee, New Hampshire 03782

INNKEEPERS: Holly and Michael Durfor

ADDRESS/TELEPHONE: 258 Stagecoach Road; (603) 763-5571 or (800) 232-5571

E-MAIL: dexters@tds.net

WEB SITE: www.bbhost.com/dextersinn

ROOMS: 17, plus 1 cottage; all with private bath. Wheelchair access to specially equipped room and bath for handicapped.

RATES: $115 to $165, double occupancy; EPB. $390 per day for 4 guests in cottage, MAP; $1,600 weekly (no meals).

OPEN: June 15 to October 15.

FACILITIES AND ACTIVITIES: Tennis, swimming pool, recreation barn, horseshoes, shuffleboard.

The main house was built in 1801 by an artisan, Adam Reddington. He earned his living by carving, from the huge knurls of the many fine maples on the grounds, the bowls in which sailing ships carried their compasses. In 1948 the house became a small country inn.

Dexter's is a nice family inn that welcomes children. Holly and Michael run the inn with the help of two young innkeepers, Hartwell and Hayley-Marie, born in 1985 and 1988. Never too soon to start learning.

Your day starts with juice and coffee served in your room at a time you set the night before. Or you can be really spoiled and have a New England breakfast tray in bed. How about some eggs Benedict, French toast, or pancakes to start your day right? These are rooms you'll want to linger in. They are a bit above average, with marvelous wallpapers, heavenly pillows made of feathers, fresh fruit and flowers, and antique beds.

The living room–library has more than 500 books, magazines, and newspapers. It offers lots of comfort and charm, along with a fireplace. Two television rooms and a breezy screened porch offer more room for relaxing.

Outdoor sports? You name it. Tennis is taken seriously here. Three all-weather Plexicushion tennis courts with a pro and shop (run by outside management) are provided for your enjoyment. After a game you can cool off in the lovely outdoor swimming pool. A horseshoe pit and shuffleboard are also available. In springtime the lake trout and salmon are close to the surface and hungry, so come all you anglers. Spring is always late up here, so you have a longer season. For a good summer or fall activity, some of the loveliest walking and hiking trails are right on the inn's property.

There is a special recreation room in the barn for all ages, but it is keyed to those under seventeen who need a place of their own.

HOW TO GET THERE:
Take I–89 out of Concord and follow exit 12 to Route 11 West for 5½ miles. Turn left on Winn Hill Road for 1½ miles to the inn. Or take I–91 out of Springfield and follow exit 8 to Claremont, New Hampshire, to Route 103/11 East for 18 miles to Newport. Follow Route 103 left onto Young Hill Road for 1²/10 miles to the inn.

League of New Hampshire Craftsmen's Fair

The oldest continual crafts fair in the nation, dating from the 1930s, is held annually at the base of Mount Sunapee during the second week of August. For nine splendid days, the fair features craft demonstrations, artists' workshops, displays and sales of hand-crafted clothing, furnishings, jewelry, weaving, basketry, metalsmithing, and much more. A fabulous collection of the region's finest juried craftspeople are an inspiration to the thousands of visitors who come to the fair. The talent—well, let me just say, wow. Live theater and musical performances are a part of the excitement here.

The fair runs from 10:00 A.M. to 5:00 P.M. daily. Call for this year's exact dates. Admission (about $7.00 per adult, $4.00 for seniors, and free to children under twelve) includes all the exhibits and performances—and a return trip the next day so you can see anything you missed the first time. For information call (603) 224-3375.

The Inn at Sunapee
Sunapee, New Hampshire 03782

INNKEEPERS: Ted and Susan Harriman

ADDRESS/TELEPHONE: Burkehaven Hill Road (mailing address:
P.O. Box 336); (603) 763-4444 or (800) 327-2466; fax (603) 763-9456

E-MAIL: innatsunapee@kear.net

WEB SITE: www.innatsunapee.com

ROOMS: 16, plus 5 suites; all with private bath.

RATES: $70, single; $95, double; $110 to $140, suite; EPB.

OPEN: All year except two weeks in November and April.

FACILITIES AND ACTIVITIES: Dinner. Bar, lounge, full license. Pool,
tennis, hiking. Nearby: Downhill skiing, cross-country skiing.

The Inn at Sunapee, an 1800s farmhouse with a classic wraparound porch, is nicely situated on a hilltop that overlooks beautiful Mount Sunapee. Nearby, Lake Sunapee is the second largest in New Hampshire, and it's a great spot for sailing, fishing, and waterskiing.

Attached to the house is a barn that has been turned into a lounge with a fieldstone fireplace and good couches. The views from the windows in here and in the dining room are spectacular any season of the year. If you like animals, you'll especially like watching the cows in the field across the road.

Most of all you'll enjoy the good food served here. The menu changes quite often. When I was here, there were New England crab cakes and Chinese spring rolls with spicy dipping sauce as appetizers. Poached salmon, a daily veal special, beef, and chicken are but a few of the foods served here. Holidays, I'm told, are really special.

Ted and Susan lived in the Far East and Southeast Asia for more than twenty-five years, and their wonderful collection of furnishings is used throughout the inn. Rooms are decorated with oak and iron furniture. Some rooms have wide-board pine floors. There is a cute and small, separate cottage; five accommodations are family suites. Everything about this inn is very gracious.

Children are welcome here. They'll enjoy the outdoor swimming pool, tennis court, and ten acres of woodland for hiking. They will also want to curl up with the inn Labrador or the cats. A sign on the door reads: DON'T LET THE INN CATS OUT.

HOW TO GET THERE: From Boston take I-93 north to Concord, New Hampshire. Then take I-89 north to exit 12 and follow Route 11 west to Sunapee. At the blinking light turn toward Sunapee Harbor. At the harbor you will see a park with a bandstand. Take the first right after the bandstand and go ½ mile up the hill to the inn.

The Tamworth Inn
Tamworth Village, New Hampshire 03886

INNKEEPERS: Virginia and Bob Schrader

ADDRESS/TELEPHONE: Main Street; (603) 323-7721

E-MAIL: inn@tamworth.com

WEB SITE: www.tamworth.com

ROOMS: 16, including 7 suites; all with private bath.

RATES: $115 to $235, double occupancy; EPB.

OPEN: All year except April.

FACILITIES AND ACTIVITIES: Sunday brunch, dinner. Pub, swimming pool, fishing, skiing, hiking. Nearby: Downhill skiing, Barnstormer's Theater.

Built in 1833, The Tamworth Inn is a rambling building in a lovely New England town. The inn sits across from the Congregational Church and a thoroughbred horse pasture.

The Swift River, true to its name, flows swiftly behind the inn. If you're looking for a memorable spot for your wedding, the riverside gazebo is great; if you're inclined toward fly-fishing, this is also the place for you. The hale and hearty might want to walk about a ¼ mile to the swimming hole. Anyone less adventuresome will find the inn's swimming pool just right.

The main attraction in town in the summer is the Barnstormer's Theater down the street, the oldest summer theater in New England. An "equity house," the theater offers eight different professional performances each summer. It certainly is nice to stay at the inn, have a tasty dinner, and walk to good theater.

There are lots of hiking trails in this area, and they are maintained by the Appalachian Mountain Club, the Tamworth Outing Club, and the Wonalancet Outing Club. They are within walking distance of the inn. In winter these trails become cross-country ski and snowshoe trails.

Back at the inn, guests enjoy sitting by the fireplace; tea is served here in the afternoon. The Library is a quieter spot for reading, having a go at the games or puzzles, or watching a movie from the inn's selection of videos. There's a fireplace here, as well.

A big country breakfast is served in the breakfast room, or in good weather, on the patio overlooking the Swift River. The dining room is drawing food lovers from the city who enjoy having gourmet fare in a rural village setting. Lighter pub fare is served in the pub, known for its antique sled collection. When the bartender is off duty, guests do the honors and pay on the honor system.

Virginia and Bob have considerably upgraded the inn decor since they arrived. Rooms are decorated with antiques and original art; beds have firm orthopedic mattresses and down comforters. "We are in the sleep business, after all," says Bob. The Family & Friends suite, with four king-size beds, is ideal for larger families or groups of friends traveling together.

It's lovely here in summer, with the pool set amid landscaped gardens, and nearly two acres of lawns and gardens to enjoy. The gazebo on the banks of the Swift River has a hammock for two, plus several gliders and Adirondack chairs, the perfect spot to relax and be lulled to the sound of the gently rippling water. The cares of real life seem very far away.

HOW TO GET THERE: Tamworth is on Route 113, 3 miles northwest of the intersection of Routes 25 and 16.

The Birchwood Inn
Temple, New Hampshire 03084

INNKEEPERS: Judy and Bill Wolfe

ADDRESS/TELEPHONE: Route 45; (603) 878–3285; fax (603) 878-2179

E-MAIL: wolfe@birchwood.mv.com

ROOMS: 7; 5 with private bath.

RATES: $70 to $80; EPB. No credit cards.

OPEN: All year except two weeks in April and one week in November.

FACILITIES AND ACTIVITIES: Dinner served Tuesday through Saturday, weekends only in winter. Wheelchair access to dining room. BYOB. Nearby: Antiquing, downhill and cross-country skiing, hiking, hunting, golf, summer theater, lakes.

*T*he inn is in the Mount Monadnock region of New Hampshire, so there is plenty to do and see here. From the top of the mountain you can see four states, a nice reward for you hikers. There are trout waiting for the angler, much game for the hunter, plus golf, summer theater, horseback riding, and walking.

Bill and Judy are the owner-chefs and are very good at what they do. Roast duckling, chicken piccata, and creative seafood dishes are examples of their good food. They have she-crab soup, which is hard to find north of South Carolina. It is excellent. Homemade breads and desserts are created daily.

The dining room walls are covered with simply beautiful Rufus Porter murals.

Bill is an avid collector of model trains. I'm a train buff myself, so I got a real kick out of seeing Bill's collection all over the inn.

The inn history stretches back some two centuries to circa 1775. During this time many people have come and gone, one notable personage being Henry David Thoreau. A room at the inn is named for him. Other rooms have different themes and rather different sorts of names, such as "The Bottle Shop" and "The Music Room." The innkeepers will entertain you with the stories of how the rooms became so named. Say hello to Barney the bassett hound when you visit.

HOW TO GET THERE: Take Route 3 out of Boston to Nashua, New Hampshire, exit 8. Follow Route 101 to Milford to Route 45 to Temple.

The Chesterfield Inn
West Chesterfield, New Hampshire 03466

INNKEEPERS: Judy and Phil Hueber

ADDRESS/TELEPHONE: Route 9; (603) 256–3211 or (800) 365–5515; fax (603) 256–6131

E-MAIL: chstinn@sover.net

WEB SITE: www.chesterfieldinn.com

ROOMS: 13, plus 2 suites; all with private bath, air-conditioning, refrigerator, phone. Many rooms have a fireplace and/or a garden terrace; 1 has wheelchair access. Pets are welcome.

RATES: $150 to $275, double occupancy; EPB.

OPEN: All year.

Dinner Monday through Saturday. Wheelchair access to dining room. Full license. Ice skating. Nearby: Fishing, boating, skiing, swimming.

A tavern from 1798 to 1811, and then a farm, the inn opened in 1984 after extensive renovations by talented architect Rod Williams of The Inn at Sawmill Farms. Exposed beams, many of them part of the original structure, and walls paneled with boards that came from an old barn make for a warm and friendly atmosphere.

The guest rooms are spacious. Some rooms have balconies or garden patios, others have a fireplace, and all are scrumptious. They are done in soft shades of blues, greens, and pinks. They have nice amenities like clock radios and telephones (all different), including one in the bathroom. Good fluffy towels and an assortment of toiletries are here. To top it all off, each room has a refrigerator with juice, bottled spring water, beers, and wine.

The foyer has a large fireplace holding a bright red woodstove, and nice couches. It's a good place for cocktails.

Off the foyer is the parlor, with a fireplace and good couches. A window seat overlooks an outdoor patio.

The chef here rates three diamonds, and you'll see why when you taste his creations. What about starting with pumpkin risotto or an apple, smoked Gouda cheese, and proscuitto turnover? Main courses might include house-smoked duck breast fanned over a sweet potato and soy bean succotash or a boneless pork loin with chestnut stuffing. Or maybe halibut fillet wrapped in bok choy over a leek, pearl onion, and turnip ratatouille, or twin quails braised in a Moroccan stew accompanied by a spiced polenta.

The menu changes often, but whatever the choices, you'll dine well, right through to the tempting desserts. Not the least of the pleasures of the two dining rooms are the outside views.

The inn's grounds are full of perennial, herb, and vegetable gardens. The beautiful Connecticut River is a short walk from the inn, so bring along your canoe or fishing pole. Lake Spofford has boats for rent. Pisgah Park has hiking trails and two spring-fed ponds for swimming. In winter, skiing is close at hand, and the inn's pond is lighted for night skating under the stars. And all year you'll find good antiques shops and arts and crafts shops.

HOW TO GET THERE: Take exit 3 off I–91. Take Route 9 east, going over the border from Vermont to New Hampshire. The inn is 2 miles on your left. Turn left on Cross Road, then right into the driveway.

Spalding Country Inn
Whitefield, New Hampshire 03598

INNKEEPERS: Diane Cockrell and Michael Flinder

ADDRESS/TELEPHONE: 199 Mountain View Road; (603) 837–2572 or (800) 368–VIEW; fax (603) 837–3062

E-MAIL: dianeec@landmarknet.net

WEB SITE: www.spaldinginn.com

ROOMS: 36, plus 6 cottages; all with private bath and phone, cottages with fireplace.

RATES: $169 to $189, double occupancy, MAP; $109 to $139, double occupancy, EPB; $89 to $109, double occupancy, EP. Packages available. Six two-bedroom suites, $150, EPB; $200 MAP.

OPEN: June through October.

FACILITIES AND ACTIVITIES: Bar, TV room, library, card room, swimming pool, clay tennis courts, croquet lawn, and junior golf course. Nearby: Weathervane Theatre, Mountain View Golf Course, hiking, fishing.

*I*f you care to see how our parents and grandparents might have spent their summers years ago, come to the Spalding Country Inn. It's been welcoming people since the early 1800s.

It's easy to see the attraction. The inn is located on more than 200 acres with glorious White Mountain views. Families are welcome; many suites have two or three bedrooms, and some cottages as many as four. The cottages also have a living room, and each has its own fireplace; some have porches. For adults in search of a quiet getaway, the carriage house offers large, romantically furnished rooms. All the rooms and cottages are tastefully appointed, with direct-dial telephones and extra pillows and blankets.

White linen in the dining room is always a sign of good things to come, and starting with breakfast the choices are grand. Fresh juice, seasonal fruit, granola and yogurt, hot and cold cereals, pancakes, French toast, eggs any style, home fries, bacon, ham, omelets—the list goes on.

Everyone gathers for sociable cocktails before dinner, in the living room or on the front porch. The dinner menu changes nightly, except on Friday, which is always lobster night. Thai coconut soup sounds good. The salads are made of locally grown greens. Entrees range from the very popular Duck Bombay—a roasted duck covered with bacon and toasted almonds—to roasted tenderloin of beef with rosemary and madeira butter; grilled salmon fillet; shrimp scampi; roast loin of pork; and grilled lamb chops. These are but a few of the many choices. Did I hear dessert? Come on up and try some.

There is no dress requirement at the inn other than to be comfortable. And that's easy here. This is a glorious spot, inside and out, so do come up and enjoy a taste of yesteryear.

There's a bear or two—stuffed, of course—in the inn. Look for them. The children's corner is great; Buttermilk, the rocking cow, is here along with small wicker chairs and games.

HOW TO GET THERE: Take I-93 north to exit 41. Follow Route 116 through the village of Whitefield. Continue 1½ miles north of town and turn right on Mountain View Road.

Select List of
Other New Hampshire Inns

Rosewood Country Inn

67 Pleasant View Road
Brandford, NH 03221
(603) 938–5253 or (800) 938–5273
E-mail: info@rosewoodcountryinn.com
Web site: www.rosewoodcountryinn.com

11 rooms and suites, all with private bath; 1896 Victorian B&B inn. Special-event weekends held year-round.

Three Chimneys Inn/ffrost Sawyer Tavern

17 Newmarket Road
Durham, NH 03824
(603) 868–7800 or (888) 399–9777; fax (603) 868–5011
E-mail: chimney3@threechimneysinn.com
Web site: www.threechimneysinn.com

23 rooms, all with private bath, four-poster bed; 4 rooms with Jacuzzi and some with two-person tub; inn built in 1649 on the Oyster River.

Maple Hill Farm Country Inn B&B

200 Newport Road
New London, NH 03257
(603) 526–2248 or (800) 231–8637
E-mail: info@maplehillfarm.com
Web site: www.maplehillfarm.com

10 rooms, 6 with private bath; B&B in 1824 farmhouse. Six-person hot tub spa, indoor basketball court, farm animals. Full-service country inn in winter; B&B in summer. Specializes in group and family package deals with meals.

Nereledge Inn

River Road
P.O. Box 547
North Conway, NH 03860
(603) 356-2831
E-mail: info@nereledgeinn.com
Web site: www.nereledgeinn.com

*11 rooms, 5 ½ with private bath; full breakfast; game room, fireplace in
sitting room; B&B in 1787 farmhouse.*

The Inn at Kinney Hill

96 Woodman Road
South Hampton, NH 03827
(603) 394-0200 or (888) 687-4455
E-mail: dsoconnor@aol.com

*3 rooms plus 1 suite, all with private bath; full breakfast, afternoon tea, gourmet
French dinner on request; indoor heated lap pool, eight-person hot tub, and
workout area; billiard room.*

The Wolfeboro Inn

90 North Main Street
Wolfeboro, NH 03894
(603) 569-3016 or (800) 451-2389
Web site: www.wolfeboroinn.com

*44 rooms, all with private bath; original part of inn dates from 1812; banquet
facilities, swimming beach, cruise boat on Lake Winnepesaukee.*

Rhode Island

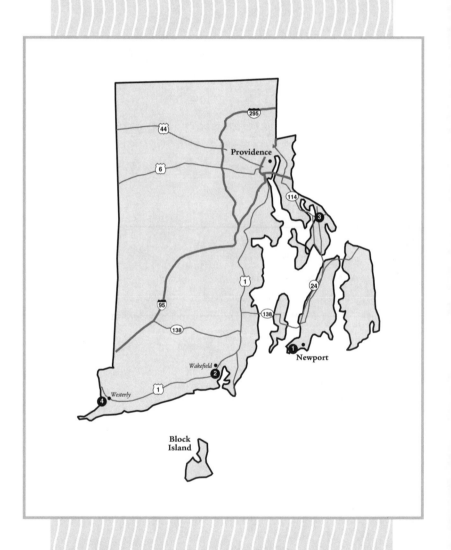

Rhode Island

Numbers on map refer to towns numbered below.

* A Top Pick Inn

Castle Hill Inn
Newport, Rhode Island 02840

INNKEEPER: Chuck Landers, manager

ADDRESS/TELEPHONE: 590 Ocean Drive; (401) 849–3800 or (888) 466–1355; fax (401) 849–3838

E-MAIL: info@castlehillinn.com

WEB SITE: www.castlehillinn.com

ROOMS: 25 rooms, including 2 suites; all with private bath, air-conditioning, TV, phone with data ports, voice mail, radios, CD players; most with fireplaces; many with whirlpools. 10 beach cottages available in summer only.

RATES: June to mid-September, $395 to $600, EPB; rest of year, $145 to $550, EPB. Beach house suites open late June to mid-September; $4,200 (weekly rentals only).

OPEN: All year except some weeks in January.

FACILITIES AND ACTIVITIES: Breakfast, lunch, Sunday jazz brunch, dinner. Decks with ocean views, Victorian garden and reflecting pool, private beach, walking trails. Nearby: Newport mansions, shops, sightseeing, dining.

If you can't have your own shingled summer home overlooking the ocean, here's the next best thing. The very Victorian mansion on a forty-acre peninsula was built in 1874 by Alexander Agassiz, a renowned scientist and explorer, whose photo hangs in the lobby. Near the house was his summer laboratory, where he pioneered in the study of marine life and oceanography.

Step into the wood-paneled sitting room of the inn and admire the intricate marquetry over the fireplace, an Oriental symbol for good fortune. The William Morris wallpaper in the halls and throughout the house set a proper Victorian mood. The main floor includes four dining rooms, including the Agassiz room, with its own fireplace, and the striking round Sunset Room, with a draped ceiling and windows all around to bring in the view.

Rhode Island Monthly magazine called Castle Hill the best all-around dining experience in the state, an evaluation you may second when you taste the chef's appetizers, such as white truffle mushroom and ricotta ravioli, and main courses like pan-roasted, pecan-crusted risotto di Mare; lobster, salmon, red snapper, and littlenecks cooked in Westport Gewürztraminer with arborio rice, winter vegetables, herbs, and Parmagiano-Reggiano; lightly smoked and grilled duck breast and leg confit with smoked Gouda mashed potatoes; or grilled aged beef tenderloin with three aioli. In good weather, you can have a drink and dine outside on the terraces, watching the yachts sail into Newport harbor.

Because the dining rooms are so popular, the first floor tends to be busy at mealtimes, so a more private small sitting room has been built on the second floor just for inn guests, who also enjoy a formal tea service here every afternoon.

Some of the nine bedrooms in the main house are paneled, and some have wallpaper. Second-floor rooms tend to be larger, but the top floor is cozy, with eaves, and many rooms have wonderful views. Six rooms in the recently remodeled Harbor House are more modern and have the bonus of private terraces with water views. The Chalet, Agassiz's former studio, has been transformed for functions such as the many weddings held on the property, and the rooms upstairs include a bridal suite. The remodeled beach houses near the entry to the estate are directly on the water, luxurious lairs that are available in summer by the week.

Wherever you stay, you'll enjoy the best in service and amenities, and just outside is a view a millionaire might envy.

HOW TO GET THERE: From Boston take I-93 South to Route 24 South to Route 114 South, which becomes Broadway in Newport. Continue down Broadway to Washington Square. Take a left onto Thames Street, pass the Brick Marketplace, and then bear right to the traffic light. At the light take a left (south) onto America's Cup Avenue and stay in the right-hand lane. Take a right onto Thames Street (just past the "Wave" statue and in front of the Red Parrot Restaurant). Continue down Thames to Wellington Avenue. Go right onto Wellington (across from the Shell station), and from this point on take every available right. This will take you past Fort Adams, Hammersmith Farm, Oceancliff, and the Coast Guard station. After going past the Coast Guard station, the road turns sharply to the right and then to the left. Castle Hill Inn is the first driveway on the right.

From I-95 North take exit 3A (in Rhode Island) to Route 138 East. Follow Route 138 over the Jamestown and Newport Bridges. Take first exit (Scenic Newport) off bridge. Take a right at the end of the exit ramp. At the second light take a right onto America's Cup Avenue. Stay in the right lane and go right onto Thames Street at the "Wave" statue. Follow the directions from above.

Vanderbilt Hall
Newport, Rhode Island 02840

INNKEEPER: Ted Horan, manager

ADDRESS/TELEPHONE: 41 Mary Street; (401) 846–6200 or (888) VAN–HALL; fax (401) 846–0701

WEB SITE: www.vanderbilthall.com

ROOMS: 50 rooms and suites, all with private bath, TV, telephone with data port, hair dryers, turndown service; many with whirlpool baths and heated towel bars.

RATES: Rooms, $95 to $445; suites, $295 to $645; EP. Service charge added to room and food bills. Many packages available.

OPEN: All year.

FACILITIES AND ACTIVITIES: Breakfast, lunch, dinner, afternoon tea. 24-hour room service, bar, roof deck, sitting rooms, billiards room, indoor pool, fitness room, sauna, steam room, whirlpool, patio. Nearby: Shops, beach, mansions, historic sites, scenic walks.

*T*he Vanderbilt family never lived in this fine hall; they gave it to the town of Newport, their longtime summer home, to serve as a rather opulent YMCA. But they would no doubt feel at home now that the 1909 building has been grandly renovated as a lodging, allowing visitors a taste of life as it was in Newport's gilded age.

You know you've arrived somewhere special when you enter the chandeliered entry, facing a lovely curved double stairway. But while the setting is grand, it is not pretentious. The sitting room is enormous, but the seating has been arranged into comfortable settings conducive to conversation, and there are books and magazines inviting you to settle in. And there are several intimate side rooms for more privacy.

Beyond is the music room, where afternoon tea is set out; a bar area; and the newly added Orangery, with plants, a greenhouse roof, ceiling fans, and latticework along the brick wall. Breakfast is served here along with light meals available from 11:00 A.M. to 11:00 P.M. Outside is a patio, and across the street, visible through the glass walls of the Orangery, is Newport's landmark Trinity Church, circa 1726.

The restoration was no mean task. The placement of the old rooms made for unusual spaces. When you ascend the graceful stair you'll find that rooms vary tremendously in size and shape, some long and narrow, others square, depending on how the configurations worked best. The result is five room categories, making it possible for almost everyone to afford some type of lodging. Furnishings are equally eclectic, with some canopy beds, some iron beds, and some Victorian wooden headboards, and there is a different magnificent armoire in every room. The former ballroom and theater became suites, and the third-floor quarters under the eaves were turned into skylit accommodations. Many rooms have themes, from tennis or polo to art deco or Victorian. All the rooms have high ceilings and well-appointed bathrooms, many with whirlpool baths and heated towel warmers. Don't miss going up to the fourth floor roof deck for a fabulous view of the harbor.

On the lower level is a very masculine billiards room with an antique-style table and leather furnishings, as well as the restored swimming pool, with a delightful sailing mural on the wall. You can work out in the adjacent small fitness room, equipped with a treadmill, bicycle, and rowing machine, then enjoy a sauna, whirlpool, or steam room, or maybe arrange for a massage.

The dining room, with fireplace, paneling, and electrified pewter gaslights, is a fitting setting for true gourmet fare. The seasonal menu might begin with such pleasures as foie gras terrine served with toasted brioche and muscat jelly, or wild mushroom risotto with spring asparagus. A duo of beef tenderloin and braised flank with baby vegetables and a red wine essence is an unusual main course, or there are classics such as lobster thermidor or chateaubriand for two. What to have for dessert? What a delicious dilemma. You won't go wrong with choices like the white chocolate and strawberry torte served with fruit compote—or the Key lime, pecan, chocolate, and bourbon pie, not to mention the cinnamon bread-and-butter pudding with ice cream.

When you step out the door of Vanderbilt Hall, you are in the midst of Newport's large historic district, a prize Colonial neighborhood, as well as 1 block from shops and the waterfront, and not far from the fabled mansions where the Vanderbilts did reside.

HOW TO GET THERE: From the north take Route 24 South and follow it until it becomes Route 114 South. Follow Route 114 South into downtown Newport until you can go no farther. At the traffic light turn left onto Thames Street and continue straight for approximately 50 yards. Take the first left onto Mary Street, and Vanderbilt Hall will be on your right, 1 block up.

From the south take I-95 North to Rhode Island exit 3, Route 138 East. Follow this for approximately 35 miles, follow the signs for the Jamestown and Newport Bridges, and cross over the two bridges. Take the first exit off the Newport Bridge, marked "Scenic Newport," and turn right at the bottom of the ramp. Proceed straight to the second light and bear left onto Thames Street. Continue straight through the next set of lights for approximately 150 yards and take the first left onto Mary Street. Vanderbilt Hall will be on your right, 1 block up.

Larchwood Inn
Wakefield, Rhode Island 02879

INNKEEPERS: Francis and Diann Browning

ADDRESS/TELEPHONE: 521 Main Street; (401) 783-5454 or
(800) 275-5450; fax (401) 783-1800

ROOMS: 19, in 2 buildings; 12 with private bath; some with phone.

RATES: $65 to $140, double occupancy; EP.

OPEN: All year.

FACILITIES AND ACTIVITIES: Breakfast, lunch, dinner. Bar, tavern,
Nearby: Swimming, fishing, skiing.

Over the fireplace in the homey bar is carved "Fast by an Ingle Bleez-ing Finely," a quotation from the Scots' Robert Burns. The Tam O'Shanter Cocktail Lounge serves up a delectable lunch that includes huge sandwiches, good salads, hamburgers, and quiche.

There are four other lovely rooms for dining or private entertaining. Dinner ideas are rack of lamb for one or two, lots of fresh fish, and a beefeater's special: a thick slice of prime rib Angus. Breakfast is very ample. I really like the special French toast topped with either sour cream or whipped cream and warmed strawberries. Perhaps you'd enjoy croissants or poached eggs with hollandaise and mushrooms and artichoke hearts. Come summer, the meals are served on the covered patio in the garden.

Some of the nicely decorated rooms are in the Holly House across the street. It is the same age as the inn; both were built in the 1830s. Diann has a real touch. The wallpapers are glorious, and one room is an especially lovely salmon color. The furnishings are beautiful. Butch, the inn cat, is a also beauty; maybe you can rent him for a night.

The inn is situated in the heart of Rhode Island's beautiful South County. Saltwater beaches for bathing, fishing, and sunning are close by. In the winter it is only a short drive to Pine Top and Yawgoo Valley for skiing.

Rhode Island isn't all that big, you know, so it's never very far from anywhere to the Larchwood Inn.

HOW TO GET THERE: Take I–95 to Route 1. Exit from Route 1 at Pond Street, follow it to the end, and the inn will be immediately in front of you.

South County Museum

Not far from Wakefield is the town of Narragansett, on the western side of beautiful Narragansett Bay. Take Route 1A to the Narragansett Town Beach and Pier. A bit north of the pier, opposite the beach pavilion, you'll find Canonchet Farm and the South County Museum (401–783–5400). It holds a collection of more than 10,000 artifacts that demonstrate the history and culture of this area and its varied settlers. From farm tools and domestic implements to a gentleman's study and children's dolls, dollhouses, and trains, the museum imaginatively presents a real sense of the passage of time through three centuries. Next to the main museum building is a barn with displays of carriages and wagons; on the property are hiking trails, a fitness course, and lots of pretty places to picnic. The museum is open from May through October. A small admission fee is charged; parking is free. The farm and museum host frequent festivals throughout the summer; call for a schedule of such events as a quilt show, an herb gardening day, a children's fair, and an antique car show.

Nathaniel Porter Inn
Warren, Rhode Island 02885

INNKEEPERS: Viola and Robert Lynch

ADDRESS/TELEPHONE: 125 Water Street;
(401) 245-6622

ROOMS: 3, all with private bath.

RATES: $90, single or double occupancy; continental breakfast.

OPEN: All year except Christmas Eve, Christmas Day, July 4, and Labor Day.

FACILITIES AND ACTIVITIES: Dinner. Tavern. Nearby: Boating and swimming at town beach.

*T*he inn is named after Nathaniel Porter, who, at the age of twelve, established his place in history when he was among the seventy-seven Minutemen who stood on Lexington Green and fired the first shots of the American Revolution in 1775. The current owners are direct descendants of that young man.

The restored inn dates back to 1795, when it was built by a wealthy sea captain. It is listed on the National Register of Historic Places. Some of the earliest documented stencils were discovered under numerous layers of paint and wallpaper. The parquet floors, dating back to the early 1800s, are just beautiful, and so are the wide-board floors. The French mural in one of the parlors dates from about 1810, and all the window glass was hand-blown in Germany.

The front parlor has nice romantic tables for two, and there are five fireplaces in the dining rooms. The waitresses here are called hostesses. They describe everything on your plate to you. Very professional. The menu changes twice a year and is extensive, offering more than enough choices for all tastes. There are many appetizers as well as a soup of the day. I had grilled shrimp in a strawberry-thyme sauce. What a nice and different flavor it had! I also tasted the smoked mussels and the excellent seafood chowder.

I get hungry just thinking about the entrees. I had filet mignon with roasted hazelnuts, flamed with cognac. It was tender and delicious. The next time I visit the inn, I'm going to try the whiskey cream shrimp. The shrimp are sautéed in butter, flamed with Jim Beam, finished with cream and Dijon mustard, and served in puff pastry.

Everything is spectacular and well presented. Need I mention desserts? Ambrosia. Add to this a wonderful wine list with some interesting Australian wines.

So off to bed. Two rooms have canopied double beds with lovely antiques, and the other has twins. At night the inn is lighted by window candles and chandeliers.

HOW TO GET THERE: From Providence take I–195 east to Route 114. Go south on Route 114 to Warren. At the first traffic light in town, go right onto Water Street. The inn is in 4 blocks on the right.

A Colonial Christmas Celebration

Each December at the Nathaniel Porter Inn dinner guests can join the colonial yule log festivities. Five or six such evenings are planned within the second and third weeks of the month, and each of these full-evening events begins about 6:00 P.M. and ends around 10:00 P.M. The Pawtuxet Rangers fife-and-drum corps performs outside the inn, and guests parade into the inn under their crossed swords when their initial performance ends. Cocktails and fruit and cheese are served in one of the inn's pretty dining parlors, then a full four-course dinner is served while the corps performs inside throughout the evening and toasts the guests at tableside. After dinner the corps plays the Christmas hymn "Joy to the World" as they carry in the traditional yule log, which is set ablaze in the inn's fireplace. Each guest makes a wish for the New Year on a sprig of holly and tosses it into the flames. A Christmas carol sing-along follows, and the evening ends with the sharing of wassail. A night to remember.

If this event ($49.95 per person, by reservation only) is fully booked, perhaps you could make arrangements to come to the inn in early January to join in the Twelfth Night celebration. This single-night event ($39.95 per person, by reservation only) includes a traditional roast goose dinner with all the trimmings and a light-hearted appointment of the King and Queen of Misrule from among the guests.

Shelter Harbor Inn
Westerly, Rhode Island 02891

INNKEEPER: Jim Dey

ADDRESS/TELEPHONE: 10 Wagner Road; (401) 322-8883; fax (401) 322-7907

ROOMS: 24, all with private bath, TV, and phone; some with fireplace and private deck.

RATES: $96 to $172, double occupancy; EPB.

OPEN: All year.

FACILITIES AND ACTIVITIES: Breakfast, lunch, dinner, Sunday brunch, bar. Private ocean beach, two paddle tennis courts with night lighting, hot tub, croquet court. Nearby: Golf, boat-launching area, tennis, summer theater, Block Island ferry, Mystic Seaport, Mystic Marinelife Aquarium.

BUSINESS TRAVEL: Desk and phone in all rooms; conference room; fax available; corporate rates.

*I*f you would like guest passes to a 3-mile stretch of uncluttered ocean beach located just a mile from a lovely old country inn, find your way to Rhode Island and the Shelter Harbor Inn. Bring the children. When they're not playing in the ocean surf, there's a salt pond near the inn for them to explore.

Ten of the guest rooms are in the restored farmhouse, and ten more are located in the barn. The rest of the rooms are in the carriage house, which is a lovely addition to the inn. There is a large central living room in the barn that opens onto a spacious deck—how ideal for families! Or, if your business group is small, have a meeting right here. There is also a library with comfortable leather chairs where you can relax with a book.

The menu reflects the location of the inn, and at least half the items offered are from the sea. The finnan haddie is specially smoked in Narragansett. You can choose your place to eat—the formal dining room, the small private dining room with a fireplace, or the glassed-in terrace room. The sunporch has been turned into a pub bar, and plants are everywhere. If weather permits, take a drink out to the secluded terrace. On a clear day you can see Block Island from the third floor of the inn. There's a hot tub up here, plus a barbecue grill.

If you can tear yourself from the beach, there is much to see around here. You are about halfway between Mystic and Newport. The ferry to Block Island leaves from Point Judith. It is an hour-long ride, and when you arrive on Block Island, you will find it a super spot for bicycling. You can charter boats for fishing or stand at the edge of the surf and cast your line into the sea. In the evenings there are Theater by the Sea in nearby Matunuck and the Colonial Theatre in Westerly.

HOW TO GET THERE: From the south take I-95 to exit 92. Turn right onto Route 2 for 1 mile to Route 78. Continue to a stoplight and turn left onto Route 1. The inn can be seen 4 miles farther on the right. From the north take exit 1 and turn left. Follow Route 3 to Route 78 and proceed as above.

Colonial Theatre

Theater lovers may want to make plans to see an Actor's Equity professional performance at Westerly's Colonial Theatre (401-596-0810), in the Greek Revival former First Congregational Church on Granite Street. Contemporary musicals, dramas, and comedies are on the bill from late April through Labor Day, and a special annual performance of Charles Dickens's *A Christmas Carol* or a similar holiday show suitable for the whole family is the traditional fare between Thanksgiving and Christmas. Tickets for the regular season are reasonably priced between $15 and $25; all seats for the holiday show are $10.

Also popular is the theater's Shakespeare in the Park summer festival for three weeks each July. These outdoor performances at nearby Wilcox Park are free; bring a picnic and enjoy.

Select List of
Other Rhode Island Inns

The Atlantic Inn

P.O. Box 188
High Street
Block Island, RI 02807
(401) 466-5883 or (800) 224-7422; fax (401) 466-5678

21 rooms, all with private bath and phone; children welcome.

The Blue Dory Inn

P.O. Box 488
Dodge Street
Block Island, RI 02807
(401) 466-5891 or (800) 992-7290; fax (401) 466-9910
E-mail: rundezvous@aol.com
Web site: www.blockislandinns.com

11 rooms, 3 suites in additional buildings, and 5 cottages; 100-year-old Victorian inn.

The 1661 Inn and Hotel Manisses

1 Spring Street
Block Island, RI 02807
(401) 466-2421 or (401) 466-2063; fax (401) 466-2858
E-mail: BIRESORTS@aol.com

18 rooms at the inn, 17 at the hotel; most with private bath, some Jacuzzis; breakfast and dinner; conference area.

Spring House Hotel

Spring Street, Old Harbor
Block Island, RI 02807
(401) 466-5844 or (800) 234-9263
Web site: www.springhousehotel.com

49 rooms, studios, and suites in 2 buildings, all with private bath; 1862 hotel.

Vermont

Vermont

Numbers on map refer to towns numbered below.

* A Top Pick Inn

A Top Pick Inn

A Top Pick Inn

The Inn at High View
Andover, Vermont 05143

INNKEEPERS: Greg Bohan and Sal Massaro

ADDRESS/TELEPHONE: 753 East Hill Road; (802) 875–2724;
fax (802) 875–4021

E-MAIL: hiview@aol.com

WEB SITE: www.innathighview.com

ROOMS: 6, plus 2 suites; all with private bath.

RATES: $90 to $155, double occupancy; EPB. Packages available.
No-smoking inn.

OPEN: All year except the first two weeks in April and November.

FACILITIES AND ACTIVITIES: Dinner on weekends, BYOB. Conference
room, swimming pool, dry sauna. Nearby: Skiing, theater, antiquing, golf.

I felt like a mountain goat getting up to The Inn at High View, but once up there I was overwhelmed with the breathtaking views from the big porch. I would love to see it in the winter, surrounded by snow. It must be truly beautiful. The inn's seventy-two acres hold many trails for cross-country skiing.

You enter through the screened porch into a large living room with a huge fireplace and a large, curved gray sofa. It's very cozy and comfortable. A checkerboard is laid out on a table inviting you to play a game of checkers, but you play with apples instead of checkers. Also in the room are lots of books, an old Victrola with vintage records that sound really great, and a piano inviting to be played.

The dining room has a fireplace, one large rectangular table, and a smaller square one. The kitchen is very open and the views are superb, no matter which direction you look.

Once a month on a Thursday night is a sort-of-private party for the neighbors; however, if you're here, you are invited to join in. The only other nights dinner is served are during the weekend. Then it's a four- or five-course affair prepared by Sal. He might offer you salmon mousse on cucumber slices, stuffed mushrooms, prosciutto and melon, or Sal's Memorable Italian Olives. After salad and the pasta course, the main course might feature stuffed pork chops, chicken Florentine, or saltimbocca. Greg's famous cheesecake is not to be missed.

The basement holds the conference room. It is fully equipped, and the inn is a perfect location for productive, private meetings. They even offer word processing, reproduction, and other support for your needs. Also in the basement is a dry sauna and a television/movie room for all ages. The pool-house has a waterfall, and all of this is watched over by Brenda, a cocker spaniel.

The rooms have interesting names. Ask for Ozzie and Harriet or the Cheshire Cat.

HOW TO GET THERE: Take I–91 north to exit 6 (Route 103 north) to Chester. Follow Route 11W to Andover-Weston Road. Watch for signs to the inn; turn right. It is the second farmhouse, ½ mile up the hill on the left.

Rowell's Inn
Andover, Vermont 05143

INNKEEPERS: Louise Riehl-Haley

ADDRESS/TELEPHONE: 1834 Simonsville Road, Chester, VT 05143; (802) 875-3658 or (800) 728-0842; fax (802) 875-3680

E-MAIL: innkeeper@rowellsinn.com

WEB SITE: www.rowellsinn.com

ROOMS: 6, all with private bath.

RATES: $125 to $195, double occupancy; EPB. MAP available.

OPEN: All year except April and November.

FACILITIES AND ACTIVITIES: Dinner on weekend; full-service bar. Nearby: Skiing, fishing, biking, summer theater, and more.

Built in 1820 as a stagecoach stop, this inn has served many purposes over the years. It was once a post office and general store, and then in 1910 F. A. Rowell came along and purchased it, and it became Rowell's Inn. He added the elegant tin ceilings, cherry and maple planked dining-room floors, central heating, and indoor plumbing. The brochure says that during the mid-1900s the inn was a preferred luncheon stop on the "Ideal Tour" between Manchester, Vermont, and the White Mountains for a hearty fare of trout and chicken. Today the inn is on the National Register of Historic Places.

In Rowell's Tavern you will find an old icebox, a soda fountain, a wood-burning stove, and a booth to play games or work on a jigsaw puzzle. Now where else but a country inn would you find a room such as this?

One entree is offered each night at the four-course dinner that is served on weekends. Some examples are beef tenderloin, cognac-glazed hens, or a New England boiled dinner. This course is preceded by homemade soups and a garden salad topped with the inn's own dressing. Dessert may be caramel fudge pecan pie, pumpkin cake, or another dreamy thing. All this good eating is served in the dining room lit by candlelight. Breakfast is a good, full one.

Two of the lovely rooms have working fireplaces. Some brass beds, quilts, and hooked rugs add to the tasteful decor.

Close at hand you'll find hiking, golf, tennis, biking, trail riding, and fishing in trout streams. The area provides summer theater, great shopping, and antiquing. All this plus—as you'd expect in a good Vermont country inn—alpine and cross-country skiing nearby.

HOW TO GET THERE: The inn is on Route 11, 7 miles west of Chester.

The Arlington Inn 🖤 📱
Arlington, Vermont 05250

INNKEEPERS: Bill and Sherrie Noonan

ADDRESS/TELEPHONE: Route 7A (mailing address: P.O. Box 369); (802) 375-6532 or (800) 443-9442; fax (802) 375-6534

E-MAIL: stay@arlingtoninn.com

WEB SITE: www.arlingtoninn.com

ROOMS: 22, in 4 buildings; all with private bath and air-conditioning; 10 with fireplace; 3 with whirlpool tub.

RATES: $90 to $265, double occupancy; EPB.

OPEN: All year.

FACILITIES AND ACTIVITIES: Dinner. Tennis. Nearby: Fishing, hiking, skiing, shopping, and much more.

You can recapture the gracious living of the Victorian period in this historic Greek Revival mansion. It was built in 1848 by Martin Chester Deming. The lovely rooms in the inn are named after Deming's family members. There are Sylvester's Study, Pamela's Suite, Martin Chester's Room, Sophie's Room, Mary's Room, and (I love this name) Chloe's Room.

They are all beautifully furnished and very comfortable. Rooms are located in four buildings, with six in the main house. The Parsonage has six rooms with televisions and phones, really beautiful beds, and delightful

peace. Many rooms also have fireplaces, a few offer Jacuzzis, and two provide private porches.

It matters not what season you are here; there is much to do year-round. Tennis is right on the inn grounds, the famous Battenkill River nearby is loaded with fish, and you can find opportunities for hiking, biking, golf, swimming, and canoeing. Winter brings cross-country and downhill skiing just a short drive away. If you'd prefer to go shopping, it's very close by.

Dining at The Arlington is very gracious. Start your dinner right with Maine crab crakes, chilled duck breast, or a selection of other first courses. Move on to entrees like rainbow trout, grilled swordfish, stuffed pork chops, quail, or sweet potato ravioli—a new one for me. The Deming Tavern has its own delightful menu. The house salad is a winner. The inn uses authentic Vermont products whenever possible.

Breakfasts, served in the cheerful solarium, are ample. You'll find omelets, eggs any style, blueberry and strawberry pancakes, French toast, huge blueberry muffins, and fresh fruit cup.

When looking for the ideal spot to host your management retreat or workshop, look no farther. Weddings, rehearsal dinners, anniversaries, and parties are done very well here at The Arlington. The Victorian garden gazebo is a favorite spot. All are watched over by Zig the inn dog—a bichon like mine—and B. J. the cat. I sure like it here.

HOW TO GET THERE: The inn is located on Historic Route 7A between Bennington and Manchester in the center of Arlington.

West Mountain Inn
Arlington, Vermont 05250

INNKEEPERS: The Carlson family; Paula Maynard, manager

ADDRESS/TELEPHONE: P.O. Box 481; (802) 375-6516; fax (802) 375-6553

E-MAIL: info@westmountaininn.com

WEB SITE: www.westmountaininn.com

ROOMS: 10, plus 6 suites and 2 cottage rooms; all with private bath; 1 specially equipped for handicapped.

RATES: $165 to $236, double occupancy, MAP; $104, per room, EPB. Corporate rates available.

OPEN: All year.

FACILITIES AND ACTIVITIES: Wheelchair access to all common rooms. Bar. Hiking, cross-country skiing, fishing, canoeing, swimming. Nearby: Antiquing.

he Carlsons are really the ideal innkeepers. From the minute you arrive until you leave, you feel at home. The inn is always being updated. Recent additions include a lovely suite of rooms with a gas fireplace and a room and bath with complete facilities for the handi-capped. The nicest touch is the thought. There are too few people who care enough to spend a bit more for other people's comfort.

The family's love of nature is evident in the busy bird-feeding station, pond with a collection of exotic goldfish, and the llamas. Each guest takes home a homegrown African violet.

The rooms, all named for famous people, are quite different. Their stories are found in a cookbook filled with wonderful inn recipes, found in each room. I have stayed in the Norman Rockwell Room, which is up in the tree-tops. Down comforters and wool blankets are provided to keep you toasty warm.

Children have their own room for fun, with a television, huge stuffed animals, books, and games and an aquarium.

Across the lounge area are tables set with games, rockers, and a view of the birdfeeders and beyond to Red Mountain.

There are three suites at the historic mill located close to the river. In each are two bedrooms and a bath upstairs and a living room and kitchen downstairs. Two of the suites have private decks, and two have open-hearth fireplaces. The Cottage in the Pines has lovely rooms, some with housekeeping facilities.

The inn prepares great dinners and has some excellent wines in an extensive wine cellar. They are the perfect complement to the meal. The crab cakes are delicious, and the pasta primavera is excellent, as are the nightly specials. Desserts, well, I gained a pound—but it was worth it.

This inn is truly in the country, with 150 acres of trees, trails, pastures, and ponds, all on the mountainside overlooking the village of Arlington. Cross the trout-filled Battenkill; wind your way over the bridge, which is flower-laden in summer; go by the millhouse, up past the main cottage and spring-fed rock quarry, to the seven-gabled inn. The grounds around the inn are reputed to have more species of evergreens than any other place in New

England. There are lovely trails for hiking, jogging, or cross-country skiing, depending on the season, and the inn provides a trail map for your pleasure.

HOW TO GET THERE: Midway between Bennington and Manchester, the inn is ½ mile west of Arlington on Route 313. Turn onto River Road, cross the river, turn left, and go up the hill until you come to the inn.

Twin Farms
Barnard, Vermont 05031

INNKEEPERS: Shaun and Beverley Matthews; Thurston Twigg-Smith, owner

ADDRESS/TELEPHONE: Barnard; (802) 234-9999 or (800) 894-6327; fax (802) 234-9990

ROOMS: 4 suites, 8 cottages, 2 suites in lodge; all with private bath, phone, TV, air-conditioning, minirefrigerator, and CD player.

RATES: $900 to $1,600, double occupancy; all inclusive. $16,000 per day for the whole property.

OPEN: All year except April.

FACILITIES AND ACTIVITIES: Full license. Spa, fitness center. All winter sports, mountain bikes, tennis, croquet, swimming, canoeing.

Twin Farms is a 235-acre hideaway estate that was owned by novelist Sinclair Lewis and given to his wife, Dorothy Thompson, as a wedding present. During the 1930s and '40s, they came here to rest and entertain many literary figures of the time.

You arrive at the entry gate and dial a number indicating who you are. Then you enter an unbelievably unique and luxurious property. Drive down the lane and along a circular drive to the main house.

The game room, with a beautiful fireplace, has many games and Stave wood puzzles. Off this is the Washington Suite, where my friend Audrey and I stayed. It has beautiful quilts and down-filled beds, two televisions, a CD player, and a bathroom with a large skirted antique tub and a huge shower. The sitting room has a bay window with a nice view, good couches, and a beautiful fireplace. There's a fireplace in the bedroom, too.

Red's Room, the original master suite, is glorious, with a view of Mount Ascutney. Red was Sinclair's nickname.

The Guest Room walls and curtains are covered in toile de Jouy, a green-and-ivory French linen that tells a story. It's just beautiful.

The cottages have fireplaces, sumptuous baths, very private screened porch es, and lots of comfort. They all have names. The Studio is splendid and has a huge copper soaking tub and front and back porches. The Treehouse is beautiful, with Chinese fretwork in the bedroom. Orchard Cottage is set amid the old apple orchard and features two handcarved granite fireplaces. The two-story Barn Cottage offers grand views, and the Meadow, with its Moroccan interior reminiscent of a desert king's traveling palace, is stunning; the tent ceiling is something you'll just have to see. Wood Cottage has an Italian oak writing table and much charm. And the Log Cabin is an authentic old Tennessee log cabin refurbished the Twin Farms way. It's very hard to choose here, so come a lot of times—you won't be disappointed.

A covered bridge takes you to the pub. Here are a self-service bar, pool table, fireplace, and television. Below this is a fully equipped fitness center. In-room massages are available. Up the road is a Japanese Furo. There are separate tubs for men and women, separated by fragrant pine walls, and one larger one for both men and women.

The main dining room is rustic; however, you can dine wherever you choose. We were in the original dining room, and both the food and the service were incredible. Cocktails are at 7:00 P.M. There are two bars where you may help yourself any time of the day or night. Lunch may take any form, and you can have it anywhere. Tea is glorious.

There is much to do here, whatever the season. Tennis and croquet; a lake for swimming, canoeing, or fishing; walking; biking. You can use the inn's mountain bikes. The inn also has its own ski slopes, ski trails, snowshoes, toboggans, and ice skating.

This is an experience few may be able to afford, but what a wonderful trip. The inn was awarded five stars by the *Mobil Travel Guide*. Say hello to Maple, the golden inn dog.

HOW TO GET THERE: The inn is 10 miles north of Woodstock, Vermont. Driving directions are supplied when you make reservations.

The Black Bear Inn
Bolton Valley, Vermont 05477

INNKEEPERS: Ken Richerdson and Suzanne Wallace

ADDRESS/TELEPHONE: 4010 Bolton Valley Road; (802) 434–2126 or
(800) 395–6335; fax (802) 434–5161

E-MAIL: blkbear@wctv.com

WEB SITE: www.blackbearinn.com

ROOMS: 24, all with private bath and color TV; 15 with Vermont
firestove or a fireplace.

RATES: $69 to $109, double occupancy; EP.

OPEN: All year.

FACILITIES AND ACTIVITIES: Breakfast, dinner, lounge. Heated swimming pool, hot tubs, Jacuzzis, sauna, cross-country skiing, downhill skiing, hiking. Nearby: Tennis, fishing, golf.

*F*our miles up twisting, curving Bolton Valley Road, you come across this contemporary country inn, nestled in the mountainside as if it had been here forever. Once inside, you are greeted by the warmth of a wood-burning stove and the aroma of freshly baked breads and muffins that fills the air.

Everything is homemade. You could stay here for two weeks and not be served the same thing twice, and that even includes the breads and muffins. You can begin your dinner with some good soups, like cream of broccoli, chilled gazpacho, or a roasted onion, corn, and sweet potato chowder. Yum. There are always five entrees offered, one

of which is seafood. You might find rack of lamb, sea scallops baked with mushrooms and herbs, and vegetarian pasta as some of the choices on the menu one evening. For a happy ending, try the blueberry raspberry cobbler.

The rooms are well appointed, with color televisions, good beds, and lovely balconies, where in summer you may sit and smell the good clean air and enjoy the views of the grounds, covered with wildflowers. The heated pool beckons you, comfortable lawn furniture is all around, and the beautiful blue skies are yours to enjoy. They are spectacular this far up in the mountains.

Some of the rooms have a fireplace and some a Vermont firestove. The inn's 54 miles of cross-country ski trails make good paths for a hike. When you return to the inn, there are outdoor hot tubs or a nice cozy bar with four bar stools and a sign behind the bar that says TEDDY BEAR CROSSING.

The inn comes alive in winter. You can ski out the door on a trail that connects to the main mountain for downhill skiing at Bolton Valley. Cross-country enthusiasts can also strap on their skis right outside the door and enjoy a 120-kilometer network of trails. Snow tubing and sleigh rides are other ways to have fun in the snow.

Bolton Valley's nearby indoor sports center, with swimming, exercise rooms, saunas, and tennis, is the place to be when you're not skiing. There is so much to see and do in the area in all seasons, you'll find it a great place to bring your children.

There are a lot of bears up here (stuffed, of course) in many different poses. There is Burt Bear sitting on a chair, and he's huge. A real live basset hound called Oscar also lives here and will greet you when you arrive—provided he is awake.

HOW TO GET THERE: Coming west on I-89, take exit 10 at Stowe-Waterbury. Turn left, then turn right onto Route 2 and follow it 7 miles. Turn right onto Bolton Valley Road in Bolton where I-89 passes over Route 2. The inn is 4 miles up the mountain.

The Brandon Inn
Brandon, Vermont 05733

INNKEEPERS: Sarah and Louis Pattis

ADDRESS/TELEPHONE: 20 Park Street; (802) 247-5766 or (800) 639-8685; fax (802) 247-5768

E-MAIL: slpattis@sover.net

WEB SITE: www.historicbrandoninn.com

ROOMS: 35, all with private bath and phone; 25 with air-conditioning.

RATES: $115 to $200, double occupancy; EPB.

OPEN: All year.

Walking Around Brandon

Established 200 years ago between the Neshobe River and Otter Creek, Brandon has one of the most unusual town layouts in New England. Distinguished by its two greens, one on each bank of the Neshobe, the town also boasts a collection of nearly 250 nineteenth-century homes, ranging in styles from late Georgian through Federals, Greek Revivals, and Queen Anne Victorians. Almost every one of these homes is on the National Register of Historic Places. The Brandon Chamber of Commerce (802-247-6401) has published a walking tour around the village. You might see the birthplace of Stephen A. Douglas, a U.S. senator famed for his debates against Abraham Lincoln.

Brandon also borders the Green Mountain National Forest, which has miles and miles of hiking and cross-country ski trails. Ask at the inns for the best access routes to these trails or pick up a copy of the Green Mountain Club's *Day Hiker's Guide to Vermont*.

FACILITIES AND ACTIVITIES: Lunch in summer only, Tuesday through Saturday. Wheelchair access to dining room. Bar, lounge, elevator, meeting facilities, TV rooms, swimming pool, trout fishing, summer theater.

Facing the village green in lovely Brandon is this Queen Anne–style brick inn, which is listed on the National Register of Historic Places. The inn has been here since 1786.

The rooms at the inn all come with private bath. There are king, queen, double, and twin beds. The choice is yours. Each room is different and has a charm of its own, perhaps created by a cozy easy chair for curling up in with a book or an intimate corner desk perfect for letter writing.

Your room is not the only place to relax. There are cheery, comfortable sitting rooms on each floor, just right for watching television on a rainy day. The main floor also offers various spots where you can unwind: the main foyer, for example, where you can enjoy a roaring fire in the winter and gentle breezes in the summer. There are puzzles and chess and books.

The inn has excellent facilities for weddings, meetings, and conferences. The mirrored ballroom is perfect for an elegant reception.

The five acres of inn grounds provide outdoor recreation. The swimming pool is great, and the Neshobe River on the inn's grounds is perfect for trout fishing. The lower barn is the home of the Vermont Ski Museum.

Luncheon might be soup, sandwiches, pizzas, or burgers from the grill. In warm weather, you can enjoy dining on the terrace. At dinner try ravioli Tuscany. Doesn't it sound great? Go on to the special house salad with the chef's special nightly dressing. It's excellent. In winter there is a tavern menu. Very nice.

A special feature at the inn is the "Barbecue Pit," with a choice of ribs or Cornish game hen or a combination of the two, slow cooked over a hickory fire. Delicious! What to have for dessert? Well, the apricot-filled chocolate gâteau and dairy-fresh Vermont cheesecake with fresh fruit sauce have won culinary awards, so if they are on the menu, don't hesitate.

The oldest elevator in Vermont is here; it's checked very regularly, so it's safe. Sarah has it decorated in checks, and it looks like a bird cage.

HOW TO GET THERE: The inn is on Route 7 in Brandon, on the village green.

The Churchill House Inn
Brandon, Vermont 05733

INNKEEPERS: Linda and Richard Daybell

ADDRESS/TELEPHONE: 3128 Forest Dale Road (Route 73 East); (802) 247–3078 or (877) 248–7444

WEB SITE: www.churchillhouseinn.com

ROOMS: 9, all with private bath; 3 with whirlpool tub.

RATES: $85 to $120 per person; MAP.

OPEN: All year except April.

FACILITIES AND ACTIVITIES: Swimming pool. Guided tours for treks, hikes, bikes. Nearby: Fishing, golf, horseback riding, museums.

*T*his is an inn for active people. The inn sits at the edge of the Green Mountain National Forest and provides numerous recreational opportunities, such as hiking, biking, skiing, and fishing. All are right here at the door, and the inn has a nice pool to relax in during the summertime.

The Churchill House participates in activities that originated here—hiking, biking, or skiing. These self-guided vacations are custom-planned according to your wishes. Several guided trips are scheduled from mid-May through October; these treks cover a variety of terrain, and all of them are great. There is also cross-country skiing from inn to inn—wonderful. The Catamount Trail runs the length of the Green Mountains, with inns along the way, beautiful scenery, and quiet everywhere except for your skis. As the saying goes, this one's for me.

Guests have access to a variety of cross-country trails, including the 17-kilometer loop to Silver Lake. Ski rentals can be arranged at the inn.

Anglers, do not despair. Native and rainbow trout exist in the nearby Neshobe River, Furnace Brook, and the Middlebury and White Rivers. A guide can be provided for fishing trips, too.

Churchill House has a great reputation for fine food. My spies tell me that the cottage-cheese pancakes at breakfast are sinful, and a favorite at dinner is the cedar-planked salmon. The breads and desserts are all made here. What a treat after a busy day!

HOW TO GET THERE: Go up Route 7 to Brandon and turn right on Route 73 east; the inn is in about 4 miles.

The Lilac Inn

Brandon, Vermont 05733-1121

INNKEEPER: Michael Shane

ADDRESS/TELEPHONE: 53 Park Street; (802) 247-5463 or
(800) 221-0720; fax (802) 247-5499

E-MAIL: lilacinn@sover.net

WEB SITE: www.lilacinn.com

ROOMS: 9, all with private bath; 1 with whirlpool tub; 3 with fireplace.
Phone available.

RATES: $100 to $250, double occupancy; EPB. MAP rates available.

OPEN: All year. Restaurant closed to public between Easter and
Mother's Day.

FACILITIES AND ACTIVITIES: Sunday brunch, dinner Wednesday
through Saturday. Catering and room service, wedding planning. Jazz
and classical concerts in summer.

BUSINESS TRAVEL: Ballroom for meetings. Function planning, secretarial services, telephone, computer, fax, and modem available.

*W*ow! This is a beauty. It's a 10,000-square-foot Georgian Revival
mansion that was built in 1909 as a summer cottage. Adorned with
yellow and white paint, it is a lovely country inn that has recaptured
the charm of the era in which it was built.

To the left of the coach entrance is the library, which has a nice fireplace,
books galore, chess, and a ton of comfort and charm. On the right is a stupendous butler's pantry hall leading to the tavern. Here is a beautiful copper-
topped bar with six leather
chairs with backs. Boy, are they
comfortable!

The tavern has its own
menu, full of glorious food.
How about a Loaf of Soup—a
freshly baked mini-boule, filled
with the soup of the day?

The dining room menu

changes weekly. Usually there are four appetizers and soup du jour. A few of the choices when I visited were grilled Angus sirloin, baked cheddar scrod, raspberry lamb, and baked stuffed salmon. Two of the desserts take thirty minutes to prepare. I won't tell you what they are. Come up and find out; they are wonderful.

The staircase is grand. In 1991 a time capsule was inserted into its newel post. At the top of the stairs is an ornate Chinese chest from the 1850s.

The rooms are spacious and well appointed. The bridal suite has a two-person whirlpool tub and wedding dolls on the fireplace mantel. It is used frequently, as the inn specializes in weddings. Televisions are in armoires, and there also are VCRs.

The innkeeper is assisted by two inn cats—White and Sebastian, a wonderful Himalayan. The inn dogs are pugs called Winston and Emma Rae.

HOW TO GET THERE: Follow Route 7 to Brandon. Turn right on Route 73 east (Park Street). The inn is about the fourth building on the right.

The October Country Inn
Bridgewater Corners, Vermont 05035

INNKEEPERS: Richard Sims and Patrick Runkel

ADDRESS/TELEPHONE: Upper Road Route 4 (mailing address: P.O. Box 66); (802) 672–3412; fax (800) 648–8421

E-MAIL: oci@vermontel.com

WEB SITE: www.octobercountryinn.com

ROOMS: 10; 8 with private bath.

RATES: $140 to $170, double occupancy; MAP.

OPEN: All year except April and two weeks in November.

FACILITIES AND ACTIVITIES: Pool. Nearby: Downhill and cross-country skiing, antiquing, horse shows.

There are a lot of comfortable things about this inn. It has a very cozy living room, with overstuffed furniture and a fireplace at one end and an old, old woodstove at the other. The fire is usually blazing, and the library offers an extensive supply of books as well as a great selection of games and puzzles. The innkeepers are always buying new books

Bridgewater Mill Mall

Built in 1825 as a cotton mill, the Bridgewater Mill Mall on Route 4 also had a long history as a woolen textile mill. For many years it processed the fine wool from the 9,000-plus sheep that lived in Bridgewater in the 1840s, and during World War I and World War II, uniforms and blankets for soldiers were made here. In 1925 the owners of the Bridgewater Mill changed its name to Vermont Native Industries.

The mill was closed in 1973 because flood waters from the Ottauquechee River destroyed the dye room, but in 1978 the mill building was reopened for a new life as the Bridgewater Mill Mall, also known as the Old Mill Marketplace. Home again to Vermont native crafters and artists, it also houses the Sun of the Heart Bookstore, a furniture workshop, a ski/sports outlet, and the Mountain Brewery. Visit such artists as David Crandall, born in Springfield, Vermont, and a jewelry maker since the age of fourteen! His beautiful work in gold, platinum, diamonds, and gemstones is glorious. The mall is open seven days a week, but some artists have hours by chance or by appointment only. See what's open on the day you visit or call (802) 672-3332 for more information.

and games for you to enjoy. This room is a nice place for guests to relax and meet each other.

The rooms are also comfortable, with good beds and mattresses. Some rooms have skylights, which I always like.

On a summer day you can sit by the pool and enjoy a glass of lemonade. The pool is in a peaceful meadow, and the view is great. If you want to stay out of the sun, relax under an apple tree or on the secluded deck.

Of course, if you can tear yourself away from all the comfort and relaxation, there are lots of things to do in this area. The Quechee Hot Air Balloon Festival is in June, and the Scottish Festival is in August; there are horse shows, antiquing, and Calvin Coolidge's birthplace. Winter brings a winter carnival, and downhill and cross-country skiing are nearby.

Dinner is a real experience. The French menu has onion soup, French baguette, sole au gratin, vegetable strudel, oven-roasted potatoes, salad, and apple cheese torte. The Italian menu offers summer-garden minestrone soup (the inn has its own vegetable and herb gardens), Italian bread, garlic-baked chicken, eggplant parmigiana, homemade pasta with garlic and olive oil, salad, and chocolate cake with raspberry cassis sauce. Also here are African, Greek, Scandinavian, Mexican, and good old American menus. I'm impressed that the innkeepers are so inventive. Breakfast includes fresh fruit, homemade granola, freshly baked small muffins, breads, and something hot, such as pancakes with Vermont maple syrup.

There are lots of reasons why I like it here, but two more are Zoe and Persephone, the inn's beautiful cats.

HOW TO GET THERE: From I-91 North take exit 9 to Route 12, then go west on Route 4. From I-89 North take Vermont exit 1 to Route 4. The inn is at the junction of Routes 4 and 100A, halfway between Killington and Woodstock.

Shire Inn
Chelsea, Vermont 05038

INNKEEPERS: Jay and Karen Keller

ADDRESS/TELEPHONE: Box 37; (802) 685–3031 or (800) 441–6908

E-MAIL: stay@shireinn.com

WEB SITE: www.shireinn.com

ROOMS: 6, all with private bath; 4 with working fireplace. No-smoking inn.

RATES: $145 to $225, double occupancy; MAP. On weekdays, $120 to $155, double occupancy; EPB. Two-night minimum stay on weekends in fall and on all major holidays.

OPEN: All year.

FACILITIES AND ACTIVITIES: Dinner for inn guests. Bicycles and cross-country skis available. Meeting facilities for small parties and social events; fishing, biking, snowmobiling. Nearby: Downhill and cross-country skiing, swimming, boating, theaters.

Constructed in 1832 of Vermont brick, this inn was truly built to last. It is situated in a lovely part of the state. The White River is close by—actually, it's in the backyard. It's a paradise for fisherfolk. Cross-country skiing is in Chelsea, and downhill skiing is good at the Sonnenberg Ski Area near Woodstock. Lake Fairlee is the place to be for swimming and boating in the summer and ice skating in the winter. Hanover, New Hampshire, the home of Dartmouth College, isn't far and offers theaters, art, and more.

The living room/library with its neat fireplace beckons all who pass through the door. Lots of books and a good collection of *National Geographic* magazines make this room very enticing on a cold or rainy day. Be sure to ask about the history of the antique French buffet in the living room. A circular stairway goes up to some of the rooms, and they are lovely. Four rooms have working fireplaces. They are furnished with period antiques. A canopy bed is in one room; a king-size bed is in another. Good feather or foam pillows assure you of a good night's sleep. The inn is not well suited to children under five.

Climb the hill to the Adirondack chairs under the apple tree and just sit and enjoy the view of the town. If you want to take a walk, there's a bridge over the river leading to an open field. In the wintertime this is a great spot for sledding or skiing—or take a ride on the skimobile trail. There is also a nature trail about 1 mile above the inn.

Breakfast is not to be missed. There are six different muffins and all sorts of fresh fruits, Maine blueberry or apple pancakes, waffles, French toast, omelets, and quiche. I hope you like to start your day with a stupendous breakfast.

Dinner means such goodies as spinach, sweet pea, and mint soup; oven-baked crusty mustard chicken; Italian stuffed flank steak; scallops with mushrooms and tomato cream sauce served on angel hair pasta; apple-cranberry crumble topped with French vanilla ice cream; chocolate raspberry cake; and chocolate mint cheesecake. Oh my! This is a fine inn.

HOW TO GET THERE: From I–89 take the Sharon exit via Route 14 to South Royalton, then Route 110 north to Chelsea.

Chester House Inn
Chester, Vermont 05143

INNKEEPERS: Randon Guy and Paul Anderson

ADDRESS/TELEPHONE: 266 Main Street; (802) 875–2205 or (888) 875–2205; fax (802) 875–6602

E-MAIL: randy@chesterhouseinn.com

WEB SITE: www.chesterhouseinn.com

ROOMS: 7, all with private bath, phones, and modems; 5 with gas fireplaces; 2 with Jacuzzi; 1 with steam shower.

RATES: $89 to $169, double occupancy; EPB. Packages available.

OPEN: All year.

FACILITIES AND ACTIVITIES: Full breakfast, dinner by reservation for house guests only, wine and beer license. TV in the bar area.

*T*he inn was built in 1780, and the rooms are named for King George IV, his wife, and children. There's a booklet in each room with a short biography of the person for whom that room is named. I was in the room named for Prince Oclavious; he was the thirteenth child of King George and Queen Charlotte-Sophia, born on February 23, 1779—my birthday, but not the year. Ho ho. He died only four years later. The rooms are all very different. One has a table made from English stovepipes, and a sleigh bed; all are very comfortable.

The inn is on the village green, where there are good shops and restaurants also. Dinner at the inn is served in the keeping room by a colonial fireplace, and I enjoyed their spring menu. Antipasto and bread sticks, garden salad, a choice of shredded pork tenderloin with lime sauce (it was excellent), Gorgonzola ravioli with butter herb sauce, or chicken Wellington, plus vegetable du jour. Tea or coffee and ice cream or rhubarb ice finished that wonderful meal.

For winter activities, the inn is close to the major ski mountains, cross-country-skiing touring center, ice skating, and sleigh rides.

There are three lovely inn cats named Purrsistence, Tom-E-Cat, and Suki. I love cats.

HOW TO GET THERE: From I-91 take exit 6 and watch for Chester signs; the inn is on the green.

Mountain Top Inn
Chittenden, Vermont 05737

INNKEEPERS: Margaret and Michael Gehan

ADDRESS/TELEPHONE: Mountain Top Road; (802) 483-2311; (800) 445-2100 from out of state

WEB SITE: www.mountaintopinn.com

ROOMS: 35, plus 11 cottage and chalet units; all with private bath; chalets with kitchenette. No smoking in chalets or dining room. Two rooms specially equipped for handicapped.

RATES: $134 to $246, double occupancy; EP. MAP is available.

OPEN: All year except April and November.

FACILITIES AND ACTIVITIES: Lunch, bar, lounge. Wheelchair access to dining rooms. Heated pool, tennis, lawn games, 5-hole pitch and putt with full-size greens, game room, horseback riding and lessons, sauna, cross-country skiing, horse-drawn sleigh rides, kayaking, canoeing, ice skating, sledding, golf school, fly-fishing clinics, claybird shooting. Nearby: Downhill skiing.

*I*n the 1870s the Mountain Top property was part of the Long family's turnip farm. In 1940 William Barstow, an engineer and philanthropist from New York, purchased the farm and converted the barn into a wayside tavern as a hobby for his wife.

Today, the inn is just beautiful, with views that no money can buy. At a

2,000-foot elevation, the inn overlooks Mountain Top Lake, which is surrounded by fantastic mountains. When you enter the inn, you are in a very inviting living area with a large fireplace. Ahead of you are the view and a spectacular two-story glass-enclosed staircase that leads to the "Charlie James" lounge and the dining room. The food served here is superb. On my most recent visit here, I ordered veal piccata, which came with a baked potato and salad. It was very good. Medallions of pork loin are also delicious.

The rooms, most overlooking the lake and mountains, are large and luxuriously furnished. All have spacious baths. An electric pot for boiling water for your early morning coffee is a nice convenience.

The inn has an excellent ski touring program. With more than a thousand acres to ski on, the views are awesome. There are two warming huts on the property. The inn has a ski shop with instructors and all the latest equipment. Ice skating and sledding are also fun, and downhill skiing is nearby at Pico and Killington.

Summer brings walking or hiking through the lovely countryside, and in fall the color show of the trees is breathtaking. And in winter, riding in sleighs drawn by draft horses is a wonderful yesteryear experience.

HOW TO GET THERE: From Rutland head north on Route 7. Pass the power station, turn right on East Pittsford Road, and follow it into Chittenden. Follow the signs up to the inn.

Tulip Tree Inn 🖤
Chittenden, Vermont 05737

INNKEEPERS: Alex and Ann Volz

ADDRESS/TELEPHONE: Chittenden Dam Road; (802) 483-6213 or (800) 707-0017

E-MAIL: ttinn@sover.net

WEB SITE: www.tuliptreeinn.com

ROOMS: 9, all with private bath; 6 with Jacuzzi; 3 with fireplace.

RATES: $159 to $299, double occupancy; MAP.

OPEN: All year except April, early May, and part of November.

FACILITIES AND ACTIVITIES: Full license. Fishing. Nearby: Swimming, hiking, golf, tennis, canoeing, bicycling, horseback riding, skiing.

This inn was once selected as one of the top ten country inns in the nation. You can't beat that! You arrive, and a lovely front porch with wicker chairs beckons you at once. Beautiful woods surround you. You hear a brook babbling, and a feeling of sheer peace comes over you. Inside you find a nice living room with a fireplace, a small bar and library, a den with a fireplace, and a great assortment of chairs, love seats, and couches throughout.

The rooms are the sort you never want to leave. Puffy comforters on the beds are inviting to curl up under, and the Jacuzzi tubs in six of the rooms feel so great after a long day. There are nice antiques, including a huge pine bed with a pineapple on top.

Dining is very special here at the inn. Pretty, too, with yellow and white napery in the summer and red, white, and blue in the winter. Ann's breakfasts are full Vermont style. That means you'll find cold

cereals; yogurt; juices; sweet breads; and apple, cheese, or blueberry pancakes or French toast, all with pure maple syrup.

If you think that's good, come back at dinnertime, when Ann really shines. There are homemade breads and soups like zucchini and curried carrot. A sorbet is brought to you to cleanse your palate, and then it might be medallions of pork with apricot-orange sauce, chicken with curry sauce, or fillet of beef with béarnaise. Oh my, and her desserts! . . . Well, just save some room, because they are so good.

The inn is only a mile from the Chittenden Reservoir, where the fishing and swimming are superb. East Brook runs right by the house. Trout anyone? There's a saying up here that a traffic jam in Chittenden is one farmer with one tractor towing two wagons.

HOW TO GET THERE: From Rutland drive north on Route 7. Just outside Chittenden you will see a redbrick power station on the left. Just beyond it is a Y in the road, with a red country store in the middle. Keep right of the store and follow the road approximately 6 miles. Just past the fire station, go straight ahead ½ mile to the inn, which will be on your left.

Heermansmith Farm Inn
Coventry, Vermont 05825

INNKEEPERS: Jack and Louise Smith

ADDRESS/TELEPHONE: Heermansville Road, Box 7; (802) 754–8866

E-MAIL: hersmith@sover.net

ROOMS: 6, all with private bath.

RATES: $75, double occupancy; EPB.

OPEN: All year.

FACILITIES AND ACTIVITIES: Breakfast and dinner, extensive music and book library, wonderful walking and hiking, cross-country skiing and snowmobiling from door, and fishing in the Black River. Nearby: Skiing at Stowe or Jay Peak is 45 minutes away.

*F*itting in with the simplicity of life in the valley, life within this inn is equally low key. A gravel road meanders by. Street lights don't exist—the twinkle of stars is spectacular. The clean fresh country air is shared by plants, animals, and guests. Innkeepers Jack and Louise are not in the forefront directing the ebb and flow of guests at the inn. At Heermansmith you're simply enjoying a home that has been in their family for generations without a bit of pretense. This is from their brochure, and I could not say it any better.

The inn has been here since 1807, and it's lovely. When you come in the door and turn left you are in the bar area; the living area and dining room are close by. The food is glorious. A few ideas for appetizers are New England codfish cakes, baked stuffed mushrooms, and good soups. An entree may be duck, a house special, roasted crisp with a strawberry and chambord sauce—

oh my, I wish I lived closer—or shrimp Louise or Delmonico steak. Or sample the chef's choices: Cajun grilled scallops, fresh veal cutlets, or fresh salmon. Save room for dessert.

There's a nice library and a model of a four-masted schooner named *Maude Ritter*—it's a beauty. The rooms are spotless and very comfortable.

Do go wandering while you are up here. Visit country stores, walk through acres of wildflowers. Northern Vermont has better autumn colors than any place I know. Winter is a picture, so are spring and summer. Do yourself a favor and come on up.

HOW TO GET THERE: Take I-91 to exit 26 (Orleans) and pick up Route 5 north. Go about 6 miles to Coventry. At the sign COVENTRY VILLAGE SCHOOL, take a left into Coventry Village. Take the next left onto Heermansville Road. Go uphill ⁶⁄₁₀ mile; the inn is the fourth place on the right.

The Craftsbury Inn
Craftsbury, Vermont 05826

INNKEEPERS: Bill and Kathy Maire

ADDRESS/TELEPHONE: Main Street; (802) 586–2848 or (800) 336–2848; fax (802) 586–8060

E-MAIL: cburyinn@together.net

WEB SITE: www.craftsburyinn.com

ROOMS: 10; 6 with private bath. No-smoking inn. Pets accepted with prior approval.

RATES: $140 to $190, double occupancy, MAP; $90 to $150, single occupancy, EPB. EP rates available.

OPEN: All year except April and November.

FACILITIES AND ACTIVITIES: Dinner for public, by reservation, Tuesday through Saturday. Bar, cross-country skiing. Nearby: Canoeing, swimming, fishing, horseback riding, tennis, golf.

The inn is a lovingly restored Greek Revival house that was built circa 1850. The little town of Craftsbury, said by the *Boston Globe* to be Vermont's most remarkable hill-town, was founded in 1788 by Col. Ebenezer Crafts and lies in what is called the Northeast Kingdom. The population today is something less than 900, and that includes Craftsbury, East Craftsbury, and Craftsbury Common.

One year I arrived here on a chilly day in the middle of June and was greeted by a lovely fire in the fireplace. Boy, did it feel good! Speaking of fireplaces, the one in the living room is the original that warmed the first post office in Montpelier, Vermont's capital.

The rooms here are filled with antiques, and the beds have handsome heirloom quilts. Fresh paint and paper have made this lovely old inn even nicer.

Innkeeper Bill Maire is your talented chef. He was trained in France and before coming to Vermont was at the prestigious Arizona Biltmore Resort, so you know good things are ahead. The menu changes with the season to take advantage of fresh ingredients. Hostess Kathy sees that the ambience and service match the food, and though the table settings are formal, there is no dress code, and the mood is comfortably casual.

There is much to do in this area. Cross-country ski trails connect the inn to the Craftsbury Sports Center and the Highland Lodge trail systems. In the summer you can rent a canoe, swim, or fish in the center's lake. You can also ride horseback, play tennis, or play golf at Vermont's oldest course in Greensboro, where the greens are fenced to prevent intrusion of the grazing cattle. Throughout July and August the Craftsbury Chamber Players perform every Thursday evening. Come and enjoy.

HOW TO GET THERE: Take I–91 to St. Johnsbury, pick up Route 2 west, and at West Danville take Route 15 to Hardwick. Follow Route 14 north to Craftsbury. Take a right off Route 14 onto South Craftsbury Road. The inn is 2 miles down on the right, across from the general store.

The Inn on the Common
Craftsbury Common, Vermont 05827

INNKEEPERS: Penny and Michael Schmitt

ADDRESS/TELEPHONE: Main Street; (802) 586–9619 or (800) 521–2233; fax (802) 586–2249

E-MAIL: info@innonthecommon.com

WEB SITE: www.innonthecommon.com

ROOMS: 17, in 3 buildings; all with private bath; 5 with fireplace or woodstove.

RATES: $125 to $150, per person, double occupancy; MAP. Ski touring and ski packages available. B&B rates available.

OPEN: All year.

FACILITIES AND ACTIVITIES: Food and drinks to the public by reservation. Solar-heated swimming pool, clay tennis court, English croquet, boating, cross-country skiing.

*I*t is a long way up here, but it's worth every mile you travel to be a guest of the Schmitts.

There are three buildings that make up the inn. In the main house are six luxurious rooms that Penny loves to show off. The north annex is on the common, with a lovely picket fence around it. All of its rooms are beautifully appointed. The wallpapers are

Scalamandre reproduction from a South Carolina historic collection. There's a very unusual sofa; try to figure out how the arms go down. Two of the bedrooms in the north annex have a fireplace. One of the bathrooms has such a cute, tiny bathtub. There's a lovely canopy bed in one room.

Across the street is the south annex. The guest lounge has a fireplace, comfy sofas, and a large television. You can fix lunch, make tea, or concoct whatever else you may wish in the guest kitchen.

In the main house is the dining room with a glass wall overlooking the rose gardens. All the gardens are lovely. Penny has a green thumb and is a faithful gardener. The dining room has the perfect atmosphere to savor the sumptuous food. Iced purple plum soup and grilled scallop bisque were two offerings on my most recent visit here. Rabbit was one of the entrees, braised in a rich broth of stock, beer, fresh herbs, and cloves. Salads are so good. I never had a vegetable baklava before, and it is delicious. The menu changes all the time, and the choices are really spectacular and tasty. Off the dining room a deck is where summer dinner will be served.

There is a superb wine cellar with many wines to complement your meal. Cocktail hour in the library is a fun, social time. The inn has won the *Wine Spectator* Award of Excellence for nine years in a row.

The solar-heated swimming pool has a little waterfall to let the water in. It disturbs nothing in its peaceful location behind the south annex. Tyler, the inn dog, enjoys watching it.

A staff of naturalists runs a sports complex near the inn. One hundred and forty acres include lake swimming, sculling, canoeing, cross-country skiing, nature walks, and bird-watching. There is a summer walking map of Craftsbury, with walks along the appropriate ski trails, logging roads, and back roads. Come on up. There is something for everyone.

HOW TO GET THERE: Follow I–91 to St. Johnsbury, take Route 2 west, and at West Danville take Route 15 to Hardwick. Take Route 14 north to Craftsbury, and continue north into the common. The inn is on the left as you enter the village.

Silas Griffith Inn
Danby, Vermont 05739

INNKEEPERS: George and Carol Gaines

ADDRESS/TELEPHONE: 178 South Main Street; (802) 293–5567 or (800) 545–1509; fax (802) 293–5559

E-MAIL: stay@silasgriffith.com

WEB SITE: www.silasgriffithinn.com

ROOMS: 15 rooms and 2 suites in 2 buildings; all with private bath and fireplace.

RATES: $129 to $229, double occupancy; EPB.

OPEN: Year round.

FACILITIES AND ACTIVITIES: Dinner most weekends, bar, heated pool, gazebo with whirlpool. Nearby: Hiking, biking, horseback riding, golf, 5 ski areas, tennis, fishing, factory outlets.

*I*n 1891 lumber baron Silas Griffith built this large, stately mansion on a bluff overlooking the town of Danby as a gift for his wife. The workmanship is grand. I was really taken with the round, cherry pocket door that leads into the music room, with its lovely German grand piano. Birch, cherry, maple, and other woods have been used throughout the inn.

When you are past the reception room of the inn, you are in a huge great room full of books, chairs, couches, and a welcoming fireplace. An adjoining parlor has a television and is a good spot to meet the other guests.

Rooms are in the mansion or the adjacent carriage house, and all are Victorian beauties with cozy fireplaces. Most of them have queen-size beds with fluffy quilts. Carol says she had fun remodeling and redecorating all the rooms, making each a unique experience for guests. Vermont-made products are used in the baths, including natural soaps, shampoos, conditioners, and lotions.

The restaurant is in the carriage house. You'll find a good-size bar, a fireplace, and attractively set tables. Every night there is a new dinner menu. The night that I visited the inn, guests were able to start their dinner with Brie baked with peach chutney or Vermont cheddar-cheese soup. A choice of marinated pork tenderloin served with a delicate cherry wine sauce, boneless breast of chicken stuffed with crabmeat, steak, shrimp, or salmon was offered. There are fresh vegetables in season and assorted homemade desserts.

This is a nice area of Vermont with many activities to enjoy. Hikers like the inn's proximity to the Appalachian Trail; shoppers enjoy the factory outlets for bargain shopping; skiers think it's super to have five ski areas to try; and historians like the nearby marble museum. The world's largest underground marble quarry is in Danby; marble from here was used to build the Jefferson Memorial and most of the other marble buildings in Washington, D.C. Even if you're not a historian, you will find the museum worth a visit.

Do say hello to the inn cats, Miss T, Jessie, Chi Chi, and Ocito.

HOW TO GET THERE: On Route 7 about 12 miles north of Manchester, look for the inn's sign on the right. It's a left turn into the inn.

Barrows House
Dorset, Vermont 05251

INNKEEPERS: Jim and Linda McGinnis

ADDRESS/TELEPHONE: Route 30; (802) 867-4455 or (800) 639-1620; fax (802) 867-0132

E-MAIL: innkeepers@barrowshouse.com

WEB SITE: www.barrowshouse.com

ROOMS: 18, plus 10 suites, in 9 houses; all with private bath and air-conditioning; 5 with fireplace; 1 room specially equipped for handicapped. Pets welcome.

RATES: $200 to $250, double occupancy; MAP. EPB and off-season rates available.

OPEN: All year.

FACILITIES AND ACTIVITIES: Wheelchair access to dining room. Cross-country ski shop, rentals, heated swimming pool, tennis courts, bicycles.

Nearby: Golf, skiing, shopping, hiking, horseback riding.

BUSINESS TRAVEL: Meeting facilities; fax available; corporate rates.

*T*he Barrows House is an inn for all seasons and all reasons. The unique facilities and extensive grounds make the inn a special place for a family gathering, honeymoon, small business meeting, or spur-of-the-moment vacation.

There is a story to every Barrows House room or cottage. Each is a furnished unit with its own restful style, antiques, old family pieces, and modern bedding. Each of the nine houses has its own sitting room and porch or terrace, as well as its own fire control system.

Sitting on twelve acres, the Barrows House is a 200-year-old estate. The house was built for the pastor of the Dorset Congregational Church (you can walk there from the inn), and in 1888 it became an inn. The first innkeepers were Theresa and Experience Barrow. Don't you love his name? The front living rooms and entryways have some of the original stenciling, which was found after removing thirteen layers of wallpaper.

The menu changes nightly. The chef and sous chef do a fine job. Two of the appetizers are sweet potato, leek, and garlic soup, and batter-fried mushrooms with honey-mustard dipping sauce. There are entrees like pork medallions or grilled venison medallions, calf's liver, Vermont-raised trout, lamb medallions with honey-thyme sauce, and grilled peppered tuna with tomatoes, olives, garlic, and feta cheese. For "finishers," well, come on up and taste. Just a hint—the Maine crab cakes Chesapeake-style are a house specialty. Heart-healthy cuisine is available here.

There's so much to do in this area. The skiing is superb, antiques shopping is near, and the Dorset Playhouse is here. Horseback riding and hiking or golf are available in nearby Manchester. And when you're tired of all the activity, come back to the inn to enjoy the cozy tavern, the glowing fire in the main living room, or the eleven acres of grounds. Bring the whole family—children of all ages are welcome.

HOW TO GET THERE: The inn is 6 miles northwest of Manchester, Vermont, on Route 30.

Cornucopia of Dorset
Dorset, Vermont 05251

INNKEEPER: Donna Butman

ADDRESS/TELEPHONE: Route 30 (mailing address: Box 307);
(802) 867-5751 or (800) 566-5751; fax (802) 867-5753

E-MAIL: cornucop@vermontel.com

WEB SITE: www.cornucopiaofdorset.com

ROOMS: 4, plus 1 cottage; all with private bath, phones, CD players,
robes, and air-conditioning. No-smoking inn.

RATES: $130 to $180, double occupancy, EPB; cottage, $225 to $270,
double occupancy, EPB.

FACILITIES AND ACTIVITIES: Full breakfast only meal served. Nearby:
Good restaurants, theater, art centers, shopping, and more.

*H*ere's a small charmer just off the village green in Dorset. There
are several rooms where you can relax and enjoy your stay. The
living room has comfortable love seats and an inviting wood-
burning fireplace. The small den is cozy, with a leather overstuffed chair that
invites reading—or napping. My favorite is the big plant-filled solarium with
full-length windows overlooking the grounds. Here's where you'll find the
television set, games, and books.

Breakfast is served at the large oak tables in the dining room adjoining
the solarium. And what a breakfast! It begins with fresh fruit juice and a fruit
course and then moves on to entrees such as baked blueberry French toast,
egg frittatas, croissants a l'orange, or maple-swirl soufflés.

There are four lovely rooms in the inn, most with fireplaces. The cottage
has a queen-size bed and cozy comforter. Downstairs is a TV/VCR and
French doors that open to a private patio facing the back lawn—very nice.

Dorset is old and lovely. The
marble quarries at the edge of
Dorset are said to be the oldest
in the country. They provided
marble for the New York City
Library, the sidewalks in town,
and the all-marble church next
to the village green. Yesterday's
quarries are today's swimming
holes.

HOW TO GET THERE: The inn is 6 miles northwest of Manchester, Vermont, on Route 30.

Dorset Inn
Dorset, Vermont 05251

INNKEEPERS: Sissy Hicks; Kimberly Ragonnet, manager

ADDRESS/TELEPHONE: Route 30; (802) 867–5500

ROOMS: 31, including 2 suites; all with private bath.

RATES: $95, single; $125 to $150, double occupancy; EPB; suites $225 to $250.

OPEN: Closed first two weeks in November and last two weeks in April.

FACILITIES AND ACTIVITIES: Breakfast, lunch, dinner (restaurant closed Monday and Tuesday from November 1 to May 1), bar. Wheelchair access to dining room. Nearby: Golf, theater, hiking, bicycling, skiing.

*B*uilt in 1796, this is the oldest continuously operating inn in Vermont. Today the inn has been completely restored and is listed on the National Register of Historic Places. There are wide-board floors, and beautiful Vermont pine is around the fireplace in the living room.

While the inn has retained the feeling of the eighteenth century, it is modern in its conveniences. It has been completely insulated. The bathrooms have been redone, some of the rooms have been air-conditioned, and firm mattresses have been purchased. There is no crowding in this large and rambling inn.

Sissy Hicks, who presides over the kitchen, is a very well-known lady. So many people requested recipes, she has put them into a book, *Flavors from the Hearth*. Some of the luncheon items are curried mussels and noodles on spinach, beef and scallions with rice, and biscuit-crust apple and turkey pie. Sounds great! At dinner the appetizers are numerous. One is New England cheese chowder. Sissy's entrees are really different. Sautéed breast of chicken stuffed with Brie and coriander. Fresh Atlantic salmon with creamy fennel and leek sauce. The most requested dish? Her calf's liver with bacon and onions. The breakfast menu is pure ambrosia.

I like it here. I think you can tell.

The recently restored tavern has its own menu, and it's lovely in here. Try the baked eggplant crepe or the grilled marinated shrimp.

A fine golf course is nearby for anyone who likes to play. Swimming is a lot of fun in a huge marble quarry up the road. If culture turns you on, the Southern Vermont Arts Center and the Dorset Playhouse will provide the comedy and drama of good theater. There are four inn dogs—three Labs and a bassett hound. Christmas is special up here, and the inn is glorious with lights.

HOW TO GET THERE: Leave I-91 at Brattleboro and go left on Route 30 to Dorset. Or take Route 7 to Manchester Center and go north on Route 30.

Inn at West View Farm
Dorset, Vermont 05251

INNKEEPER: Christal Siewertsen

ADDRESS/TELEPHONE: 2928 Route 30; (802) 867-5715 or (800) 769-4903; fax (802) 867-0468

E-MAIL: stay@westviewfarm.com

WEB SITE: www.innatwestviewfarm.com

ROOMS: 10, all with private bath; 1 with wheelchair access.

RATES: $115 to $165, double occupancy; EPB.

OPEN: May through October and mid-November through March.

FACILITIES AND ACTIVITIES: Breakfast, dinner, tavern. Dining room closed on Tuesday and Wednesday. Nearby: Tennis, golf, swimming, skiing.

This is an authentic Vermont country inn. Informal and relaxed is the style. The living rooms, with their glowing fireplaces and good couches and chairs, are restful after a day of skiing or shopping. The guest rooms are warmly furnished with four-poster beds and antique dressers. One room has facilities for handicapped guests.

The dining room, known as the Auberge Room, is just beautiful. It is highlighted by a tin ceiling and a broad bay window. The room seats forty-five people. The stunning place plates are a floral pattern from Villeroy and Boch, and Botanica made in Luxembourg. Needless to say with such magnificent surroundings, the food served here is excellent. The menu changes often, but you can expect appetizers such as Maine crab cakes or cauliflower soup with applewood-smoked bacon lardons, and interesting main courses that might include braised Niman Ranch beef short ribs, rabbit and papardelle, pan-seared diver scallops, or house-cured pork tenderloin. There is always a nice selection of wines by the glass.

What's for dessert? The warm chocolate cake is delicious, not to mention the walnut tart with homemade maple-bourbon ice cream. A pastry tray has an enticing variety of tarts, tortes, and pastries. Or you can enjoy sorbet or ice cream. What a way to go!

A lovely stained-glass window separates the dining room from the tavern. The bar is done in rich, warm wood and is a real beauty.

The inn is only 5 miles north of Manchester, where there are shops for your every wish. Three downhill ski areas and cross-country skiing are all nearby, and the Dorset Playhouse is less than a walk around the block from the inn.

To see this beautiful inn in the snow is a picture to remember. And in the warm weather, the porch with its wooden rocking chairs beckons. What a great view from here!

HOW TO GET THERE: Take I–91 North to Brattleboro, then take Route 30 to Manchester. At the blinking lights, take a right and an immediate left, which brings you back on Route 30 North. Go about 5½ miles north of Manchester. Look for the inn on your right.

Blueberry Hill 🖤
Goshen, Vermont 05733

INNKEEPERS: Tony Clark and Shari Brown

ADDRESS/TELEPHONE: Blueberry Hill, RD 3; (802) 247–6735,
(802) 247–6535, or (800) 448–0707; fax (802) 247–3983

E-MAIL: info@blueberryhillinn.com

WEB SITE: www.blueberryhillinn.com

ROOMS: 11, plus 1 cottage; all with private bath; 1 specially equipped
for the handicapped. No smoking inn.

RATES: $115 to $150 per person, double occupancy; MAP.

OPEN: All year.

FACILITIES AND ACTIVITIES: Packed lunch available, BYOB. Sauna
across the pond. Cross-country skiing, swimming, fishing.

*S*tart with the location, a nature lover's dream, 120 secluded acres of forest, woodlands, lakes, ponds, and alpine terrain. The pristine environment includes miles of marked hiking and walking trails and more than 75 kilometers of groomed cross-country ski trails. The property has a spring-fed freshwater pond for swimming. The Cross Country Skiing Center, a barn-style building offering rentals and lessons, also houses cycling equipment and the building containing a sauna. To add to the peace and privacy, the property is surrounded by 22,000 acres of Moosalamoo, a lush nature preserve with well-maintained trails.

The inn itself, an 1813 farmhouse, was to be the owners' dream house, restored to its early nineteenth-century appearance. Instead, in 1971, the Clarks hung out the Blueberry Hill shingle and began new careers as

innkeepers. They seem to have been made for the job. Guests are immediately at home here. The common rooms invite company, with comfortable seating and a warming fire in the hearth. An open kitchen is the focal point of the inn, enticing with its aromas. And everyone loves the plant-filled greenhouse, cheerful even on the dreariest day. Complimentary hors d'oeuvres are served here before dinner.

Guests also tend to linger over their candlelit dinners in the congenial dining room, hung with herbs and with a crackling fire to warm chilly nights. Tony Clark, a Welshman, was raised in Bordeaux, and good food is among his passions. Entrees include such dishes as Truite Antoine, lobster and crab ravioli with roasted garlic cream sauce, beef tenderloin with Irish whiskey sauce, and soufflé roll with chicken béchamel filling and roasted red pepper coulis. So many people ask for recipes that he has published *Tony Clark's New Blueberry Hill Cookbook*.

One recipe Tony won't give out is for the inn's famous oversize chocolate-chip cookies. The inn does a brisk mail-order business with guests who long for them.

Rooms are in the original inn or in an added wing overlooking the pond. Each has antiques, a handmade quilt, and amenities including inn-made herbal bath salts and body lotion.

The herbs used for these products and also instrumental in the kitchen are from the inn's own gardens, where more than fifty culinary and twenty-five medicinal herbal varieties are grown. Shari, who has done extensive study on herbs, looks after the gardens, which also include lovely flowers that adorn the rooms and your dinner plate.

Glorious in summer, a skier's haven when the snow falls, Blueberry Hill is truly an escapist's inn for all seasons.

HOW TO GET THERE: From Rutland take Route 7 north to Brandon, then Route 73 east for 6 miles. Turn left at the inn's sign, and follow the signs up the mountain on a dirt road to the inn.

The Old Tavern
Grafton, Vermont 05146

INNKEEPER: Kevin O'Donnell

ADDRESS/TELEPHONE: Route 121 (mailing address: P.O. Box 9); (802) 843–2231 or (800) 843–1801; fax (802) 843–2245

E-MAIL: oldtavern@vermontel.net

WEB SITE: www.old-tavern.com

Grafton's Renaissance

In the early nineteenth century, Grafton's 1,400 or so citizens managed pretty tidily from the profits derived from the 75,000 yards of wool produced annually from the 10,000 sheep that grazed in Grafton pastures. Thirteen soapstone quarries produced sinks, stoves, and other household goods. The Phelps Tavern—now known as The Old Tavern—was upgraded with innkeeper Marlan Phelps's gold rush profits and entertained illustrious guests from poets to presidents.

Unfortunately, Grafton lost scores of its citizens in the Civil War, sheep farmers went looking for bigger pastures out West, and floods and new highways changed the look and the lure of this once-prosperous village. By 1940, the town's economy had trickled down to nearly nothing. Along came the Windham Foundation in 1963, and suddenly Grafton had new life in its center. Find out the history of the remarkable transformation of Grafton in its "new" Old Tavern Inn and in its three museums dedicated to the human and natural history of the town. Call the Grafton Historical Society (802-843-2564), the Grafton Museum of Natural History (802-843-2111), and the Windham Foundation (802-843-2211) for information about historical exhibits and tours. You can also visit the Grafton Village Cheese Co. (802-843-2348) for a look at its cheese-making operation, and you can see "demonstration" flocks of sheep at the village's sheep barn viewing area. Horse-drawn sleigh rides are offered in the village in the winter, and the village's many walking paths, also popular in summer, are opened to cross-country skiers. Inquire at The Old Tavern about bicycle rentals and the Windham Foundation's horse stable.

ROOMS: 51 rooms, 7 suites, in 7 houses; all with private bath.

RATES: $135 to $225, double occupancy; EPB. Rate includes afternoon tea. Higher in fall foliage season. Senior citizen discounts.

OPEN: All year except April, Christmas Eve, and Christmas Day.

FACILITIES AND ACTIVITIES: Breakfast, lunch, dinner, bar, cafe, retail store. Wheelchair access to inn, bar, lounge, and dining room. Television in lounge, parking, elevator, conference facilities for up to forty, swimming. Nearby: Tennis, nature walks, cross-country skiing, bicycle rentals.

If you're looking for perfection in a country inn, go to a charming Vermont village called Grafton, where you'll find The Old Tavern. It has been operated as an inn since 1801. Since the inn was purchased by the Windham Foundation in 1965, it has been restored and is now one of those superb New England inns we are all seeking.

When you turn your car off pounding interstate highways to the tree-

shaded route that winds to this quaint village, you step back in time. The loveliest of the old combined with the comfort of the new makes this an unbeatable inn. No grinding motors can disturb your slumber when you are in the best beds in all New England. The sheets and towels are the finest money can buy, and there are extra pillows and blankets in each room. The spacious rooms are filled with antiques, all in mint condition. The guest houses across the street that are also part of the inn are enchanting.

There is no "organized activity" at The Old Tavern. The swimming pool is a natural pond, cool and refreshing. There are tennis courts nearby and marked trails in the woods for walkers. This is the place to calm your spirits and recharge your batteries.

The cocktail barn is charming, connected to the inn by a covered walk. There are flowers everywhere, in hanging baskets, in flower boxes, and on various tables in the gracious public rooms. The cuisine is excellent, with unusual soups and varied entrees, all cooked well and served by pleasant waitresses.

Up the street a bit, there is a six box-stall stable that will accommodate guest horses, plus a four-bay carriage shed, if you care to bring your own carriage. All this is for the exclusive use of Old Tavern guests.

The Old Tavern has a heritage that goes back almost as far as our country's. It first opened twelve years after America's independence. The Old Tavern looks very much as it did in former days, when, over time, it accommodated the likes of Daniel Webster, Oliver Wendell Holmes, Ulysses S. Grant, Rudyard Kipling, Ralph Waldo Emerson, and Henry David Thoreau.

HOW TO GET THERE: From I-91 take exit 5 at Bellows Falls. Take Route 5 north to Route 121, on which you will get to Bellows Falls (12 miles from I-91) and the inn. As you come down the exit ramp, watch for Route 121, which you'll take to the inn.

Highland Lodge

Greensboro, Vermont 05841

INNKEEPERS: Wilhelmina and David Smith

ADDRESS/TELEPHONE: 1608 Craftsbury Road; (802) 533-2647; fax (802) 533-7494

E-MAIL: HLodge@connriver.net

WEB SITE: www.highlandlodge.com

ROOMS: 11 rooms, plus 11 cottages; all with private bath; 1 cottage equipped for handicapped.

RATES: $194 to $250, double occupancy; MAP. Off-season rates.

OPEN: All year except March 15 to Memorial Day and October 15 to December 20 (or nearest weekend thereto).

FACILITIES AND ACTIVITIES: Lunch, dinner, and Sunday brunch; beer and wine license. Wheelchair access to dining room. Tennis, bicycle rentals, lawn games, hiking trails, swimming, boating, fishing, nature trail, cross-country ski touring center. Nearby: Working dairy farm, golf.

When the snow starts falling up here, it has to be one of the most beautiful places in the world. And you can bet that it's popular with cross-country skiers. There is a complete ski touring center with daily instruction, ski shop (sales, rentals, and repairs), guided tours, marked trails, and skier's lunch. All this is at an altitude of 1,800 feet, a minisnowbelt where there are miles of ski touring through the wonderful scenery.

Winter isn't the only fun time of year to be here. Caspian Lake, with the lodge's own beach house, is just across the road for swimming, canoeing, and sailing. Fishing is good in June and from September to mid-October for salmon, lake trout, rainbow trout, and perch. Tennis, golf, and riding are available for those so inclined.

Any inn that sends its chef to Italy to train for the kitchen surely gets my nod. The food has always been outstanding here, and now it is even better. The menu is inventive, and there are great grilled black Angus sirloin steaks to prove it. The innkeepers grow all their own herbs in a lovely herb garden.

I love the desserts. They have great names and taste equally great. Ishk-abibble is a brownie topped with ice cream and homemade hot fudge. Forgotten Dessert is a meringue with ice cream and strawberries. It's nice to find these old favorites on a menu.

Children of all ages are welcome here. Baby-sitters are available. In July and August a play lady comes in for the three-to-nine set. The playroom offers amusement for kids of all ages, and the playhouse has a supervised play program for youngsters. With the children happily occupied, the living room and library remain free and quiet for you.

This is the place to get away from it all. The views and utter peace are so wonderful, they are hard to de- scribe. Come and enjoy.

HOW TO GET THERE: Greensboro is in the Northeast Kingdom of Vermont, 35 miles northeast of Montpelier. From the south take I–91 to St. Johnsbury and follow U.S. 2 west to West Danville. Continue west on Vermont 15 to the intersection with Vermont 16, about 2 miles east of Hardwick. Turn north on 16 to East Hardwick and follow signs west to Greensboro, at the south end of Caspian Lake. Highland Lodge is at the north end of the lake, on the road to East Craftsbury.

Three Mountain Inn
Jamaica, Vermont 05343

INNKEEPERS: David and Stacy Hiler

ADDRESS/TELEPHONE: Route 30; (802) 874-4140 or (800) 532-9399; fax (802) 874-4745

E-MAIL: stay@threemtn.com

WEB SITE: www.threemountaininn.com

ROOMS: 14 in 2 buildings, 1 cottage; 10 with fireplace or cast-iron stove.

RATES: $125 to $275, double occupancy; EPB.

OPEN: All year except for occasional weeks in November, April, and May.

FACILITIES AND ACTIVITIES: Dinner, pub, lounge, outdoor swimming pool. Nearby: Downhill and cross-country skiing, ice skating, Jamaica State Park, tennis, golf, fishing, horseback riding, summer theater.

he inn is well named, since it is within a few minutes of Stratton, Bromley, and Magic Mountains. Mount Snow is also within easy range. Skiers should love this location. Cross-country buffs will find a multitude of trails in nearby Jamaica State Park, including a dramatic trail along the long-defunct West River Railroad bed, and in summer there are lovely walks along the West River. Tennis is available both indoors and out at nearby Stratton. Horseback riding is superb on lovely trails in the area, or go swimming in the inn's own beautifully landscaped pool.

This small, authentic country inn was built in the 1780s. The living room has a large, roaring fireplace, complete with an original Dutch oven. The floors and walls are of wide, planked pine, and there are plenty of comfortable chairs. A picture window offers views of the Green Mountains to complete the scene.

A cozy lounge and bar area make you feel very comfortable for sitting back to enjoy good conversation and a before- or after-dinner drink. A good wine selection is at hand.

The rooms are tastefully decorated. One room has a four-poster king-size bed and two have wood-burning fireplaces. Another has a private balcony overlooking the swimming pool and garden. A charming Hansel and Gretel cottage is also available. The beds have lovely sheets, and there is a whirlpool tub. Perfect for honeymooners, especially since the inn can host small weddings.

Everything has been upgraded since the Hilers arrived in 1999, and amenities like gas-burning stoves are being added to the guest rooms all the time.

Dining is set in two intimate rooms with original wood-burning fireplaces. The ground-level Library, entered from the living room through French doors, can seat thirty and is a popular spot for private functions, but when it is not in use, it is another nice place to relax by the fire or play a game of cards or Scrabble. The eclectic menus offer something for almost everyone, from traditional French cuisine to regional Indian or Southeastern specialties. Homemade soups and breads baked in the beehive oven are longtime inn favorites, as are the chef's breakfast scones and famous Three Mountain Inn cookies.

HOW TO GET THERE: Follow I-91 to Brattleboro and take the second exit to Route 30, to Jamaica.

Mountain Meadows Lodge
Killington, Vermont 05751

INNKEEPER: Michelle Werle

ADDRESS/TELEPHONE: 285 Thundering Brook Road; (802) 775-1010 or (800) 370-4567; fax (802) 773-4459

WEB SITE: www.mtmeadowslodge.com

ROOMS: 18 rooms, including 2 family suites; all with private bath; some with phones and television;1 handicapped accessible room. No-smoking inn.

RATES: $114 to $240, double occupancy, MAP; $85 to $200, double occupancy, EPB. Children ages 3 and under stay free, ages 4 to 10 are an additional $31 per night per child.

OPEN: All year except the end of March to June 15 and mid-October to Thanksgiving.

FACILITIES AND ACTIVITIES: Handicapped-accessible dining room;

full-license bar. Game room, hot tub, pool, sauna; hiking, swimming, boating, fishing, cross-country skiing, shoeshoeing, sledding; children's programs, farm animal activities. Nearby: Tennis, alpine slide, downhill skiing, golf, horseback riding.

This inn welcomes families with children. Mountain Meadows Munchkins is the name of their state-licensed program. It introduces children to farm animal care, nature, outdoor activities, and art. A playroom includes games, books, craft supplies, and dress-up clothes for those rainy days. The inn also has a petting zoo.

The Appalachian Trail crosses the inn grounds. Many years ago I met Bear, a mostly red setter who had just come off the trail carrying his own backpack. If you are hiking inn to inn, this is the southernmost inn on the trail and a good place to start.

The inn is very casual and relaxed and overlooks 110 acres of lovely Kent Lake. The lake is stocked with rainbow trout and largemouth bass. You can borrow a fishing pole if you haven't brought one. There are rowboats, canoes, and sailboats for your pleasure, and you can swim in the lake or the inn's pool.

The food served here is delicious. Vegetarians are well taken care of, and us meat and fish people will have plenty to choose from, with items like

prime rib, apple and cheddar–stuffed chicken, vegetarian pasta, and all sorts of fish. Salmon in puff pastry comes to mind. Do you enjoy a good breakfast? The inn is famous for its sky-high blueberry griddle cakes.

Children may dine at 5:30 P.M. with other youngsters in the children's center, and they can select from a special kid's menu. There are also theater nights for children.

Right next door to the inn is the largest cross-country ski touring center in the area. The alpine skiing areas at Killington and Pico Mountains are but five minutes away.

HOW TO GET THERE: The inn is 10 miles east of Rutland, just off Route 4. Follow Route 4 from Rutland for 12 miles, and at Thundering Brook Road you will come to the inn's sign. Turn left. The inn is ¼ mile beyond.

The Vermont Inn 🏨
Killington, Vermont 05751

INNKEEPERS: Megan and Greg Smith

ADDRESS/TELEPHONE: Route 4; (802) 775-0708 or (800) 541-7795 (outside Vermont); fax (802) 773-2440

E-MAIL: relax@vermontinn.com

WEB SITE: www.vermontinn.com

ROOMS: 18, all with private bath; some with fireplaces; 1 specially equipped for handicapped.

RATES: In summer, $45 to $75 per person; in winter, $60 to $110 per person. MAP.

OPEN: All year except mid-April to Memorial Day.

FACILITIES AND ACTIVITIES: Dinner every day, bar. Wheelchair access to dining room. TV, game room, sauna, hot tub, pool, tennis, lawn games. Nearby: Gondola ride, alpine slide, summer theater, Norman Rockwell Museum, farmers' market, skiing.

*Y*ou may be greeted at the door of this friendly red house by the inn cats, Sunshine, Eloise, and Angel. Innkeepers Megan and Greg are always here, and a nicer couple you'd have to travel a long way to find. The Vermont Inn is well known locally for the fine food it serves in its lovely dining room. As a matter of fact, three years in a row the restaurant was awarded the Killington Champagne Award for fine dining. To give you an idea of what awaits you: There are six appetizers, including mussels Dijon. There are excellent entrees, with rack of lamb persillé, Delmonico steak au poivre, and Vermont Inn baked stuffed chicken being some of the best known. There is a fine wine cellar to enhance the good food, and a special children's menu.

The inn's guests are a mixed bag and include many Canadian visitors. You'll run into young professional people from Boston or New York, a grandparent or two, families—anyone from honeymooners to golden oldies.

The room for handicapped guests has a ramp, a queen-size bed, a beautiful daybed, a specially equipped bathroom, and air-conditioning.

This old house has sturdy underpinnings. Some of the original beams still have the bark on them, and how the rocks of the foundation were ever put in place I cannot imagine. Everything was changed around—the old dining room became a lounge to make the inn cozier—so take advantage of the glorious view of Killington, Pico, and Little Killington, straight ahead across the valley. The bar was handmade locally of Vermont cherry wood, and it's a beauty. Couches and a woodstove make this room a great spot for relaxing. There is also a room that houses a hot tub, exercise machines, and lots of plants and offers a wonderful view. It's handsome and is ideal for anyone who wants to unwind after a day on the trails of the slopes.

HOW TO GET THERE: The inn is 6 miles east of Rutland, on Route 4. It is also 4 miles west of the intersection of Route 4 and Route 100 North (Killington Access Road).

The Landgrove Inn
Landgrove, Vermont 05148

INNKEEPERS: Jay and Kathy Snyder

ADDRESS/TELEPHONE: 132 Landgrove Road; (802) 824–6673 or (800) 669–8466

E-MAIL: vtinn@sover.net

WEB SITE: www.landgroveinn.com

ROOMS: 18; 16 with private bath; some with fireplace, jet tubs.

RATES: $90 to $235, double occupancy; EPB.

OPEN: All year except April 1 to May 22 and October 20 to mid-December.

FACILITIES AND ACTIVITIES: Dinner, except Monday and Tuesday during the summer. Pool, tennis, stocked pond, ice skating, hiking trails, hay and sleigh rides, bumper pool, Ping-Pong, volleyball, cross-country skiing. Nearby: Downhill skiing, alpine slide, summer theaters, golf.

This is a family-run inn that especially welcomes families. Yes, that does mean you can bring your children. They will be well entertained, and so will you. Indoors is a fun game room, and outside are playthings, a heated swimming pool, two Plexipave tennis courts, and a volleyball court. A hike through the national forest is unbelievably scenic, and summer theater is nearby.

Winter means snow, and there is plenty of it. It's only a short hop by car to Bromley, Stratton, Snow Valley, or Okemo. Cross-country skiing begins at the inn's door, or try your skills at snowshoeing or ice skating. After a long day revive yourself in a deluxe room with jet tub and fireplace, and then enjoy the fireside warmth in the Rafter Room lounge. A room near the lounge holds a big-screen television with a VCR.

The architectural style of the inn is peculiar to Vermont, with one building added onto another building. It turns out to be charming. The first part was built in 1810. It has been an inn since 1939. The rooms are spick-and-span, spacious, and very comfortable. The common rooms, dining room, and just everything about this quiet spot are relaxing. And the Snyders, who are cordial and welcoming innkeepers, make you want to return year after year.

The food is excellent. Just a few choices are angel hair pasta with sun-dried tomatoes, basil, artichokes, pine nuts, garlic, olive oil, and goat cheese; a wonderful seafood strudel, consisting of puff pastry filled with shrimp and scallops in a light clam sauce; and beef roulades. Desserts? Well, do save room.

From horse-drawn sleigh rides in winter to the blueberry pancakes, this is a nice place to be—with Mar, the beautiful inn dog.

HOW TO GET THERE: From I–91 use exit 2 and take a left to Route 30 to Bondville. Take a right onto Route 100 to Londonderry, then go left on Route 11 and right on Landgrove Road. Go 4 miles to the inn, on your right.

From Manchester take Route 11 past Bromley Ski Area, and turn left into Peru Village. At the fork in Peru, bear left and continue 4 miles through the national forest to the crossroads in Landgrove. Turn left toward Weston, and the inn will be on your right.

The Meadowbrook Inn
Landgrove, Vermont 05418

INNKEEPERS: Tony and Madeline Rondella

ADDRESS/TELEPHONE: RR 1, Box 145, Route 11; (802) 824–6444 or
(800) 498–6445; fax (800) 824–4335

E-MAIL: innkeeper@meadowbinn.com

WEB SITE: www.meadowbinn.com

ROOMS: 8, all with private bath; 4 with two-person whirlpool; 5 with
fireplace.

RATES: $85 to $200, double occupany; EPB. MAP is available.

OPEN: All year except April.

FACILITIES AND ACTIVITIES: Full breakfast. 26 kilometers of trails for
all seasons, hiking, cross-country skiing, and snowshoeing on the property.

*N*ice to have this inn back in the book. The new owners changed the
name from Nordic to Meadowbrook (for a meadow here on the
property), refurbished the old inn, and added some comfortable
sofas and chairs in the living room. It is the perfect place to relax at the end
of the day and enjoy a cup of tea and Madeline's homemade biscotti. The old
stone fireplace is still here and wonderful. The solarium dining room has
had a fireplace added for warmth and romance.

Breakfast is served in the solarium, with awesome views for dessert. All of
the breads and cakes are homemade and are wonderful. A fruit course follows,
perhaps a wine-poached pear or a seasonal fruit kebab served with ginger
cream. Then the main course arrives hot from the kitchen. Some of the inn's
favorite entrees are marscarpone-stuffed French toast, breakfast pizza, lemon-
lift pancakes, and Vermont omelets
with apples and cheddar.

Landgrove is on the Catamont
Trail and near the Long and
Appalachian Trails; trout streams are
in the area. Playhouses and shopping
are close by.

The rooms are very lovely. Some
have two-person whirlpool tubs and
fireplaces; all are nice. Foxglove's iron
bed is a beauty.

HOW TO GET THERE: The inn is between Bromley and Londonderry on Route 11, 14 miles east of Manchester.

Frog's Leap Inn
Londonderry, Vermont 05148

INNKEEPERS: Kraig and Dorenna Hart

ADDRESS/TELEPHONE: RR 1, Box 107, Route 100; (802) 824–3019 or (888) 376–4753; fax (802) 824–3657

E-MAIL: Info@frogsleapinn.com

WEB SITE: www.frogsleapinn.com

ROOMS: 16, in 4 buildings; all with private bath, down comforters, hand-crafted quilts, hair dryers, iron and ironing board, alarm clocks.

RATES: $125 to $163, double occupancy; EPB. Many MAP packages available. Children age 16 and under free in parents room; added roll-away, $10.

OPEN: All year.

FACILITIES AND ACTIVITIES: Dinner Tuesday through Sunday July 1 to mid-October, Thursday through Sunday rest of year. Full liquor license. Pool, all-weather tennis court, 32 acres of field and forest, hiking/biking/cross-country ski trails, Ping-Pong, croquet, volley ball, golf-driving cage, gardens. Nearby: Skiing, fishing, golf, horseback riding.

High on a hill with wonderful views, this is a quiet retreat on thirty-two acres. Sammy, the resident cat, and Chloe, the inn dog, will welcome you to the handsome rambling inn, built in 1842. If there is a chill in the air, you can gather round the toasty Franklin stove in the comfortable living room. A second seating area is fine for readers, with a love seat and chair and bookshelves. A new 3,600-square-foot addition includes a dining/pub area, and more couches and chairs in front of a Rumford-style fireplace. An original Natalee Everett mural is painted above the fireplace.

Rooms are in pleasant country decor, each one different, with many prints and accessories by Vermont artists. There are many nice furnishings, such as sleigh beds. All are queen size and have hand-crafted quilts or down comforters. Six rooms are in the main house, while Lily's House houses eight more accommodations, four of them suites. On the second floor of the Tad Pool House is a spacious set-up with two bedrooms, a kitchen, living room with TV, bathroom, and kitchen. One of the living room couches is a sleeper, making this a grand place for families. The new Forest Glen House has a similar arrangement.

You'll not lack for activity here. On the expansive property are a hilltop heated pool with more of those heavenly views, an all-weather tennis court, and trails for hiking or cross-country skiing. Trout fishing, golf, and horseback riding are nearby. Go picnicking and hiking in the Green Mountain National Forest. Weston is close by, and its summer playhouse is fun. Fall foliage is spectacular throughout the area, or you can sit right here and watch the inn's 200-year-old maples turn color. Winter brings downhill skiing at Bromley, Stratton, or Okemo. All are within twenty minutes of the inn. In addition to cross-country skiing on-site, three ski touring centers are nearby.

The dining room is charming, and the food is glorious. It's especially nice when the weather is brisk and you can dine by the fireside. Menus take advantage of each season's bounty. A sample fall menu might start with baked sweet onion soup with Vermont cheddar cheese or sun-dried tomato pasta. Typical entrees are baked red snapper with pumpkin, apple, and raisin sauce; boneless duck breast with mandarin oranges, honey, and thyme; chicken cutlet with white wine and capers; or roast pork with Vermont cider sauce. What to have for dessert? You simply can't go wrong.

HOW TO GET THERE: Take exit 2 from I-91 at Brattleboro. Take Route 30 north to Route 100, and the inn is just north of town on Route 100.

Rabbit Hill Inn 💚
Lower Waterford, Vermont 05848

INNKEEPERS: Brian and Leslie Mulcahy

ADDRESS/TELEPHONE: Lower Waterford Road; (802) 748–5168 or (800) 76–BUNNY; fax (802) 748–8342

E-MAIL: info@rabbithillinn.com

WEB SITE: www.rabbithillinn.com

ROOMS: 21 rooms: 8 luxury (fireplace and whirlpool tub for two), 4 rooms and suites with fireplaces, and 9 classic rooms; all with private bath, CD player, hair dryer, robes, coffeemaker. 1 room specially equipped for handicapped (wheelchair access to dining rooms). No-smoking inn.

RATES: $245 to $380, double occupancy; MAP, includes all gratuities. Midweek, winter rates available.

OPEN: All year except first two weeks of April and first two weeks of November.

FACILITIES AND ACTIVITIES: Breakfast and dinner served. Bar, game room, library, video den. Snowshoeing, sledding, cross-country and downhill skiing, hiking, biking, swimming, and canoeing. Nearby: Ice skating, golf. Two quaint towns are within a ten-minute drive.

BUSINESS TRAVEL: Access to fax machine and copying services; two guest phone rooms.

*R*abbit Hill Inn is one of the lovingly restored crisp white buildings that make up Vermont's tiny "White Village." This Historic District is one of the state's prettiest and most photographed places. The inn was built by Samuel Hodby in 1795 as a tavern, general store, and lodging for those traveling between Canada and the ports of Boston and Portland. In 1825 Jonathan Cummings built his home and workshop here (it is now part of the foyer and front dining room). The two properties have operated as one since the 1830s. In the 1930s the inn was renamed the Rabbit Hill Inn for the many rabbit warrens then found on the property. The inn's present owners have preserved the charm of this lovely old inn. And what a job they've done!

Accommodations are grand. Every room or suite has its own enchanting theme. Some of them are the Toy Chamber (inspired by *The Velveteen Rabbit*), the Music Chamber (with a 1857 pump organ and antique Victrola), and Top of the Tavern (a real beauty with a grand four-poster bed, fireplace, and Victorian dressing room). I was in Victoria's Chamber, a lovely room with a king-size 1850s reproduction bed, empire sofa, and glorious mountain view. A diary is in each room for people to write in during their stay. What fun they are to read! In every room you'll find pretty things, wonderful touches, and a stuffed rabbit sitting on the bed.

The first- and second-floor porches face the Presidential Range. It is a special place to just sit and rock with Zeke, the inn cat.

Do spend some time in the inviting common rooms. Afternoon tea and pastries are served in the Federal Parlor. The old crane in the fireplace here is still used in the winter for hearth cooking on Saturday afternoons. The Snooty Fox Pub is modeled after Irish pubs of the eighteenth century. Oh boy, what a place! There's also a comfortable library full of books and games to enjoy.

Everything is very nice indeed at the award-winning restaurant. The intimate, candlelit dining rooms feature good Windsor chairs and polished tables set with crystal and fine china.

Five-course gourmet dinners here are a true joy. It takes two hours to dine; it is all done right. The menu changes seasonally and frequently, each time bringing new delights. Everything is prepared from scratch. Try the seared Nantucket scallops or venison and pork pâté to start. Then sample the grilled tenderloin of beef with a maple molasses sauce; roasted chicken breast stuffed with shrimp, basil, and pine nuts; or sautéed monkfish. There are always heart-healthy and vegetarian options available. Be sure to savor the homemade sauces, mustards, and salsas prepared with herbs and edible flowers from the inn's garden. Save room for dessert. Chocolate hazelnut cheesecake and espresso crème caramel are a sampling of the goodies you might find.

In the evening while you're dining, your bed is turned down, soft music is turned on, and oil lamps and candles are lit. A handcrafted fabric heart is placed on your doorknob. You are invited to use it as your do-not-disturb sign and then to keep it as a memento of your visit.

You'll wake in the morning to a full candlelit breakfast of homemade granola (not to be missed), fruits, yogurts, juices, and hot entrees. Delicious!

The inn is splendid. So is the pretty little village. You will not be disappointed.

HOW TO GET THERE: From I–91 (North or South): exit 19 to I–93 south. Take exit 1 onto Route 18 south and go 7 miles to inn. From I–93 North: Take exit 44 onto Route 18 north and go 2 miles to inn.

The Andrie Rose Inn
Ludlow, Vermont 05149

INNKEEPERS: Michael and Irene Maston

ADDRESS/TELEPHONE: 13 Pleasant Street; (802) 228–4846 or (800) 223–4846; fax (802) 228–7910

E-MAIL: andrierose@mail.tds.net

WEB SITE: www.andrieroseinn.com

ROOMS: 9, plus guest house with 13 suites; all with private bath; all suites and 5 rooms with whirlpool tub; steam showers in 2 suites. 2-, 3-, and 4-bedroom family units. No-smoking inn.

RATES: $90 to $325, double occupancy; EPB.

OPEN: All year.

FACILITIES AND ACTIVITIES: Dinner Friday and Saturday, full liquor license. Meeting facilities. Nearby: Skiing, hiking, fishing, theater, antiquing.

Andrie Rose was the former owner of this lovely inn, built in 1829. She would be pleased to have her name connected with this very gracious inn, a AAA four-diamond award winner for the past ten years.

When you arrive, a personalized welcome card is in your room, highlighting area activities and events. If you are celebrating a special event, you may receive chilled champagne, flowers, or a Vermont specialty product. You can help yourself at any time to the cookies and candies found throughout the inn. In the fall and winter, guests enjoy hot chocolate, cider, tea, or coffee; in the summer lemonade and iced tea are served. All of these are very nice, thoughtful touches.

The front porch is a great place to just relax, have a cocktail, or read a book. A fireplace is in the living room, and games are in the front room. Bombay paddle fans are in all of the common rooms and guest rooms. These are lovely at any time of the year. The innkeepers are always thinking about what will make your stay memorable.

The rooms are decorated beautifully. Some are done in Laura Ashley prints. Caswell-Massey almond-scented bath accessories are in all the bathrooms. Soft pastel colors are used on the walls, towels, and linens. I found them very restful. There are thirteen whirlpool tubs, so nice after a day of skiing. The beds are turned down in the evening, and soft music plays through the stereo system in each room.

On Friday and Saturday nights a four-course dinner is served, with a choice of four entrees. The menu changes seasonally. On a recent fall menu, interesting appetizers included grilled duck and mango sausage with Asian spiced red cabbage slaw or curried butternut squash soup. Medallions of pork tenderloin with cider sauce, herb grilled lamb chops, confit of duck with glazed apples and green peppercorn sauce, and dill-and-pepper-crusted salmon were some of the divine dinner entrees. This is also a great place to be a vegetarian, with choices like wild mushroom risotto with black truffle oil and roast tomatoes, and roast artichoke tart with caramelized onions, roast tomatoes, wilted spinach, and Vermont chèvre.

My last trip was made during the week, when dinner is not available, so the innkeepers sent me to a nearby restaurant called Cappuccino's at 41 Depot Street. The food was so good. It was a wonderful recommendation.

Breakfast comes in a basket by your door, ordered the night before. One highlight is the inn's "cuckoo's nest," a small soufflé.

Ludlow is a wonderful town. It is home to Okemo, a very popular downhill ski area. During the rest of the year, the inn has bicycles for your use, so go and have a Vermont adventure. Be sure to take along a picnic lunch.

The entire inn is available for a small business retreat or other function, including weddings. Murder mystery weekends are offered during the summer and late fall. What great surroundings you'd have!

Echo Lake Inn
Ludlow, Vermont 05149

INNKEEPERS: Laurence and Beth Jeffery and Peter and
Joanne Modisette

ADDRESS/TELEPHONE: Route 100 (mailing address: P.O. Box 154);
(802) 228-8602 or (800) 356-6844; fax (802) 228-3075

WEB SITE: www.echolakeinn.com

ROOMS: 21; 11 with private bath.

RATES: $79 to $380, double occupancy; EPB. MAP available.

OPEN: Closed first three weeks in April and November.

FACILITIES AND ACTIVITIES: Lunch in-season, dinner, full license.
Swimming, tennis, boating, and activities suited to all four seasons.

Built in 1840, the Echo Lake Inn is one of the few inns remaining
in Vermont that was originally constructed to operate as an inn.
This is an authentic "old Colonial inn." But you do not have to
worry; it has an automatic
fire-alarm system.

There are family suites
and deluxe rooms with
queen-size beds and ceil-
ing fans. All the accommodations are comfortable.

The Basketcase Lounge
is on the right as you enter
the inn. On the left is a
nice living room with good
chairs, television, and books.

Now for my favorite pastime—food—which I certainly enjoyed in the cozy
dining room. The menu changes twice a year, and there are always specials.
The daily soup selections are really good. I have some of the recipes so I can
make them at home. Among the entrees are grilled sirloin, sautéed fresh rain-

bow trout, and roast country duckling. I had veal, which was yummy.

Be sure to save room for breakfast. A 2-2-2 Scramble is two eggs scrambled with two kinds of cheeses and two herbs. It comes with toast. There's more, of course.

On a warm day you're sure to enjoy the lighted tennis courts, the pool, the steam bath, and the old-fashioned porch with rockers. You must see the chipmunks to believe them. They eat peanuts right from your hand, and one called Stripes will take a peanut from your pocket.

Take a walk and pan for gold. It was found near here years ago. The inn will lend you pans so you can try your luck. There are also boats on the lake, good fishing, secluded waterfalls, golf, skiing, and much more nearby. But if you decide to stay in, you can head for the six-person Jacuzzi or the Stoned Tavern, which has a pool table, Ping-Pong, darts, and video games.

Any season here is beautiful, but the lakes mirror the brilliant colors of fall like nowhere else in New England. Spectacular! Echo is the middle lake of the three-stream, spring-fed Plymouth Lakes.

HOW TO GET THERE: From I–91 take exit 6 to Route 103 to Ludlow. One and a half miles north of Ludlow, turn right on Route 100. The inn is in 3½ miles on the left.

The Governor's Inn
Ludlow, Vermont 05149

INNKEEPERS: Cathy and Jim Kubec

ADDRESS/TELEPHONE: 86 Main Street; (802) 228–8830 or (800) GOV–ERNO (468–3766)

E-MAIL: kubec@thegovernorsinn.com

WEB SITE: www.thegovernorsinn.com

ROOMS: 8, plus 1 suite; all with private bath. No-smoking inn.

RATES: $105 to $165, double occupancy; includes full breakfast and afternoon tea. Dinner by advance reservation only, $45 per person.

OPEN: All year except December 23 to December 26.

Afternoon tea, picnic hampers available for lunch. Bar. Cooking seminars (send for brochure). Nearby: Skiing, boating, fishing, golf, historical attractions.

Cathy is the chef, and she really does justice to the title. She is not only an honors graduate of the Connecticut Culinary Institute but has a certificate from the Cesar Ritz Course at the Ritz Escolier École de Gastronomie Française in Paris. Needless to say, this is an inn known for fine food!

The treats begin at breakfast. Have you ever tasted ice-cream-dipped French toast?

It's special. So is the inn's "cuckoo's nest," a small soufflé. To make things even nicer, the table is set with crystal, silver, and antique china.

Dinner in the formal lantern-lit dining room is different every night. Here's one sample: eastern crab cake appetizer, wine broth soup, pepper-crusted beef tenderloin or stuffed game hens, and Apricot Victorian for dessert.

Cathy regularly offers Culinary Magic Cooking Seminars for those who want to learn her secrets.

The inn itself is very Victorian. It was built in 1890 by William Wallace Stickney for his bride, Lizzie. Eight years later, Stickney became governor of Vermont, hence the inn's name. The parlor has a magnificent 1890s corner slate fireplace where guests tend to congregate, and lots of period antiques.

Cozy rooms have lovely printed wallpapers, and many have Victorian era iron headboards. I'm partial to the third-floor rooms under the eaves, each with a gas-lit Vermont firestove.

The Governor William Wallace Stickney Suite is the grandest. It has a living room, a large bedroom with king-size brass bed, a seating area, a whirlpool bath, and a walk-in closet. The rooms have windows overlooking the village church steeples and Okemo Mountain 1 mile away.

There's much to see and do in this area, and the innkeepers will gladly fill you in on the best places. Ask for one of Cathy's gourmet picnic lunches and enjoy the sights.

HOW TO GET THERE: Take exit 6 north from I–91 and follow Route 103 west to Ludlow and the inn.

The Wildflower Inn
Lyndonville, Vermont 05851

INNKEEPERS: Mary and Jim O'Reilly

ADDRESS/TELEPHONE: Darling Hill Road; (802) 626-8310 or (800) 627-8310

WEB SITE: www.pbub.com/vermont/wldflwr.htm

ROOMS: 12, plus 10 suites; 10 with private bath; 10 with kitchenette; 1 specially equipped for handicapped. No-smoking inn.

RATES: $95 to $220, double occupancy; EPB.

OPEN: All year except April, the last week in October, and the first three weeks in November.

FACILITIES AND ACTIVITIES: Dinner. Gift shop, meeting room, heated pool, children's pool, sauna, spa, ice-skating pond, cross-country skiing, petting barn and farm animals, summer children's theater, art gallery.

*H*ere's an inn that makes children feel more than welcome. It has a special children's playroom that comes complete with dress-up clothes and toys for all ages. There are also bumper pool and air hockey, television, and nightly games and a movie.

The inn is situated on its own 500 acres on a ridge overlooking the valley of Vermont's Northeast Kingdom. What a beautiful view it has! You're sure to enjoy roaming over the inn's property, discovering the pond, drinking in the fabulous view, petting the kittens, or walking up the hill to see the Burkland Mansion. Families will enjoy summer performances of the

Vermont Children's Theater, which has taken up residence in one of the inn's barns. And in the winter, of course, cross-country skiing and ice skating are right here.

The main inn has four bedrooms with shared baths. The dining rooms are located here. One overlooks the glorious valley. Help yourself at the appetizer buffet while having a cocktail, and then dig into the main entrees, which change daily. Besides a daily special and fresh fish of the day, there are rib-eye steak, chateaubriand for two (a wonderful treat), and more. Black Forest cake and raspberry cheesecake caught my eye for dessert, but there are many more choices.

The carriage house has suites with kitchenettes and lots of beds and is wonderful for families. An old schoolhouse is a bit removed from the inn. It's the honeymoon cottage. More suites are located near the pool—and what a pool it is! It is heated and has a spectacular view. There is also a children's pool out here. The all-purpose room (also with a view) is nice for conferences or meetings. After a day of work or play, relax in the delightful sauna and spa.

HOW TO GET THERE: Take exit 23 off I-91 in Lyndonville. Go north through town on Route 5 to Route 114. Follow Route 114 for ½ mile. Darling Hill Road is a left turn immediately after the second bridge you cross. The inn is in 2 miles.

The Inn at Manchester
Manchester, Vermont 05254

INNKEEPERS: Ron and Mary Blake

ADDRESS/TELEPHONE: Route 7A; (802) 362–1793 or (800) 273–1793

E-MAIL: stay@innatmanchester.com

WEB SITE: www.innatmanchester.com

ROOMS: 14, plus 4 suites; all with private bath; 3 suites with fireplace and air-conditioning.

RATES: $120 to $180, double occupancy; EPB.

OPEN: All year.

FACILITIES AND ACTIVITIES: Beer, spirit, and wine license. Swimming pool. Full country breakfast and afternoon tea. Saturday wine and cheese social. Nearby: Skiing, golf, tennis, theater, shopping outlets.

*L*ush greenery in the bay window of the living room is the sight that greets you when you walk in the front door of this inn. The many fireplaces surrounded by restful sitting areas, the numerous good antiques, and the dining room with Tiffany lamps add up to a warm country inn atmosphere. The antique Champion oak stove is the focal point in the game room, which is an ideal spot to unwind after a day on the ski slopes. Here you can watch television or play games or cards at a card table.

The guest rooms are spotless and so very nice. Sheets, comforters, dust ruffles, and towels are color coordinated, and the beds are perfect for a good night's sleep. The carriage house rooms are inviting. Each room has its own private bath and is individually decorated with coordinating sheets, comforters, towels, and antiques. There are Tiffany-style lamps, queen-size beds, cast-iron and brass beds, and a beauty in cherry. Attractive artwork hangs throughout. All very nice indeed. The inn is not well suited to children under eight.

Breakfast is a treat. The homemade granola and apple pancakes with local maple syrup can start anyone's day right. Dinners are served family-style. The menu changes daily.

The inn is conveniently located in the heart of just about everything, with skiing, downhill and cross-country, only minutes away. Summer brings great antiquing, summer theater, specialty craft shops, and boutiques. Golf and tennis are within walking distance of the front door, and the swimming pool is in a lovely meadow between the carriage house and the creek.

HOW TO GET THERE: The inn is approximately 22 miles north of Bennington, Vermont, on Route 7A. It is on the left.

The Inn at Ormsby Hill
Manchester Center, Vermont 05255

INNKEEPERS: Chris and Ted Sprague

ADDRESS/TELEPHONE: Historic Route 7A (mailing address: 1842 Main Street); (802) 362–1163 or (800) 670–2841; fax (802) 362–5176

E-MAIL: stay@ormsbyhill.com

WEB SITE: www.ormsbyhill.com

ROOMS: 10, all with private bath, air-conditioning, double whirlpool tub, fireplace, phones, and robes.

RATES: $190 to $370, double occupancy; EPB.

OPEN: All year.

FACILITIES AND ACTIVITIES: Hammock, porch. Nearby: Golf, bicycling, antiquing, fishing, tennis, hiking, downhill and cross-country skiing.

What a beautiful inn this is! When you enter, the first room on the left is a beautifully furnished formal living room. Go on into the gathering room, which has a huge fireplace, games, and books. Continue into the conservatory–dining room. It's great. When the inn is full, three tables are in use. There's a really different-looking fireplace in here. The mantel came from either Europe or Newport. It's a beauty. The glass windows at the end of the room remind me of a ship, and Chris has nice plants all around and an apple checkerboard at the ready. The view of the mountains is awesome.

The inn was built around 1760 and added onto in the 1800s. The new wing was constructed in 1996. You cannot tell where the old and new meet. Innkeepers are clever people. The rooms are just beautiful. Almost all have two-person whirlpool baths and fireplaces, either gas or wood. The beds are kings and queens and so comfortable. There are four-posters and canopies. Everything is restful, and the colors are muted. The towels are big and fluffy. The inn reminds me of a gracious manor house in the English countryside, and it has a full sprinkler system and alarms.

The tower room is the latest addition, and it's a dream. There are some steps, so be prepared (but it's worth every step). Up seven steps from the second floor to a queen-size canopy bed, a gas fireplace, and lots of windows. Up a few more to an unbelievable bathroom with a Jacuzzi for two as well as a two-person shower/steam shower and more windows. Wow.

Chris Sprague is an exceptional chef, winner of many awards, and breakfast at Ormsby Hill is an extravaganza; you may not need to eat again until dinnertime. After juice and fresh-fruit starters, you get delicious treats like lemon almond bread fresh from the oven, then unusual main courses like breakfast bacon-and-egg risotto, raisin bread-and-butter pudding, or Chris's famous baked pancakes. Then she serves dessert! Honest. Things like blueberry and peach crisp with vanilla ice cream or warm gingerbread with vanilla ice cream. Delicious.

Ask Chris or Ted to tell you about the inn's unusual past. The original portion of the house still contains Manchester's first jail cell in the basement, complete with marble floor. It was part of the Underground Railroad used by runaway slaves. In the late 1800s it was bought and expanded by Edward Isham, a law partner of Robert Todd Lincoln, son of Abraham Lincoln. As you might expect with all that history, the house is listed on the National Register of Historic Places.

HOW TO GET THERE: From Route 30 go north to Historic Route 7A in Manchester. Turn left. Go south about 3 miles to the inn.

The Reluctant Panther
Manchester Village, Vermont 05254

INNKEEPERS: Maye and Robert Bachofen

ADDRESS/TELEPHONE: 17–39 West Road (mailing address:
P.O. Box 678); (802) 362-2568 or (800) 822-2331; fax (802) 362-2586

E-MAIL: stay@reluctantpanther.com

WEB SITE: www.reluctantpanther.com

ROOMS: 21 rooms and suites in 2 buildings; all with private bath, TV,
air-conditioning, and phone; most with fireplace; 5 with Jacuzzi; 1 specially equipped for handicapped. No-smoking inn.

The Jelly Mill . . . & Friends

On Historic Route 7A, you can visit the restored four-story
dairy barn called the Jelly Mill. This barn, the brick home
next door, and the surrounding acreage were once home to
Loveland Munson, former Chief Justice of the Vermont
Supreme Court. The barn now houses a wonderful country
store that had its beginnings in an old cider jelly mill and
later moved here. The proprietors still sell cider jelly plus
eighty-eight other flavors of jellies, jams, and preserves.
Along with these goodies you'll find jelly beans, chocolates,
and Vermont maple sugar products and cheeses. Also here
are "the Friends"—other businesses that sell country furnishings and accessories, jewelry, Christmas collectibles,
handblown glass, pottery, handcrafted teddy bears, toys,
doll furniture, and much more. The Buttery Restaurant
serves breakfast and lunch daily from 10:00 A.M. to 3:00 P.M.
The rest of the Jelly Mill is open from 10:00 A.M. to 6:00 P.M.
daily, except for New Year's Day, Easter, Thanksgiving, and
Christmas Day.

RATES: $129 to $425, double occupancy; bed-and-breakfast. Inquire about packages.

OPEN: All year.

FACILITIES AND ACTIVITIES: Dinner on weekends and holidays only from November through May, daily during rest of the year. Bar lounge. Nearby: Golf, tennis, hiking, skiing, American Museum of Fly Fishing, health club.

BUSINESS TRAVEL: Phones in all rooms, desks in some; conference room; fax and audiovisual equipment available; midweek corporate rates.

*T*he inn is mauve on the outside, and a good bit of lavender and wine colors are inside. These are colors I love, and, believe me, the inn is hard to miss with its yellow shutters. There are marble sidewalks and beautifully manicured gardens and lawns.

Accommodations here are grand. The rooms are beautifully decorated, and all have a private bath. The suites have a whirlpool tub. All of the beds, no matter the size, are comfortable. I saw a wonderful king-size brass bed. The goose-down quilts are heaven. Some of the rooms and all of the suites have a fireplace. There is nothing more restful than a crackling fire in your own fireplace. The suites in the Mary Porter House even have a fireplace in the bedroom and a second fireplace in the bathroom.

Robert is a Swiss-trained hotelier and former food and beverage director for the Plaza Hotel in New York. He was born and educated in Switzerland. Don Gatewood, formerly the chef of The Palace Arms Restaurant in the Brown Palace Hotel in Denver, joined the team at The Reluctant Panther as exectutive chef in 1999. His menu is a fine blend of European and American specialties. The greenhouse extension of the dining room is a spectacular setting for Don's creations. His dinners begin with appetizers such as Swiss raclette, or steamed mussels with saffron-thyme sauce. Of course there are more. Some of the tempting entrees are Swiss veal—thinly sliced veal with

Olive Metcalf

mushrooms and white wine. Wiener schnitzel with homemade spaetzle also sounds grand, as does pan-seared pork tenderloin or grilled tuna steak. The choices change every night. The wine list is extensive and very good.

The tavern is cozy, with comfortable chairs, fireplace, and the sort of good company that is found only in a country inn.

HOW TO GET THERE: As you approach Manchester Village from the south on Route 7A, keep an eye on the left. Soon The Reluctant Panther will pop into view, 1 block north from the Equinox Hotel.

The Village Country Inn ♥
Manchester Village, Vermont 05254

INNKEEPERS: Jay and Anne Degen

ADDRESS/TELEPHONE: 3835 Main Street (Route 7A); (802) 362–1792 or (800) 370–0300; fax (802) 362–7238

E-MAIL: vci@vermontel.com

WEB SITE: www.villagecountryinn.com

ROOMS: 12 standard rooms, plus 21 luxury rooms and suites; all with private bath, phone, and air-conditioning; some with TV; 4 with fireplaces. No-smoking inn.

RATES: $183 to $409 per room, double occupancy; MAP. $129 to $345, EPB. Special packages available.

OPEN: All year.

FACILITIES AND ACTIVITIES: Bar-lounge, boutique, swimming pool, tennis, ice skating. Nearby: Golf, skiing, shopping.

*M*anchester's favorite front porch beckons you as you arrive at The Village Country Inn, located in the heart of town. The porch is 100 feet long, with wicker furniture and rockers covered with rose chintz.

This is a beautiful French country inn, done in shades of mauve, celery, and ecru and stunning inside and out. Anne was a professional interior decorator, and the inn reflects her expertise. Mauve is a color I adore. The boutique is The French Rabbit, with well-dressed rabbits to greet you. Anne has wonderful taste, and the boutique is full of very nice things.

Tavern in the Green, the bar and lounge, has an upright piano and nice people who play and sing. One night when I stayed here, a playwright was in this room with a marvelous selection of music and songs. What an unexpected treat! A door from here leads out to the swimming pool and gardens. During the winter the large patio is flooded for ice skating. The inn has a large collection of skates for guests to use, and twinkling lights are hung in the trees all around the patio. In the summertime breakfast and dinner may be served out here.

There is a large fieldstone fireplace dating back to 1889 in the living room, with comfortable couches and chairs around it. Tables are provided for all sorts of games.

The rooms are magnificent, and each one is different. They are done in ice-cream colors. Lots of canopied beds, lace, plush carpets, down pillows, and nice things on dressers and tables give the rooms an elegant atmosphere. Good towels are such an important feature to inn guests, and, needless to say, they are here.

I was in a suite called Chantel's Boudoir. Done in soft greens, the king-size bed is a beauty. There's also a fireplace, television, phone, chaise lounge, and couch. I could live in here.

Victoria's Room has a queen-size bed with a lovely spread, a gas fireplace, a chaise lounge, air-conditioning, a television, phone, and a two-person soaking tub in a lovely large bathroom. It all overlooks the pool area.

Dining is a joy in the lovely Rose Room. The bishop-sleeve lace curtains and trellis alcoves create a cozy and romantic atmosphere for the glorious food. Truffle mousse pâté with proscuitto melon is excellent. Salads aren't run-of-the-mill, and entrees are creative. Grilled lamb chops with goat cheese natural sauce, and charcoal-grilled half pheasant with a lingoberry glaze are just two of the selections. I chose crème brûlée for dessert. It was grand. Breakfast is a full one, with many choices.

Affairs of the heart are wonderful up here. Rekindle the romance by having a "Time for Two" romantic getaway, an affair for the "too busy" and "too stressed." Also offered is the "Blooming Affair," a romantic champagne picnic lunch in the lovely gazebo and formal gardens. These special packages are offered spring, summer, and winter. Christmas, as you can imagine, is very special up here.

HOW TO GET THERE: Coming north on historic Route 7A, you will find the inn on your left in Manchester Village.

Wilburton Inn
Manchester Village, Vermont 05254

INNKEEPERS: Georgette and Albert Levis

ADDRESS/TELEPHONE: River Road (mailing address: P.O. Box 468); (802) 362–2500 or (800) 648–4944

WEB SITE: www.wilburton.com

ROOMS: 11 in main house, 19 in other 5 houses; all with private bath.

RATES: $115 to $315, double occupancy; EPB (includes full breakfast mid-May through October and holidays). MAP rates available.

OPEN: All year.

FACILITIES AND ACTIVITIES: Breakfast, dinner. Tennis, heated pool, sculpture garden. Nearby: Skiing, shopping, art gallery, theater, music festivals, hiking, swimming, canoeing, trout fishing, golf.

This inn was built in 1902 for a friend of Robert Todd Lincoln. In 1906 James Wilbur purchased the estate and lived here until his death in 1929. Later, during World War II, it was a boarding school for daughters of European diplomats. In 1946 the estate became a very elegant inn, and in 1987 Georgette and Albert became the new owners. The inn is set on a twenty-acre knoll that rises above the lush Battenkill River Valley.

When you enter the inn, you are in a large living room with couches and chairs, a huge table for serving tea, and a wonderful fireplace with set of huge carved brass andirons. A library and a porch where breakfast is served are also on the ground floor, along with the dining rooms.

The food here is glorious. For starters I was able to try the vegetarian ravioli with a tomato-sage cream sauce. On another night the gravlax was ambrosia, as were the rack of lamb and the salmon, sweet potato crusted with raspberry gastrique. Very different. Salads are excellent, and the desserts—well, you'd better come up here and see for yourself. Breakfast? Usually I could turn it down, but not when it's this grand. Fresh blueberry muffins and, of course, much, much more. The menus change monthly, and specials abound. The pink-and-white napery add to the pretty ambience.

Accommodations in the main inn are luxurious. Most beds are queen- or king-size, with lovely bedspreads. Wonderful large windows provide a view of the surrounding mountains. Five other houses on the estate are just as well appointed and so nice for families, wedding parties, or corporate meetings.

After a day of whatever you do, return to the inn for tea or cocktails in the living room by the fireplace. This is truly a grand inn.

HOW TO GET THERE: From the blinking light in Manchester, go 1½ miles south on Route 7A to River Road. Go left for 1 mile—the driveway is on the left.

Red Clover Inn
Mendon, Vermont 05701

INNKEEPERS: Mary and Dave Strelecki and Melinda Davis
ADDRESS/TELEPHONE: 7 Woodward Road; (802) 775-2290 or (800) 752-0571; fax (802) 773-0594
E-MAIL: innkeepers@redcloverinn.com
WEB SITE: www.redcloverinn.com

ROOMS: 14 in farm house and carriage house, all with private bath and air-conditioning; 6 with fireplace; 5 with whirlpool tub. TV in some rooms. No-smoking inn.

RATES: $170 to $495, double occupancy; MAP. Packages available.

OPEN: All year except mid-April to mid-May.

FACILITIES AND ACTIVITIES: Dinner every night except Sunday. Pub. Nearby: Skiing at Killington and Pico, shopping, lakes, hiking, golf.

*B*uilt as a summer estate for Gen. John Woodward of Washington, D.C., the inn is nicely tucked off the main road, about 5 miles east of Rutland. All you hear are the sounds of nature.

The inn is very comfortable. The living room has cozy chairs and couches. This is also the library. Curl up in front of the fire with a good book or a friend. Adjacent to the living room is the pub, which will provide you with your favorite drink. The guest rooms are nicely appointed and restful—just what you expect in a good inn.

The dining rooms are lovely, and the food is just glorious. The chef has a good background, and his menu changes daily. There are fine soups and appetizers like broccoli and Gorgonzola cream soup. Roasted tomato, garlic, and garden basil soup is a real winner. Medallions of beef, fettucine, vegetarian pasta, sautéed duck breast, pork tenderloin, and venison are sometimes served as the entrees. Save room, everyone; the desserts are all homemade.

There are several four-legged assistant innkeepers here. There's an elderly, slow-moving Scottish terrier, Ghillie, and the lively Maggie, a Yorkshire terrier. A young, energetic, soft-coated Wheaten terrier named Dillon watches over the grounds from the owner's quarters. Wilson, a tabby cat, stays in hiding most of the time but the barn cat Dink roams about the farm. Every year Mallard ducks return to the inn's pond to raise their ducklings. This is quite a menagerie!

The area offers a lot to do. Killington and Pico are near-by for skiing, or you can go hiking, golfing, swimming or fishing in nearby lakes, and shopping. Do go and have a great time. They have won the *Wine Spectator*'s award of excellence since 1995, and they have a grand wine cellar.

HOW TO GET THERE: Take Route 4 east from Rutland. The inn is on the right, down narrow Woodward Road.

Middlebury Inn
Middlebury, Vermont 05753

INNKEEPERS: Frank and Jane Emanuel

ADDRESS/TELEPHONE: Route 7; (802) 388-4961 or (800) 842-4666; fax (802) 388-4563

E-MAIL: midinnvt@sover.net

ROOMS: 73, including 6 suites; all with private bath, air-conditioning, cable TV, and phone; 3 specially equipped for handicapped.

RATES: $95 to $185, rooms; $134 to $375, suites; double occupancy; EP. Package rates available. EPB available.

OPEN: All year.

FACILITIES AND ACTIVITIES: Breakfast, lunch, afternoon tea, dinner, bar. Wheelchair access to dining rooms and all public areas. Parking, elevator, gift shop. Nearby: Skiing, swimming, golf, fishing, boating, museums.

*T*here has been an inn standing at this same location since 1788. There have been some changes, due to fire and the inroads of time, but the current brick building, known as the Addison House, was constructed in 1827. One hundred years later, when the Middlebury Hotel Company took over, extensive repairs were made, and in 1977 Frank and Jane Emanuel became the innkeepers. Their efforts to restore the inn to its former elegance have been aided by a grant from the Vermont Historic Preservation Division.

The inn has an excellent central location in the delightful town where Middlebury College is situated. There are many historic buildings, museums, and shops to visit in the town, and all around is an abundance of outdoor activities.

The Addison House has a spacious veranda and a really large lobby. The dining room is beautiful, and the food that is served here is delicious. The elegant candlelit buffets should not be missed, from the served appetizer and sherbet courses to the finishing touch of a fingerbowl. Summer dining on the porch is a special delight. The Morgan Room Tavern and Terrace offers excellent liquid refreshment, including the inn's own Candied Apple. Upstairs, the wide halls wander and dip, up one step and down three, wide enough for those ladies of long ago to have maneuvered their hoop skirts with grace.

Additional rooms are in adjacent buildings or wings off the original building. The Jonathan Carver Wing was constructed in 1897, and the Thomas Hagar House, which was built in 1816, is now attached to the Addison House. The Porter Mansion, built in 1825, has five handsome guest rooms, several fireplaces of rare black marble, and a lovely curving staircase in the front parlor. More contemporary-style rooms are found in the Governor Weeks House and the Emma Willard House. The East Wing has been completely and beautifully refurbished.

Whatever type of room you need, you'll find a wide variety of good choices here.

I could stay forever, mooning over the jigsaw puzzle in the lobby or eating their nightly popovers.

HOW TO GET THERE: Go up Route 7, and you will run right into Middlebury. The inn is in the middle of town, overlooking the town green.

Swift House Inn
Middlebury, Vermont 05753

INNKEEPER: Karla Nelson Loura

ADDRESS/TELEPHONE: 25 Stewart Lane; (802) 388-9925;
fax (802) 388-9927

E-MAIL: shi@together.net

WEB SITE: www.swifthouseinn.com

ROOMS: 21, all with private bath, air-conditioning, and phone; some
with cable TV, working fireplace, double whirlpool baths, patios, or
wheelchair accessibility. One room specially equipped for handicapped.

RATES: $90 to $235, double occupancy; continental breakfast.

OPEN: All year.

FACILITIES AND ACTIVITIES: Breakfast. Wheelchair access to dining
room. Sauna, steam room. Nearby: Downhill and cross-
country skiing, hiking, fishing, golf.

Three historic buildings make up this lovely inn. The handsome
Federal-style main house was built in 1814, the Carriage House
added in 1886, and the very Victorian Gate House was constructed
in 1906 near the entrance to the house on Stewart Road. I stayed in a glorious room with a patio in the Carriage House, which has been renovated to
hold six luxurious rooms, all with fireplaces and double whirlpool tubs.

The main house also has many lovely accommodations, especially the
Garden Room, which has a whirlpool tub and its own entrance from a private patio, and the Swift Room, which has a fireplace and canopy bed as well
as a private terrace. Rooms in the Gate House are more modest, but still
inviting; the round turret room is especially appealing. The inn living rooms
have fireplaces and comfortable chairs and couches, nice places to relax.

The complimentary continental breakfast is grand, a buffet spread that
includes juices, yogurt with fresh and dried fruits, granola, cereals, bagels
with cream cheese and smoked salmon, homemade quiche, and all sorts of
delicious muffins, breads, and pastries.

This inn has an interesting history. The original portion was built by
Samuel Swift, who had a long career of public service in Vermont as a lawyer,
judge, legislator, and local historian. After his death in 1875, the home was
purchased by John W. Stewart, another attorney, whose political career
included eight years in Congress and one term as governor of Vermont. By

romantic coincidence, his daughter Jessica married Charles M. Swift, grandson of the original owner of the house. Ask the innkeepers to tell you more about the many accomplishments of the Swift and Stewart families, who continued to live in this home until 1941.

HOW TO GET THERE: Take Route 7 to Middlebury. The inn is 2 blocks north of the center of town on the corner of Route 7 and Stewart Lane.

Zack's on the Rocks 💟
Montgomery Center, Vermont 05471

INNKEEPERS: "Zack" and Gussie Zachadnyk

ADDRESS/TELEPHONE: Route 58; (802) 326–4500

ROOMS: 1 housekeeping cottage for two.

RATES: $100 per night, double occupancy; EP.

OPEN: All year except Monday and Christmas Day.

FACILITIES AND ACTIVITIES: Dinner by reservation only, bar. Wheel-chair access to the dining room.

After you finally find Zack's, you really will not believe what you see. His cottage home and restaurant are literally hanging on the rocks over an incredible valley.

This is my smallest inn. A cottage that sleeps two has a living room, a dining ell, a kitchen, two fireplaces, a bedroom, and an incredible bathroom with a sunken tub. Even if you cannot stay here, stay in town and come up here to eat Zack's food. It is fantastic, and so are he and Gussie, his wife.

Zack's is so unique that it is almost impossible to describe. When you approach the door of his restaurant, you will find it is locked. Ring the sleigh bells, and the door will be opened by Zack. He will be in a wondrous costume, and the performance will begin. I will tell you no more except about the food. The menu is printed on a brown paper bag, which is in beautiful contrast to his restaurant and Gussie's bar. Zack does all of the cooking. He is the most inventive chef and innkeeper I have had the pleasure to meet. The dining room has to be seen to be believed.

And Gussie's bar is something special. It has an organ with a full grand piano top built over it. This is my first organ bar. The room has a stone fire-

Jay Country Store

Just north of Montgomery Village on Route 242 in Jay is the Jay Country Store (802–988–4040), the perfect place to go for a taste of the real Vermont. "Sustenance for both body and spirit" is what they say you'll find here—and they are right. It's just fabulous, a destination in itself, filled to the brim with everything Vermont—handmade quilts, hand-forged lamps, gallery-quality primitives, trunks and boxes, cookbooks by Vermont authors, wonderful hand-painted pottery, lead-free ceramics, and tons more. Two levels of art galleries include lots of American folk art, including the largest selection anywhere of limited-edition lithographs by Will Moses, great-grandson of Grandma Moses. Also here are limited-edition prints by a famed New York naturalist and lithographer—come spend the afternoon and see for yourself.

Don't be afraid to come in hungry. The store also has a terrific deli counter and lunch room where you can feast on an old-fashioned country-style sandwich, a steaming bowl of homemade chili or soup, crispy pickles, and Green Mountain coffee. Fine wines, Vermont cheeses, honey, maple syrup, and a full line of groceries and baked goods are also here. The Christmas World shop includes decorations and ornaments from around the world as well as some handcrafted by local artisans. I've probably left out a whole other list of the things the shop carries—come to discover whatever I left out. Hours are 8:30 A.M. to 7:00 P.M. (and until 9:00 P.M on Friday) every day of the year except Christmas and Thanksgiving. Say hello to owners Peggy and Art Moran.

place and is done pub-style but with flair. The bar has five stools, but to go with it is the best-stocked back bar in Vermont. To top it all, the inn plays music from the forties. What a pleasant sound!

Pyewacket is the name of both of the inn cats.

Zack's cottage is called Fore-the-Rocks. The private home is called Off-the-Rocks, and the inn is called On-the-Rocks. Gussie's bar is After-the-Rocks. Lots of rocks up here. Some of them are even purple.

Reservations here are an absolute must.

HOW TO GET THERE: Going north from Stowe on Route 100, turn left on Route 118 at Eden. When you reach Montgomery Center, turn right on Route 58. The inn is up the hill on the left, after the road becomes dirt.

Black Lantern Inn
Montgomery Village, Vermont 05470

INNKEEPERS: Rita and Allan Kalsmith

ADDRESS/TELEPHONE: Route 118; (802) 326-4507 or (800) 255-8661; fax (802) 326-4077

E-MAIL: blantern@together.net

WEB SITE: www.blacklanterninn.com

ROOMS: 10, plus 6 suites; all with private bath, fireplace, whirlpool tub, and TV.

RATES: $90 to $150 per person, double occupancy; EPB. MAP is available. Kayak- and canoe-trip packages.

OPEN: All year.

FACILITIES AND ACTIVITIES: Bar, outdoor hot tub, cross-country skiing. Nearby: Downhill skiing, fishing, swimming, golf, tennis, bicycle rentals. Breakfast and dinner.

When you get to Montgomery Village, you are nearly in Canada, perhaps 6 or 7 miles from the border. This is a quiet Vermont village, and the Black Lantern has been nicely restored by its hardworking owners. Whether you come in the snow for a skiing vacation or on a green summer day, there is a warm welcome at this friendly inn. It is also surprising to encounter a rather sophisticated menu in this out-of-the-way corner of the world—French onion soup, stuffed mushrooms, and entrees like lamb Marguerite, Drunken Bird, veal cavalier, salmon steak, and much more.

You can ski at Jay Peak, where there are 50 miles of trails for every kind of skier, outright novice to expert. Not too far away, over the border, there are four Canadian mountains, and ski-week tickets are available. Cross-country skiing starts at the inn door and is undoubtedly the best way to see beautiful Vermont in the winter.

Summer brings the joy of outdoor life. Fishing, swimming, golf, tennis, and hiking are all very near, and the inn offers canoe and kayak trips. You've heard about those country auctions, haven't you? Or would you rather spend the day browsing through antiques shops? Whatever you choose to do, there will be a superbly quiet night to catch up on your sleep. The inn's guest accommodations are very comfortable, and the three-room suite is a joy. It has a fireplace and a whirlpool tub. This is heaven. The Burdett House next door has more suites, all of which have a fireplace, a whirlpool tub, and a television with VCR. Some of these suites have a balcony. There is also a nice and bright lounge area.

The bar was the front desk in a hotel in Ohio—now that's recycled furniture.

The double-peaked roof on the old, 1803 farmhouse covers a typical north-country inn. Small, friendly, just a little bit different, and well enjoyed by Nellie, the inn's springer spaniel.

HOW TO GET THERE: Go north from Stowe on Route 100 and turn left on Route 118 at Eden. This will take you into Montgomery Center. Continue down the main street and out of town, and before too long you will reach Montgomery Village and the inn. From I-89 in Burlington turn right at St. Albans onto Route 105, toward Enosburg Falls. Pick up Route 118 at East Berkshire and follow it to Montgomery Village and the inn.

The Four Columns Inn
Newfane, Vermont 05345

INNKEEPERS: Gorty and Pam Baldwin

ADDRESS/TELEPHONE: West Street (mailing address: P.O. Box 278); (802) 365-7713 or (800) 787-6633; fax (802) 365-0022

E-MAIL: innkeeper@fourcolumnsinn.com

WEB SITE: www.fourcolumnsinn.com

ROOMS: 9, plus 6 suites; all with private bath and air-conditioning, many with gas fireplace.; some with gas-log woodstove, whirlpool or soaking tub for two. No-smoking inn.

RATES: $115 to $340, double occupancy; continental breakfast. MAP packages available.

OPEN: All year.

FACILITIES AND ACTIVITIES: Restaurant closed Tuesday. Wheelchair access to dining room and bar. Bar, swimming pool. Nearby: Hiking, ice skating, skiing.

The inn is located on the most photographed town common in Vermont. The area is just beautiful, and so is the inn. Innkeepers Gorty and Pam are truly marvelous, with a friendly staff and a nice dog named Jack.

The rooms are full of antiques. One lovely room has a brass bed. Another room has a canopy bed with a lace top, and four-poster beds are in others. Fresh flowers and plants in your room are a wonderful touch. Big towels and good pillows and mattresses; all these things make up a fine inn. The third-floor suite has a lovely porch with wicker furniture facing the common. A nice place to sit and watch the world go by.

The inn has an attractive living room with a fireplace where you can gather to visit with other guests, read, watch television, or just relax. The dining room with a fireplace has pale green and pink napery. A beautiful armoire is used to display the superb wines served here.

The inn was given three well-deserved stars in the *Mobil Travel Guide* for its food and rooms and a four-diamond rating from AAA for its restaurant.

Chef Greg Parks is the reason. With the inn for more than twenty years, he is nationally known and has attracted many celebrities to the dining room. He loves to use local suppliers. I've tasted the Vermont-raised, milk-fed veal he insists on, and it is heavenly. His menus always have a delicious soup of the day, as well as appetizers such as spicy Vermont quail with greens, goat cheese, and smoked bacon, or smoked salmon mousse. A salad with balsamic vinaigrette and a slice of Pecorino cheese comes before the main course.

Deciding on an entree is not an easy matter, when you have choices like North Atlantic salmon in a hearty bouillabaisse broth, Peking duck breast, seared venison loin with a spiced zinfandel glaze, or a veal T-bone with a sauce of five peppercorns, roasted garlic, and mushrooms. And the rest of the menu is glorious—the desserts are outstanding. Breakfasts may include fresh fruit with a dipping sauce, flaky croissants, granola, and more.

The lounge has a pewter bar, which is very unusual, lots of plants, and more country charm than you can shake a stick at. Do I like it here? Just wish I lived closer!

Outside is a lovely swimming pool. And down at the stream is a hammock waiting for you. The trout pond is stocked. Try your luck or let the staff catch you one. Can't get them much fresher than this.

HOW TO GET THERE: The inn is 220 miles from New York and 100 miles from Boston. Take exit 2 from I-91 at Brattleboro to Route 30 north. The inn is in Newfane, 100 yards off Route 30, on your left.

Old Newfane Inn
Newfane, Vermont 05345

INNKEEPERS: Eric and Gundy Weindl

ADDRESS/TELEPHONE: Court Street; (802) 365-4427 or (800) 784-4427

WEB SITE: www.oldnewfaneinn.com

ROOMS: 10, all with private bath.

RATES: Rooms, $105 to $115; suites, $135 to $155; double occupancy; continental breakfast. No credit cards.

OPEN: All year except April to mid-May, late October to mid-December, and Monday.

FACILITIES AND ACTIVITIES: Dinner, bar. Parking. Nearby: Skiing, swimming, hiking.

The inn is well named, for old it is—1787, to be exact. It has been carefully kept, however, and the weary traveler will find great comfort and fabulous food.

Almost all the rooms have twin beds and are large and tastefully furnished. Gundy is a very good decorator. There is an informal bar and lounge, and the dining room has tables with pink cloths over white ones. Very effective. There is a huge brick wall with a fireplace in the dining room that gives a wonderful feeling of warmth and good cheer. The floors here are polished to a turn and beyond. And not just run-of-the-mill glassware for the inn. The drinks I had before lunch were served in crystal.

Like his counterpart at the Four Columns Inn, Eric Weindl has been here for a long time, more than thirty years, and he has built a notable reputation for his prowess in the kitchen. It is unusual for one small hamlet to have two such talented chefs, and Newfane has become a popular destination with gourmets. Eric trained in Switzerland, and his menu remains European, with dishes such as veal goulash with spaetzle and snails, Burgundian style.

His soups are a bit different and very good. I have tried both the cold strawberry and the creamed watercress. Loved them both. By the way, I hate calf's liver, but Eric asked me to try his. What magic he performed I do not know, but I ate every bite. Veal is king here. Eric butchers his own, so he gets the exact cuts he wants. Of course, the menu also has seafood, lamb, fowl, pheasant, venison, and fine steaks. The dessert menu reads like poetry, from the flaming suzette and jubilee to a fabulous omelet surprise. There are also some cream pies demanding that you do not even think of calories.

HOW TO GET THERE: Take exit 2 from I–91 in Brattleboro, and follow Route 30 North. The inn is on the corner of Court Street and Route 30, on the left in Newfane.

North Hero House
North Hero, Vermont 05474

INNKEEPER: John Martinez; Walter Blasberg, owner

ADDRESS/TELEPHONE: Route 2 (mailing address: P.O. Box 106); (802) 372-4732 or (888) LAKENH; fax (802) 372-3218

E-MAIL: NHHLAKE@aol.com

WEB SITE: www.northherohouse.com

ROOMS: 26 in 4 buildings; all with private bath; most with screened porch overlooking the lake; some with fireplaces and Jacuzzis.

RATES: $69 to $249, double occupancy; continental breakfast in winter, full breakfast May to October. $129 to $309 MAP.

OPEN: All year.

FACILITIES AND ACTIVITIES: Dinner, full license. TV in living room, outdoor hot tub, games, swimming, boating, tennis, shuffleboard, fishing, ice skating, cross-country skiing, ice fishing.

Getting here is a treat for the eyes. North Hero is the county seat of Grand Isle, one of the Champlain Islands. This is one huge lake. It's so scenic and offers so much to do. And as you look across Lake Champlain, you see Mount Mansfield.

Most of the rooms, located in four buildings, have screened porches overlooking the lake. There are spacious lakeside rooms in Homestead, which is done in barn siding; Southwind, made out of pine; and Cove House, in brick. North Hero House was founded in 1891.

There is outdoor dining on the patio overlooking the lake. Inside are a regular dining room and a very bright greenhouse–dining room behind it.

Dinner is a real treat. There are several different appetizers, often including delicious house-cured gravlox. Entrees include steak, chicken, and veal, all done in many interesting ways, as well as seafood—salmon, fresh walleye, scallops, and shrimp. For vegetarians the pasta of the day is a good choice, and the main course salads are delicious. Do save room for dessert.

In the morning, breakfast offerings are fresh fruit, coffee, tea, cold cereal, and freshly baked muffins (blueberry, cinnamon apple, and carrot are some of the favorites). During the warm-weather season, May to October, guests may order from the full menu as well.

There are boat rentals—paddleboats, canoes, Sunfish, sailboats—or come in your own boat. Looking for another sort of adventure? Fishing is good for bass, walleye, and Northern pike. Need to relax? The sandy beach and lawn chairs are inviting. Bird-watchers will enjoy the inn's birding weekends.

In winter, there's still plenty to do, what with ice skating, cross-country skiing, ice-fishing excursions, and special events such as murder mystery weekends and wine tasting dinners.

The outdoor hot tub is a perfect ending to the day whatever the season.

Champ is a cousin of Scotland's famous Nessie and lives in the lake. Come up and see if you can spot her.

HOW TO GET THERE: Take exit 17 from I-89 onto Route 2 West about 17 miles to North Hero. The inn is in the center of the village.

The Norwich Inn
Norwich, Vermont 05055

INNKEEPERS: Sally and Tim Wilson

ADDRESS/TELEPHONE: Main Street; (802) 649-1143;
fax (802) 649-2909

ROOMS: 27, including 4 two-bedroom suites; all with private bath, cable TV, and phone.

RATES: Winter, $69 to $129, double occupancy, EP; summer, $79 to $149, double occupancy, EP.

OPEN: All year.

FACILITIES AND ACTIVITIES: Breakfast, lunch, dinner, Sunday brunch, bar; dining room closed Monday. Nearby: Swimming, canoeing, golf, skiing, tennis, biking, hiking.

*R*ight on the sign for the inn it says SINCE 1797, and it is truly said, because travelers up the beautiful Connecticut River Valley have been finding a warm welcome at this grand old house ever since. It is just a mile away from Dartmouth College, and alumni, skiers, tourists, and commercial travelers find a special homelike atmosphere here that is dignified but a lot of fun.

The friendly bar and lounge area is named The Jasper Murdock Ale House after the inn's first owner. All the draft beers are brewed on the premises, just as they were in colonial "public houses" before the advent of commercial breweries. Some of them are Whistling Pig Red Ale, Jasper Murdock's Old Ale, Pompanoosuc Wheat Beer, and Fuggle & Barley Corn, and there are more. Go and have fun.

The food is glorious. The Sunday champagne brunch offers you a glass of bubbly or a mimosa, along with eggs Benedict, a crepe or quiche of the day, or chicken duffina (sautéed with artichoke hearts in Madeira and cream). Dinner is always good here. Blackened carpaccio is an appetizer done with thinly sliced sirloin, capers, and garlic rounds. For entrees there are poached North Atlantic salmon, crisp roasted boneless duckling with raspberry glaze, and escallops of veal with julienne prosciutto, among others. The desserts are wonderful. The wine list is one of the most extensive I have seen.

Montshire Museum of Science

A beautiful woodland setting of one hundred acres along the Connecticut River is the site of the Montshire Museum of Science (802-649-2200) on Montshire Road in Norwich. Two floors of exhibit space include dozens of interactive displays about nature, space, and technology. Fresh- and saltwater aquariums, live animal exhibits, a gift shop of science and nature-related books and toys, and an outdoor network of walking trails and picnic areas await visitors of all ages. The museum is open year-round daily from 10:00 A.M. to 5:00 P.M.

Breakfasts are ample, with fruit, cereals, toast, muffins, eggs any way, crepes, French toast, pancakes, and a deep-dish quiche of the day. There is a very full lunch menu; if you can't find something to eat, then you must not be very hungry.

The rooms have very good beds and mattresses. There are canopied beds and some iron and brass beds. All rooms are beautiful, and each one has its own telephone. Guest pets are welcome in the carriage house rooms.

Make sure you ask for a copy of the history of the inn—it's fascinating.

HOW TO GET THERE: Take exit 13 from I-91. Go west a bit less than 1 mile to the center of town. The inn is on your left.

The Four Chimneys 🍂
Old Bennington, Vermont 05201

INNKEEPERS: Christine and Harold Cullison

ADDRESS/TELEPHONE: 21 West Road; (802) 447-3500 or (800) 649-3503; fax (802) 447-3692

E-MAIL: innkeeper@fourchimneys.com

WEB SITE: www.fourchimneys.com

ROOMS: 11; all with private bath, air-conditioning, phone, and TV; 9 with Jacuzzi; 9 with fireplace; 1 specially equipped for handicapped.

RATES: $95 to $200, single; $110 to $215, double; continental breakfast.

OPEN: All year.

FACILITIES AND ACTIVITIES: Dinner, bar and lounge. Full license. Nearby: Facilities at Mount Anthony Country Club.

When you come into the inn, straight ahead is the bar and lounge. The lounge is so comfortable, with a fireplace and light-colored couches and chairs. If you turn right down the hall, you'll find the dining room, and the food is grand. For dinner, appetizers might include Burgundy-style snails in garlic butter or crisp taro root Napoleon with crabmeat, spiced tomato, avocado, and shrimp. Main courses could be seared tuna, lamb rack, beef medallions, roasted chicken, or lots more really good choices. Desserts? Oh boy—one is crème caramel. In summer the porch overlooking the gardens is ambrosia.

There are eleven guest rooms, and they are beauties. They have queen- or king-size beds, quilts, and color-coordinated sheets and towels. Cut-glass lamps in the bedrooms are pretty and give good light for reading. On the third floor the bathroom has a huge Jacuzzi for two, with seats. The icehouse has a wonderful suite; so does the carriage house.

The inn is a wonderful setting for weddings or family reunions.

HOW TO GET THERE: From Boston take I-90 to Lee. Go up Route 7 to the center of Bennington, and then take Route 9 west to the inn. From Lee take Route 20, which becomes Route 7.

Willough Vale Inn
Orleans, Vermont 05680

INNKEEPERS: Randall and Katherine Johnson

ADDRESS/TELEPHONE: Route 5A South; (802) 525-4123 or (800) 594-9102; fax (802) 525-4514

E-MAIL: info@willoughvale.com

WEB SITE: www.willoughvale.com

ROOMS: 8, plus 4 cottages; all with private bath; 1 specially equipped for handicapped. Fireplaces in cottages.

RATES: $79 to $125, double occupancy; $99 to $179, cottages; continental breakfast. Higher in fall.

OPEN: All year.

FACILITIES AND ACTIVITIES: Dinner for guests in season, bar, and lounge. Wheelchair access to dining room and rest rooms. Fishing, swimming, and boating at the lake. Nearby: Snowshoeing, snowmobile trails, hiking. Snowmobile trail from back door.

*T*his is a scenic paradise with one of the most beautiful lakes I've seen in many a country mile. Do you like to fish? There are lake trout, landlocked salmon, perch, and rainbow trout just waiting for your line.

A porch with a gazebo at one end overlooks the lake. Around it are beautiful flowers. Lupine and wildflowers are all over the place.

The inn is full of antique and Vermont-handcrafted furniture. The guest rooms are all furnished differently, but all have comfortable queen beds. There's even a whirlpool for two in one lovely bathroom. Clock radios are in all the rooms. I liked the nice parlor and library. It's a quiet spot for cards, writing, reading, or just relaxing after an active day.

The taproom has an elegant bar and tables and is a pleasant gathering place. Dinner is available for guests only, by reservation, and the menu has a nice variety of entrees to be enjoyed along with the lake view.

There are climbing trails on Mount Hor and Mount Pisgah and skiing at nearby Burke Mountain. Snowmobiling across the frozen lake is invigorating. A canoe ride on a moonlit night would be wonderful.

The fully equipped cottages have a fireplace, screened porch, deck, and private dock. There are two-bedroom cabins and one with one bedroom. Pets less than fifty pounds are welcome here in certain rooms.

HOW TO GET THERE: From the south leave I-91 at Lyndonville (exit 23) and proceed north on Routes 5 and 5A. From Canada get off I-91 at Barton and follow Route 16 to Route 5A.

Johnny Seesaw's
Peru, Vermont 05152

INNKEEPERS: Gary and Nancy Okun

ADDRESS/TELEPHONE: Route 11; (802) 824–5533 or (800) 424–2729

E-MAIL: jseesaws@sover.net

ROOMS: 30, all with private bath; some with fireplace.

RATES: Summer, $38 to $75, per person, EPB; winter, $50 to $97, per person, EPB. Pets welcome.

OPEN: All year except end of skiing season to Memorial Day and end of foliage season until Thanksgiving.

FACILITIES AND ACTIVITIES: Dinner, liquor license. Wheelchair access to dining room. TV, game room, swimming, tennis. Nearby: Skiing, hunting, golf, horseback riding, fishing, hiking, biking.

Skiing Magazine once said that this inn has the best Yankee cuisine in New England. The food is good, tasty country food prepared with imagination, featuring home-baked bread and homemade soup. Val is the talented chef who turns out all this fine fare.

The inn has a unique character, mostly because of the guests who keep coming back. It is set 2,000 feet up, on Bromley Mountain. The 65-by-25-foot marble-rimmed pool is a great summer gathering place, and the tennis court is always ready. There are six nearby golf courses, and riding horses can be hired in Peru.

For the many skiers who come to Vermont, Bromley's chairlifts and GLM Ski School are right next door. Stratton Mountain, the Viking Ski Touring Center, and Wild Wings X-C are but a few minutes away.

For fishers and hunters, or those who wish to take up the sport, the Orvis

Fly-Fishing and Wing Shooting schools in nearby Manchester have excellent instruction. Classes are held regularly and participants can stay at the inn. The nearby towns boast many attractive and interesting shops.

The circular fireplace in the lounge really attracts me at the end of a long day, to say nothing of the cushioned platform along one side of the library. Stoker, the inn dog, will keep you company here.

There is a lot of history in this inn. The back of the extensive menu details the legend of the inn and is well worth reading. On the menu are such appetizers as crab cakes, tortellini Alfredo, and good soups. Entrees are veal, meat, fish, fowl, and vegetarian.

HOW TO GET THERE: The inn is 220 miles from New York, 150 miles from Boston. From Route 7 take Route 11 right at Manchester Depot. The inn is 6 miles east, on Vermont Route 11. From I-91 follow exit 6 to Route 103 to Chester. The inn is 20 miles west, on Vermont Route 11.

Wiley Inn
Peru, Vermont 05152

INNKEEPERS: Judy and Jerry Goodman

ADDRESS/TELEPHONE: Route 11 (mailing address: P.O. Box 37); (802) 824-6600 or (888) 843-6600; fax (802) 824-4195

E-MAIL: wileyinn@sover.net

WEB SITE: www.wileyinn.com

ROOMS: 16, all with private bath; 2 with Jacuzzis; 4 with fireplace.

RATES: $105 to $95, winter; $85 to $165, rest of year; double occupancy; EPB.

OPEN: All year except two weeks in May.

FACILITIES AND ACTIVITIES: Breakfast, picnic lunch available, dinner for inn guests, by reservation. Swimming pool. Large Jacuzzi outside. Gift shop. Nearby: Hiking, skiing, horseback riding, fishing, golf, canoeing, antiquing, skiing, sleigh rides, ice skating, snowmobiling.

The Wiley Inn has been greeting guests for more than half a century. The main house was built in 1835 and was turned into an inn in 1943. Over the years it has been a farmhouse, stagecoach stop, and tearoom. It has changed a lot since it was built, having had at least ten additions, which is typical of Vermont's continuous architecture.

Jerry and Judy are friendly and pleasant innkeepers who do a good job of making guests feel right at home. The lower living room has a fireplace, a bar, a huge couch, and tons of things to do, such as a player piano with a lot of rolls, a television and VCR with a library of films (including a lot of Disney films for the kids), and games.

The library has an old-fashioned phone booth from a Philadelphia drugstore. The phone still works. There are a lot of books in here. Would you like to surf the Net? Well, there's a cyber cafe in here, and next to it is a small bar and a fireplace.

You will always find something to do at the inn. The swimming pool is heated and has a deck; there's an outdoor children's play set for climbing, sliding, and swinging; and the Long and Appalachian Trails are nearby. So are several golf courses, horseback riding, fishing, and the alpine slide and other

amusements at Bromley. During fall the foliage is king, and in winter there are Bromley, Stratton, Magic, and Okemo Mountains for you downhill skiers. Cross-country ski touring centers are within minutes. Go and enjoy.

Dinner is offered by reservation for guests of the inn in season; families are most welcome. The fireside bar in the living room offers aprés-ski refreshments and year-round evening bar service, with a nice selection of wines and both local and imported beers.

HOW TO GET THERE: From I–91 take exit 6 to Route 103 to Chester. Go left on Route 11. The inn is 20 miles west, in Peru.

Pittsfield Inn
Pittsfield, Vermont 05762

INNKEEPER: Tom Yennerell

ADDRESS/TELEPHONE: P.O. Box 685; (802) 746–8943 or (877) 746–8943

E-MAIL: escapert@vermontel.net

WEB SITE: www.pittsfieldinn.com

ROOMS: 9, all with private bath.

RATES: $90 to $150 per person, double occupancy; EPB.

OPEN: All year.

FACILITIES AND ACTIVITIES: Breakfast and dinner, 7 days when open. Full liquor license.

Nice to have Tom back as innkeeper of his inn. When you arrive the living room is to your right and just beyond is the bar, a television, woodstove, and good bar stools. To the left is the dining room, named Sweet Peas. The menu changes weekly. Some good ideas of what they have are great beginnings like Vermont chevre and fresh herb crepes, fresh garden herbs wrapped in a delicate crepe served with a tomato-basil medley—yum yum—peanut soup, onion soup, and shrimp in beer batter. Entrees may be salmon with puff pastry, chicken a la Sweet Pea or Marsala, filet mignon, or rib-eye steak. Homemade desserts are a treat to come back to after a day of hiking.

The inn offers Escape Routes, guided and self-guided outdoor adventures in the Green Mountains of Ver-

mont. They include biking, hiking, trout fishing, snowshoeing, and backcountry skiing. Something for every season. The activities are customized to meet your desires and abilities. It would be just beautiful to ski in snow that no one else has ever seen.

The Tweed and White Rivers are close by and full of trout and salmon, so come on, you anglers.

The inn has been here since 1835. A lot of history is around New England. Come and enjoy. The bar itself is antique; it's old marble.

HOW TO GET THERE: The inn is 20 miles northeast of Rutland. Take 4 east and Route 100 north to the village of Pittsfield. The inn is on the green.

The Golden Stage Inn
Proctorsville, Vermont 05055

INNKEEPERS: Sandy and Peter Gregg

ADDRESS/TELEPHONE: 399 Depot Street, off Route 131; (802) 226-7744 or (800) 253-8226

E-MAIL: goldenstageinn@tds.net

WEB SITE: www.virtualvermont.com/countryinn

ROOMS: 9; 6 with private bath; 1 suite.

RATES: $89 to $214, double occupancy; EPB.

OPEN: All year.

FACILITIES AND ACTIVITIES: Beer and wine license. Swimming pool, bike tours. Nearby: Hiking, skiing, alpine slide, gondola rides, antiquing, golf, biking, fishing, summer theater.

The Golden Stage Inn still is known locally as the Skinner place, for Otis, the actor, and his daughter Cornelia Otis Skinner, the author. The house was built more than 200 years ago, shortly before Vermont's founding in 1791. It was once a stagecoach stop and is reputed to have been a stop on the Underground Railroad.

When you drive in, you immediately notice the rockers on the porch and the abundance of flowers that surround the inn. It's very pretty in the summertime. Sit and rock on the porch and enjoy the breathtaking views of the Black River Valley and Okemo Mountain.

One of the rooms has its own little porch. There are lovely quilts, many antiques, and lots of books. The living room, with its cozy fireplace, is very comfortable after a day of doing your own thing. There are all sorts of games and puzzles, too, but maybe all you want to do is sit and knit or read.

The food is delicious. Tomato wine soup is my favorite appetizer. Veal and mushrooms with a wine sauce and pork tenderloin in an orange-ginger sauce are just two of the good entrees. A chocolate walnut torte makes any chocolate lover swoon, and the fallen chocolate soufflé is a big hit, too. Croissants on Sunday morning are a heavenly way to start the day. The inn also has a huge vegetable and herb garden, so necessary to the good cooking here.

Ten acres of rolling lawns, beautiful gardens, and trees are just what you need for a picnic, a long walk, or simply being alone. Surrounding this haven of loveliness are thousands of acres of forests to hike in and four mountains noted for their good skiing. They are Okemo Mountain, Mount Ascutney, Bromley (fun in summer, too, with its exciting alpine slide down the mountain), and Killington Peak, which has year-round gondola rides, the longest in the United States. Killington often has one of the longest ski seasons in the East.

Biking from inn to inn is another way to see this wonderful country. While you bike to the next inn, a support van transfers your luggage. This is my idea of neat.

The whole first floor is handicapped accessible. A nice touch for deaf guests are rooms specially equipped for the deaf; they have Strobe lights for the fire alarm. The Otis room has a print of Otis Skinner as Romeo—this room has a double hide-away bed, an iron double bed, and books.

Also in residence are the inn's two sheep, 'Lil April and Shayla.

The inn has a cookie jar that is never empty. Nice.

HOW TO GET THERE: From I-91 take exit 6 to Route 103, then take a right off Route 103 at the Proctorsville sign. The inn is the first driveway immediately on the right.

Okemo Lantern Lodge
Proctorsville, Vermont 05153

INNKEEPERS: Jennifer Keegan and Alex Bordas

ADDRESS/TELEPHONE: P.O. Box 247; (802) 226-7770 or (800) 732-7077

ROOMS: 10, all with private bath.

RATES: $90 to $140 per couple; EPB.

OPEN: All year.

FACILITIES AND ACTIVITIES: Beer and wine license. Swimming pool. Nearby: Golf, tennis, bicycling, skiing, skating, hiking, antiquing, fishing, horseback riding.

The inn was built in the early 1800s. It is a lovely Victorian with natural butternut woodwork and original stained-glass windows. The living room is all comfort, with armchairs, couches, and a crackling fire to warm your toes after a day on the slopes. A sunny bay window is the perfect place to settle in at the table with one of the inn's many board games.

Each bedroom is unique, some with king-size beds, many with four-posters and canopies. Some are large enough to accommodate families. Guests are welcomed with chocolate truffles and bottled water in their rooms. TV/VCR combinations are available so that you can enjoy selections from the inn's large video library.

Heavenly aromas are always coming from the kitchen, whether they are from the homemade bread in the oven, freshly perked coffee, or bacon sizzling on the grill. Breakfast is served family-style at tables in the formal dining room. The larger of the two tables has been with the property for more than one hundred years, and the detail in the woodwork is amazing.

At the end of the day, Jennifer and Alex invite guests to a cocktail hour with delicious hors d'oeuvres such as scallops wrapped in bacon, tenderloin–bleu cheese crostinis, and shrimp canapés. A typical dinner menu might include homemade butternut squash soup, spinach salad with fresh raspberries and chèvre, and for the main course, ginger-honey glazed salmon, London broil with bérnaise sauce, or a traditional New England clambake. Lovely cut flowers on the table and around the inn are from the gardens on the property.

When the weather is mild, the wraparound porch is the perfect place to enjoy a drink, read a book, or watch the world go by, and the swimming pool is ready to refresh after a day of hiking or biking. In winter, skiers will find Okemo Mountain just 3 miles away, and Killington is 20 miles to the north. The inn offers ski-and-stay packages.

HOW TO GET THERE: Take I–91 to exit 6. Go north on Route 103 to its junction with Route 131 and turn right. The inn is ¼ mile on the left.

Parker House
Quechee, Vermont 05059

INNKEEPERS: Walt and Barbara Forrester and sons Jay and Nick

ADDRESS/TELEPHONE: 16 Main Street; (802) 295-6077

E-MAIL: parker_house_inn@valley.net

WEB SITE: www.theparkerhouseinn.com

ROOMS: 7, all with private bath; some with air-conditioning.

RATES: $115 to $140, double occupancy; EPB. Package plans available.

OPEN: All year.

FACILITIES AND ACTIVITIES: Dinner every night but Tuesday. Weekends only in winter and spring. Ask about Italian night (summer and fall only)—it's grand. Lounge, full license. Inquire about cooking classes. Nearby: Full privileges at Quechee Club, fly-fishing, canoeing.

Parker House Inn, a registered National Historic Site, was built in 1857 by Vermont state senator Joseph C. Parker for his family. The Ottauquechee River flows along the rear of the property, and 2 miles away is the Quechee Gorge, 165 feet deep and an amazing sight.

All the rooms, which are furnished in a Victorian style, have names. My friend Audrey and I had Emily. At the top of the steps is another beauty, Rebecca; down the hall are Joseph and Walter, which look over the river. The third floor has more rooms. There is also a cozy sitting room with a small television and games.

Up in one room is a desk that you have to see—an early Victorian Murphy-style bed that, when put together, looks like a desk. It's from the late 1800s.

The dining rooms are lovely. The tables are nicely spaced, and the food prepared by Walt and Barbara is glorious. He is a graduate of the Culinary Institute of America, and Barbara is a natural chef. The grilled portobello mushrooms, served on spinach salad with warm Vermont goat cheese, were superb. I think I could also have eaten this for breakfast. Walt and Barbara offer a sampler—a tasting of three selected appetizers—which is a nice idea.

The menu changes quite often. When I was visiting, some of the entrees were roast rack of lamb, beef tenderloin, breast of chicken, and Vermont rabbit. And the desserts were heavenly, but you'll have to come see for yourself.

On the porch, which is shaded by an awning, are tables and chairs. Sit out here and watch the river. There's also a brick side patio. This is a very nice inn, with wonderful innkeepers.

Guests of the inn can enjoy full club privileges at the Quechee Club. It has two 18-hole golf courses, skiing, tennis, swimming, and a fitness center. There are golf and tennis packages and also a sports widow package for those who want to indulge in a massage, facial, pedicure, and manicure. And, of course, there's the wonderful river for fly-fishing or canoeing. The pleasant bar has a view of the river. Here you'll find two game boards; one is Life's Little Instructions—very funny.

HOW TO GET THERE: Take exit 1 off I-89 North. Turn left on Route 4 for 4 miles, crossing the Quechee Gorge. Turn right at the flashing traffic light. Cross the covered bridge and turn left. The inn is on the left.

The Quechee Inn at Marshland Farm
Quechee, Vermont 05059

INNKEEPERS: Meghan and Myles Ostroff; Rodger Perry, owner

ADDRESS/TELEPHONE: Quechee Main Street; (802) 295–3133 or (800) 235–3133; fax (802) 295–6587

E-MAIL: info@quecheeinn.com

WEB SITE: www.quecheeinn.com

ROOMS: 24, all with private bath and TV.

RATES: $90 to $240, double occupancy; EPB.

OPEN: All year.

FACILITIES AND ACTIVITIES: Lounge, full license. Wheelchair access to dining room. Cross-country ski learning center, fly-fishing school, bicycles and canoes to rent, fishing, hiking. Nearby: Downhill skiing, golf, tennis, squash, swimming, boating.

The first time that I saw and heard Quechee Gorge, I was standing on the bridge that spans it. Now I know another way to see this remarkable quirk of nature. The inn is but a ½ mile from it, and the innkeeper will show you how to see it from an unusual angle.

The inn was a private home from 1793 until 1976 and has been beautifully converted to an inn. Rooms in the inn have a variety of beds, doubles to king size, and some lovely queen canopy beds. Seven more guest rooms, in the wing off the original building, have windows overlooking the meadow and lake. All rooms are equipped with color cable television, and the whole inn is air-conditioned.

Arts and Crafts in Quechee

Downer's Mill in Quechee is now the site of Simon Pearce's beautiful glassworks, operated in part through the harnessing of the Ottauquechee River's hydropower. In the center of Quechee overlooking the waterfall of the dam and the covered bridge, you will find the mill and its glassworks. Visitors can watch the glass-blowing process and view the hydroelectric turbine that fuels Simon's glass furnace. You might also see a potter throwing a piece of pottery on the wheel. You can admire or shop for the finished products; both first-quality pieces and seconds are sold in the lovely retail shop. Along with the glassware are Simon Pearce pottery, plus quilts, sweaters, baskets, linens, jewelry, and other Vermont-made handcrafts. The Simon Pearce Restaurant at the mill serves lunch and dinner daily. For information on the glassworks and shop, call (802) 295-2711. For restaurant information or reservations, call (802) 295-1470.

Right at the Quechee Inn at Marshland Farm is the Quechee Inn Gallery. Visit during your stay for a look at paintings, prints, etchings, lithographs, and other work by fine artists from Vermont and elsewhere. Changing exhibitions of featured artists are hung frequently throughout the year.

There are paintings by local artists in the dining room and a beautiful awning over the porch. Adjoining the dining room is a small library used for meetings or private dining. It's a real treat to be able to have a business meeting at a place like this. The living room has an abundance of comfortable chairs and couches, a piano, color television, books, and a fireplace. One feels at home here any season of the year.

Breakfast is a sumptuous buffet. Everything is delicious. Dinner is equally good. Appetizers include Maine lobster bisque and smoked Scottish salmon. Among the varied entrees might be Gulf shrimp scampi, veal saltim bocca, sautéed chicken breast with sage cream, India green curry with basmati rice, and a fresh fish of the day. Homemade breads and scones are always a treat.

The inn guests have full club privileges at the nearby private Quechee Club. The two championship golf courses are breathtakingly scenic and are challenging. You can also play tennis and squash here for a fee.

HOW TO GET THERE: From I-91 take I-89 North to exit 1. Go west on Route 4 for 1²⁄₁₀ miles, then right on Quechee Main Street for 1 mile to the inn.

Three Stallion Inn
Randolph, Vermont 05060

INNKEEPERS: Martina F. L. Rutkovsky; Sam and Jinny Sammas, owners

ADDRESS/TELEPHONE: Lower Stock Farm Road; (802) 728-5575
or (800) 424-5575; fax (802) 728-4036

E-MAIL: tsi@quest.net.com

WEB SITE: www.3stallioninn.com

ROOMS: 15; 13 with private bath.

RATES: $127 to $170, double occupancy; EP; continental breakfast. Packages available.

OPEN: All year.

FACILITIES AND ACTIVITIES: Dinner. Two all-weather tennis courts, pool. 1,300 acres with 35 kilometers of trails for mountain biking or cross-country skiing, two stocked trout ponds. Nearby: Downhill skiing, golf, swimming and fishing in White River, Chandler Music Hall.

The full name of the inn is Three Stallion Inn at the Green Mountain Stock Farm, a sign that this valley is the original birthplace of the Morgan horse. The emphasis used to be on riding, but today this is an inn with all kinds of recreation. The 1,300-acre property includes a swimming pool, two tennis courts, two stocked trout ponds, and 35 kilometers of trails for mountain biking or cross-country skiing. You can rent equipment right on the property. The Montague Golf Club, one of the oldest in the state, adjoins the inn's property along the White River. Swimming and fishing in the river is also fun, and at the end of the day, you can relax in the inn's whirlpool and sauna or take advantage of the fitness center.

Guest rooms and suites are spacious and decorated with lovely floral prints and antiques. Two-bedroom suites are perfect for families. Guests wake up to a bountiful continental breakfast of fresh fruit, juices and cereals, homemade breads, and freshly made granola from a local farm.

Dinner at Lippitt's Restaurant changes monthly and emphasizes foods of the season. The winter menu might begin with onion soup or New England clam chowder, blackened shrimp and scallops, or baked eggplant crepes. Main dishes include sea scallops, tempura coconut shrimp with orange-horseradish dipping sauce, prime rib of beef, or wild game. In summer, you can enjoy a cocktail or dinner on the covered deck overlooking the lawns, trout pond, and lovely gardens.

Morgan's Pub is more informal and has its own light menu of burgers and pasta; winter pub guests enjoy the warmth of a Vermont iron castings stove.

With all these attractions, part of the inn property is being devoted to lots for private homes.

An added bonus in the town of Randolph is the Chandler Music Hall, featuring chamber music, jazz, and popular concerts. If you want more amusement, the town also offers a movie theater, bowling alley, and ice-skating rink.

HOW TO GET THERE: Take exit 4 off I–89. Go 1⁸/₁₀ miles toward Randolph. Turn left on Stock Farm Road and go ⁷/₁₀ mile to the inn.

The Inn at Saxtons River
Saxtons River, Vermont 05154

INNKEEPERS: Jeremy Burrell and Steven Griffiths; Ilene and Sandy Freiman, owners

ADDRESS/TELEPHONE: 27 Main Street; (802) 869–2110; fax (802) 869–3033

E-MAIL: theinn@sover.net

WEB SITE: www.innsaxtonsriver.com

ROOMS: 16, all with private bath; 2 with porch.

RATES: $120, double occupancy; EPB.

OPEN: All year.

FACILITIES AND ACTIVITIES: Dinner, Sunday brunch. Pub. Nearby: Downhill and cross-country skiing, horse-drawn sleigh rides, country fairs.

This wonderful Victorian inn started life in 1903 as a hotel and then became an inn several years later. It's a rare gem. When you see it, you'll see what I mean.

The guest rooms are well decorated, and two have private porches, so you can sit and listen to the quiet. There's a Victorian pub, and the porches have rockers. What a comfortable way to spend a summer evening. Winter is glorious. Take a sleigh ride through the pristine white snow or just enjoy the warmth of the inn and the fireplace.

When you enter the inn, the parlor is on the left. It has a baby grand

piano, fireplace, and good couches and chairs. On the right is the pub. Ahead is the dining room. I like Toby jugs, and there is a nice collection over the fireplace.

The menus are enticing. One really excellent appetizer is the baked cheese; it's a blend of three cheeses, sun-dried tomatoes, tarragon, and Dijon mustard, all wrapped in puff pastry. Go on to delicious soups, salads, and entrees like roast Vermont turkey, sautéed pork medallions, boneless roast duck, and pasta of the day. Espresso and cappuccino and lovely desserts cap off the meal.

The brochure says a lot: Service is the key word, and the service is the same that has been practiced in small English hotels and inns for more than a century. It is "above and beyond."

HOW TO GET THERE: Take I–91 to exit 5. Proceed on Route 5 North to Route 121 to Saxtons River and the inn.

The Londonderry Inn
South Londonderry, Vermont 05155

INNKEEPERS: Chrisman and Maya Kearn

ADDRESS/TELEPHONE: P.O. Box 2038, Route 100; (802) 824–5226

E-MAIL: londinn@sover.net

WEB SITE: www.londonderryinn.com

ROOMS: 25; 20 with private bath.

RATES: $79 to $156, double occupancy; EPB. No credit cards.

OPEN: All year.

FACILITIES AND ACTIVITIES: Dinner served weekends and holidays only, bar. Restaurant closed late October to mid-December and April to mid-June. Pool tables, Ping-Pong, swimming. Nearby: Skiing, horseback riding, hiking.

The location is lovely, high on a hill overlooking the West River. Once a dairy farm, circa 1826, the house has grown into a comfortable rambling inn with many common areas, a great place for families as well as grown-ups. You can relax in the living room in front of the big stone fireplace, play Ping-Pong or pocket billiards in one of the game rooms, or head for the movie room with a cup of hot cocoa or apple cider and cookies. Three major ski areas are within a ten-minute drive, and there's sledding on the expansive property. A spring-fed swimming pool and nearby hiking trails call in summer. With so much to do for all ages, and dormitory rooms available, this is an ideal inn for family reunions.

The old woodshed is now the dining room, where you'll have a hearty buffet breakfast. The only problem is making a choice. Pancakes are a specialty—multigrain with Maine blueberries or bananas and pecans. The inn's baked French toast is so popular the recipe is available for guests; it comes with pecans and, of course, delicious Vermont maple syrup. Or you can choose scrambled eggs with scallions, tomatoes, and Vermont cheddar, served with Chris's famous home-fried potatoes and onions.

Guests also enjoy fresh-baked cookies every afternoon, and in winter hot soup and fresh bread is served, tempting lots of folks to forget going out for dinner and just staying by the fire, gathering around the piano, or watching a movie.

In your room, you'll find teddy bears, quilts, and Maya's charming paintings. Several rooms can be combined to form a family suite. Romantics will find two special rooms with king-size beds and fireplaces.

There's something for everyone in this welcoming country inn.

HOW TO GET THERE: Take exit 2 from I-91 at Brattleboro, and follow Route 30 north to Rawsonville. Then take Route 100 to South Londonderry. The inn is on your left.

The Inn at South Newfane
South Newfane, Vermont 05351

INNKEEPERS: Neville and Dawn Cullen

ADDRESS/TELEPHONE: 369 Dover Road; (802) 348-7191 or (877) 548-7191; fax (802) 348-9325

E-MAIL: thecullens@innatsouthnewfane.com

WEB SITE: www.innatsouthnewfane.com

ROOMS: 6, all with private bath.

RATES: $95, single, EPB; $99 to $130, double, EPB. MAP is available.

OPEN: All year except two weeks in April.

FACILITIES AND ACTIVITIES: Breakfast, dinner daily for inn guests; for the public, July through October, six days, closed Wednesday; during rest of year, Thursday through Sunday. Full liquor license, swimming and skating pond, lawn games. Neaby: Skiing, snowshoeing, hiking, biking, antiquing, horseback riding, and much more.

This is an inviting inn. The living room has an old original Estey pump organ. There's a fireplace in here, comfortable couch and chairs, lots of games and chess.

The morning room is where breakfast is served to house guests and outside guests. Here are some ideas of what you might have: fresh orange juice, muffins, scones, pancakes, hot or cold cereals, eggs, omelets, coffees, and tea—all very nice. In the warmer months the French doors open onto a lovely porch for dining and looking. There are rockers out here, and the porch looks out on the grounds and pond. We sat out here and watched robins and their little ones in training—it sure was fun.

Neville, the chef, who apprenticed in Europe, is very good at what he does. He uses local and regional produce. I had Maine lobster bisque, and was it good. So the are salads, fettuccine Alfredo, grilled teriyaki, marinated tofu, steak au poivre, veal dishes, and more. In the dining room each table has different colored napkins, picking up colors in the set plates. It looks like a rainbow. Fresh flowers are also on the tables.

Accommodations are lovely. The room I was in had a king-size bed and a lovely rose-colored wing-type chair, and it was very comfortable. There are three queens, two kings, and one set of twins. Ceiling fans are in all. A grand place for a wedding.

HOW TO GET THERE: The inn is located 11 miles northwest of Brattleboro. From I-91 take Brattleboro exit 2 and turn left at end of ramp, following signs for Route 5 North/Route 30 into the center of Brattleboro. Turn left at the traffic light and bear left at the split of Route 5 and Route 30. Follow Route 30 North for 9 miles. You will see the sign for The Inn at South Newfane on your right. Take next left toward Williamsville/South Newfane, etc.

and continue for 2 miles, turning left at end of cement bridge, through Williamsville, over the covered bridge, and proceed for about 1 mile to The Inn at South Newfane. (It's on the left.)

Kedron Valley Inn 💙
South Woodstock, Vermont 05071

INNKEEPERS: Max and Merrily Comins

ADDRESS/TELEPHONE: Route 106; (802) 457–1473 or (800) 836–1193; fax (802) 457–4469

E-MAIL: kedroninn@aol.com

WEB SITE: www.information.com/vt/kedron

ROOMS: 23 rooms and 5 suites, in 3 buildings; all with private bath; many with fireplace or Franklin stove and TV; 4 with Jacuzzi.

RATES: $201 to $318, double occupancy, MAP; $131 to $248, double occupancy, EPB. Substantial discounts midweek.

OPEN: All year except April and a few days before Thanksgiving.

FACILITIES AND ACTIVITIES: Bar, lounge, meeting facilities, private beach on pond, hiking. Dinner 5 nights (not on Tuesday or Wednesday). Nearby: Golf, horseback riding, tennis, skiing.

T he inn's quilt collection alone is worth the trip here. There are more than fifty of them, some of which came from Merrily's family. Two of them were made by her great-grandmother more than a hundred years ago. I was fascinated to find on display stories and pictures of the women who made these beautiful quilts.

There's wonderful history throughout the inn. Two of the inn's buildings date from the 1820s. A secret attic passageway is rumored to have been used by runaway slaves during the Civil War. Another room has a walk-in safe with an iron door. The main building was once a post office, dance hall, tavern, and country store. More recently the inn has been used in the Christmas Budweiser commercial with the Clydesdale horses pulling a sleigh.

Nine of the rooms have a fireplace, and six have a woodstove. I slept in a very comfortable queen-size canopy bed. There are twins and doubles in the log house. All the rooms have a television. One of the largest rooms has a three-sided fireplace and lounge chairs on its private porch. Three other rooms have a private deck or veranda, and five rooms have a Jacuzzi. This is real comfort, folks. There are also new suites, and they're beauties. In Room 12 do ask to see the wood drawer.

Dining at Kedron Valley is wonderful. The menu changes quite often, and the chef is inventive. My spies tell me great stories about his food, and, of course, I've checked up on them, and they're right. I thought the stuffed Cape bay scallops were very different and good. The cool mixed-fruit soup is very tasty. I had chicken breast studded with fresh roasted pistachios in a beurre blanc sauce. Another entree that looked tempting was the salmon stuffed with an herbed seafood mousse, wrapped in puff pastry, baked, and served with a different sauce each night. Desserts are grand. This is truly excellent food. The air-conditioned dining patio is flanked by bulb and perennial gardens.

There's a tavern menu for lighter appetites featuring such treats as pizza baked on a pizza stone, grilled shrimp and mixed green salad, and more. There's also a nice children's menu.

The inn dog is a yellow Lab. The inn allows well-behaved pets to stay here.

HOW TO GET THERE: Take Route 4 to Woodstock. Turn south on Route 106 and go 5 miles to South Woodstock and the inn.

The Hartness House
Springfield, Vermont 05156

INNKEEPERS: The Blair Family

ADDRESS/TELEPHONE: 30 Orchard Street; (802) 885–2115 or (800) 732–4789; fax (802) 885–2207

E-MAIL: innkeeper@hartnesshouse.com

WEB SITE: www.hartnesshouse.com

ROOMS: 39, including 1 suite; all with private bath, air-conditioning, and TV.

RATES: $99 to $150, double occupancy; EP. Package rates available.

OPEN: All year.

FACILITIES AND ACTIVITIES: Breakfast, lunch on weekdays, dinner. No smoking in main house. Lounge and bar, swimming pool, nature trail. Nearby: Cross-country and downhill skiing.

The Victorian mansion was built in 1903 for James Hartness, inventor, astronomer, and one-time governor of Vermont. The rooms are all different in size and decor. There are period wallpapers, some antiques, and twins, doubles, and queens—even some canopies. The Charles Lindbergh Room is in a corner. It's really lovely and has a wonderful window seat.

For relaxation try the swimming pool and nature trails. For winter exercise a snowshoe trail, ice skating, and skiing are nearby.

The dining-room chandeliers set an elegant tone for meals at the inn. The lunch offerings include soups; salads; quiche; a variety of sandwiches, hot and cold; and platters such as a tuna melt, fish 'n' chips, or breaded chicken cutlets topped with marinara sauce and melted mozzarella, served on a roll or over pasta. The special Hartness House Grill is turkey and ham with barbecue sauce, cheddar cheese, and tomato on grilled Texas toast. For dinner, a good start is the inn's terrific onion soup or maybe sautéed shrimp with mushrooms and spinach in a roasted red-pepper cream sauce tossed with penne pasta. The entrees are equally enticing. How about filet mignon with béarnaise sauce? Or maybe a roast half-duckling with black currant demi-glace. Many tasty dishes come from the grill, everything from halibut and scallops to pork chops and sirloin steak.

The telescope lounge overlooks the pool, and the porch is a small, private dining room. There is no smoking in the main house.

Although James Hartness was something of a recluse and needed absolute quiet, he married a lovely butterfly of a lady. Do visit the house they created together.

The Hartness House Observatory

Unique among all the inns in this book, the Hartness House is the only one with a historic observatory. James Hartness was an aviator, the builder of Vermont's first airport, an inventor who patented more than 120 different machines, as well as the governor of the state from 1920 to 1922. As if that were not enough, he was also an astronomer. When he completed his stone-and-shingle mansion, he added an observatory and a 600-power Turret Equatorial Telescope. Built in 1910, it was one of the first tracking telescopes in the nation. Guests can tour the 240-foot underground tunnel that links the observatory to the main house, and they can also see the Stellafane Museum where Hartness created his inventions. Tours are given daily at 6:00 P.M.

HOW TO GET THERE: From the police booth in downtown Springfield, go up Summer Hill, starting at the light. Keep going up the hill as it curves around the left until it levels off (a cemetery is on the right) at the five-street intersection. Bear left on Orchard Street. The inn is 300 yards ahead of you.

Edson Hill Manor
Stowe, Vermont 05672

INNKEEPERS: William and Juliet O'Neill

ADDRESS/TELEPHONE: 1500 Edson Hill Road; (802) 253-7371, (802) 253-9797, or (800) 621-0284

WEB SITE: www.stowevt.com

ROOMS: 9, all with private bath, in the manor; 16, all with private bath and fireplace, in the carriage houses. Smoking in carriage houses only. Handicapped bathroom in 1 carriage house.

RATES: $119 to $179 per room, EPB; $159 to $219 per room, MAP.

Package rates available.

OPEN: All year.

FACILITIES AND ACTIVITIES: Dinner, fully licensed bar, après-ski lounge. Wheelchair access to dining room. Pool, fishing, horseback riding, cross-country skiing with rentals and instruction, ice skating. Nearby: Ice skating and golf at Stowe Country Club.

*H*ere you are, halfway between Stowe and Mount Mansfield, 1,500 feet above the hubble-bubble of that lively village of Stowe, living the good life in a house that was built in 1939 for a family that loved to ski and ride.

The swimming pool here is beautiful. It won an award from Paddock Pools of California. The stocked trout pond is a must for anglers, and you can use the inn's boat. How nice to go catch a fish and have it for your breakfast! When the snow comes, the stables turn into a cross-country ski center, so there you are, taking off practically from the inn door.

This attractive house has been run as an inn since 1953, and there are still homelike touches. The old delft tiles around many of the fireplaces are so appealing. The pine-paneled living room has an aura of quiet elegance that reflects the feeling of gracious living all too often missing from our busy lives. Look closely at the living-room curtains. Somebody shopped hard for that material.

Downstairs are a bar and lounge. A skier's lunch is served here. The dining room is splendid, and the food is grand. The menu changes quite often, but to give you an idea, here are some of the summertime offerings: chilled melon soup with honey and lime; summer beefsteak tomato with grilled eggplant; warm fresh mozzarella crostini with balsamic vinegar; grilled Vermont rabbit; barbecued shrimp; swordfish, salmon, steak. . . .

One wintertime favorite is the homemade butternut squash ravioli. There are also sweetbreads, calf's liver, and pork tenderloin; this is really good food. Choose a wine from the wonderful wine cellar, or complete your meal with one of the great hot beverages.

The inn has very nice guest accommodations. The rooms in the carriage house have beamed ceilings, brick fireplaces, and private baths.

This is a beautiful inn, and the view from here is spectacular.

A note of particular interest to all you moviegoers is that Edson Hill Manor was the winter filming location for Alan Alda's *The Four Seasons*.

HOW TO GET THERE: Take Route 108 North from Stowe 4⁹/₁₀ miles, turn right on Edson Hill Road, and follow the signs uphill to the manor.

Foxfire Inn
Stowe, Vermont 05672

INNKEEPERS: Bob and Kate Neilson

ADDRESS/TELEPHONE: 1606 Pucker Street (Route 100); (802) 253–4887; fax (802) 253–7016

E-MAIL: foxfireinn@aol.com

ROOMS: 5, all with private bath.

RATES: $75 to $115, double occupancy; EPB.

OPEN: All year.

FACILITIES AND ACTIVITIES: Dinner, bar, full license. Wheelchair access to dining room. Parking. Nearby: Downhill and cross-country skiing, fishing, skating, hiking.

*L*ots of people know the Foxfire best as a great Italian restaurant, but it actually began as a bed-and-breakfast more two decades ago and still offers five cozy guest rooms furnished with antiques and inviting living rooms where you can sit and talk or maybe play a few rounds of checkers in front of a crackling fire. The owners like to say that the inn glows with warmth, like the iridescent moss it is named for.

When the family arrived in 1975, they began serving family-style dinners to guests, and that grew into the restaurant that is now a local tradition, presided over by the Neilsons. For starters, wait until you taste the home-baked bread sticks, still warm from the oven and drizzled with olive oil and fresh garlic. Besides the usual Italian dishes like veal parmigiana or lasagna, there are not-to-be-missed house specialties such as chicken Ripieno and their own special eggplant parmigiana. Desserts? Taste the Killer Mousse, so thick they call it "a slice of chocolate."

And when you can push yourself away from the table, you have the charming town of Stowe at your door, with some of New England's best skiing, plus ice skating, an-tiques, shops, summer hiking, fishing, and more.

Pass me another tortoni, please. I am settled in for the season.

HOW TO GET THERE: Take I–89 to Route 100 North into Stowe. The inn is on the right, 1½ miles north of town.

Green Mountain Inn
Stowe, Vermont 05672

INNKEEPER: Patti Clark

ADDRESS/TELEPHONE: 18 Main Street (mailing address: P.O. Box 60); (802) 253–7301 or (800) 253–7302; fax (802) 253–5096

E-MAIL: info@gminn.com

WEB SITE: www.greenmountaininn.com

ROOMS: 100 rooms, suites, and apartments in 7 buildings; all with private bath, TV, air-conditioning, and phone; many with canopy beds, Jacuzzis, fireplaces; 22 with DVD/CD players; some suites with personal computers with high-speed Internet access.

RATES: $89 to $259, single; $99 to $269, double occupancy; $139 to $409, suites; EP. Higher rates in fall and during Christmas week.

OPEN: All year.

FACILITIES AND ACTIVITIES: Breakfast, lunch, dinner, afternoon tea. Lounge; health club with sauna, whirlpool, massage, exercise machines, heated outdoor swimming pool, game room, 120 private acres with trails. Nearby: Skiing.

*T*his venerable inn, built as a private residence in 1833, has been receiving visitors since the mid-1800s, but never in such style as you'll find here today. In the past few years, it has expanded to one hundred rooms, suites, and apartments, in several buildings in the center of the village. The original inn and annex rooms still offer antiques, stenciling, Early American–design draperies, and country quilts to give you that warm, old-fashioned feel, but the inn also has updated with many added luxuries.

Fifty of the rooms and suites offer canopy beds, large Jacuzzis, and fireplaces. Rooms in the Mill House, Clubhouse, and Depot have added VCRs and CD players. Sanborn House suites have full kitchens. The newest addition, the Mansfield House, opened in 2000 with twenty-two rooms and additional amenities such as marble baths, fireside Jacuzzis, large-screen TVs, and DVD/CD players. Suites and grand rooms provide large desks and personal computers with high-speed Internet access.

A bountiful breakfast for all guests is available in the Colonial-style Main Street Dining Room looking out on the village. Dinner is also served here in season. Year-round, the downstairs Whip Bar and Grill, named for its collection of antique buggy ships, serves lunch, dinner, and Sunday brunch. The dinner entrees include seafood, steaks, pasta and vegetarian choices, along with homemade soups, breads, and desserts. Guests are treated to afternoon cookies and hot cider or lemonade, depending on the weather.

You can work off dessert on the inn's private 120-acre property, located a short drive from the inn, where miles of trails winding through field and forest are ideal for cross-country skiing, snowshoeing, or walking. They connect to even more trails preserved by the Stowe Land Trust. The inn's health club has state-of-the-art exercise equipment, plus Jacuzzi, sauna, steam room, and massage services, and the heated outdoor pool is open year-round.

When you step out the door, you are in the heart of Stowe, surrounded by shops and scenery. What more could you wish for?

HOW TO GET THERE: Take I–89 to Route 100 North into Stowe. The inn is at the intersection of Routes 100 and 108.

Ten Acres Lodge
Stowe, Vermont 05672

INNKEEPERS: Grace and Albert Obarzanek

ADDRESS/TELEPHONE: 14 Barrows Road; (802) 253–7638 or
(800) 327–7357; fax (802) 253–6589

E-MAIL: tenacres@stowevt.net

WEB SITE: www.tenacreslodge.com

ROOMS: 15, plus 2 guest cottages; all with private bath, phone; some
with fireplace, TV. 1 room equipped for handicapped. Pets welcome in
cottages.

RATES: $175 to $215, double occupancy; EPB. Cottage rates on request.

OPEN: All year.

FACILITIES AND ACTIVITIES: Dinner nightly in season, Thursday to
Sunday off season. Liquor license. Outdoor pool, tennis court, hot tub.
Nearby: Skiing (downhill and cross country), skating, Stowe recreation
path, shopping.

The living rooms at Ten Acres Lodge are inviting, with soft couches
and large chairs, fireplaces, books, and windows looking out on
sheer beauty year-round. In summer, dairy cows graze in the
rolling fields across the road, and in winter, cross-country ski trails crisscross
the hillside. Around the inn, maples more than a century old provide lazy
New England shade.

The dining rooms are beautifully appointed, from the artwork to the
napery. The menus use the freshest local ingredients, changing with the seasons. Starters could include crisp confit of duck with cider-poached cranber-
ries, braised greens, and balsamic syrup, and the main course might be
pan-seared yellowfin tuna steak with a three-grain pinenut pilaf, grilled scallions, and ginger and chervil sauce.

The comfortable, newly redecorated main lodge guest rooms have pine
walls or wallpaper with pine
trim. Beds are all king or
queen size, with down duvet
comforters. Each room has
been individually decorated
and has its own New England
country charm. All have nice
sitting areas with a sofa or

two chairs and are air-conditioned in summer.

The Hill House suites are more deluxe, with wood-burning fireplaces, cable television, and private balconies with views. The four upstairs rooms have an airy cathedral ceiling. The guest cottages have two or three bedrooms and even more amenities, including kitchens, fireplaces, TV, VCR, and CD players.

The inn has a sociable bar area with a large selection of fine wines, as well as liquors. Outside in winter, you are in the ski capital of the East. But the mountains are simply beautiful anytime, whether covered in snow or painted in blazing autumn colors.

HOW TO GET THERE: From Route 100 North in Stowe, turn left at the three-way stop onto Route 108. Proceed about 2 miles, then bear left onto Luce Hill Road. Ten Acres is located about ½ mile up, around the sharp left, then on your right.

Tucker Hill Inn
Waitsfield, Vermont 05673

INNKEEPERS: David Jackson

ADDRESS/TELEPHONE: Marble Hill Road (off Route 17) (mailing address: P.O. Box 707); 802–496–3983 or (800) 543–7841; fax (802) 496–3203

E-MAIL: tuckerhill@tuckerhill.com

WEB SITE: www.tuckerhill.com

ROOMS: 16 rooms and 3 suites; all with private bath, TV/VCRs, telephone with data ports; 1 suite with fireplace, Jacuzzi.

RATES: Rooms, $79 to $199; suites, $249 to $399; double occupancy; continental breakfast.

OPEN: All year.

FACILITIES AND ACTIVITIES: Dinner at The Steak Place nightly in season, Friday through Monday rest of year except closed mid-April to end of May. Full-service pub. Outdoor pool, two red clay tennis courts, 14 acres of property with hiking trails. Nearby: Skiing, golf, canoeing, fishing, biking, shopping.

*I*f you knew the venerable 1940s vintage Tucker Hill Lodge in the past, you'll hardly recognize the place. The new owner, David Jackson, has renovated and refurbished everything—rooms, restaurant, pub—and added more rooms and suites. Rooms have been furnished with antiques and Ethan Allen furnishings and updated with telephones, TV/VCRs, and computer data ports.

How well did things work out? Well, *Ski* magazine named Tucker Hill its "Inn of the Month" in February 2000. Even the name has been changed from *lodge* to *inn* to tell you things are less rustic now.

The welcoming living room has pine floors and a big fieldstone fireplace, and there is another fireplace in the restaurant, now transformed into The Steak Place, serving Angus Certified Beef steaks. If you can finish the 48-ounce giant in one sitting, you get a free lift ticket for Mad River Valley. Of course, steak isn't the whole story. The restaurant also serves wood-smoked barbecued ribs, fresh seafood, and vegetarian fare. Before or after dinner, you can relax in the fireside pub.

The Mad River Valley is a beautiful, peaceful area of Vermont, with the quaint villages of Waitsfield and Warren waiting to be explored. In winter, you are in prime ski country, with Sugarbush and Mad River Glen nearby. In summer, the inn offers an outdoor pool, two clay tennis courts, and lots of walking trails on its fourteen acres.

Try to come up sometime for the famous Fourth of July parade in Warren, a wonderful bit of small-town Americana come to life.

HOW TO GET THERE: Turn west off Route 100 onto Route 17 in Waitsfield in the Mad River Valley. Go 1½ miles west; the sign for the lodge will be on your left.

Thatcher Brook Inn
Waterbury, Vermont 05676

INNKEEPERS: Lisa and John Fischer, managers

ADDRESS/TELEPHONE: Route 100 North (mailing address: P.O. Box 490); (802) 244–5911 or (800) 292–5911

ROOMS: 24, all with private bath, phone, clock radio; 6 with whirlpool tub; 1 specially equipped for handicapped; 3 with wheelchair access.

RATES: $75 to $210, double occupancy; EPB.

OPEN: All year.

FACILITIES AND ACTIVITIES: Dinner, tavern. Wheelchair access to dining room. Nearby: Canoeing, biking, hiking, cross-country and downhill skiing, golf, tennis.

*T*hatcher Brook, named after Col. Partridge Thatcher, was quite a powerful stream in the late 1800s. It had two sets of beautiful waterfalls, and during the nineteenth century two mills were constructed at these falls. In 1894 Stedman Wheeler purchased the upper sawmill and a small house. He became so prosperous in his business that he decided to construct a larger house on land directly across from the mill. Today that house is Thatcher Brook Inn.

It is obvious from the fine attention to detail and workmanship in the inn that old Stedman spared no expense. The house took two years to construct. Several types of lumber were used in the inn, including oak, bird's-eye maple, spruce, cherry, and birch. The hand-carved fireplace and stairway are original to the house, as are the pocket doors between the two front dining rooms and the window seat in the lobby. Especially attractive is the gazebo-type front porch.

The rooms are colorful, neat, and clean. One has a canopied bed. The shower curtains are remarkably lovely. The decorating has been done well. A sitting area, well equipped with books and games, is up by the rooms. Another building has been added to the inn. It alone is worth a trip.

There are six dining rooms and a lovely deck with

umbrellas. The tables are lovely, with restful pink cloths and darker, complementary napkins. Dinner is memorable. One favorite appetizer is Mushrooms a la Thatcher (I won't explain them; come see for yourself). Another is baked Brie, and the dipping sauces change quite often. A great soup is country red potato and cheddar au gratin. These are followed by entrees like roast stuffed pork tenderloin, grilled lemon and rosemary duck breasts, seafood in parchment, and vegetarian pasta. The possibilities are truly wonderful. With all this good food, you can imagine that the desserts are delicious.

Bailey's Tavern opens at 5:00 nightly and serves its own menu. It has beef and black bean chili, Vermont hamburger, barbecued pork sandwich, and more.

Be sure to wander across the street to look at the two sets of beautiful waterfalls.

HOW TO GET THERE: The inn is ¼ mile north of exit 10 off I-89, on Route 100, the road to Stowe.

The Inn at Weathersfield
Weathersfield, Vermont 05151

INNKEEPERS: Mary and Terry Carter

ADDRESS/TELEPHONE: Route 106, Box 165; (802) 263-9217;
fax (802) 263-9219

WEB SITE: www.weathersfieldinn.com

ROOMS: 9, plus 3 suites; all with private bath; 8 with fireplace.

RATES: $95 to $185, double occupancy; EPB.

OPEN: All year, except Christmas Day.

FACILITIES AND ACTIVITIES: Dining room closed Monday and Tuesday April 1 to 15. Tavern, recreation room with aerobics equipment, tennis, sauna; pool table, TV and VCR with movies, large library, gift shop. Outside amphitheater, gardens, and recreation area suitable for weddings or small conference groups.

This beautiful old inn was built circa 1795 and has a wonderful history. Prior to the Civil War, it was an important stop on the Underground Railroad, sheltering slaves en route to Canada. The inn is set well back from the road on twenty-one acres of property. Your rest is assured.

Everything that has been done to improve the inn has been undertaken with class and lots of care. In the reconstructed barn attached to the inn are five beamed-ceiling guest rooms with sensational old bathtubs. These are real honest-to-goodness Victorian bathrooms. There are twelve fireplaces in the inn, and each of these rooms has one. Two of the suites have a bedroom and sitting room—the innkeepers say that these are ideal for honeymooners; the other sleeps four and is good for families. All the rooms are beautiful with fresh flowers, fresh fruit, and canopy beds.

The tavern is modeled after eighteenth-century Massachusetts taverns. The nonsmoking greenhouse–dining room is a handsome complement to the other rooms. Stencils copied from those used in the early 1800s decorate many of the rooms.

Excellent, four-diamond-rated food is served here. The menu changes daily, taking advantage of what is in season. They grow their own herbs in a special space in the gar-den. Expect elegant appe-tizers such as smoked trout on toast points with Chantilly cream and red onion confit. Main courses might be roasted half duckling with a homemade fresh rasp-berry glaze or honey-Dijon marinated rack of lamb. Be sure to save room for desserts, as they are glorious. The culinary staff are an extraordinary team.

HOW TO GET THERE: Take I–91 North to exit 7 (Springfield, Vermont). Take Route 11 to Springfield, and then take Route 106 in town to the inn, which is on your left, set well back from the road.

TOP PICK
Inn

Deerhill Inn 🖤
West Dover, Vermont 05356

INNKEEPERS: Linda and Michael Anelli

ADDRESS/TELEPHONE: Valley View Road (mailing address: Box 136); (802) 464–3100 or (800) 993–3379; fax (802) 464–5474

E-MAIL: deerhill@sover.net

WEB SITE: www.deerhillinn.com

ROOMS: 13, plus 2 suites; all with private bath; many with fireplace; 2 with decks; 2 with porches; 3 with balconies.

RATES: $180 to $320, double occupancy, MAP; $105 to $240, double occupancy, EPB.

OPEN: All year.

FACILITIES AND ACTIVITIES: Bar, full license. Wheelchair access to dining room. Swimming pool. Nearby: Golf, fishing, cross-country and downhill skiing, tennis court, beaches, hiking, mountain biking, theater, and music hall.

*T*he setting for the Deerhill Inn is perfect. Surrounded by lovely maple and fruit trees, it is perched on a hill with views of the countryside's beautiful mountains and lush meadows. Everything is nice and quiet up here.

The inn dogs, Chuck and Tiff, may greet you when you arrive. The downstairs parlor has a beautiful copper-topped table, couches, and good chairs. There's a fireplace in here, too. As you wander on, you arrive in the dining rooms with their wonderful views and a magnificent mural done by a local artist. The artwork on the other walls is for sale. The plants are delightful.

For appetizers you may find grilled skewered shrimp with hot mustard sauce, smoked Atlantic salmon, the day's fresh pasta, and soup. Entrees may include fresh fish of the day, veal medallions hunter-style, pork loin, steak, or roast duckling. Save room for the chocolate desserts, or perhaps you'd like a lemon parfait. Oh my!

Upstairs is a great library, good couches, that view again, a fireplace, and television. The accommodations are lush. There are quilts on most beds, and flannel sheets in winter. Two rooms have decks. One room has a canopy bed, Oriental furniture, and a lovely Oriental fan on the wall.

The Anellis won the Room of the Year award from Waverly fabrics; I saw the room, and it's a real beauty, as they all are.

If ever I had wanted to own an inn, this would have been the one.

There's much to do in the area. For skiing there are Mount Snow and Haystack, Stratton, and Bromley, as well as cross-country places. In the summertime cast for trout on the Battenkill River, go play a game of golf, or use the inn's pool. It's beautiful up here.

A flash for all anglers: The inn is a short drive to Lake Whitingham, the second largest lake in Vermont, and just 20 miles from the Connecticut River and New Hampshire lakes, so come on up! This gives you very productive fishing in the Northeast.

For something different at the end of summer, there's the wicked wild mountain bike race.

HOW TO GET THERE: Take Route 9 to Wilmington; turn north onto Route 100 at the traffic light and continue to West Dover village. Pass the church and post office; at the antiques store turn right onto Valley View Road. The inn is 300 yards up the road, on the right-hand side.

Doveberry Inn
West Dover, Vermont 05356

INNKEEPERS: Michael and Christine Fayette

ADDRESS/TELEPHONE: Box 1736, Route 100; (800) 722–3204 or (802) 464–5652; fax (802) 464–6229

E-MAIL: duveberry@aol.com

WEB SITE: doveberryinn.com

ROOMS: 8, all with private bath; some with fireplaces, TV, and VCR.

RATES: $95 to $175, double occupancy; EPB. MAP rates available.

OPEN: All year except last two weeks of April and first two in May.

FACILITIES AND ACTIVITIES: Breakfast and dinner (no dinner on Tuesday night), sugar house nearby has swimming pool, sauna, basketball, exercise room. Nearby: Skiing, cross-country trails (small fee).

*T*his inn is just 1¾ miles from Mount Snow on Route 100 in a lovely area with much to do. The Marlboro Music Festival is but a short drive away.

Accommodations are lovely. Some are small and very neat. Some are larger. It's really your choice. One has a sundeck; all are pretty and clean with televisions and VCRs. So you have lovely countryside and the modern world.

There's a Christmas village in the living room, along with a fireplace, a good couch, and a small bar. Next is the dining room. Two or three different table runners vary with the season and are very pretty. Christine does the desserts, and Michael is the head chef. The menu changes seasonally. Some appetizers on my last visit were grilled shrimp served on a bed of cucumber noodles, vegetable risotto topped with fresh reggiano Parmesan, and calamari sautéed with baby leeks, black olives, and roasted red peppers. There are good, very fresh salads. Entrees may be sautéed halibut or soft-shelled crabs, lobster ravioli, pork chops, chicken breast, steak, or veal chops. Do save room for glorious homemade desserts. There's a wine rack between the two dining rooms.

Nicholas is the innkeepers' young son, and I'm so glad I got to meet him. What a future he has!

HOW TO GET THERE: Take exit 2 from I–91 in Brattleboro, then take Route 9 west to Wilmington and Route 100 North about 7½ miles to West Dover. The inn is on the right.

The Inn at Sawmill Farm
West Dover, Vermont 05356

INNKEEPERS: Rodney, Ione, and Brill Williams and Bobbie Dee Molitor

ADDRESS/TELEPHONE: Cross Town Road (mailing address: P.O. Box 367); (802) 464–8131

ROOMS: 10, plus 10 in cottages; all with private bath; some with fireplace.

RATES: $350 to $420, double occupancy, MAP; cottage rooms, $450 to $520, MAP.

OPEN: All year.

FACILITIES AND ACTIVITIES: Bar, lounge. Swimming pool, tennis court, trout pond and two bass fishing ponds.

The Williamses have transformed an old Vermont barn into the gayest, warmest, most attractive inn that I have seen in a long time. Ione is a professional decorator and Rod is a noted architect, which makes for a wonderful marriage of talents and an almost perfect inn. The Williamses' son, Brill, runs the kitchen, and he does a superb job of it.

The inn's copper collection is extensive. The oversized fireplace in the living room is surrounded with it, and there's a huge copper-topped coffee table that's a beauty. They also have a handsome brass telescope on a tripod for your viewing of Mount Snow. A most incredible bar made of solid copper also is here.

Accommodations are very different, with some rooms done in Victorian motif, some in Chippendale, and all with the flavor of New England at its best. The cottage rooms have fireplaces. I was in Farm House, and my room was done in the softest pastels, with a king-size bed and a lovely dressing room and bath. All the rooms are color coordinated and come with thick towels and extra pillows. Little boxes of chocolates are in each room. A very nice touch. The inn's facilities are not well suited to children under ten.

Dinner is beyond belief. Brill is a fine chef. There are eight appetizers. Coquille of crabmeat imperial under glass was my choice. The soups are inventive and good. One entree is medallions of pork tenderloin with Robert sauce and baked stuffed apple. There are many others, like rack of lamb, potato-crusted grouper, and grilled loin of venison. They are perfectly complemented by wines from Brill's impressive wine cellar, winner of *Wine Spectator*'s "Grand Award." Desserts are all homemade. Breakfast is also special. Fresh orange juice and homemade tomato juice are just starters. The staff who serve all these goodies are very courteous.

The inn makes a specialty of special occasions. Do try to get up here for Christmas. It's something you will never forget.

HOW TO GET THERE: Take I-91 to exit 2 in Brattleboro. Take Route 9 west to Wilmington, and then follow Route 100 north for 6 miles to West Dover.

West Dover Inn
West Dover, Vermont 05356

INNKEEPERS: Monique Phelan and Greg Granas

ADDRESS/TELEPHONE: Route 100 (mailing address: P.O. Box 1208); (802) 464–5207; fax (802) 464–2173

E-MAIL: wdvrinn@sover.net

WEB SITE: www.westdoverinn.com

ROOMS: 8, plus 4 suites; all with private baths and TV; suites have Jacuzzis and fireplaces.

RATES: $100 to $200, double occupancy; EPB.

OPEN: All year except mid-April through Memorial Day weekend and first and second weeks in November.

FACILITIES AND ACTIVITIES: Dinner (fall and winter, Wednesday through Sunday; summer, Thursday through Saturday); cocktail lounge. Nearby: Mountain biking, golf, swimming, hiking, skiing (all types).

*I*t's a lovely old place, an inn since 1846. When you come in the door, to the left is the office and on the right is an inviting living room with a fireplace, good couches, books, a television, and a VCR. Comfortable accommodations offer many queen-size beds and a beautiful collection of antiques and hand-sewn quilts. For a family, a pair of twins and a double are nice. The suites are a joy; all have a fireplace and Jacuzzi tub. There are bears on the bed, unique and handmade.

There is much to do here in the area, whatever season you would like to come. The inn is just a short hop to every type of outdoor activity.

Breakfast is served in a cherry breakfast room, and, as they say, anything you can put syrup on they have, along with fruit and eggs. The pleasant dining room has a tempting menu. There are appetizers like bruschetta with an antipasto of marinated tomatoes, roasted onion, olives, and capers or pan-seared scallop and lobster cakes served with a spicy tomato remoulade sauce. Entrees could be grilled salmon fillet, honey Hoisin glazed duck, steak, pork, chicken, pasta, plus chef's specials. Save room for dessert. The lounge has a pub menu in keeping with its more casual ambience. Guests like to mingle at the full-service bar, where ten stools invite socializing.

The two inn dogs, Sam and Zoe, are Hungarian Vizslas. I had a friend in Essex, Connecticut, who had one named Buda—what a character he was.

HOW TO GET THERE: From Brattleboro, take exit 2 off I-91 North to Route 9 West. Go 20 miles to Wilmington. Turn right at the traffic light onto Route 100 north. Proceed 6 miles to the inn. From Bennington take Route 9 East 21 miles to Wilmington. Turn left at the traffic light onto Route 100 North. Proceed 6 miles to the inn.

Windham Hill Inn
West Townshend, Vermont 05359

INNKEEPERS: Pat and Grigs Markham

ADDRESS/TELEPHONE: 311 Lawrence Drive; (802) 874–4080 or (800) 944–4080; fax (802) 874–4702

E-MAIL: windham@sover.net

WEB SITE: www.windhamhill.com

ROOMS: 21, all with private bath, phones, and air-conditioning; some with fireplace or porch; 1 equipped for the handicapped; some with Jacuzzi or soaking tub.

RATES: $190 to $315, single; $200 to $325, double; EPB. Special midweek packages available.

OPEN: All year except one week in late December.

FACILITIES AND ACTIVITIES: Dinner by reservation, full liquor license. Conference facilities. Pool, tennis, hiking, cross-country skiing, ice skating. Nearby: Downhill skiing.

*T*fyou are a dreamer as I am, and you dream of a perfect country inn, this is as close as you will come. At Windham Hill you are sitting on top of the world, and it is beautiful up here. The West River valley stretches as far as the eye can see. The 160-acre site was a working dairy farm when the house was built about 1825, and in 1962 it was converted to an inn.

When you arrive at the inn, on the right is one of the living rooms with a fireplace. Keep on walking into the next room, where there are a nice bar and three bar stools. Take another right into a room with a porch and a fantastic view. Here's where you'll find a piano, books, chess, and games.

Straight ahead are the lovely dining rooms. The Frog Pond dining room has a view of Frog Pond, of course, and the great beyond. It has a fireplace, private tables, and the "Big Table," which is a nice way to meet other inn guests.

The menu for the four-course dinner changes nightly. When I was visiting, there were crab cakes, sautéed sea scallops with a tomato-corn relish, sun-dried tomato ravioli with a pesto beurre blanc, good soups, and salads. For entrees I had my choice of grilled veal medallions, fillet of salmon, and grilled medallions of beef tenderloin. The desserts were very tempting—fresh peach almond tart, chocolate mousse cake, spiced rhubarb, raspberry cobbler, and fresh seasonal fruit. All this, plus you have your pick of wines from a wonderful wine cellar.

The accommodations are awesome. All have views that are enough to keep you in bed all day. Beds are queens and kings, and some rooms have a fireplace or porch. The White Barn has glorious rooms—always has, but now there are three more. I was in Meadowlook with a million-dollar view. Full of comfort, Marion Goodfellow has its own cupola and North Loft. The Markhams have really added to this wonderful inn. The new conference room is 1,000 square feet of sheer beauty. Birch and cherry floors, a fieldstone fireplace, Oriental rugs, and all of the business equipment necesary for anything. Up here you're so close to heaven.

There's a heated pool and tennis courts, and all with a view. Ten kilometers of groomed cross-country trails are also here at the inn, as are lessons and rental equipment. Hiking on the inn's trails is breathtaking. Downhill skiing is close by, or you can ice skate on the inn's pond. There is so much to do here; why go anywhere else?

What in the world are you waiting for? At least come and say hello to Bart the Bear in the lounge area and the real live goldens, Taylor and Monty, the inn dogs.

HOW TO GET THERE: The inn is located just off Windham Hill Road, approximately 1½ miles from Route 30.

Autumn Harvest Inn
Williamstown, Vermont 05679

INNKEEPER: Carolyn White

ADDRESS/TELEPHONE: Clark Road; (802) 422–1255; fax (802) 433–5501

E-MAIL: autumnharv@aol.com

WEB SITE: www.central-vt.com/web/autumn

ROOMS: 18, all with private bath, TV, VCR, phones, and air-conditioning.

RATES: $69 to $139; EP. Horseback riding packages available.

OPEN: All year except Christmas day.

FACILITIES AND ACTIVITIES: Breakfast, dinner served Tuesday to Saturday spring through fall, Wednesday to Saturday in winter. Full liquor license. Horseback riding. Nearby: Cross-country skiing.

What a heavenly location for an inn, high on a knoll overlooking 1,000 acres of mountains and rural Vermont countryside. The property was known as Autumn Crest Farm for more than a century before the name was changed to Fogged Inn. The original name has now been reinstated. It was a dairy farm for most of those years, and then a horse farm before being completely restored as a country inn. Five of the guest rooms and the breakfast area were part of the original farmhouse and still have their wide-board wooden floors. On chilly days, the large common room welcomes with a great brick fireplace, and the wraparound porch is wonderful on a summer day. In keeping with the rural setting, the bedrooms are simple country with Bates bedspreads and ruffled curtains.

The surroundings are part of the pleasure of this inn. You can dine with a view of the countryside and in warm weather, be served outside on the veranda. Horseback riding is a favorite pastime, and abandoned town roads across the hillsides are ideal for walking or mountain biking. In winter these become snowmobile trails and connect with the expansive trail system of the Vermont Association of Snow Travelers.

Dinner is a highlight of the day. Typical appetizers are crab cakes with Dijon sauce or bacon-wrapped scallops. For your main course you can choose from dishes like medallions of beef, prime rib, chicken Dijon, or baked salmon. Dinner always comes with a crisp house salad and homemade bread. Desserts are sinfully delicious.

After dinner you can relax in the lounge and compare stories of your day in the great outdoors.

HOW TO GET THERE: The inn is just two minutes from I-89; take exit 5 onto Route 64 East.

The Hermitage
Wilmington, Vermont 05363

INNKEEPERS: Jim and Lois McGovern

ADDRESS/TELEPHONE: Coldbrook Road; (802) 464–3511;
fax (802) 464–2688

E-MAIL: hermitag@sover.net

WEB SITE: www.hermitageinn.com

ROOMS: 15; all with private bath, wheelchair accessibility, phone, TV,
VCR, and fireplace.

RATES: $112.50 to $125 per person, double occupancy; MAP.

OPEN: All year.

FACILITIES AND ACTIVITIES: Brunch every Sunday. Wheelchair access
to dining room. Restaurant is air-conditioned. Sauna, wine cellar, trout
pond, hiking, cross-country skiing from the door.

*H*igh on a windy hill facing Haystack Mountain, you will find a
unique and heartwarming country inn, The Hermitage. The owner
is a man with many interests. He also has a certain charm. Maybe
it is the quick smile or a fleeting twinkle as he says, "No piped-in music in my
inn." You might, though, find a classical guitarist some night or someone at
the piano in the lounge.

Come in the very early spring and you will find maple sugaring going full
blast. There are four sugarhouses on the property, and Jim McGovern makes
about 700 gallons of maple syrup a year. In summer the big kettles are kept
simmering making homemade jams and jellies.

Sporting clays, a shotgun game imported from England, simulates the
flight patterns of game birds in their natural settings. The clay "birds" are
thrown from ten different fields, so there are grand challenges. Also here is a
500-acre hunting preserve.

Along with this talent for making the most of nature's bounty, Jim is an
oenophile (wine lover) and has a wine cellar with a stock of 30,000 bottles.
You are never at a loss for the perfect wine to enjoy with this inn's first-rate
food.

Dining at The Hermitage is truly gourmet and includes homegrown game and fresh vegetables. The dining rooms are lovely. The Delacroix Room was named for Michael Delacroix, whose paintings are featured throughout the inn. (Michael has done the Hermitage—a beautiful winter snow painting, available here, of course.) The fireplace will warm you while you enjoy some of Jim's wines.

Rausan, the inn dog, may come by to say hello, but he is likely to be distracted by a passing gaggle of geese that will fly off in a flurry of wings. Jim also has a large collection of decoys of every description on display and for sale.

The comfortable rooms, all with their own working fireplace, are furnished with antiques and, oh, those brass beds! In the carriage house you will even find a sauna.

Brook Bound, down the hill from The Hermitage, is also owned by the McGoverns. It has fourteen rooms with ten private baths. Dinner is at The Hermitage.

HOW TO GET THERE: Take Route 9 to Wilmington; follow Route 100 North 2 miles to Coldbrook Road on the left. The Hermitage is 3 miles down Coldbrook Road.

Red Shutters Inn
Wilmington, Vermont 05363

INNKEEPERS: Tad and Renée Lyon

ADDRESS/TELEPHONE: Route 9 West; (802) 464–3768 or (800) 845–7548; fax (802) 464–5123

ROOMS: 7 rooms, 2 suites; all with private bath; some with fireplace and TV.

RATES: $110 to $240, double occupancy; EPB.

OPEN: All year except Easter to May 15.

FACILITIES AND ACTIVITIES: Full license, breakfast, dinner every night except Monday. Nearby: Shopping, skiing.

*N*estled among many well-established maples, pin oaks, and evergreens on a lovely hillside is the Red Shutters Inn, located on the edge of Wilmington. There are five acres around the inn, which dates back to 1894. It is a handsome Colonial-style structure.

The carriage house, also built in 1894, was recently renovated. It has three rooms and a suite that has a skylight, a fireplace, and a magnificent brass bed. Of course, there's plenty of charm and comfort no matter where you are. There are ceiling fans in all of the rooms. The suite in the main house has a private deck overlooking the hillside.

There's a woodstove in the living room and pub. The dining room is air-conditioned for your comfort. And the food is delicious. Choose from appetizers like a smoked seafood plate, baked Brie with fresh fruit, and very good soups, and try entrees like lamb racks, pork tenderloin, venison with green peppercorn sauce and pickled red cabbage, chicken, and veal. The desserts and coffees are ambrosia. There's a nice fireplace in here and a dining porch with wicker furniture. A nice place to sit and read or just listen to the stream that goes by—very comforting. You are just steps away from the town, but you are in a country setting.

HOW TO GET THERE: The inn is located on Route 9, just west of the intersection of Route 100.

The White House

Wilmington, Vermont 05363

INNKEEPER: Robert Grinold

ADDRESS/TELEPHONE: Route 9; (802) 464–2135 or (800) 541–2135;
fax (802) 464–5222

E-MAIL: whitehse@sover.net

WEB SITE: www.whitehouseinn.com

ROOMS: 16 in main house and 7 in guest house; all with private bath;
9 with fireplace.

RATES: $108 to $178, double occupancy; EPB. MAP available.

OPEN: All year.

FACILITIES AND ACTIVITIES: Sunday brunch, skier's lunch in winter,
dinner served all year except Easter to Memorial Day. Wheelchair access
to dining rooms and common room and two guest rooms on first floor.
Bar, lounge. Swimming pool inside and out, health spa with sauna,
steam room. Cross-country skiing. Nearby: Downhill skiing and tubing
on the inn's own hill.

You would expect an inn named The White House to be elegant,
and, believe me, this one is. Built in 1914, the mansion has much
to offer.

The gallery on the main floor has an extremely unusual wallpaper that
was printed in Paris in 1912. There are high ceilings throughout the inn, and
the living room is large, with a fireplace and beautifully covered couches and
chairs. The Casablanca bar has wicker chairs, couches, pretty flowered pillows, and Bob's collection of angels all around. So nice to come back to after
a day on the ski trails.

There are two dining rooms, both of which are very elegant, and a small
private dining room. The food served in this three-star inn is superb, but
would you expect anything else in The White House? Here's just a sampling
of what is offered: There are nine appetizers, including baked Brie, carpaccio
of beef, and interesting soups. Entrees are numerous and varied. One is boneless stuffed duck. Of course, all the desserts are homemade. I get hungry just
writing about Bob's inn.

The grounds are sumptuous, with a lovely rose garden and fountain, and below this is a beautiful 60-foot swimming pool. There's another small fountain outside the lounge, and from this delightful room you watch spectacular sunsets over the Green Mountains.

The guest rooms here are all sizes. The wing that faces west has four rooms with, as Bob says, two-passenger whirlpool tubs.

It seems appropriate that the inn dogs, both golden retrievers, are named Eleanor and Roosevelt.

The health spa is what you need after a day of fun: sauna, steam room, and showers. There's also an inside pool to relax in. Ah, what an inn!

Intrigue: Why did the original owner of the house put in a secret staircase? You will have to ask where it is.

HOW TO GET THERE: From I–91 take Route 9 to Wilmington. The inn is on your right, just before you reach the town.

The Inn at Windsor
Windsor, Vermont 05089

INNKEEPERS: Larry Bowser and Holly Taylor

ADDRESS/TELEPHONE: 106 Apothecary Lane; (802) 674–5670

ROOMS: 2 rooms and 1 suite, all with private bath and fireplaces.

RATES: $125 to $145, double occupancy; EPB.

OPEN: All year.

FACILITIES AND ACTIVITIES: Breakfast only meal served. BYOB.

*T*he inn is perched on a hill overlooking The Historic Village and shaded by tall trees. There's a driveway up the hill, next to the town's old burying ground; you park at the top and proceed through the gate into a terraced garden. The door is here, and you may find shoes and slippers here because no one wears shoes inside—the innkeepers provide clean slippers for you.

There is so much history connected to this house it would take pages to tell it all, so come on up and ask because it's really a lovely story.

The bedrooms and suite are very pretty and comfortable. The suite has a TV and VCR, a library, a king-size bed, and the original Indian shutters. Bathrobes are provided along with natural Vermont soaps. The living room looks out at a 250-year-old sugar maple.

The homestead, begun in 1786, was the home of an early physician and apothecary named Green, who added the carriage house in 1804 as a distribution center for his patent medicines. It stayed in the Green family until 1963, when it was sold to the Knights of Columbus. During restoration they discovered hand-hewn beans, hand-planed planks on the walls, spruce flooring, and even pencil inscriptions on the bedroom walls made by Green's daughter Ann Elizabeth in 1847.

Breakfast may be orange Julius, fruit salad with yogurt and nuts, apple walnut French batter pancakes, hot glazed pears with cool yogurt topping, or baked herbed eggs. Before breakfast, coffee, tea, or juice may be brought to your room to wake you up.

HOW TO GET THERE: From I-91 take exit 9. Go down Main Street in Windsor to number 106; it's on the right.

Juniper Hill Inn 💛
Windsor, Vermont 05090

INNKEEPERS: Rob and Susanne Pearl

ADDRESS/TELEPHONE: 153 Pembroke Road; (802) 674–5273 or

(800) 359-2541; fax (802) 674-2041

E-MAIL: innkeeper@juniperhillinn.com

WEB SITE: www.juniperhillinn.com

ROOMS: 16, all with private bath; 11 with fireplace. No-smoking inn.

RATES: $95 to $175, double occupancy; EPB. MAP rates available.

OPEN: All year except two weeks in April and November.

FACILITIES AND ACTIVITIES: Dinner by advance reservation six days a week; open to the public by advance reservation Wednesday through Sunday. No smoking in dining room. Full license, swimming pool. Nearby: Downhill and cross-country skiing.

*T*he upper valley of Vermont is lovely and full of history. Windsor is the birthplace of Vermont, and the longest covered bridge in America is here. The inn is a 1902 Colonial Revival mansion that is listed on the National Register of Historic Places. It was once known as a summer White House because former presidents Rutherford Hayes, Benjamin Harris, and Theodore Roosevelt were frequent guests of the original owners.

Large white columns lead into a 30-by-40-foot oak-paneled entry hall. You'll think it's big enough to be a ballroom, and it once was. Hunting trophies used to be displayed here. Today it is one of the parlors and called the Great Room. There are two smaller parlors for reading or quiet conversation.

There is a beautiful grand staircase centered under a large Palladian window in a very private library wing. There are two guest rooms at the top of the stairs. One has a canopied bed, the other has a porch, and both are charming.

Some of the other rooms have marble sinks, and one has a summer porch. Two rooms offer balconies with a view of Lake Runnemeade and Ascutney Mountain. Beds include a sleigh bed, canopies, and four posters. They all afford a good night's sleep.

Please note the great table in the Great Room. Its top weighs more than 1,000 pounds. It is the original dining table of the house; now it holds a swan, books, and a lamp.

Some of the goodies from the chef are herb-crusted rack of lamb, roast duck, chicken boursin, halibut, and steaks. There's no smoking in here; Tucker, Cuddler, and Jane, the inn dogs, don't care for smoke.

Windsor Attractions

Whether you are interested in history or arts and crafts, there are several good reasons to visit Windsor. The Vermont State Crafts Center at Windsor House (54 Main Street; 802-674-6729) has a fine inventory of handmade furniture, quilts, pottery, wood crafts, weavings, baskets, and sculpture by more than 150 Vermont artisans, as well as a stock of Vermont-made foods. It is open Monday to Saturday from 10:00 A.M. to 5:00 P.M. and Sunday from 11:00 A.M. to 4:00 P.M. North of town off Route 5 is the workshop and showroom of Simon Pearce (802-674-6280), where you can watch glassblowers creating exquisite goblets and home accessories by hand and pick up seconds at good prices in the shop.

On the history side, Windsor is known as the birthplace of Vermont; the state constitution was adopted here in 1777 in a tavern that is now a museum of state history known as the Old Constitution House (17 North Main Street, 802-828-3051). It is open Wednesday to Sunday 11:00 A.M. to 5:00 P.M., Memorial Day to Columbus Day.

This small town also boasted one of the nation's first modern systems of industrial production. The American Precision Museum (196 Main Street; 802-674-5781), housed in an 1846 armory and machine shop, has the National Machine Tool Collection, a notable gun collection, and a scale model collection of actual working models of various manufacturing processes. See the products of Thomas Edison and Henry Ford; learn about the famed Sharps, Enfield, and Springfield rifles; and peruse the outstanding collection of photographs, drawings, catalogs, and other documents related to the history of industry in the United States. The museum is open from Memorial Day through October.

Just outside of town on Hunt Road, visit the beautiful gardens at Cider Hill (802-674-5293). Browse the footpaths through gardens and greenhouses, and visit the gallery for lithographs and prints. Plants and garden accessories are also for sale here. Cider Hill Gardens is open daily from May through July and on Friday through Sunday from August through October.

HOW TO GET THERE: From I–91 South take exit 9. Go about 3 miles on Route 5 South, then take a right onto Juniper Hill Road. Go ½ mile to the end of Juniper Hill and take a right. At the first junction turn left and go ½ mile up the hill to the driveway on the right.

The Jackson House Inn
Woodstock, Vermont 05091

INNKEEPERS: Carl and Linda Delnegro

ADDRESS/TELEPHONE: 114–3 Senior Lane; (802) 457–2065 or (800) 448–1890; fax (802) 457–9290

E-MAIL: innkeepers@jacksonhouse.com

WEB SITE: www.jacksonhouse.com

ROOMS: 9, plus 6 one-room suites; all with private baths, Casablanca fans, and air-conditioning; phones in the suites.

RATES: $195 to $380, double occupancy; EPB.

OPEN: All year.

FACILITIES AND ACTIVITIES: Full breakfast and dinner. Nearby: Glass blowing, art galleries, biking, hiking, horseback riding, canoeing, swimming, golf, tennis, theater, skiing, sleigh rides, and more.

What a beauty this is! The long porch with both rockers and chairs and beautiful hanging plants is the first thing you see. And this that follows was said so well from the brochure.

The Jackson House was built with devotion in 1890 by Wales Johnson, a local sawmill owner. His aim was to erect the finest example of late Victorian architecture possible. Floors of cherry and maple complement fine furniture, walls, and moldings of the finest workmanship. The many exterior eaves and twin chimneys are a statement of pure classical design and dignity of workmanship. The building is listed on the National Register of Historic Places.

In 1940 the house was bought by the Jackson family and opened as the Seven Maples Tourist Home. In 1983 it was sold to the third owners in one hundred years. Later owners completely renovated the inn, and in 1996 four opulent suites and the restaurant were added. The most recent owners, the Delnegros, are continuing the long tradition of excellence.

The dining room is elegant, with white napery and a double fireplace. There's a chef's tasting menu—that's a grand idea—a spring vegetable menu, and a prix fixe menu. One appetizer that took my eye was wild ramp soup.

Entrees include veal tenderloin, free range chicken, lobster, beef, and fish. Desserts—well, as you can imagine, save room. Before the evening meal, complimentary wine or champagne and hors d'oeuvres are served. Breakfast the next morning is ample; almond-crusted French toast is just one idea.

A spa in the basement holds up to six people. A treadmill, stationary bicycle, and stair climber are also here for the guests' use. Those who prefer to relax may rest on the wicker furniture and enjoy a huge TV and VCR. Movies are provided. A juice bar is also here.

Handicapped access is to the first floor. Accommodations are grand. Four guest rooms are on the first floor; the rest are on the second and third floors. Two of the suites are on the third floor and are beauties. They open to a deck overlooking the landscaped gardens. One room has a Jacuzzi, and a few more have thermal massage tubs.

HOW TO GET THERE: Go through Woodstock, and from the town green it is 1⁶⁄10 miles to the inn, which is on the right on old Route 4.

The Lincoln Inn
Woodstock, Vermont 05091

INNKEEPERS: Kurt and Lori Hildbrand

ADDRESS/TELEPHONE: Route 4; (802) 457–3312; fax (802) 457–5908

E-MAIL: Lincon2@aol.com

WEB SITE: www.lincolninn.com

ROOMS: 6, all with private bath.

RATES: $125, double occupancy; EPB. Higher rates in foliage season.

OPEN: All year except after Easter to May 1 and November 1 to Thanksgiving.

FACILITIES AND ACTIVITIES: Dinner Tuesday through Sunday. Bar, lounge, TV room, games, VCR for movies. Nearby: Golf, fishing, cross-country and downhill skiing.

The Lincoln Covered Bridge is the only remaining wooden bridge of its kind and design left in America. In 1844 T. Willis Pratt invented and patented the bridge plans. In 1869 storm waters pushed the bridge from Dewey's Mill in Woodstock Village to an island downstream. In 1877 Charles Lincoln (cousin of Abraham) had the bridge moved to its current location by floating it on "jack" skates. It was renovated in 1947. It spans the Ottauquechee River and is at one end of the inn's property.

The inn, a 200-year-old farmhouse, sits on about six acres of rolling lawn alongside the river. It is a nice spot to go fishing or wading, so you anglers should bring your pole and catch some fish.

There is an old stone fireplace for cookouts and a picnic table, so do come and relax. The gazebo on a knoll overlooking the river beckons me. In the wintertime it's snowmobiles and skiing that will keep you busy.

The nice living room offers a television and VCR with a library full of good movies. This is a great place to unwind on a snowy winter night. Accommodations are cozy. The beds are new and comfortable.

The dining room offers a full country breakfast and, in the evening, fireside dining. The chef-owner Kurt is a native of Switzerland—he has trained extensively in fine hotels. One of his appetizers is porcini ravioli with red pepper coulis, plus there are good soups and salads. Entrees include breast of chicken with tomatoes, basil, and a confit of garlic; loin of lamb; veal medallions; steak; and good seafood such as shrimp in phyllo with an orange-ginger-lime sauce or broiled lobster tail. Desserts—well, there's chocolate truffle cake with vanilla sauce and raspberries. There are more, but why go on after that one?

There is so much to do in this area. What are you waiting for? Come and enjoy.

HOW TO GET THERE: From I–91 take exit 9 and follow Route 12 north to Route 4. Take Route 4 to the inn; it is 3 miles west of the village green in Woodstock.

The Village Inn
Woodstock, Vermont 05091

INNKEEPERS: Kevin and Anita Clark

ADDRESS/TELEPHONE: 41 Pleasant Street; (802) 457–1255 or
(800) 722–4571

WEB SITE: www.villageinnofwoodstock.com

ROOMS: 8, all with private bath and air-conditioning; 1 with fireplace.

RATES: $95 to $185, double occupancy; EPB.

OPEN: All year.

FACILITIES AND ACTIVITIES: Dinner five nights, bar, lounge. Nearby:
Golf, tennis, skiing, swimming, boating, shopping.

*W*oodstock is a beautiful town with a classic village green. The inn
was once part of a forty-acre estate on the Ottauauechee River.
The Victorian mansion and carriage house, built in 1899, are all
that remain of the estate. The location, within walking distance of the town's
many shops and the green, couldn't be better.

Lots of charm and comfort are found in the bar. The very pretty ceilings
are of pressed tin, and there is a beautiful stained-glass window. The room
also has a nineteenth-century oak bar. Upstairs is a large common room with
a porch, television, and games. And—this is a good thing to know—the inn
has a fire-alarm system.

Rooms are gracious, comfortable, and furnished nicely. Some have marble sinks in them. One has a king-size bed and a working fireplace.

I loved the romantic dining room, complete with a working fireplace, the
original tin ceilings, and natural oak woodwork. A chef-owned inn is always a
plus. The menus are enticing. Among the appetizers I saw were grilled mini-
pizzas and fettucine Anita. I chose the stuffed baked potato skins, which were
very good. Roast Vermont turkey
is an entree that is too often forgotten on menus. Roast lamb,
roast prime rib of beef, fresh
seafood catch of the day . . . and
the menu goes on. Desserts, well,
all I'll say is that they're homemade and delicious. The wine list
is extensive and includes good
wines at low prices.

Covered bridges, elegant shops, skiing, sleigh rides, golf, or tennis anyone? Go swimming or boating in one of the many lakes. Come on up and enjoy yourself. This whole area and this lovely refurbished inn get my applause.

HOW TO GET THERE: From I-91 take I-89 North to exit 1. Turn left into Woodstock. The inn is on the left.

The Woodstock Inn
Woodstock, Vermont 05091

INNKEEPER: Tom List

ADDRESS/TELEPHONE: Fourteen the Green; (802) 457-1100 or (800) 448-7900; international 0101-802-457-1100; fax (802) 457-6699

E-MAIL: email@woodstockinn.com

WEB SITE: www.woodstockinn.com

ROOMS: 176 rooms, 7 suites, 1 house; all with private bath, color TV, phones; 23 with fireplaces; some with VCR (tapes for rent at the front desk).

RATES: $174 to $550, double occupancy; EP. Special package rates starting at $119 and MAP are available. No surcharges, no limits.

OPEN: All year.

FACILITIES AND ACTIVITIES: Breakfast, lunch, dinner. Richardson Tavern, full license. Country club, golf, tennis, health and fitness center, pool, classes, tennis, ski touring center, and downhill ski area. Nearby: Horseback riding, hunting and fishing, bicycling.

BUSINESS TRAVEL: Located 260 miles from New York; 166 miles from Hartford; 148 miles from Boston; 180 miles from Providence; 206 miles from Montreal, Canada; 138 miles from Albany; and 89 miles from Burlington.

What a beautiful inn! I cannot help but wonder why it's taken me so long to put it in this guide. The grounds and flowers are lovely, and when you walk into the inn, it's glorious. The old

Woodstock Inn opened in 1892, and the new inn opened November 23, 1969. There are nooks to sit in and wonderful comfort. Accommodations? They are handsome. Twenty-three rooms have fireplaces; all are air-conditioned, have color televisions, are beautifully furnished, and are so restful. The inn provides air mattresses for kids and they love them—like camping, you know, for a kid.

The dining rooms are elegant, and so is the food. They have been awarded four diamonds and four stars. Besides the ample menus, the inn's culinary staff gladly accepts special requests, and they pride themselves on featuring Vermont products on the menus.

You might begin with baked onion soup or Michelle's soup of the day—they are always yummy. Fresh seasonal and exotic fruit, marinated chicken salad, and Caesar salad with grilled chicken or shrimp are some of the other appetizers. Among the grand sandwiches are hot shaved country ham on marbled rye or char-grilled sirloin burgers. There's also baked scrod and pizzas—wow! And freshly baked desserts.

The main dining room menu offers about six choices of first courses. The house-made tri-color lobster ravioli was wonderful. Of the delicious soups, well, a duet of tomato and wild mushroom bisque was oh so good. The main course menu has suggested wines with each entree. Roast rack of lamb got me, but there were some other wonderful choices of beef, pork, chicken, duck, and, of course, fish. The desserts are sinful.

Can't stop now, because it's on to Sunday brunch, and it's a beauty. The way the food is displayed boggles my mind. A display of domestic, imported, and Vermont cheeses with assorted crackers was awesome. Tri-colored pasta and vegetable salad, country pâtés, baked herb-encrusted chicken breast, lamb chop on lentil mushrooms, and couscous with sun-dried tomato madeira sauce is just a sample. There is much more. The Woodstock Inn's pastry display—well, it's just spectacular.

For a hike, ski tour, trail ride, or the trip home, hearty box lunches are ideal. The names alone are great. The Hiker, the Long Haul, the Daydreamer, the Light Haul, and Wildflowers Picnic Basket for Two. I won't tell you what they are. Come on up and try some.

There is a shuttle bus to the inn's sports center and country club. No need to use your car.

Woodstock is one of the most beautiful villages in New England, and the unspoiled grandeur of Vermont is everywhere.

HOW TO GET THERE: From Boston take I-93 North to I-89 North to Route 4 West. From Connecticut, eastern New York, or New Jersey, take I-95 or the Merritt Parkway to I-91 North, to I-89 North, to Route 4 West. Then travel 10 miles to the village green (traffic rotary). Keep the village green on your left, and the inn will come up on your right. From western New York and other points west, take I-87 to Route 9 North to Route 149 East to Route 4 East. Travel 12 miles to Whitehall and bear right on Route 4 East near the Silver Diner, then travel 35–40 miles into Rutland. At the end of the four-lane road, turn left on Route 4 East/Route 7 North, travel about 3 miles, and take Route 4 East after the Grand Union on your right. Follow Route 4 for 31 miles to Woodstock. As you begin to circle the village green, the inn will be on your right.

Billings Farm and Museum

Established in 1871 by Frederick Billings, Billings Farm is still a working dairy. Come here to see its fine Jersey cows and learn about the concepts of responsible agriculture and land stewardship that distinguished this farm. Reforestation and selective breeding were among the practices of scientific farm management that led to the success of this dairy. Visit the fields, the barns, the 1890 farmhouse, the heirloom garden, and the farm museum. A museum shop and a dairy bar are also here. Be sure to watch the wonderful short film documenting farm life, the passage of the seasons, and the history of farming and logging in Vermont. Come to enjoy such seasonal activities as wagon rides and sleigh rides during November and December. The farm and museum (802-457-2355) are open daily from May 1 through October 31, plus weekends in November and December and daily from December 26 through 31. Admission is charged. This place is grand for the whole family.

Select List of
Other Vermont Inns

The Willow Inn B&B

Historic 7A
Arlington, VT 05250
(802) 375-9773

3 rooms, 1 with private bath; in 1840 farmhouse.

Alexandra B&B

Historic Route 7A
Bennington, VT 05201
(802) 442-5619 or (888) 207-9386; fax: (802) 442-5592
Web site: www.alexandrainn.com

6 rooms, all with private bath; in 1859 Victorian house.

Willard Street Inn

349 South Willard Street
Burlington, VT 05401
(802) 651-8710 or (800) 577-8712
Web site: www.willardstreetinn.com

14 rooms, all with private bath; B&B in brick Victorian mansion.

Hugging Bear Inn and Shoppe

244 Main Street
Chester, VT 05143
(802) 875-2412 or (800) 325-0519
Web site: www.huggingbear.com

6 rooms, all with private bath; B&B in Victorian house.

The Sumner Mansion

4 Station Road
Hartland, VT 05048
(802) 436-3386 or (888) 529-8796
E-mail: sumnerm@vermontel.com
Web site: www.sumnermansion.com

3 rooms, 1 suite in mansion, all with private bath; 2 rooms in carriage house, 1 with private bath. Mansion on National Historic Preservation List.

1811 House

Route 7A
Manchester Village, VT 05254
(802) 362-1811 or (800) 432-1811
Web site: www.1811house.com

14 rooms (3 in cottage), all with private bath; full breakfast; B&B in 1770 home.

Basin Harbor Club

on Lake Champlain
Vergennes, VT 05491
(802) 475-2311 or (800) 622-4000
Web site: www.basinharbor.com

40 rooms, 77 cottages, all with private bath; two restaurants; private airstrip, 18-hole golf course, tennis courts, and pool. Open mid-May through mid-October.

West Hill House Bed and Breakfast Inn

1496 West Hill Road
RR 1, Box 292
Warren, VT 05674
(802) 496-7162 or (800) 898-1427
E-mail: westhill@madriver.com
Web site: www.westhillhouse.com

7 rooms, all with private bath; 5 with fireplace, 2 with Jacuzzi, 1 with steam shower; B&B in 1850s farmhouse; sometimes serves dinner on Saturday nights.

Indexes

Alphabetical Index to Inns

Romantic Inns

Inns Serving Lunch

Inns Serving Sunday Brunch

Inns with Accommodations for Families

Lakeside Inns

Inns on or near Saltwater
(* denotes on beach)

Inns with a Swimming Pool

Inns with Golf Course or Tennis Court

Inns with Cross-country Skiing on Property

Inns with Rooms Specially Equipped
for Handicapped

Inns for Business Travelers

About the Author

The "inn creeper" is the nickname ELIZABETH SQUIER has earned in the more than twenty-five years she's been researching this guide to the country inns of New England. And a deserved name it is, for she tours more than 200 inns every year, from top to bottom, inside and out, before recommending the best ones to you.

A recognized author on fine food and lodging, Elizabeth is a gourmet cook and has written travel and food columns for many periodicals. Like you, she recognizes readily the special ingredients that make a good inn exceptional.

For many years Elizabeth called Essex, Connecticut, home. She now resides in Florida and has a rather long commute!